Bitches, Bimbos and Virgins

Women in the Horror Film

Midnight Marquee Press, Inc.
Baltimore, Maryland, USA

Copyright © 2011 Gary J. Svehla and Susan Svehla
Interior layout and cover design by Susan Svehla

Without limiting the rights under copyright reserved above, no part of this publication may be reproduced, stored in or introduced into a retrieval system, or transmitted, in any form, or by any means (electronic, mechanical, photocopying, recording or otherwise), without the prior written permission of the copyright owner or the publishers of the book.

ISBN 978-1-936168-22-4
Library of Congress Catalog Card Number 2011918154
Manufactured in the United States of America
Revised First Editon October 2011

This book is dedicated to
all the women who have
helped put the scare
into scary movies.

TABLE OF CONTENTS

6	Introduction to Original Edition
8	150 Years of Women and Horror: She Has Always Lived in the Castle
18	He Done Her Wrong: The Fate of Women in Golden Age Horrors
26	Women Take a Bite Out of Classic Horror: Dracula's Daughter and Mark of the Vampire
43	The Golden Age of the Scream Queen
63	Empowered Women in the Val Lewton Canon
84	Bad Girls Meet Bad Ends
96	Attack of the Alien Women from Outer Space!
104	Harlots, Hedonists and Heroines: The Women of Hammer Films
127	Queen Bitches of the Universe

147   **Scream and Scream Again!**

        Horror's Honor List of Scream Queens

158   **Women to Die for—1960s Onward:**

        Midmar Readers Have Their Say...

167   **Attack of the Movie Poster**

        Pin-Up Girls

174   **Middle Earth's Heroines**

178   **Deadly Delights—**

        Movies Featuring Our

        Favorite Queens of Evil

198   **Dominatrix Divas:**

        MidMar Readers

        Pick Their Faves

Introduction to Original Edition

Bitches, Bimbos and Virgins!...Oh my!

To many, this may sound like an exploitative title, a book that caters to prurient tastes and features cheesecake photographs of pseudo-actresses from direct-to-video basement/bedroom productions. Those so-called Scream Queens.

But this is not that type of book

No, *Bitches, Bimbos and Virgins* is the history of women in the horror cinema, profiling their evolution from coffee maker to scientist, from seductress and victim to kick-ass heroine, and finally detailing their emergence as well-drawn characters who play important roles in horror movie history—past, present and future.

And don't expect this history to be definitive, stuffy or academic, for the history of women in horror cinema should be as enjoyable to read as it is to watch. A fun read with plenty of photos! But also, at the same time, it must remain both an intelligent analysis with controversy and food for thought, while remaining well documented and carefully researched. This volume, I trust, meets all these requirements.

Simply stated, horror films provided meaty roles and made stars out of male icons such as Boris Karloff, Bela Lugosi, Vincent Price, Lon Chaney, Jr., Peter Cushing and Christopher Lee—their roles include unsavory anemic royalty with questionable origins and unquenchable appetites, doctors with mad imaginations harvesting dreams of gods and monsters, grotesque creatures with criminal brains but innocent souls, flamboyant maniacs with well-carved personalities and periodic lapses in good taste, and cruelly ravished artists whose well-plotted revenge remains their only motive for being. Such characters stalked movie houses for decades.

But what of the women?

Generally, women's roles were subservient, underwritten, colorless, unimaginative, predictable and demeaning. Women were depicted as beautiful window dressing on the arms of more recognizable male stars. Women often became screaming, panicking and frightened victims, who were bitten, stabbed, sliced, crushed, beaten, throttled, shot or pushed off cliffs. Or, women became nasty seductresses luring both innocent and not-so-innocent male victims to their doom because of their sexual charms. In horror/monster movies of the 1950s, they might be scientists or curvy companions to the male heroes, but most likely they would be powdering their faces at the office, answering the phone and taking messages, or fixing the best cup of coffee available in town. Women were written into scripts almost begrudgingly, almost as if they had to occupy secondary roles in a male-dominated universe, someone for the monster to threaten and the hero to save. As young children we always used the "gooey love scene" required in every horror film as our excuse to go to the bathroom or run to the concession stand. During those missing few minutes we knew nothing of note would transpire. Writers, producers and directors drew the same conclusions.

But in spite of such predictability in female roles throughout the history of horror movies, something profound occurred. Many female actresses rose above the standard listless scripts and slapdash productions to create memorable characterizations that broke free of stereotypes and created performances that rank right up there with the substantial male roles. True, such well-written and well-acted roles are exceptions to the norm, but they cannot be denied or ignored.

Mirian Hopkins as the doomed Ivy is murdered by Hyde (Fredric March) in *Dr. Jekyll and Mr. Hyde* (1932).

During the decade of the 1930s, such exceptional talents as Zita Johann, the tragically doomed reincarnated Egyptian Princess of the past, who once again in the present denies her love for the persistent Boris Karloff in *The Mummy*, proves that female love-interests could be beautiful, tortured, strong and enigmatic, worthy to share the screen with icon Karloff and hold their own in the acting department. Also in 1932, Miriam Hopkins, playing the lower-class seductress Ivy in Rouben Mamoulian's *Dr. Jekyll and Mr. Hyde*, proves that a well-drawn female character could be both sexy and manipulative and also tragic and sad in a complex performance that becomes so much more than mere window dressing.

During the decade of the 1940s, the Val Lewton RKO B-feature unit created most of the outstanding female horror film performances of the decade. Simone Simon was more than a sex kitten in *Cat People*, but she is aggressive, manipulative and defensive while also being tragically doomed, vulnerable and caught between a world of wanton passion and respectable sexual restraint. Hers was a character cut from original fibers and sewn into a patchwork that displays the full complexity of femininity during this era. Other notable Lewton females include the teaming of Jean Brooks and Kim Hunter, who portray opposing sisters, in the darkly pessimistic *The Seventh Victim*, featuring a young innocent's bravery in leaving her boarding school cocoon to venture forth to the sinful New York cityscape to find her doomed sister, a cutting-edge character, who gets involved in a Satanic cult sworn to secrecy. Such opposites become more and more similar as their determination and courage mold them into original and memorable characters that demand the viewers' attention. Such plum roles are the norm rather than the exception in the universe of Val Lewton.

Women regressed during the 1950s, settling down into comfortable stereotypes: the prim and proper asexual scientist, the sexually alluring but all-business assistant/ secretary/scientist's daughter, the cheap tramp barfly, the bored and boozed-out rich bitch wife, the alluring space babe whose all-female civilization is invaded by men, the screaming and kicking monster victim, the "other woman" of the sordid triangle affair, etc. Very few juicy and innovative female roles appear during this decade.

But by the late '60s and throughout the '70s (due in part to the feminist movement) prominent female roles re-emerged, characterizations written that allow women to break free from stereotypes and become assertive, intelligent and equal companions to the men with whom they share the screen. Characters such as Princess Leia (from *Star Wars*) and Ripley (from the *Alien* series) created the new subgenre of "kick-ass" heroines who now fill the shoes formally inhibited solely by males. And the evolution of women's roles in horror cinema continues to this day.

Unlike film noir and detective/suspense cinema, women are generally not respected in the horror film genre. Not because of any lack of talent involved, but because of the limitations placed upon the film genre by the studios and screenwriter. Yet this book exists to document those starting exceptions, to illustrate the evolution of women's roles in the horror film genre and to show that even within the narrow artistic limits, women's characterizations and performances could still impress and rise above the mediocre.

In no way does *Bitches, Bimbos, and Virgins* mock the extraordinary work delivered by women in horror movies throughout the decades. It is instead a long-overdue tribute to their often neglected film work. Hopefully this book will provide some of that much-deserved recognition.

—Gary J. Svehla
October, 1996

Dr. Frankenstein's Monster (Boris Karloff) threatens Frankenstein's bride (Mae Clarke) in the 1931 *Frankenstein*.

150 Years of Women and Horror: She Has Always Lived in the Castle

by James J.J. Janis

The story of women in horror is a simple one simply told: Once upon a time, women in the horror genre, especially film, were inferior and degraded. Pathetic and marginalized, a woman existed only to be saved from the monster by the virile young male hero who would then carry her off to wedded bliss where she would assume her rightful place in the world...that of unpaid servant and prostitute. Brainwashed to be barefooted, bake bread and be bloated with babies, many of the women in the reading/viewing audience were likewise only helpless victims of the monstrous horror film which, once unmasked, was revealed to be just another powerful poison of the pernicious oppressive patriarchy.

However, when all seemed lost, in the early 1960s and 1970s, feminism, a vital young political movement, marched into battle against the bumptious bastions of the barbaric blowhards and, after much bra-burning and blistering bursts of bitter bluster, saved helpless womanhood, carrying her off to a happy utopia where her consciousness would be raised and the pornographic horror film would be re-educated into becoming a progressive power for positive persuasion.

It is a happy story with a happy ending. Pleasingly short and uncluttered with any annoying facts or unwanted dissenting voices, it has the advantage of being able both to rally the cadres to action and to keep them in line. No thinking is required or desired. All that need be known is included and in fact, with little effort, as Helen Reddy demonstrated, it can be made into a rather little nice song. All in all, the story is a beautiful thing.

Except.

What if it is not so?

Woman has always been a force in horror. After the genre, as it is now known, was created by Horace Walpole with his classic Gothic novel, *The Castle of Otranto*, in 1764, there was a singular 14-year period when this was not the case. But by 1777, as the Gothic movement began to build momentum, nearly all of its earliest primary champions and geniuses were female. There was author Clara Reeve who, in *The Old English Baron*, introduced such standards as castles with haunted wings, groans, clanking chains and the rest of "Gothic machinery" that the reader now might view as clichés. This would be the driving force behind the genre for over 100 years and became, on film, the Old Dark House subgenre with such descendants as *Horror Island, The Monster Walks* and, not surprisingly, *The Old Dark House*. Reeve was the first to use dreams as a harbinger of terror, thus paving the way for (in the Universal series) Elizabeth Frankenstein's precognitive visions and for Freddy Krueger. And Reeve introduced to the horror tale sentimental morality, more of which we will encounter later. Women writers such as Sophia Lee, Anne Fuller and Agnes Musgrave soon followed.

While Stephen King has often been used as an adjective to praise a work of fear, be it in print or celluloid, that is through a surfeit of ignorance. If

Clara Reeve

Walpole is horror's Columbus, then its Washington is undeniably Ann Radcliffe. Born the same year as the genre itself, Radcliffe's contributions are immense. In her works such as *The Italian* or *The Mysteries of Udolpho*, she created the fairy-tale world of breathtaking castles or ruined abbeys set in deep valleys or jagged crags (such as Ludwig Frankenstein's castle in Vasaria and a Realtor's show list of Castle Draculas—from the Lugosi original to Hammer's *Scars of Dracula*) and old dark houses set near the pounding surf of an ocean (as in *Dr. X* or *Abbott and Costello Meet Frankenstein* or *The Pit and the Pendulum*).

Radcliffe created the "hero-villain" who, though evil, is so impressive in mind and almost supernatural abilities that he becomes the focus of the reader's attention and near-sympathy; a character type so much larger than life that it would later demand actors such as a Lugosi (as in *The Devil Bat*), an Atwill (as in *Murders in the Zoo*), a Price (*The Abominable Dr. Phibes*) or a Gough (*Horrors of the Black Museum*) to play them. In spite of all other elements that were before and have arrived since, it could be suggested that these almost elemental figures of darkness *are* the horror genre. It is undeniable that the great monsters/villains are what/who the story is ultimately about, what drives the plot, and whose psychological makeup is the most clearly delineated. The great hero-villain can sometime carry a lesser vehicle simply by his/her own dramatic power and it is this character that enthralls the genre's disciples. Would there be any interest in the Lugosi Monograms if the films lacked Lugosi or if *The Mad Doctor of Market Street* featured Van Heflin in the Lionel Atwill role? Can the reader contemplate *Black Zoo* without Michael Gough or a horror world without a Creeper or a Phantom or a Frankenstein Monster? Even today, in a modern horror world that lacks much in the way of hero-villains, there are the likes of a Jason Voorhees or a Michael Myers to satisfy the need, if only on a basic level. With Radcliffe, one can see the progenitor of the great supervillains, be it a Dr. Fu Manchu from print or a Dr. Victor Von Doom or a Green Goblin from the comic books—all of which have been brought to the screen. What has been called, mistakenly, Byronic should properly be called Radcliffian.

Radcliffe pioneered horror's use of masterly dialogue as a means of revealing character and of advancing the action. If one loves the riches of an "Even the phone is dead" or an "I stole bodies....they said" or the exquisite monologues of a "Do you know where you are, Bartolomy?" or the various "mad" speeches, then it is Radcliffe one must thank.

Ann Radcliffe

Radcliffe created the basic dramatic structure of horror with its sudden plot twists at strategic moments, the withholding of information, or an added mystification. In short, the story structure of the horror film's Golden and Silver ages follows this basic pattern: Their slow build-ups toward the introduction of the menace (usually at the 30-minute mark) and then the twist (the Monster is revealed, attacks or escapes, the scientist conceives of a plan, someone is murdered or the pursuit begins, etc.) followed by the menace discussion/rules scene and then another twist (usually the Monster kidnapping the girl or some type of death trap) followed by a resolution (menace destroyed) followed by the moral/explanation of why things happened as they did.

Radcliffe created the sudden spotlighting of certain individual scenes where the plot pauses to cause or increase the suspense by focusing on a certain element. This can be seen in James Whale's habit of halting his films to introduce his main menaces by a series of progressive close-ups or in the grave-opening

Illustration from 1830 volume of *The Mysteries of Udolpho*.

scene in Mario Bava's *Black Sunday*. Dracula's various resurrections—particularly in the Hammers—are Radcliffian spotlights, as is every famous unmasking from *The Phantom of the Opera* to *The Fly* to the shark's first appearance in *Jaws*.

Radcliffe demanded that her nightmares be infused with intelligence, and her books are filled with quotes from Shakespeare, Milton and others. Is it even necessary to restate again just how, from the highest MGM to the lowliest PRC, from scripts made up of complex, clever and many times beautiful dialogue to the consistent use of actors and actresses who could actually speak, the classic horror film is miles above its modern sub-literate counterparts such as *Jeepers Creepers 2*, where characters do not so much as talk as shriek obscenities in a bizarre tonal mantra only the imbecilic could truly find meaningful?

Radcliffe expanded upon Reeve's innovation and also insisted that horror must have sentimentality and morality—in short, a respect for human decency. It is amazing and depressing to reflect just how low the body counts are in the great horror films and just how memorable each of those deaths is. Little Maria or Tante Berthe. The villager ordered to shoot the Monster. Gino. Chris the dog. Meanwhile who died again in the fifth Freddy film? Or the fourth *Alien* film? Does anyone truly care beyond the gore crowd and only then if the death was coolly wet?

Lastly, it was Radcliffe who developed the principle of suggestive obscurity to a fine art. It was Radcliffe who discovered the terror of the unseen or the partially glimpsed or the not shown. The gust of wind. The drop of blood seen by candlelight on a dark staircase. A strain of music coming from someplace in the dark. Radcliffe was "the mistress of hints" who preferred her audience use its imagination. Here is the true origin of Val Lewton and his famous "buses," and many of the Italian horror films of the '60s such as *The Whip and the Body* or *Terror-Creatures from the Grave* were knowingly or otherwise influenced by the Radcliffian style.

Radcliffe's impact was vast. Her book *Udolpho* was called the most interesting novel in the English language. Besides such straight writers such as Byron, Balzac, the Brontes, Keats, Wordsworth, Dumas, Scott and others, it should not surprise that she inspired genre figures such as Mary Shelley, Victor Hugo, Edgar Allan Poe, almost all of the Victorians from Dickens to Stoker and from Conan Doyle to Stevenson right into the 20th century and beyond. Her work heavily affected the German Gothic horror story from 1798, which, in turn, would influence the German Expressionistic horror films of the silent and sound eras. Radcliffe probably would not have found much amiss with the Production Code of 1934-1967 nor the horror film's Golden Age from Universal to Lewton and Curtiz to the Silver Age's Roger Corman productions, all of which could properly be called The

Illustration from the gore-filled *The Monk*.

Felicity Jones as Jane Austen Gothic heroine Catherine Morland is overwhelmed by the Tilney mansion in the 2007 *Northanger Abbey*.

Radcliffian Age. *Seven Footprints to Satan* is Radcliffe. *The Black Castle* is Radcliffe. *House on Haunted Hill* is Radcliffe. Except for the frog, *The Maze* is Radcliffe. She is even responsible, with her tendency toward explaining away the supernatural, for…sigh…Scooby Doo.

No one is perfect.

When, in 1796, Matthew Gregory Lewis wrote his novel *The Monk*, filled with gore, sensuality and a "daylight orgy of horrors," he was purposely defying the Radcliffe school and creating the other side of the genre... the terror story as a collection of "charnel house horrors and lust." Condemned by the Radcliffians (Samuel Coleridge called *The Monk* "a poison for youth and a provocative for the debauchee"), one can see, as what Lewis wrought in his novels and was later preserved in the Penny Dreadfuls, the pulps such as *Weird Tales*, Lovecraft, the films of Tod Slaughter, *The Human Monster*, the Hammers, the Cohen/Gough films right up to the Freddy and Jason movies of today, that it was not in 1957 but 1796 that the great Universal vs. Hammer debate truly began.

Let us now step from behind the curtains obscuring these darkling muses working with quill and paper to examine, if we would, one of their creatures moving about upon the printed page before the eyes of the reader. Let us now be introduced to the horror heroine. The horror genre, as early as 1789, has been much maligned by those unsympathetic, ignorant or hostile to the form. Jane Austen's *Northanger Abbey* is probably the most infamous example where the *Udolpho* novel provides much conversation among the *Northanger Abbey* characters. And one of the targets of choice—and of convenience—has been the Gothic horror heroine. Even today, within the ranks of terror's acolytes, there are those self-defeating agenda-driven fanatics and their ignorant desperate-to-please flatterers who persist in misrepresenting the Gothic heroine as being some passive dullard who shrieks, faints at a moment's notice and is utterly helpless unless saved by whoever the hero happens to be in that novel. Yet, the literary daughter of Samuel Richardson's *Pamela* and *Clarissa*, all Gothic heroines, is a character who would be perfectly at home and accepted in an Austen or a Bronte novel. There she would cleverly and subtly navigate the rocky shoals of upper class society until she achieved her goals. Instead, in the Gothic, she gets stuck in a haunted castle, pursued by lustful madmen in very bad weather, locked in black catacombs, threatened with insidious torture and gets no critical respect at all.

While attempting to mock, in 1813, one of Gothic's enemies, Eaton Barrett described the heroine thusly, though nevertheless letting some truth shine through: the "heroine is a young lady rather taller than usual, and often an orphan, at all events, possessed of the finest eyes in the world. Though her frame is fragile, that a breath of wind might scatter it like chaff, it is sometimes stouter than a statue of cast iron." She is

Richard Stapley, Sally Forrest and Charles Laughton in *The Strange Door*

intelligent beyond reason, can paint, sew, compose, sing and usually play a musical instrument. While, when "reduced to extremities," she might faint "on the spot," she might also exhibit "energies almost superhuman." She may be filled with "tears, sighs, and half sighs" but she can also take "journeys on foot that would founder 50 horses." She can live a month on a handful of food, and trapped in a fetid dungeon for extended periods will emerge finally "glittering like a morning star, as fragrant as a lily, and as fresh as an oyster."

No matter what the outrage, indignity or ungodly terror, the Gothic heroine will endure. Yet this writer would wonder why this is not to be considered strength? This "endurance girl" is usually accused, often simultaneously, of lacking initiative and of being foolish when she elects to explore the dark recesses of castles and convents. Yet this writer would suggest that these two libels are self-negating. If the endurance girl behaves intelligently then she lacks initiative. However, if she takes the initiative then she lacks intelligence. It's little wonder that she is subject to fits of melancholia and suffers from the vapors.

Author Donald Westlake once derided the Gothic novel as being about "a girl who gets a house." And so it is, but what does *that* mean exactly? The founding fathers of this country recognized that one of the foundations of human freedom and democracy is the right to own property. For with property comes security and with security comes freedom. Every totalitarian movement in the 20th century has identified itself as being the enemy of human freedom by its denial of the right of property. And so, in almost every instance, from Radcliffe to *London after Midnight* to *The Ghoul* to *Sherlock Holmes Faces Death* to *The Strange Door* to *Shadow of the Cat* to, surprisingly, *Hellraiser*, the heroine is set upon by villains preternatural, outré or mysterious who seek to deny her birthrights, her honor, her freedom, her happiness and frequently her life—to make it trendy—to take her away her right of choice. If she gets the house then she has attained freedom. If not then she loses all. The "endurance girl," while perhaps not to the taste of modern audiences, should nonetheless, have her respect and sympathy. The Gothic novel, created around the time of the American Revolution, is about the attaining of liberty from the old medieval feudal order still in power in Europe. What is *Dracula* if not the story of two modern independent women on the verge of choosing how their lives will be, having that choice either threatened or destroyed by a literally medieval aristocratic monster from Europe who, by turning them into vampires, hardly "liberates them" as has moronically been suggested but rather enslaves them, returns them to his castle where they will assume a subservient place in his scheme of things—as vassals—as *his* property. The Gothic terror novel was molded by women, written by women and features women who, through endurance and courage, do get a house and, by doing so, gain choice, independence and freedom. And this is bad?

The Radcliffian model—in terms of form, theme and the endurance girl —would continue into the 19th century. Despite much silliness written about the period regarding women, the Victorian Era would prove to be a remarkably fertile period for women, for horror and for women in horror. In England and America, women began to promote motherhood as being of a sacred importance, declaring that it was a woman's duty to bring about a true Christian civilization whereby men must become more like women and the women more like angels. Using motherhood as the rallying cry, women demanded and received almost complete control of the nursing and teaching occupations. (And it is of note that, besides reporters, the profession of choice of women in classic horror has been a nurse or a medical assistant of some type, be it *Captive Wild Woman, House of Dracula* or *The Gorgon*. And what did Laurie Strode become when she grew up? A teacher.) Women displaced most ministers and became the spiritual guides of their congregations or towns. (Frieda Inescourt's function in *Return of the Vampire* illustrates the concept.) Women effectively removed much paternal influence in the home and in the raising of children, which appears to be what is happening to poor old Kent Smith in *Curse of the Cat People*, what appears to be the case with Henry Frankenstein regarding his sons Wolf and Ludwig, as well as Lawrence Talbot (implied), Philippe Delambre (from *The Fly*) and certainly—though for the worse—Baron Meinster in *Brides of Dracula*. And anything that threatened their new powers and rights or attempted to marginalize them in any way such as atheism, demon rum or certain types of scientific or intellectual trends would be fought. Perhaps the best genre manifestation of this can be seen in the early cinematic versions of *Dr Jekyll and Mr. Hyde* in which Henry Jekyll is a perfect Victorian femininized man who is undone by his interests in strange unwomanly scientific and theological notions along with the worst case of "demon rum" imaginable.

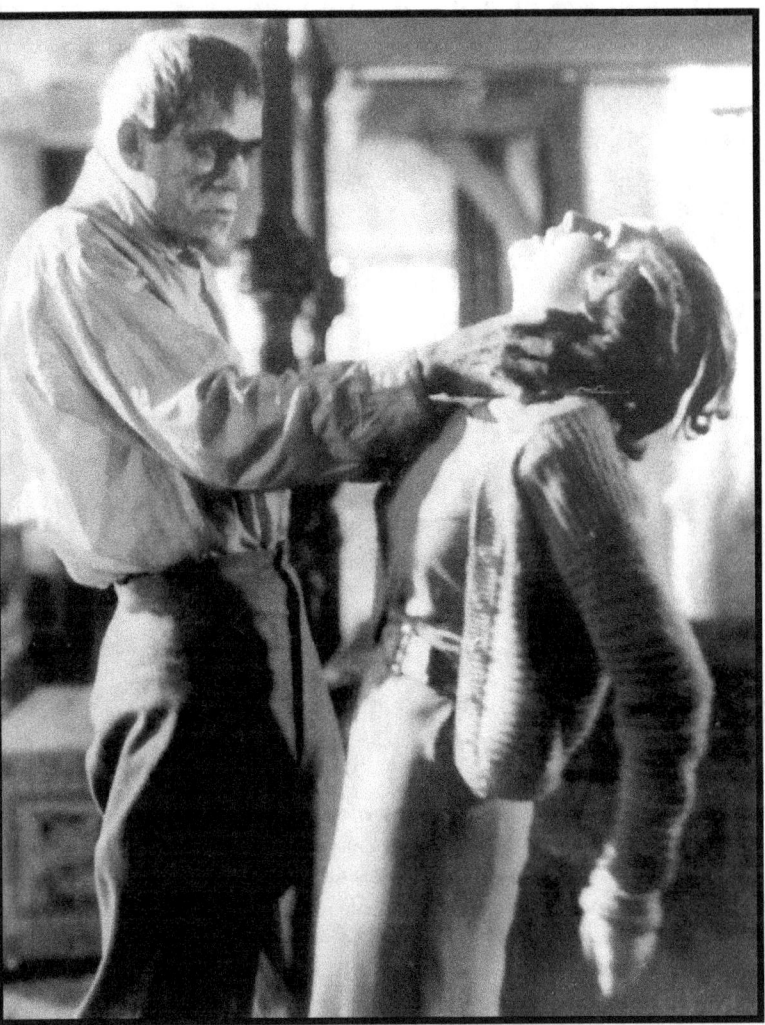

Prof. Henry Morlant (Boris Karloff) aka The Ghoul terrorized Betty Harlon (Dorothy Hyson) in *The Ghoul*, 1933.

And women wrote. Henry James would note that, in the 1880s, women dominated the field of fiction—being more prolific and more popular than many male authors. For example, all of the sales of the works by Hawthorne, Melville, Thoreau and Whitman did not equal that of one of the popular female-written domestic novels. Many of these women authors—the most productive ones—were spinsters, independent women—who had a house (very much like the heroine in *The Bat*). Novels appeared featuring feisty independent women who saved men or communities from sin (as in *Strangler of the Swamp*) or mistaken theological notions (usually those dour Puritans—horror's religious villain of choice after Catholics), became writers (*Little Women* being the obvious example here), detectives (the first female detective was introduced in the 1864 novel *The Female Detective*), or were the central characters of such novels as *The Story of a Modern Woman* (1894) or *The Woman Who Did* (1895). In 1890, Mary Bradley Lane even wrote a science fiction novel called *Mizora* that dealt with an all-female Utopia that we can probably—ahem—thank for such things as *Queen of Outer Space* and the *Buck Rogers in the 20th Century* episode "Planet of the Amazon Women."

As already indicated, this trickled down into horror. Women had never left horror anyway, with writers such as Charlotte Riddell, Mary Braddon and Rhoda Broughton carrying the Gothic flame lit by Radcliffe. Because of their deeply held religious beliefs, it should not surprise to learn that Victorian society on both sides of the Atlantic was fascinated with the supernatural and the occult. (Echoes of this culture can be seen in TV's *Supernatural*.) Séances were a must for all who professed an open mind and modern outlook. Many

Margaret O'Brien is the perky Mary Lennox in the 1949 *The Secret Garden*, which also starred Brian Roper (left as Dickon) and Dean Stockwell as Colin Craven.

Dracula's references to death in *House of Frankenstein* as being a place from which he has "just returned." The sense and issue of morality, the explorations of what is right and wrong, not just judged by physical action or appearance but upon what was inside, became the salvation of the genre, preventing it from deteriorating into just a pool of the putrid and the perverse as it frequently threatened to do in the Penny Dreadfuls of the period or across the channel with the Grand Guignol or across the Atlantic with the cynical tales of Ambrose Bierce. The blood of Christ, to paraphrase, was the life of horror, flowing through the greatest works of the period, be it Stevenson's *The Strange Case of Dr. Jekyll and Mr. Hyde* or Hugo's *The Hunchback of Notre Dame* (where despite his appearance and actions, who can deny that Quasimodo is a better man than his Master, the Archdeacon). Even in the genre work of one of the modern nihilist culture's icons, Oscar Wilde, be it his fairy-tales such as *The Selfish Giant* or his horror classic *The Picture of Dorian Gray* (both of which have been filmed), there exists an intense morality. Such is the definition of classic horror, separating it from its lesser-mongrelized siblings.

who wrote about the supernatural were, along with being devout Christians, devout believers in the spirit world. So now, instead of evil monks, Italians or Barons, the horror novel frequently concerned a woman who got a house—and a ghost. Films such as *The Ghost and Mrs. Muir*, *The Uninvited* or *The Canterville Ghost* are examples of descendants of these types of stories. These novels/short stories, written by well-read, open-minded and sometimes well-traveled women, were usually intelligent, with excellent characterizations and plotting.

Due to heavy involvement in things Christian, the moral ground broken by Clara Reeve would become horror's firm foundation. There would be strong moral purposes to the stories, with many of the ghosts being benevolent, rebuking abusive parents or wastrels. *A Christmas Carol*, though written by a male, is probably the most notable survivor of this type, though the films *The Scoundrel*, *The Ghost Goes West*, *Beyond Tomorrow*, *The Passing of the Third Floor Back*, *The Lady in White* and *The Changeling* can be considered linear descendants. Elizabeth Stuart Phelps wrote novels (*Gates Ajar* for example) about death, heaven and the geography of the afterlife that seem almost certain to have informed such later films as *Between Two Worlds*, *A Matter of Life and Death*, *On Borrowed Time* and even

In most of these books, as should be expected, the endurance girl remained, holding tightly to the mortgage of her house of horrors.

However, soon she would have a rival.

Along with the feisty independent ladies of regular fiction, the bright energetic, jolly girls with a passion for setting the world to right (such as *Rebecca of Sunnybrook Farm* or *Pollyanna*) were the characters of choice in another genre dominated by women authors— what is today called children's literature. At that period though, genre categories were not nearly as rigid, with many writers finding themselves being claimed by adults, children or both, regardless of their own intentions. Writers such as Radcliffian Walter Scott, James Fenimore Cooper and Jonathan Swift suddenly became children's authors, while many "children's authors" such as Robert Louis Stevenson or Louisa May Alcott found themselves being read by adults. Many others were claimed by both camps—frequently genre writers or dabblers such as Wilde, Le Fanu, Sir Arthur

Conan Doyle, H.G. Wells, Washington Irving or Jules Verne. Into this genre entanglement, the fairy-tales of the Brothers Grimm were or were about to be translated into English. Filled, as they were, with horrific tales of witches, werewolves, curses, murderers, castles and torture, these were short versions of the Gothic novel, intended for children! These charming tales of carnage—though more in the Lewis vein at times—were told to the Grimm Brothers predominantly by educated young women from the middle class or the aristocracy of Germany (and probably, this writer ventures, steeped in Radcliffe) and not surprisingly these stories featured clever perky young girls named Gretel or Red Cap or Maleen who dealt firmly with evil gnomes, witches, wolves or stepmothers—and usually got a house. The Golden Age of children's literature is roughly dated from 1865 to 1910. That period, along with Grimm's Fairy Tales, includes fantasy novels featuring dimension-jumping Alice in *Alice's Adventures in Wonderland* and witch killer extraordinaire Dorothy in *The Wizard of Oz*. Likewise, in Francis Hodgson Burnett's *The Secret Garden*, a novel about a young, perky orphan girl who goes to England, finds a tragic mystery, sets the world to right and gets a house (this was later made into a creepy 1949 film featuring a perfectly at home George Zucco and Elsa Lanchester), this perky girl dominated fantasy/children's novels, as her elder sister the endurance girl did horror. However, due to the genre's permeability, the perky girl would very slowly, and as will be seen with characteristic convolution, begin moving on up into other genres.

The two ladies, however, could not be more unalike. Where the endurance girl was a creature of classical literature, steeped in the poetic and the historic, the perky girl, an amalgam from children's stories, the social and religious novels and the just-beginning female detective story genre, tended to personify the modern. The endurance girl would frequently be, whatever her current status, from the upper middle class or the aristocracy. Her boyfriends would be earls, princes, knights or the odd viscount. The perky girl would be from the middle, lower-middle class or the poor. Hers would not be a story of restoration or inheritance but the classic Horatio Alger rags to riches story (or at least an improvement of her situation). Perky girls usually held jobs. Her boyfriends (if she had one) would be lumberjacks, first mates, reporters, pilots or, on occasion, a struggling doctor or architect. The endurance girl would be tall, a tad too thin with classical looks, wear long dresses with long hair (the better to blow gently in the ghost-like wind and reflect the moonlight) and was almost always depressed. The perky girl would be short, sometimes leaning to stoutness, have an oval face with dimples and a pert button nose, wear, perhaps, a gingham dress (but certainly nothing to interfere with her ability to run) or pants—jodhpurs preferred with riding or laced boots. Her hair, when not bobbed, would be short, barely reaching the neck, frequently curled or covered with a cap. The perky girl was always chipper. If she had one (both ladies tend to be orphans, and mother is always, no matter what, dead), the endurance girl's father, a drunkard or an opium addict in debt to the villain, would be just another hardship for her to endure. The perky girl's father would usually be a scientist or an archeologist—who would then be kidnapped by a ghastly heathen cult or the mystery menace—both seeking the secret formula. The perky girl would then set out on a quest to rescue daddy. For a comparison, think Christine from *The Phantom of the Opera* vs. the female characters from *Mystery of the Wax Museum/House of Wax*.

Anna Lee was the heroine to Boris Karloff's villain in *Bedlam*.

This tendency toward "quests" is a basic characteristic of the perky girl. As per her origins in the religious and social novels of Victorian women, the perky girl is on a mission. Be it to liberate Oz, defend the downtrodden, or save orphans or abused dogs and lead them all through the glorious gates of heaven, the perky girl *will* set the world to right. As might be expected, this can make the perky girl tend toward self-righteousness, priggishness and a great deal of narcissism (which can make her overlook the obvious—particularly who the mystery villain is). She *can* grate, is preachy, and her temper is something to note. (Anna Lee in *Bedlam* or Anne Nagel in *Man Made Monster* are perfect examples.) On the other hand, the perky girl is determined and unrelenting. She never doubts or questions her God-given purpose. While the endurance girl sort of glides, the perky girl, with head protruding rather like a ferocious fowl, runs to her goals. Like Linda Stirling in *The Tiger Woman* or *Zorro's Black Whip*, she will fly at a villain, fists flailing, unheedful of the odds because she knows her cause is just. She frequently prevails simply because she tends toward fanaticism. The perky girl, be it Nancy Drew or Miss Marple, owns the female detective genre because she *will* fight evil. The endurance girl endures evil, will wear it down and, sometimes, if honor demands, will kill it, but she would never be a detective. That would be gauche. The endurance girl, however, can play a lute and read Petronius in the original Latin. Unless her father is an archeologist and taught her Aramaic or Greek at a young age, the perky girl has no patience with such useless intellectual rot but she can shoe a horse, fly a biplane and change the sparkplugs on a Model T. She has read the Bible (King James) from cover to cover, though.

Though both are usually young women, the perky girl, when not actually a preteen, always seems much younger and can frequently be a tomboy. Hence she tends toward more action, plot-driven genres. Besides children's literature, initially and still, she would later move into the pulps (Pat Savage, Margo Lane and Nita Van Sloan) and comic books (Lois Lane, Linda Page, Barbara Gordon, The Black Canary and the Golden Age Wonder Woman—the latter the perky girl taken to nightmarish extremes) and, with Edgar Rice Burroughs and Alex Raymond's space operas, would contend with the endurance girl for, and later dominate, the science fiction genre. The endurance girl would appear in all of these genres with varying degrees of success (she is a regular feature in the Fu Manchu novels for example), but Gothic horror would always be her home.

When moving pictures arrived at the dawn of the 20th century, the horror film was born and women were still there. But the situation was different. Film is a business that sprang from commerce and the sciences—not from the arts, the Church, or the hearth. It is a group effort and not a private one like writing nor is it especially subject to morals or respect for family. Women, as a creative force in the weaning of the infant horror film, were excluded, reduced to stealing visitation rights either through adaptations of their stories, novels or plays or through their involvement in external social or religious organizations concerned (especially after the pernicious *The Birth of a Nation*) with reining in the increasingly juvenile delinquent cinema. The result was still that, as creative or moral forces, women, as they had feared they would be during the Victorian Era by these godless hard-drinking scientific intellectual masculine hordes, were left behind momentarily at the movies, while paradoxically their fictional creations, over whom they had once held ultimate

Boris Karloff and Gloria Stuart starred in *The Old Dark House*.

sway, were *now* embodied by actresses—a sort of author twice removed. As Gothic horror reached the screen, the endurance girl was there, making a noble sacrifice to defeat the vampire in *Nosferatu*, surviving Erik in *The Phantom of the Opera*, or getting a house in *The Cat and the Canary*. The perky girl, through her dominance of the fantasy/ children's novel, would make the leap into the fantasy/children's film (either through film versions of the Oz books, for example or through the persona of Mary Pickford), but her most important move would be in the adventure serials of the late teens and early 1920s. There she would begin to encounter science fiction elements, thus laying her claims in that direction, as well as hooded killers, supernatural entities and other Gothic motifs. By the end of the 1920s, she would be, in (appropriately) German productions, a *Woman in the Moon*

Faith Domerque with Jeff Morrow (left rear) and Rex Reason in *This Island Earth*

and would be setting the world to right with a feisty fire and God on her side in *Metropolis*.

By the time sound arrived, and yet decades before terms such as Scream Queen were conceived, the two ladies became such established types that certain actresses tended to specialize (either through inclination or qualification) in one or the other. It is especially hard to imagine Frances Drake, Gloria Stuart, Marian Marsh, Helen Chandler or Evelyn Ankers being anything other than endurance girls while it is equally difficult to imagine Anne Nagel, Anna Lee, Peggy Moran, Louise Currie, Helen Mack or Jane Randolph being anything else than perky. The occasional example of movie miscasting, such as Jean Rogers' wildly wrong endurance girl version of perky girl Dale Arden in the first two *Flash Gordon* serials, is only cast in starker relief when the role was finally recast with a wonderfully pugnacious Carol Hughes in the third serial. Meanwhile, Mae Clarke as Elizabeth Frankenstein kept acting as if she would have preferred helping out the *King of the Rocketmen* or getting roughed up by gangsters rather than all that high emoting that Valerie Hobson would later do so well. Fay Wray is the major exception here, somehow managing to combine many aspects of both types so seamlessly that, to this day, many horror fans still do not know what to make of this strange perky/endurance girl.

As the decades passed and science fiction came to dominate in the 1950s, the perky girl, personified expertly by Faith Domerque and Mara Corday, seemed set to sweep the endurance girl from the scene until Barbara Shelley, Yvonne Romain and Veronica Carlson got a house—of Hammer. Though again, here there is the major and very rare exception of Hazel Court, who could play endurance convincingly (*The Man Who Could Cheat Death*) and then be delightfully perky (*Dr. Blood's Coffin*).

The above is no small accomplishment, as the character of the endurance girl is, in spite of some of today's major talents who have attempted to play her, becoming a lost art. In *Theater of Blood*, it is just not possible to believe that the otherwise wonderful Diana Rigg would ever endure anything when she could inflict—thus compromising the film's "surprise" revelation. Kate Nelligan in the 1979 *Dracula* seems to have wandered in from her stage success in *Plenty* delivering a blundering wrong and fatally unattractive performance, and Helena Bonham-Carter in the 1994 *Frankenstein* comes flying in on her broom. Unlike the perky girl, always so very modern, whose very makeup allows her to be both dim and bright, arrogant and admirable, irritating and irresistible and thus is usually easier to portray and moreso to cast (getting a narcissistic

self-righteou actress is probably *not* all that difficult in Hollywood), the endurance girl, as per her origins, requires a sensitivity, intelligence and care that, at present, only Jamie Lee Curtis seems to have been able to demonstrate with consistency. The type just may end up like the fictional Miss Havisham and all those historically forgotten female horror writers—all alone in their solitary old dark houses, unremembered, unwanted and unloved.

But this is in the future.

By 1914, it was all there. It just had to be brought to life on celluloid. The heavy lifting had already been done. Women had staked a claim creatively, establishing much of what the horror genre would be both in print and later on in film. They had given horror the intelligence and intricate infrastructure that put the lie to those who say the genre is without worth. They had made of horror a fountain from which inspiration flowed to other genres of literature and to authors who *stole* the good stuff and then would frequently dismiss the genre with contempt to cover up their thievery. Women had given horror its moral foundations that convey its meaning, beauty and artistry. They had done their work so well that it would take more than five decades before horror would actually be deserving of the scorn that has been traditionally heaped upon it. In a perverse way, they had given horror its gore and sex too, as Matthew Lewis wrote *The Monk* in reaction to the Radcliffe school of fear. In ways direct or oblique, they had given us *Frankenstein, Dracula, The Hunchback of Notre Dame, The Phantom of the Opera* and so much more up to and including the next film by M. Night Shayamalan—whose work is steeped in Radcliffian aesthetic. They had staked a claim to one of the genre's iconic bedrock figures—the endurance girl—a figure, who, though beset with many difficulties that harry her both in mind and body, with strength and honor will *endure* all to find a reward of security and freedom. Women, though through a labyrinthine route, had created another of the genre's iconic and important figures—the perky girl—who, though fully formed by 1914, had not yet asserted herself. But she would, as always with good cheer and optimism, soon set the world right and become a full member of the world of horror.

And this was done before anyone reading this was born. Woman and horror. She has endured and succeeded beyond what anyone had any reason to expect. And she got a house. In fact, it can be said that—she has always lived in the castle.

He Done Her Wrong: The Fate of Women in Golden Age Horrors

by Gregory William Mank

"And All the Winds Go Sighing,
for Sweet Things Dying"
—Christina Rossetti

The trademark sound of the Horror Film, of course, is the female scream.

And among the most sensational vignettes of "Golden Age" Horror were those in which Ladies—usually in censor-pleasing penance for their own celluloid sins—met their Maker in audience-titillating fashion.

Of course, this was decades before the slasher films, which mutilated and debased women even as the Female Liberation wars were waging. Audiences of the '30s and '40s enjoyed these comeuppances, just as Shakespeare's crowds had beheld the poisoning of Hamlet's lascivious mother Gertrude, or the suicide of hysterical Juliet.

And the death scenes often revealed a lot about the Movies—and the people who watched them.

What follows is a dozen Female Death Scenes, 1931 to 1945, which lurk in my memory:

1. *Murders in the Zoo* (Paramount, 1933): "I'm not going to kiss you. *You're* going to kiss *me*!"

They're a fascinating couple. There's Lionel Atwill, "The Maddest Doctor of Them All," here the Maddest Husband of Them All as Eric Gorman—millionaire sportsman/sadist. "Pinky" Atwill, nearing birthday #48, is trying hard to look like his old Matinee Idol self: He's sporting a toupee; he looks girdled into a snug tuxedo that makes him look like a horny puffin. But the gleam in Atwill's cat eyes—*that's* genuine, as he wraps a Valentino-style clutch around the lovely Mrs. Evelyn Gorman...

Kathleen Burke, the 19-year-old Paramount starlet, fresh from playing "the Panther Woman" in the studio's *Island of Lost Souls* (1932). Eyes like a sexy rabbit, bee-stung lips, her slinky figure draped in a fur-fringed frock: Kathleen (in real life reportedly a shy, quiet gal) has the look of a 1933 hooker who worked only the best street corners. Actually, it's the perfect look for the character of Evelyn, whom her husband suspects of being a nymphomaniac.

"I *hate* you!" shrieks the lady, running to her boudoir, where the wild-eyed Atwill (perversely chuckling at her hatred) has ordered her to await him. But, even though it's Hollywood's pre-Code era, we get no boudoir show (perhaps mercifully: the sight of Atwill stripping himself of toupee and girdle probably wouldn't have been pretty). Instead, we see the lithe and limber Kathleen slip through a window, sneak into the study, get the obscene, poison-loaded, fake snake's head that Atwill had used to kill her latest paramour (John Lodge, real-life future Connecticut governor) and take off in her high heels to the zoo, to blow the whistle on her murdering, sex-maniac husband.

He follows.

Lionel Atwill and Kathleen Burke in *Murders in the Zoo*

19

Linda Darnell as Netta whoops it up in Hangover Square.

They meet on a little ornamental bridge which might be perfect for *The Music Man* and the "Till There Was You" number, but for one fact: In the pool below, alligators are swimming.

Atwill retrieves the snake's head, overwhelms his screaming mate, and tosses her into the alligator pool as the creatures joyfully growl and splash at the surprise arrival of this delectable midnight snack.

Of course, come the climax of *Murders in the Zoo*, and the kinky "Pinky" gets his own comeuppance—as a giant snake bites him on his disreputable thigh and sinuously wraps itself around him.

(I wonder, come the early 1940s, and those juicy newspaper accounts of the Atwill Christmas Holidays "orgy," did Kathleen Burke, by then retired from acting, follow the scandal of her infamous former co-star?)

2. *Hangover Square* (20th Century-Fox, 1945): Linda Darnell was (arguably) the most beautiful movie star of the 1940s. In *Hangover Square*, as predatory chanteuse Netta, preying her way through 1903 gaslit London, she's a sensation. That Toulouse-Lautrec—style dance hall costume... those fishnet stockings... and that incredible mouth, seemingly painted in black lipstick: Little wonder that Linda won *Time*'s accolade (in the magazine's *Hangover Square* review) as "Hollywood's most rousing portrayer of unhouse-broken sex."

Of course, lovely Linda pays dearly for her sensual sins in *Hangover Square*'s most famous episode (masterfully staged by director John Brahm): the Guy Fawkes bonfire. Tragic Laird Cregar (in his final and posthumously released performance) strangles his tormenting vixen as she vainly primps before her mirror (symbolically, her cat is killed in the streets below simultaneously). Later, we see him carrying her cadaver through the London streets, having disguised the dead villainess as a dummy (complete with grotesque mask) to burn on the November 5 bonfire. As the crowd chants and cavorts, Cregar carries his macabre cargo to the not-yet-lit bonfire; as he climbs up a ladder to place her corpse atop the pyre, the mask slips a bit—and we see one last time that remarkable mouth. The revelers light the bonfire with their torches, and as Bernard Herrmann's brilliant music shrills in demonic glee, Cregar, caught in the dancing celebrants, stares in horror at the cremation of his dead lover.

By the way #1: Only a little more than a year before *Hangover Square*, Linda Darnell had played the vision of the Blessed Mother in Fox's *The Song of Bernadette*.

By the way #2: Linda, who had a life-long fear of fire, truly, tragically died after being trapped in a burning house in Dallas in 1965.

3. *The Lodger* (20th Century-Fox, 1944): This classic melodrama, of course, was predecessor to *Hangover Square*: same star (Laird Cregar, a magnificent Jack the Ripper), same director (John Brahm), same second male lead (George Sanders), same producer (Robert Bassler), same writer (Barre Lyndon). Instead of Linda Darnell in fishnets, we have the spectacle of Merle Oberon in opera hosiery.

However, the big female death scene of *The Lodger* doesn't belong to Miss Oberon (who survives in the movie), but to Doris Lloyd. This red-haired, blue-eyed, middle-aged British character actress (familiar in support in such Universal fare as *The Wolf Man, Night Monster, Frankenstein Meets the Wolf Man*, et al.) plays an over-the-hill whore ("Whitechapel Hag," says *The Lodger*'s cast list), who goes home to her hovel one bleak night—only to be paid a call by Jack the Ripper. She superbly builds her rising fear as the door creaks... and she begins to shiver, so pathetically that we almost shiver with her. Then the candle blows out—and, in a wicked trick her way through the last minutes of the movie—shuddering, shaking, waking up screaming...

Come the climactic midnight, and Chaney, Gwynne, marvelous Elizabeth Russell (as widow of Ralph Morgan, whom Ankers had driven to suicide in the film), and Lois Collier all confront her with her guilt. Reginald Le Borg must have enjoyed directing Evelyn's hysterical emoting (and it's a treat to see how she manages to back out a window in a skirt, without compromising her ladylike bearing!). Then, in one of the 1940s' weirdest death scenes, Evelyn's Ilona runs across a second story arbor, falls through it, somehow gets caught in a vine—and hangs herself.

As film historian *par excellence* Doug McClelland summed it up in his book, *The Golden Age of "B" Movies* (for which Evelyn wrote the Introduction, "The 'B' and I"): "Made to think dark powers were being used against *her*, Ankers then got to give out with one of her juiciest screams (one of her specialties), go crazy, fall off a roof and, for an encore, hang herself from a grapevine."

5. *House of Dracula* (Universal, 1945): She's the type of gal any WWII guy would have been proud to bring home to Mamma in late '45: an attractive brunette, with a wonderfully sweet disposition, a job at a cliffside castle above the sea, and a promising career as nurse to a brilliant, miracle-working scientist.

Doris Lloyd in *The Lodger*

of movie magic, *we* become the Ripper himself as the camera (virtuoso cinematography by Lucien Ballard) stalks Miss Lloyd, twitching and jerking insanely, as the actress backs away, too terrified to scream, too horrified to do anything as the Hugo Friedhofer music swells and "we" the Ripper fall upon "our" victim...

Afternote: Doris Lloyd, not long before her death in 1968, reported she received fan mail from an admirer who claimed he'd watched her death scene in *The Lodger* 13 times because it "gave him a tingle."

4. *Weird Woman* (Universal, 1944): The best of the *Inner Sanctum*s from Universal, *Weird Woman* rules primarily due to the novel attraction of seeing Evelyn Ankers, Universal's late and lamented "Queen of the Horrors," play a heavy. As Ilona the librarian, Other-Woman-from-Hell, Evelyn sashays through this macabre soap opera with two major acting challenges: pretending to be love-mad over Lon Chaney (who had made life miserable for "Evie" ever since *The Wolf Man*), and play-acting insane hate of Anne Gwynne—Evie's real-life friend, here playing Chaney's Tropics-born bride.

It's fun to watch Evelyn do her jealousy bit, and try to scare Anne Gwynne with voodoo chant phone calls. But the fun really starts when our "heroes" turn the tables on the chic librarian and she slowly goes crazy, losing her cool as she gasps

Only one problem: she's a hunchback.

"DRACULA! Frankenstein's MONSTER! WOLF MAN! MAD DOCTOR! HUNCHBACK!" teased Universal's *House of Dracula* advertisement. And it was cruel of the studio to hype Jane Adams' little nurse Nina among these time-tested goblins. A former Conover model and Pasadena Playhouse alumna, Miss Adams plays deformed Nina as brave, self-sacrificing— anything *but* monstrous.

As such, her death scene is a scandal.

John Carradine's Dracula has evaporated in the rays of the dawn; Lon Chaney has been cured of his Wolf Man affliction. Our "Mad Doctor" Edelmann (Onslow Stevens), tainted by Dracula's blood, is insanely trying to strengthen Glenn Strange's Frankenstein Monster. Miss Adams' Nina (who has delicately hinted in her acting that she's in love with the doctor) comes to the lab, beholds the madman and Monster amidst the flashing electrical apparatus, and timidly approaches the bestial, transformed Edelmann...who grabs her by the throat.

Chaney, his new love Martha O'Driscoll, and Constable Lionel Atwill all race to the lab at the sound of Jane's scream, just in time to see a death scene worthy of Barnum & Bailey: "Mad Doctor!" chokes "Hunchback!", then the doctor hurls her to the floor so roughly that she practically bounces, rolls over backward (legs in the air), and falls into a hole leading to the cave below.

Monster kills Atwill, Chaney kills Mad Doctor, Monster perishes in flames, villagers mix it up in Universal fashion...but as THE END rolls on the screen, I (for one) am still wincing at the fate of poor little Nina.

P.S.: At Fanex 9, Jane Adams revealed that a stunt woman actually performed that remarkable somersault/ death scene.

We were all relieved to hear it.

6. *House of Frankenstein* (Universal, 1944): Predecessor to *House of Dracula*, the first of Universal's "Monster Rallies" was a holiday for death scene aficionados: Karloff's Mad Doctor and Glenn Strange's Monster sinking in quicksand, Carradine's Dracula screaming and decaying in the rays of the sun, J. Carrol Naish's Hunchback (actually his double, Billy Jones) tossed by the Monster through a castle window, George Zucco's Prof. Bruno Lampini strangled, and Chaney's Wolf Man shot by a silver bullet. But it was she who fired that silver bullet who got the best death scene of all: the terrific Elena Verdugo, in Esmeralda wig and Gypsy costume, performing what we in the genre affectionately recall as "the crawl."

Top: Nina (Jane Adams) is done in by the man she secretly loves, Dr. Edelmann (Onslow Stevens), in *House of Dracula*.
Bottom: Ilonka (Elena Verdugo) is killed by her lover, who's also a werewolf (Lon Chaney) in *House of Frankenstein*.

While Elena, as Ilonka, waits outside the castle, under the full moon, Chaney transforms (all but his hands—a rare Universal gaffe); he crashes through the doors, and she follows him into the misty forest. For a werewolf doesn't just die: He must be killed by a silver bullet—"fired by the hand of one who loves him enough to understand."

The mist is swirling, the moon is shining, the Hans J. Salter music is swelling, Elena is screaming and a gun is firing. Lycanthrope Chaney lunges into close-up by a gnarled branch, breathes his last and turns back into Larry Talbot. And Elena's Ilonka, fatally mauled in the bargain, crawls across the forest floor, toward the man she loved and mercifully killed, and—in a Gothic demise Shakespeare might have lifted for one of his own tragedies—she dies at peace, her head resting on his chest.

Bad girl Daisy (Jeanne Bartlett) meets two different wolves in *Werewolf of London.*

Note: When John Parnum presented the Fanex Award to Elena Verdugo in 1995, he suggested that David O. Selznick had stolen the Verdugo/Chaney death scene for Jennifer Jones (then Mrs. Selznick) and Gregory Peck in *Duel in the Sun* (1946), in which Jennifer did her own "crawl." The audience applauded in agreement.

7. *Werewolf of London* (Universal, 1935): This one's a particular personal favorite. It's the Zoo episode. The wolves are howling in their cages, for Henry Hull has turned werewolf, loping through the zoo in his natty cap and clothes, a dude of a lycanthrope. Meanwhile, in the zoo, the watchman has a visitor. She's Daisy the Slut (played by blonde Jeanne Bartlett)—a Cockney hooker who has followed her own bestial instincts to the zoo to seduce the watchman ("Me with a wife and kids!" he guiltily laments). Daisy is every wife's (and censor's) nightmare: a brazen honey, who not only gets her hands and lips on the fidgety watchman, but takes time out from her kisses and pawings to insult his wife!

"Oh, what a fool you are" sneers Daisy. "Young fellow like you—tied to a white-faced, wimpering scarecrow of a woman!"

It's werewolf to the rescue. As the watchman goes to see why the wolves keep howling, decadent Daisy checks her makeup in her hand mirror. And whom does she see leering at her from the bushes but...the Werewolf of London! And he endears himself to moralists everywhere by going after the blonde bimbo, who, in her black high heels and very tight dress, is hardly attired to outrun a werewolf.

Sic semper bimbos.

Question: Whatever happened to Jeanne Bartlett?

8. *Dracula's Daughter* (Universal, 1936): In this one, the villainess gets the shaft—literally and figuratively.

Gloria Holden, as Countess Zaleska, has glided through this sombre chiller, gracefully dominating the leading man Otto Kruger (as Dr. Jeffrey Garth) and her sinister servant, Sandor (Irving Pichel); indeed, she's The Female Liberation Monster of the '30s. (Of course, Gloria was only earning $300 per week, compared to Kruger's $2,500 and Pichel's $650; but, we won't belabor that here.)

At any rate, Ms. Holden (who should have received some variety of Oscar for being the only movie star of 1936 to make it though an entire performance without

That's not cupid's arrow—Otto Kruger and Gloria Holder in *Dracula's Daughter.*

blinking) has kidnapped Garth's loved one (Marguerite Churchill). Kruger and Edward Van Sloan (as Dr. *Von Helsing*) pursue. The Countess seems to have won... but Sandor, jealous that the Vampire Queen is offering Garth eternal life, aims his bow and arrow at the leading man... and misses. Instead, the arrow goes right through the heart of Dracula's Daughter.

One could indulge himself/herself in all variety of response to this death—which seems (despite Sandor's own death) to be Hollywood's last reel revenge on a liberated, domineering (and bisexual) female. But it all reverts to beautiful Gothic make-believe as the camera lingers on Gloria Holden's placid, wide-eyed "corpse," and Van Sloan intones:

"She was beautiful when she died—a hundred years ago!"

9. *The Body Snatcher* (RKO, 1945): This writer's choice as Greatest Horror Movie of the 1940s, *The Body Snatcher* mixes Val Lewton poetry with the blood-and-thunder acting of Karloff's Cabman Gray and Henry Daniell's proud Dr. MacFarlane. It's an actor's feast day (for Bela Lugosi, too, whose servile, creepy Joseph is too often underrated)—and features one of the great female death scenes of the era.

Our victim is the Street Singer (Donna Lee), a pretty young "lass" from the highlands. Lewton and Robert Wise (who so masterfully directed this classic) give the

Singer Donna Lee poses for a studio portrait.

Street Singer a strange, bizarre quality; we never hear her speak—she only sings, like some lost angel. And one night, Body Snatcher Karloff needs a fresh specimen...

We see the Street Singer, looking almost like a Catholic madonna, singing her way through the black streets of RKO's Edinburgh. The coach of Karloff follows, the clip-clop of the horse's hoofs echoing on the cobbled streets. As she is swallowed up in the darkness, the coach follows—and suddenly, in the middle of a high note, the singing stops!

"It was a real 'audience picture,'" Russell Wade, "Fettes" in the film, told me re: *The Body Snatcher*. "Some of those scenes, as directed by Robert Wise—such as the sudden snort of the horse, and Karloff's murder of the street singer—got tremendous audience reaction."

10. *Svengali* (Warner Bros., 1931): What a rich, Gothic, terrific melodrama this is! It features John Barrymore's greatest screen performance as sinister hypnotist Svengali, while Marian Marsh—only 17 at the time—is a beautiful, moving and perfect Trilby.

The finale is a classic in itself. Barrymore's Svengali has used his hypnotic magic to transform tone-deaf milkmaid/nude model Trilby into the World's Greatest Diva—but has never won her love. His ego and temperament have gotten the better of him; the mighty have fallen, and now Svengali, Trilby, and the loyal violinist Gecko (Luis Alberni) are appearing in a nasty Cairo nightclub—sharing the bill with Mlle. Doro and her Morocco Dancing Girls.

In the audience is our "hero," the cherubic Little Billee (Bramwell Fletcher), waiting for his chance to get Trilby back again.

"Listen, my dear," says Svengali to Trilby, backstage. "Tonight, I want you to watch me very closely. Do not take your eyes off mine, even for an instant. And, remember," says Barrymore, his eyes shining with tears, "there is nothing in your mind, nothing in your heart, nothing in your soul, but Svengali...Svengali... Svengali."

On the stage, Marian Marsh's Trilby begins to sing, Svengali conducting below, Gecko and the little orchestra playing "Ben Bolt." Then Svengali suffers a heart attack, and as his power weakens, Trilby goes woefully off-key—and collapses! Svengali is dying, the crowd is in an uproar, Little Billee races to the stage, and cradles the leading lady in his arms. We're all ready for a conventional, Happy Ending fadeout.

Then Barrymore prays...

as they play...and the heartbreaking bewilderment of the Monster (in the restored footage) after he has run out of flowers, and thrown the child into the lake: The immensely tragic scene never loses its punch. The magical chemistry that the irreplaceable King of the Horror Movies shared with this unhappy, seven-year-old child is uncanny—creating (with James Whale's direction) the most sad and haunting vignette of the Golden Age of Horror.

By the way: Marilyn Harris, whom I interviewed for *Films in Review* (10/92), and a dear friend, still remembers her "Monster" of 65 years ago with emotion: "...I just loved him. Immediately... I just loved him."

12. *Bride of Frankenstein* (Universal, 1935): It's the Golden Age of Horror-in-Excelsis, Karloff's Greatest Performance, James Whale's masterpiece, and the most strikingly theatrical Terror Genre death scene of all.

It belongs, of course, to Elsa Lanchester—the vainglorious Bride herself.

"We *belong* dead!" intones Karloff's Monster—a classic curtain line as he prepares to pull that lever and blow up Ernest Thesiger's wicked Dr. Pretorius, and the Bride, and his bolt-necked self.

Marian Marsh and John Barrymore in *Svengali*

"Oh, God! Grant me in death—what you denied me in life—the woman I love!"

Marian Marsh looks at Bramwell Fletcher, who is holding her—then, unforgettably, she turns her head away from him, and looks at Barrymore.

"Svengali," she sighs, lovingly—and dies.

And John Barrymore—proving he was, just as Warner Bros. billed him, "The World's Greatest Living Actor"—joyfully sings a little song to himself and, dropping his baton, joins his Trilby in death.

For once in a classic Horror movie, the villain gets the girl—and the angels are on his side.

11. *Frankenstein* (Universal, 1931): It's a celebrated episode that becomes more profound with the decades—the "flower game" of Boris Karloff's Monster and Marilyn Harris's "Little Maria" by the mountain lake.

The joyful laughter of Karloff's Monster as he tosses the flowers...the trust and innocence of Marilyn's Little Maria

Boris Karloff and Marilyn Harris in *Frankenstein*

Elsa Lanchester as the Bride in *Bride of Frankenstein*

And Elsa, of course, throws back her head, and—like one of the swans she used to feed at the lake in London's Regents Park—she madly hisses.

Just what is the Bride of Frankenstein hissing with such lunatic, brilliant bitterness, as the watchtower explodes? Karloff's crying Monster? James Whale, for allowing Colin Clive's Dr. Frankenstein and Valerie Hobson's Elizabeth a Hollywood Happy Ending? The ever-prurient audience of Horror Movies? Mortality itself?

All of the above?

Women Take a Bite Out of Classic Horror: Dracula's Daughter and Mark of the Vampire

by Gary Rhodes and John Paris Springer

Now the truth is, I felt rather unaccountably toward the beautiful stranger. I did feel, as she said, 'drawn toward her,' but there was also something of repulsion. In this ambiguous feeling, however, the sense of attraction immensely prevailed. She interested and won me; she was so beautiful and so indescribably engaging.—Female narrator of J. Sheridan Le Fanu's story, *Carmilla* (1872)

You won't object to removing your blouse, will you? —Gloria Holden (Countess Zaleska) to Nan Grey (Lili), *Dracula's Daughter* (1936)

Along with such screen legends as Lugosi's Dracula, Karloff's Frankenstein Monster, and Elsa Lanchester's Bride, the Golden Age of the American horror film in the 1930s produced two key depictions of the female vampire: Carroll Borland as Luna in *Mark of the Vampire* (1935) and Gloria Holden as Countess Marya Zaleska in *Dracula's Daughter* (1936). Both actresses are still best remembered for their roles in these films, their distinctive images having become horror icons which continue to influence cinematic and cultural representations of women-as-vampires. Yet the depiction of vampiric women in these seminal films draws upon a rich literary and cultural legacy in which the "Vamp" is a projection of both male fantasy and fear; a response to modern redefinitions of "the feminine" and to the social and sexual freedoms which were increasingly being demanded by women in European and American society. The power of these characters derives from the strange yoking of beauty and monstrosity, familiarity and otherness, which they present, which parallels a larger ambivalence toward the new values and changing standards of behavior which defined the "New Woman." Poster art for *Dracula's Daughter* featured the suggestive ad line, "She gives you that WEIRD FEELING," a not so subtle reference to the unresolved sexual tensions raised by the film.

Both Luna and Zaleska embody the implicit danger as well as the allure of female sexuality, thus defining what has become the dominant image of women-as-vampires in American film.

Mark of the Vampire is Tod Browning's remake of his own 1927 silent *London After Midnight*, which starred Lon Chaney, Sr. The 1935 version features Count Mora (Bela Lugosi) and his vampire daughter Luna (Carroll Borland) slinking around an old castle. The latter makes a habit of biting Irena Borotyn (Elizabeth Allan), daughter of the recently murdered Sir Karrell (Holmes Herbert). Baron Otto (Jean Hersholt) assumes guardianship of Irena, as Professor Zelen (Lionel Barrymore), Dr. Doskil (Donald Meek), and Inspector Neumann (Lionel Atwill) arrive to help solve the seemingly supernatural occurrences. The film's climax finds Baron Otto recreating his murder of Sir Karrell under hypnosis. Sir Karrell's murder is solved—the "vampires" were merely actors hired to help unravel the mystery.

Dracula's Daughter (1936) is a sequel to Universal's classic 1931 film, beginning where *Dracula* left off. Police catch Van Helsing (Edward Van Sloan)—or "Von Helsing," as he is called in the new film—at Carfax Abbey and believe he has murdered an ordinary person via a stake in the heart. After they take Von Helsing to Scotland Yard, Countess Marya Zaleska arrives to collect the body of Dracula, her father. She burns his corpse, then quickly becomes involved in London society. To her servant Sandor (Irving Pichel) she expresses hopes that her days of guilt and vampirism are over; in fact, Zaleska attempts to seek help from Dr. Garth (Otto Kruger), believing he can help free her mind of Dracula's grip. However, she not only continues her vampiric pursuits but also attempts to gain control over Garth by kidnapping his secretary Janet (Marguerite Churchill). When the doctor and Von Helsing reach her castle, the vampiress dies at the hands of Sandor.

Though contemporary reviews were on the whole more favorable than many horror films received, *Mark*

of Lugosi's absence or a cheaper-looking castle, Holden is indeed spellbinding and—under scrutiny—the film as a whole possesses a thematic richness which makes it a key text in the vampire canon. Likewise, *Mark of the Vampire*—with its atmospheric sets, strong cast, and brilliant cinematography by James Wong Howe—improves on *Dracula* in a variety of ways. Setting aside the film's disappointing conclusion, *Mark* is one of the most stylish Hollywood horror films of the 1930s and an excellent example of what sustains Browning's (somewhat battered) reputation.

Luna and Zaleska—the films' vampires—share numerous traits while at the same time each remains a unique figure. However, both characterizations draw upon a wide range of influences and antecedents. Styling their performances upon potent cultural archetypes, Borland and Holden became the two major faces of feminine vampirism in the cinema.

There were, of course, radically different depictions of female vampires in films of this period. For example, Universal's Spanish-language version of *Dracula* (1931) presents buxom, overtly erotic creatures that make sexual advances toward Renfield, in contrast to the ethereal, wraith-like specters that haunt Castle Dracula in Browning's version. Here the differences in depictions of women-as-vampires clearly embody larger patterns of cultural representation and sexual ideology. Carl Dreyer's masterful *Vampyr* (1932) presents a cinematic adaptation of Le Fanu's 1872 story *Carmilla*. However, unlike its literary antecedent, *Vampyr* rarely shows its female vampire and greatly tones down the story's sexual content. Dreyer's vampire is a more aged and androgynous carrier of disease and pestilence, and in spite of the undeniable power of the film, it contributed very little to the cinematic image of female vampires.

of the Vampire and Dracula's Daughter have often been maligned in histories and the fan press. The former has taken blows since 1935 for its trick ending that dispels all hints of the supernatural. The latter—with its mild shocks and B movie production values—pales in a comparison to *Dracula* (1931). Both also have plot inconsistencies and problems. They are also disappointing to most Bela Lugosi fans, as in *Mark of the Vampire* he appears in an essentially secondary role and in *Dracula's Daughter*—a direct sequel to his classic 1931 performance—he does not appear at all.

While critical reassessments have often found fault with Tod Browning's *Dracula*, several historians have placed *Dracula's Daughter* on a higher plane. Regardless

Of much greater influence was the lingering conception of the female vampire as represented by the "Vamp" of silent cinema. During the teens, Theda Bara came to epitomize this cultural icon, who was a vampire in name only, her real threat being the power of female sexual allure and its ability to dominate and control men. Vamps were both highly beautiful and highly dangerous

As Cher sang, "She was a scamp, a camp, and a bit of a tramp, she was a V, A, M, P... vamp." Theda Bara, the original Vamp.

women who figuratively sucked the life out of the men that fell at their feet; men who had often left wives, children and careers to be with the vamp, who would drop them on a whim to move on to her next "victim." Most importantly, the "Vamp" became an early 20th-century embodiment of women's sexual freedom and, by extension, a symbol of women's growing demands for social and sexual equality with men. Thus, the "Vamp" was a transgressive figure who violated standard patterns of feminine behavior and explicitly challenged the values of a male-dominated social order.

Clement Wood's poem "Enter the Vampire"—which appeared in an April 1917 *Saucy Stories*—offers an intriguing period description: "The Vampire was not a bit respectable; They called her quite exotic and outré; And tho' the taste was bloody, they thought her thirst too ruddy; Meals should be made in some more usual way, So ducking vampires all declared delectable—Or burning them—it didn't matter which; a maid who drank corpuscles was seized by brawny muscles and treated like an ordinary witch."

In the final verse, the "Vamp" has become a creature of movie formula: "And now she writhes and wriggles thru' the photoplay, And gloats upon her victim's very gore; She violently vexes each admirer she annexes; She vamps—need we elaborate more? Yet since she's got to thrill us the *in toto* play, She has to keep it up five weary reels. Tho' we may say, in passing, just to soften the harassing, She has to vamp, to earn her daily meals."

To her fans, Theda Bara herself possessed as much mystery as any folkloric tale of vampires. A November 1915 article in *The Theatre* told readers: "You see her act on the screen, and you know that she is a daughter of the Sphinx of Egypt, that she spent her girlhood in Babylon, that she has wandered over the frozen fields of Siberia, and that she had lounged in the tropical gardens of Morocco. There are a thousand years in her eyes." Theda, of course, was merely Theodosia Goodman of Cincinnati, a fact that the author of the *Theatre* article knew all too well. In fact, many of Bara's provocative statements to the press were apparently scripted by PR men, who carefully cultivated the aura of mystery and transgression which she came to embody. Along with exotic tales of her birth and past lives, her publicity stills themselves offered visibly macabre elements. These photographs often featured her with symbols of death, including ravens and reclined (presumably male) skeletons. Eventually the myth of Bara's screen persona trapped her in typecast parts which began to look dated next to the healthy and youthful eroticism of the 1920s flapper.

Of her surviving films, *A Fool There Was* (1915) offers one of the great vamp stories and her immortal line, "Kiss Me, My Fool." *The Theatre* article, referring to her as "Mrs. Satan," quoted her at length: "I have become so identified with 'wicked women,'" she said, "that perhaps I shall be doomed always to play that sort of character and I don't know that I am sorry for it. Women of that sort have been the greatest dramatic forces in the world, ever since the world began."

A woman of such sexual power and magnetism, of course, must be seen as "wicked" and "dangerous" within a culture which promoted chastity and submissiveness as the highest feminine virtues. At the same time, however, such overt displays of feminine sexuality are also exciting, perhaps because they intentionally set out to break taboos and violate social conventions. One pen-and-ink in a February 1921 *Theatre Magazine* showed a vamp dressed in black, seated on the back of a tiger with the caption, a "she-male of her species," highlighting the masculine quality of her sexual aggression. A Covarrubias drawing in a November 1929 *Vanity Fair* accompanied the text: "Insidious dawned the day of the screen siren—who leered upon a leopard skin and panted upon a panther. This magnificent woman had 17 bones in her right hip, every one of them dislocated." Such overt sexuality even caused a 1926 Boué Soeurs dress to be named the "Vampire" due its incredibly low-cut front (which thus came with a flesh-colored chiffon bodice).

The dangers of such women would become a recurring message in cultural representations of the "Vamp." A September 1925 *Vanity Fair* included a Benito pen-and-ink titled "The Vampire." By the 1920s, it was common for the temptresses to be pictured with short, bobbed hair—itself a sign of promiscuity and loose morals. Benito's work includes a whimsical passage that read: "Best results are obtained with hard boiling. Remove clothing to taste; add one tiger skin, three absinthe cocktails, one ounce of reserve strength in hero; keep in a warm atmosphere until suspense is exhausted. Then remove vampire and substitute one half pint of heroine." In these representations the "Vamp" is explicitly associated with the "Modern Woman," whose new styles of dress and behavior often flouted traditional notions of femininity.

While Theda Bara's own star dimmed by the 1920s, the vamp image blazed on. Ads for Janet Gaynor in *Four Devils* (1929) questioned moviegoers: "Vamp or Virgin? Which do men prefer? Sweet, enduring love... or worldly, seductive, relentless love at any price?" Many viewed Jean Harlow's persona as vampish in the 1930s, with the press never forgetting the word or its connotations. "Heroines Turn into Vampires," the *Los Angeles Times* claimed on March 21, 1932. The article mentioned several actresses supposedly returning to the "Theda Bara days, when vamps were vamps and vamping was its own reward." A *San Francisco Chronicle* of January 26, 1933 claimed that Theda Bara herself had been approached for—and subsequently turned down—a new "vamp" role in the cinema.

Yet the "Vamp" image preceded Bara's appearance in film. In his 1972 essay "Edgar Allan Poe's 'Morella': Vampire of Volition," Lee J. Hamond makes the argument that Morella lives off the narrator's vitality in the tale of the same name. A similar woman ("Miss Penelosa") also appears in Arthur Conan Doyle's 1891 novel *The Parasite*, systematically destroying the life of poor Professor Gilroy. Equally of note is Florence Marryat's book *Blood of the Vampire* (1897), which finds the character Mrs. Brandt actually drinking blood while her daughter Harriet and Harriet's adoptive mother (the "Baroness Gobelli") are metaphorical vampires.

An important visual influence on the "Vamp" image was Philip Burne-Jones' scandalous painting "The Vampire." First exhibited in 1897, the painting features a woman poised seductively above a man on a bed, a position which suggests female dominance and sexual power. Her long hair flows and a slight grin plays across her lips. She has no fangs, no blood can be seen, nor can any other supernatural elements. Her victim's arm falls toward the floor as he lays unconscious on the bed.

Burne-Jones' striking image inspired the famed 1897 Rudyard Kipling poem "The Vampire," from whose lines came the title of Bara's 1915 classic. "A Fool there was and he made his prayer (Even as you and I!) To a rag and a bone and a hank of hair (We called her the woman who did not care) but the fool he called her his lady fair—(Even as you and I!)." In 1907, Istvan Csok's painting "The Vampires" codified this conflation of images even further. His canvas shows several attractive nudes seated and relaxed, while at the center, one appears to feed at a victim's neck.

Thus, the vamp's history provided ample imagery from which the 1930s' vampire women could draw. The character was linked strongly with sex and death. Vamps were viewed not merely as sinful, but as the embodiment of evil, so great was their threat to traditional socio-sexual values. Actor John Carradine used to say that early Hollywood films were black-and-white in more than one way; along with the film stock, the characters themselves were either too good or too evil to be realistic. Vamps exemplify this unredeemed villainy, yet they were unique from other villains.

Even if dressed in black or pictured with horrifying objects, they were always beautiful. Whether taming/riding beasts such as tigers or puffing long, phallic cigarette holders, they were basically projections of male dread and desire, figures who condensed widespread anxieties about the social and sexual changes which were redefining women's roles. While conventionally the villain was a character whose inner evil was visible on the surface, the Vamp was a paradox: It was her beauty that made her dangerous, along with her irresistible sexual allure and willingness to act on her desire. In fact, the Vamp's beauty was an essential aspect of her monstrosity, her ability to manipulate and control men. And it provided a further link between the woman-as-vampire and "New Woman," who increasingly found images of herself circumscribed by a cult of beauty fostered by consumer culture.

However, female vampires have a history that reaches beyond both the aestheticism of Burne-Jones and such products of mass culture and consumer society as the movie vamp. One of the earliest such images is undoubtedly that of Lilith, the woman viewed in Hebrew folklore as the "other" wife of Adam. More than merely a temptress, some legends feature her actually drinking blood.

The Greek and Roman myths of Lamiae are a particularly important part in this lineage. H. Freimark writes in *Okkultismus und Sexualität*: "...Lamias are at the same time lewd demons and vampires. They try to get handsome strong youths to marry them. Having succeeded in this, they kill them by sucking their blood." Such legends thus feature elements of their "vamp" descendants along with supernatural activities and the drinking of vital fluids. By 1819, the poet Keats depicted a similar creature in his *Lamia*. Additionally, the succubi of the Western world are an important link in the chain. A counterpart of the male incubus, the female succubus visits and tricks males in the world of the living. These demons were detailed in various texts during the 12th–17th centuries, including Kraemer's *Malleus Maleficarum* (1501), Remi's *Demonolatry* (1595), and Sinistrari's *Demoniality* from the 1600s. The succubi were indeed seen as a very real threat, particularly because they—like Lamias—were often thought of as beautiful in appearance.

Of such a phenomenon, psychologist Ernest Jones writes in *On the Nightmare* (Grove, 1959): "The explanation for these fantasies is surely not hard. A nightly visit from a beautiful or frightful being, who first exhausts the sleeper with passionate embraces and then withdraws from him a vital fluid: all this can point only to a natural and common process, namely to nocturnal emissions accompanied with dreams of a more or less erotic nature. In the unconscious mind blood is commonly an equivalent for semen."

Beyond such physiological accounts, however, lies the symbolic significance of women's blood. In his "Contributing to the Psychology of Love," Freud speaks of possible explanations for the male view of women and blood: "The primitive cannot help connecting the mysterious phenomenon of the monthly flow of blood with sadistic ideas. Thus he interprets menstruation, especially at the onset, as the bite of a spirit animal, or possibly as the token of sexual intercourse with this spirit. Occasionally the reports reveal this spirit as one of an ancestor and then from other knowledge we have gained we understand that it is in virtue of her being the property of this spirit-ancestor that the menstruating girl is taboo."

Characteristics that became a fixture in cinematic representations of vampire women are easily apparent in these early myths and legends. Beauty, danger, eroticism, the drinking of blood, and the conflation of blood and other vital fluids all occur in the cinematic depictions of such creatures.

Given the films' portrayal of women-as-vampires, however, the relationships with other woman, their penetration of others with teeth, and their own sexual desire for blood are never fixed or made completely clear. Indeed, after her first "bite" of the movie, Zaleska returns home looking not sated or "filled" as a succubus

Philip Burne-Jones' "The Vampire," 1897

that has gorged on the fluids of another, but instead drained and tired, nonchalantly commenting about her cloak, "There's blood on it again."

James Twitchell, in his 1980 essay "The Vampire Myth" (*American Image* #37), writes of the female/male encounter that: "The female vampire is older than her male victim, knowledgeable in the ways of the world, and inducts her novitiate not into evil but into manhood. Whereas the female victim of the male attack is destroyed, the young male victim is strengthened through sex."

While this is applicable to many post-1960 vampire films, Holden's Zaleska is a more romantic figure; a doomed lover unable to consummate her desire for Dr. Garth. Despite his fascination with Zaleska, Dr. Garth remains true to his secretary Janet, who helps him with his "tie trouble" throughout the film—a Hollywood euphemism for their romantic involvement. Even before Zaleska's vampirism is exposed, Janet laughingly explains the Countess' vamp status as a sexual rival for Dr. Garth's affections:

JANET: Don't you know it's very rude to stare at strangers?
GARTH: Thought I'd gotten rid of you for awhile.
JANET: Not while there's a dangerous looking brunette like that around.

It's important, however, that Garth himself is never bitten. Moreover, regardless of his own obvious attraction for Zaleska, he declines an offer for "eternal life" with her. "I refused of course," he tells Von Helsing later, signaling a restoration of male sexual authority. Whatever "weird feeling" he has for Zaleska or gets from her, it remains unfulfilled.

Instead of passing along sexual knowledge and experience to him, Zaleska is more a would-be seductress, an unrequited lover. At first, she hopes he can free her from her own problems; indeed Zaleska's vampirism is more akin to psychosis than supernatural evil, which makes her susceptible to Dr. Garth's psychological probing. Later in the film, however, she wishes to control and possess him. The calculated strategy to gain control over the brilliant doctor eventually extends to the kidnapping of Janet.

SANDOR: Why have you left her unharmed?
ZALESKA: I want him... His life in exchange for hers.

Zaleska's servant, Sandor, is also a kind of sexual slave, whom she controls via the promise of eternal life. Rather than dominating the two men, however, Zaleska becomes the victim of her own will to dominate. Instead of two slaves, a dangerous triangulation of desires erupts. A visual allusion to this occurs earlier in the film, as Garth leaves Zaleska framed between two large, phallic candles. In the film's climax, the jealous servant Sandor shoots Countess Zaleska with an arrow through the heart, the phallic penetration of the arrow ending her vampiric/sexual desire.

After the fashion of the 1920s "vamps," both Luna and Zaleska possess great beauty. A *Los Angeles Times*

Garth (Otto Kruger) is the unwilling object of Zaleska's (Gloria Holder) affection in *Dracula's Daughter*.

article dubbed Borland "the girl so beautiful she scares you." The May 30, 1936 *Billboard* claimed Holden is "called on to do little but look ominous," an effect no doubt enhanced by her commanding, statuesque physical presence. Thus—as with Theda Bara and others—the female vampire's beauty is entwined with dangerous, and possibly evil, qualities.

Edna Tichenor, as the bat-girl in *London After Midnight,* seems more forlorn than terrifying.

Steeped as she may be in that tradition, however, Holden's Zaleska stems more directly from Tod Browning's vampire women, beginning with bat-girl Edna Tichenor in *London After Midnight* (1927) and continuing with the vampire brides of *Dracula* (1931). Though Browning did not direct *Dracula's Daughter*, his influence is clear in this regard. In all three cases, the short—although not bobbed—hair is interesting, given the use of longer hair in prior vampire tales. As she slips into London's society circles, Zaleska does wear numerous Brymer dresses which seem more stylish echoes of the loose, shroud-like dresses of Tichenor and the vampire trio in *Dracula*. These nods to current fashion suggest a vampiric persona particularly sensitive to questions of style and appearance.

As embodiments of a transgressive female sexuality, it is not surprising that Luna and Zaleska both display lesbian qualities in their choice of victims. By representing their sexual aggression as primarily directed at other women, the films attempt to mitigate the potentially subversive sexual messages they contain. In the 1930s, lesbianism had only rarely surfaced in American cinema. Many point to Dorothy Arzner's *The Wild Party* (1929) as an early example, yet this film is less overt than either *Dracula's Daughter* or *Mark of the Vampire*. Indeed, American culture rarely examined the topic directly in this period, outside of inaccurate and biased medical or psychological studies, which makes the lesbian subtext even more suggestive of unresolved cultural and sexual tensions.

Both films flaunt the 1934 Motion Picture Production Code's ban on homosexual references in film. *Mark of the Vampire*, for example, explicitly associates the vampire's search for blood with homosexuality. Lugosi's Count Mora makes advances on Irena's fiancée Fedor, though it is shown only in a brief, inconclusive manner. The seduction sequences that are thoroughly depicted, however, are Luna's advances on Irena. In these scenes Irena is a passive participant in an act that she does not resist, rather succumbs to. Toward the end of the film, Irena even becomes "gay and cheerful" after seeing Luna outside her terrace. Framed through a window, Luna gazes in at Irena and fiancé. Fedor, observing Irena's excited behavior, asks, "What are you hiding from me?" Later Irena responds, "Don't ask me... please," and Fedor exposes his frustration and jealousy. "I feel that I am losing you," he admits.

At the same time, Luna's movements as sexual aggressor are themselves almost phallic after the fashion of Max Schreck in Murnau's *Nosferatu* (1922). When walking or turning, she is erect, with her arms stiff and close at her side. Though not the careful manipulator of *Dracula's Daughter*, Luna is the most physically aggressive of the two.

Dracula's Daughter presents lesbianism more overtly in its scene between Zaleska and Lili, an ill-fated and unwilling "model" for the artist. Zaleska is an artist—a pianist and a painter—and throughout the film art is presented as a "feminine" expression of her dark side, in contrast to Dr. Garth who exemplifies the male-dominated realm of science and medicine. Along with the exchange of glances between the two women, their dialogue clearly illustrates the sexual undercurrents in the scene:

ZALESKA: You won't object to removing your blouse, will you?

LILI (referring to her own brassiere): I suppose you'll want this pulled down, won't you?

ZALESKA (glaring at her): Yes.

LILI: Why are you looking at me that way? Won't I do?

ZALESKA: Yes, you'll do very well indeed.

LILI (frightened): Please don't come any closer....

The degree to which the lesbian subplot registered with audiences is unknown. If some promotional materials claimed she gives audiences (male and female, apparently) that "weird feeling," others insisted "Look out! She'll get YOU!" as artwork showed Nan Grey—rather than Otto Kruger—shuddering in horror.

More evidence of the sexual tensions in the film can be found in the paper trail of memos between Universal Studios and Joseph Breen at the Production Code Administration (PCA). In late 1935, Breen took issue with an earlier script that covered a variety of Dracula's vampire women. He strongly advised that a "flavor suggestive of a combination of sex and horror" would need to be changed.

By the time Zaleska appeared in scripts, more memos stacked up at Universal. "[The scene between Zaleska and Lili] will need very careful handling to avoid any questionable flavor," read a communication of January 15, 1936. A later memo—dated February 6—believed that "the whole sequence will be treated in such a way as to avoid any suggestion of perverse sexual desire on the part of Marya or of an attempted sexual attack by her upon Lili." The final film did not avoid such issues, of course, which caused at least a little flutter in theater wings.

It is interesting that critics in Great Britain—the horror film's enemy during the 1930s—found *Dracula's Daughter* as released a particularly disturbing film. Their complaints against the genre went well beyond the topic of vampirism and/or the sexual undercurrents of the vampire image. Yet *Dracula's Daughter* became one of the most vilified horror films in the British press.

Lili (Nan Gray) falls under the spell of Zaleska in *Dracula's Daughter*.

The *London Times* of July 21, 1936 noted that the film garnered a "horrific" certificate, adding that theaters screening the film had to post notices (of "no less than 11-inches tall") which read: "This film is unsuitable for children." How much the lesbian aspects caused the rage is unclear, but one slogan for the film had clearly warned "Save the women of London from *Dracula's Daughter*."

In looking at the film's Swedish release, however, the lesbian aspects apparently did bring censorship. A surviving 1936 file memo at the PCA lists two scenes that had to be deleted for theaters in Sweden. One is of Zaleska hypnotizing Lili, while the other is of "Dracula's daughter and cooperator at Janet's bed." Thus, with a few scissors snips the film's most overt lesbian connotations were gone.

American critics found *Dracula's Daughter* worthwhile enough, with a May 20, 1936 *Variety* claiming it was a "stay-awake influence in the bedroom later on," dubbing Zaleska a "femme killer" without clarifying whether the "femme" referred to her or her prey.

Yet if lesbianism had appeared only rarely in the American cinema, the topic had been clear in Le Fanu's classic story, "Carmilla." As the title character explains

> ✡ ✡ ✡
> **"DRACULA'S DAUGHTER" REMAINS AT FRANKLIN**
>
> "Dracula's Daughter," the Universal film now at the Franklin, is a case of romance versus necromancy, with the accent on the neck, as far as the vampire's appetites are concerned.
>
> Necromancy is the black art practiced by Dracula's Daughter. It is her magic of invoking evil through the hold she has on human beings because of her hypnotic influence. Gloria Holden interprets the fascinating personality.
>
> Otto Kruger, Marguerite Churchill and Irving Pichel, have the leading supporting roles.

to Laura, "I have been in love with no one, and never shall," she whispered, "unless it should be you." As the tale progresses, the female narrator sees "Carmilla, standing, near the foot of my bed, in her white nightdress, bathed, from her chin to her feet, in one great stain of blood."

Closer in time to the films at hand are lesbian "vamps" that turn up in such novels as Francis Brett Young's *White Ladies* (1935). In it, "Miss Cash" is a cruel headmistress with clear lesbian tendencies. As one character explains, "You see, she's a vampire. She lives on blood."

An equally unresolved sexual dimension in these films is the incestuous relationship of Count Dracula and daughter Zaleska as well as Count Mora and daughter Luna. In *Dracula's Daughter,* Zaleska expresses guilt over the connection with her father. As she makes clear, it is the memory and guilt of her relation to Dracula that causes her to search for victims. "Someone... something that reaches out from beyond the grave and fills me with horrible impulses," she tells Dr. Garth. In another scene, she seems almost possessed: "It came to me again... that overpowering command. Wordless, insistent, and I had to obey." More detail on the subject? No... "It's too ghastly to tell," she claims. Indeed, it is guilt that plagues her throughout the film and helps lead to her downfall.

In *Mark of the Vampire*, Luna and Count Mora's incest becomes clear after one becomes familiar with earlier script ideas and the production's history. Originally, the story claimed the Count committed suicide (thus causing the never-explained bullet hole in Lugosi's head) after strangling Luna as a consequence of their incestuous affair. As a result, they rose again as vampires. Though allusions to this subplot never made it to the release print, publicity stills illustrate gazes and poses that appear more sexual than familial.

Luna and Zaleska also highlight key elements of the vampire's physical characteristics. Eyes and lips are crucial to their images, not just in their respective stories, but as permanent cinematic icons. These qualities were quite clear at the time as well. For example, the *New York Times* of May 3, 1935 referred to Borland as Count Mora's "red-lipped daughter." The description not only centers on her mouth, but even highlights the color red despite the fact that the film is black and white.

Gloria Holden in *Dracula's Daughter*

Carroll Borland as Luna in *Mark of the Vampire*

These facial features figure prominently in prior Gothic literature, where they are often evocatively linked. For example, Charlotte Brontë's *Jane Eyre* (1847) describes Bertha Rochester's appearance with "...the lips were swelled and dark; the brow furrowed, the black eye-brows raised over the bloodshot eyes."

Similarly, F. Marion Crawford's wonderful tale "For the Blood is the Life" also makes use of such imagery. First printed in *Wandering Ghosts* (MacMillan, 1911), the tale has one character encountering the creature as follows: "Though she was in the shadow he knew that her lips were red, and that when they parted a little and smiled at him she showed two small sharp teeth.... Her cheeks were not livid like those of the dead, but pale with starvation, and with furious and unappeased physical hunger of her eyes that devoured him. They feasted on his soul and cast a spell over him, and at last they were close to his own and held him."

Looking at each characteristic separately yields interesting results. Though it would seem that lips are an obvious and integral vampire characteristic, Paul Barber's wonderful *Vampires, Burial, and Death* (Yale, 1988) makes clear that "scarcely anything in the folklore provides a description of a vampire's lips." Thus, the oral fixation of such stories—which becomes a key ingredient in their eroticism—seems to originate in vampire fiction of the 19th century. For example, Edgar Allan Poe's 1835 story "Berenice" finds a lover violating the grave of his sweetheart to extract her teeth.

Author Charles Baudelaire's "The Vampire's Metamorphosis" (c. 1857, translated by Jeremy Reed in the Creation Press' 1992 *Blood and Roses: The Vampire in 19th Century Literature*), depicts the female creature as "The woman with the scarlet lipsticked mouth, crackled like a snake spitting on red coals." A few years later, Le Fanu describes Carmilla's "lips in soft kisses gently [that] glow upon [Laura's] cheek." Of her vampiric experiences, narrator Laura recalls: "Sometimes it was if warm lips kissed me, and longer and more lovingly as they reached my throat, but the caress fixed itself."

In *Dracula*, Harker finds the Count "redder than ever, for on the lips were gouts of fresh blood, which trickled from the corners of the mouth...." Moreover, Stoker's vampiresses cause Harker to write of the "ruby of their voluptuous lips." Indeed, the lips' sexual nature become particularly clear in Harker's famous line: "I felt in my heart a wicked, burning desire that they would kiss me with those red lips."

In his medical text *Female Sex Perversion: The Sexually Aberrated Woman As She Is* (Eugenics, 1935), Edward Chideckel noted the almost vampiric oral practices of some "true" case studies: "One woman practiced fellatio, for no other reason than to sink her teeth in the phallus of the man. He was so severely bitten that surgical care was necessary. In one case that came to my attention the nipples of a prostitute were almost bitten off by a female sadist who paid her to submit to the practice. The oral and dental aspect is very common among female sadists."

While descriptions of lips flower in 19th century literature, the eyes have an even greater significance and power. The double-edged nature of eyes is indeed their inherent importance in conveying both attraction and menace. Wilhelm Stekel's *Frigidity in Woman: In Relation to Her Love Life* (Liveright, 1926) speaks of the sexual significance of the eyes: "A significant role, perhaps the most significant in the choice of a love object, is played by the eyes. In this connection, color, form, lustre, and the glance play a part. The belief in the evil eye shows what all-powerfulness is popularly ascribed to the eyes. The eye is an erogenous zone of the first order and in certain cases it fulfills vicariously the function of the sex organ."

If eyes have obvious links with sexuality, their existence as a site of evil—as Stekel suggests—is ancient. In his essay on "The Uncanny," Freud examined this phenomenon. In fact, in German the "evil eye" (*"der böse Blick"*) literally means the "evil look." Thus, rather than a history of deformed, discolored, or missing eyes, the evil is in the glance or the lingering gaze. As a superstition, the evil eye has roots in numerous cultures throughout the world. In Freud's view (as well as oculist Seligmann's, who studied the subject in his 1910 *Der böse Blick und Verwandtes*), being exposed to the evil eye was one of the most feared of encounters.

References to eyes and evil glances occurred frequently in the great vampire literature. For example, Le Fanu refers to Carmilla's "large, dark, and lustrous" eyes, which on another occasion are "languid and burning." As Laura observes, "...her fine eyes under their long lashes [were] gazing on me in contemplation." Later, "She [Carmilla] was gazing on me with eyes from which all fire, all meaning had flown...." The "evil eyes" also becomes entwined with the sexual act of taking blood, when Laura recalls a vampiric encounter: "The two broad eyes approached my face, and suddenly I felt a stinging pain as if two large needles darted, an inch or two apart, deep into my breast."

Stoker's novel also uses eyes to great advantage, with lines such as those regarding poor Lucy Westenra.

No longer were hers the "pure, gentle orbs we knew," they had become "unclean and full of hellfire." Dracula is also a prime example: "His eyes were positively blazing. The red light in them was lurid, as if the flames of hell-fire blazed behind them." The Count himself is very much aware of the gaze's sexual power, as he demands of the vampire women: "How dare you cast eyes on him when I had forbidden it?"

The blazing, vampiric gaze had become a defining element of the vampire image by the time of Deane and Balderston's *Dracula: The Vampire Play in Three Acts*, in which Lucy says, "I saw two red eyes staring at me and a livid white face looking down on me out of the mist. It was horrible, horrible." The evil eye was transformed into a stage effect with two small lights beamed at Bela Lugosi's eyes on-stage and in the 1931 film *Dracula*.

For Holden as Countess Zaleska, the evil eye was achieved with close-ups which were enhanced by dramatic costuming in a hooded cape which masked everything but her penetrating eyes. Moreover, one of her best lines is the question: "Sandor, look at me. What do you see in my eyes?" Sandor's deep voice intones: "Death."

With Borland the evil eye was depicted as a constant, unblinking, and unwavering stare as she gazes toward her victim. Borland wrote in her own novel, *Countess Dracula* (written in 1929, published in 1994) of the "gray lady of the castle's" eyes, which "seemed malevolent, the unwavering gaze of an ocelot," an apt description of her own performance in *Mark of the Vampire*. Borland, a Hollywood unknown when *Mark of the Vampire* was made, was apparently selected by Browning for the role of Luna precisely because of her oddly slanted, piercing eyes.

Borland's Luna is unique in numerous ways, although, again, much of the image can be traced to earlier sources. On the whole, she is strikingly similar to Bertha Rochester in Charlotte Brontë's *Jane Eyre*. "It seemed, sir, a woman, with dark hair hanging low down her back. I know what dress she had on; it was white

Zaleska uses her blazing eyes to control Albert (Billy Bevan) in *Dracula's Daughter*.

and straight; but whether gown, sheet, or shroud I cannot tell. ...[It reminded me] of the foul German spectre—the vampyre."

The last name of Borland and Lugosi's characters is traceable to two different vampire legends. For example, J.V. Grohmann's text *Sagen aus Böhmen und Mähren* (1864) refers to a Bohemian "Mora" that drinks human blood. Additionally, F.S. Krauss' *Slavische Volkforschungen* (1908) mentions the Southern Slav "Mora," which sucks either blood or milk, the two often being linked in vampire lore.

As for "Luna," the name comes from the Latin for "moon," which again suggests the "feminine" traits of mystery, mutability and ineffable beauty. Lunar references are also important in prior tales of female vampires. Le Fanu's *Carmilla* finds Laura attracted to the title character, realizing "How beautiful she looked in the moonlight!" Carmilla herself exclaims "what beautiful moonlight" one evening, while in an earlier instance she explains the moon's ability to make visible the invisible:

"'The moon, this night,' she said, is full of idyllic and magnetic influence—and see, when you look behind you at the front of the schloss, how all its windows flash and twinkle with that silvery splendor, as if unseen hands had lighted up the rooms to receive fairy guests.'"

In Stoker's *Dracula*, four references to the moon occur in one paragraph of Jonathan Harker's journal. He writes, "In the moonlight opposite me were three young women...." Moreover, their "great dark, piercing eyes" seemed almost red "when contrasted with the pale yellow moon." Stoker also uses moonlight imagery in conjunction with a woman in the short story "Dracula's Guest" (first published in 1914). As Harker approaches the tomb of Countess Dolingen of Gratz, it is the "flood of moonlight" that allows him to read the words "The Dead Travel Fast."

Much later, in Kirk Mashburn's 1931 *Weird Tales* vampire story "Placide's Wife," an old hag—presumed to be a witch—scowls at the title character when he alludes to the moonlight: "Moonlight in her eyes while she's sleeping in the grave! Oh Placide! Stupid Placide! Why did you not drive a stake through her heart when you buried her?"

In appearance, Luna differs from Zaleska in the long hair that drapes down either side of her bodice. While different than the "bobbed haired" vamps of the 1920s, Borland created a ghastly, funereal image for the character with this look. In interviews, Borland even made clear that the part down the middle was her own idea.

Borland's Luna calls to mind the text Edvard Munch wrote to accompany his "Separation/Melancholy" of 1896-98. "...her blood red hair had entwined itself around me—it had twisted around me like blood-red snakes—its finest threads had entangled themselves in my heart." Visually, she also recalls Munch's 1895 lithograph "Vampire," in which he depicts a woman with long hair covering her face as she feeds on a male.

Spectacular and unique to Carroll Borland's portrayal is a flight sequence that pictures her flapping down to the Borotyn castle floor. Bat-girl Edna Tichenor apparently "flew" during a similar sequence in Browning's *London After Midnight*. Indeed, Philip Riley's book restoration of the film (Cornwall, 1985) cites her version as 14 feet longer than Borland's. Regardless of that, this scene from *Mark of the Vampire* is, while brief, one of the most intriguing of the entire 1930s' horror cycle.

Many legends and ingrained movie images show vampires changing shape to other animals, such as bats and wolves, and the transformation is generally a total metamorphosis into some other creature—something akin to a lycanthrope. Borland, on the other hand, has fascinating bat-like wings, and is thus a combination of both vampire and bat. Such imagery is not unknown, however, as Albert Pénot's 1890 painting of a bat woman depicts a nude with bat-like wings. Moreover, Edvard Munch's 1894 lithograph "Vampire" shows a winged woman on a male corpse, an image similar to his "Harpy" of 1900 that depicts a flying female above yet another male corpse.

Even closer in time to Borland's flight is Margaret Brundage's spectacular *Weird Tales* magazine cover of October 1933. The female vampire—which promoted the story "The Vampire Master"—wears a bat-like mask that aligns its bat wings with her arms. In addition, photographs of Madame Demidoff of the Moscow Art Theatre are quite similar to Borland. One in particular—published in a January 1921 *Theatre Magazine*—shows her in a striking pose from Nikita Balieff's ballet *La Chauve-Souris* (or *The Bat*). Her low-cut and quite "vampish" dress with arms outstretched makes the flowing outfit appear to have bat wings.

In *On the Nightmare*, Ernest Jones speaks of the act of humans and creatures in flight. To him, "the phenomenon of [phallic] erection is in both

Borland and Bela Lugosi pose for an eerie family portrait for *Mark of the Vampire.*

It is not difficult to view such vampire women as metaphorical spiders, sexual predators whose aggression toward men both fascinates and disturbs us. Indeed, the implicit appeal of such sexual scenarios was not lost on fashion designers, cosmetic companies and advertising agencies, all-powerful arbiters of feminine beauty and style. As early as 1912, Broadway stage star Valeska Suratt vamped during a performance in a wickedly designed dress that featured a spiderweb design; a matching "hat" echoed the web motif. By 1921, magazines advertised Mme. Helena Rubins' "Makeup Spider." The advertisement featured a nude woman at the center of a spider web, suggesting that the modern woman could catch a man by using the product.

Edna Tichenor—who had appeared in Tod Browning's *The Show* (1927) as a spider lady, her face in a web with tarantula-like legs—also wore a dress with a web-like design in *London After Midnight* (1927), and ads for the 1931 film, *Men in Her Life*, with Lois Moran, featured her posed in the center of a web with several men caught and helpless around her.

Perhaps the most intriguing example of the spider image is the case of Elenore Wood. After the fashion

sexes the kernel of the whole conception of flying." Seen from this viewpoint, Luna's threat to masculinity is heightened even further. This interpretation also echoes her rigid, "phallic," physical characteristics.

Luna's first encounter with Irena visually suggests vampiric flight. As she rapidly moves in to bite her victim, she raises her arms to reveal that the shroud-like costume has large, drooping sleeves suggestive of wings which flare out to entrap and conceal Irena. Previous vamps had worn similar dresses, though in particular Barbara LaMarr's in *Circe of Sorrow* (1922) reflects this look.

Though at times the low lighting of Gloria Holden's face creates spiderlike shadows of her lashes, it is Borland that is particularly likened to the arachnid. For instance, her first appearance in the film finds her and Lugosi walking through the dank and dusty castle. She is in front of Lugosi, walking behind a large spiderweb. The scene cuts away from them just as Borland is framed in the center of the web itself—a subtle but memorable visual metaphor.

Edna Tichenor as the spider lady in Tod Browning's bizarre *The Show*, 1927.

Keats, in his classic poem *Lamia*, depicts the female vamp as a serpent. Indeed, the myths of Greek and Roman Lamiae often includes mention of their "hiss."

When she does hiss, Luna is physically aggressive. More than even the vampire brides in the 1931 Spanish-language version of *Dracula*, she is reminiscent of wild-eyed Hazel Whitmore in a few close-up stills from the 1929 touring stage version of *Dracula: The Vampire Play in Three Acts* with Bela Lugosi. However, she generally approaches Irena in a more restrained, deliberate manner. This is similar to M.E. Braddon's "Good Lady Ducayne," first published in *The Strand Magazine* in February 1896. The title character of that vampire tale has a doctor offer her female companions chloroform and then methodically draining them of blood.

If Luna's hiss receives frequent comment, a more subtle motif for her of 1930s' fan dancer Sally Rand, Wood cooked up a particularly unique striptease act. The "Spider Dance"—staged by Leo Henning—found Wood disrobing, with a large, costume spider wrapped around one thigh. Presumably the dance itself alluded to the movements of a spider. She made a successful West to East Coast tour with the Coconut Grove Revels in 1935, with vamp-like ads offering the invitation "Won't you walk into my parlor?" Although the novelty of her act was fleeting, Wood did make the cover of a June 13, 1936 *Billboard*.

Another curious feature of Borland's performance is Luna's viperous "hiss." If the previous cinematic vampires had remained as silent as Theda Bara, Borland offered a break in the tradition. The most direct influence on her hiss is her own novel *Countess Dracula*. In it, she writes: "Risa's nail raked my cheek as she sprang from the bed with the open-mouthed hiss of an angry cat. [...] Her head wove sideways, as does a serpent's, seeking a place to strike."

Earlier vampiric tales often made allusions to the feline characteristics of their vampires (for example, the "sooty-blacked animal that resembled a monstrous cat" in *Carmilla*). Yet, as in the above excerpt from *Countess Dracula*, Luna's hiss is more serpentine than feline in effect.

Gloria Holden in a studio portrait as Zaleska.

(and—to a lesser extent—Count Mora) is the wind sound effect. Obviously, this is a dramatic use of sound to create atmosphere, something that, say, Browning's *Dracula* (1931) sorely needs. Moreover, it can on occasion be heard when the vampires are not seen. Yet Luna's appearances are generally connected with both the wind and—in terms of her attacks—her cold breath. Indeed, often the wind is heard as Luna walks outside, yet no movement is visible in the trees or brush.

Underscoring the connection between the wind and the vampire's breath are Irena's lines: "I felt her deadly cold breath on my throat. I must have fainted. I knew no more." To Fedor, she claims of an attack: "I heard a sound like wind at the casement. I felt a draft, then I saw her... just as she was on the terrace. I fought to keep my eyes open but they closed. I felt again that deadly cold breath." Similar to this is Bram Stoker's story "Dracula's Guest," which also connects the moon and wind with vampiric presence: "With the moonlight there came a fierce sign of the storm, which appeared to resume its course with a long, low howl, as of many dogs or wolves."

It is clear that the cinematic representations of women shown as vampires in these two films were based equally on a rich cultural legacy of vampiric imagery and lore and the unique talents of Carroll Borland and Gloria Holden, whose performances produced lasting icons of horror cinema. At the same time, the power of these characters, and the source of our ongoing fascination with them, stems from the unresolved sexual tensions which they condense and articulate. Certainly the two roles remain favorites of horror film scholars and fans. Moreover, whether it is through the more overt sexuality that entered vampire films of the 1960s or the continuing appropriation of the Luna character by Charles Addams' Morticia, or Maila Nurmi's Vampira, or even Cassandra Peterson's Elvira, these performances continue to influence cinematic and cultural representations of the female vampire. Whatever that "weird feeling" is, Luna and Zaleska (and so many characters that have drawn from them) certainly still offer it.

Bela Lugosi, Carroll Borland, Elizabeth Allen and Henry Wadsworth ham it up for a publicity shot for *Mark of the Vampire*.

The Golden Age of the Scream Queen

by Nathalie Yafet

Blonde or brunette, short or tall (usually short)—no respectable horror film of the 1930s or 1940s was complete without its leading lady. There simply had to be someone for the hero to love and the villain or monster to menace.

To be quite honest, when I first became addicted to horror films, the heroine was the least of my concerns. Her love scenes with the hero would be my chance to either close my eyes if it happened to be late, or to take a break and leave the room momentarily.

For this review of the acting ability of leading ladies in horror films of the 1930s and 1940s, my selection of films was entirely arbitrary. Most of them are from Universal, Boris Karloff is in many of them, and I have decided to include the entire Frankenstein series.

Occasionally, I hope I can be excused for interjecting my opinions about the film as a whole or some of the other actors as well, and for this I beg your indulgence.

The only traits that each of these ladies shared were attractive appearances and good screams, in most cases. Their dramatic skills varied.

Dracula, 1931—Helen Chandler

Dracula opens with Renfield, a real estate agent played by Dwight Frye, traveling from London to Transylvania in order to complete arrangements for Count Dracula's purchase of Carfax Abbey. The Count (Bela Lugosi), a centuries-old vampire, makes Renfield his servant and together they sail for England, where Dracula introduces himself to Dr. Seward (Herbert Bunston) and his daughter, Mina (Helen Chandler), her fiancé, John Harker (David Manners), and her friend, Lucy Weston, played by Frances Dade. Count Dracula soon adds Lucy to his list of undead followers and hopes to do the same with Mina. He nearly succeeds but is routed by Professor Van Helsing (Edward Van Sloan), vampire hunter extraordinaire, who ends Dracula's unnatural existence with a stake through the heart.

From the first, Miss Chandler as Mina Seward is utterly charming, though we immediately notice that she is a fragile creature. Her rapport with David Manners is equaled only by Jacqueline Wells in *The Black Cat*. She is totally at ease with Lucy, making the idea of their friendship entirely plausible. Her line reading in response to Lucy's morbid little poetic recitation at the concert, "Oh, never mind the rest, dear," is perfect. Next, a bit of good-natured teasing in the "broken battlements" speech serves to showcase her slightly offbeat comedic instincts to a T.

It is also to Miss Chandler's credit that she delivers clumsy lines such as, "...and just as I was commencing to get drowsy..." with grace and dignity. Her monologue detailing the red eyes in the mist is wonderfully evocative. In the scene with John Harker when she tries to explain why it must be all over between them, her

Helen Chandler as Mina in *Dracula*

melting vulnerability is nothing short of exquisite. By far, her strongest moment comes as her soul wavers between normalcy and vampirism. As she leans in toward her fiancé with unholy intent, her eyes gleaming, she is positively mesmerizing. That she is able to be the innocent flower as well as a creature-of-the-night wannabe with seamless skill, definitely refutes any criticisms of her acting. The only fault I can find in her performance is that her voice is a little too high-pitched for comfort, but this was a characteristic of many leading ladies of the period, so she is not unique in that respect. Helen Chandler—Mina—no other actress comes close to her in this role except for Kate Nelligan (in the 1979 Langella version), whose interpretation is vastly different.

Dr. Jekyll and Mr. Hyde, 1931—Rose Hobart

Adapted from the Robert Louis Stevenson story, *The Strange Case of Dr. Jekyll and Mr. Hyde*, the film begins with Dr. Henry Jekyll, played by Fredric March, rhapsodizing to his medical students about the possibility of separating the good from the evil self. That evening, he dines with his fiancée, Muriel (Rose Hobart), and her stuffy father, Brigadier-General Carew (Halliwell Hobbes), who adamantly refuses their pleas for an earlier wedding date. On the way home, Jekyll helps out Ivy (Miriam Hopkins), a prostitute, and is sexually attracted to her. After Dr. Jekyll does manage to separate his two selves, the disgusting Mr. Hyde appears and immediately seeks out Ivy, continuing to hound her until he murders her. No longer able to control his transformations, Hyde also murders Muriel's father before he is himself killed by the police. In death, he once again becomes Dr. Henry Jekyll.

Miss Hobart plays Muriel Carew, Jekyll's long-suffering fiancée. The role is poorly written and the actress is little more than a foil for Fredric March's histrionics. However, she does try and is straightforward and honest. Miss Hobart has two especially memorable scenes. When her fiancé is telling her how much he loves her, the actress lowers her voice, looks into his eyes and says, "I wish this moment would last forever." Then toward the end of the film, she defends Jekyll to her father, vehemently announcing, "I won't hear you say one word against him!"

Frankenstein, 1931—Mae Clarke

In a grim opening sequence, we see Henry Frankenstein (Colin Clive) and his bizarre assistant, Fritz (Dwight Frye), robbing graveyards and gallows for

Rose Hobart receives a visit from Mr. Hyde (Fredric March) in *Dr. Jekyll and Mr. Hyde.*

body parts. Fritz later mistakenly steals a criminal brain from the medical school. Henry's fiancée Elizabeth (Mae Clarke), friend Victor (John Boles), and former teacher Dr. Waldman (Edward Van Sloan) go to his laboratory to try to stop the unholy experiment. Disregarding them, the driven scientist animates his not-quite-human creature, who later kills both Fritz and Dr. Waldman. On Elizabeth and Henry's wedding day, the Monster barges in and is chased to a windmill, where he heaves his maker's unconscious body from the top before being caught in a fire set by the angry mob.

Miss Clarke acquits herself admirably in this first of the Universal *Frankenstein* series. She is frank, intelligent, and altogether proves herself strong enough to balance her fiancé's madness/genius. Her opening could be a bit more forceful, but that is not her fault; she has to cope with John Boles, who is cardboard stiff and does not seem to move his face when he speaks. She is particularly eloquent as she reads Henry's letter, evoking a frightening image when she quotes, "...at night the winds howl in the mountains." Her subsequent scenes do not disappoint. She is always aware and involved, even when in the background. The garden scene with Henry is sincere and touching. The actress

Elizabeth (Mae Clarke) is approached by the Monster (Boris Karloff) in *Frankenstein*.

speaks volumes with her eyes. She is also good in the wedding scene—demonstrating her as yet unnamed fears. When these fears finally take shape, the bride-to-be and the monster execute a surprisingly elegant *pas de deux*. This Elizabeth is not the usual lady in distress.

White Zombie, (1932)—Madge Bellamy

This moody little film starts with Madeline (Madge Bellamy) and Neil (John Harron) in Haiti where they expect to be married at the mansion of Mr. Beaumont (Robert Frazer), Madeline's shipboard acquaintance, who wants her for himself. On arriving there they meet Dr. Bruner (Joseph Cawthorn) whom Beaumont has asked to officiate at the wedding ceremony. Beaumont contracts with Murder Legendre (Bela Lugosi), a zombie maker, who gives him death-simulating poison to help him persuade Madeline—should she be unwilling. After Madeline turns down Beaumont's offer of marriage, he gives her a poisoned flower which she whiffs. Later, she collapses at her own nuptial banquet due to the combined effects of poison and voodoo spells. Horrified by soulless Madeline, Beaumont pleads with Murder to release her but is made into a zombie himself. Dr. Bruner and Neil go to Legendre's lair, where Madeline tries to stab her husband. Saved at the last minute, Neil prevents Madeline from flinging herself into the nearby ocean, whereupon Murder orders his zombie crew to kill Neil. Dr. Bruner appears and tells Neil to stand aside as the zombies mindlessly walk off the cliff into the ocean below. Murder flees, but Beaumont throws him into the ocean, afterwards jumping in himself.

Madge Bellamy essays a generalized portrayal of Madeline and gives us no idea of what her character is like. Miss Bellamy's heroine is all bee-stung lips, strangled voice and mannered acting—which, when you come to think of it, makes an excellent zombie.

Murder Legendre (Bela Lugosi) has control over Madeline (Madage Bellamy) in *White Zombie*.

Morgan (Karloff) attacks Margaret (Gloria Stuart) in *The Old Dark House.*

The Old Dark House, (1932)—Gloria Stuart

We first meet Margaret Waverton (Gloria Stuart), husband Philip (Raymond Massey), and friend Penderel (Melvyn Douglas), as they're driving through a tumultuous storm. Unable to continue on, they seek shelter for the night at the only house around, where they are admitted by Morgan (Boris Karloff), the mute butler. The owners, Horace Femm (Ernest Thesiger) and his religious fanatic sister Rebecca (Eva Moore), reluctantly allow them to stay. A bedridden Sir Roderick Femm (Elspeth Dudgeon) warns them about his pyromaniac son, Saul (Brember Wills), who is locked up.

Miss Stuart dives headfirst into the role, testily wrangling away about anything and everything in her opening scene, running the risk of making herself unattractive to the audience. Here also is an actress who knows when to let the other actor have the upper hand. As a result, her scene with Rebecca in the bedroom is grotesque, but strikingly memorable. After she fearfully flees Miss Femm's room, she has a tender moment with her husband as she makes an effort to reconcile with him. She is savvy enough to catch on to Morgan's intentions toward her very quickly. Their cat and mouse games are beautifully played by both actors. Miss Stuart telegraphs her terror admirably. She is paired well with Raymond Massey, an unconventional and rather ineffectual leading man. They're especially endearing, and not at all cloying, following the fight with Morgan. Margaret stays in the background for the rest of the film, but provides good support for her fellow players.

The Mummy, (1932)—Zita Johann

As *The Mummy* unfolds, Egyptologists Sir Joseph Whemple (Arthur Byron) and Ralph Norton (Bramwell Fletcher) along with Whemple's friend, Dr. Muller (an occult specialist, played by Edward Van Sloan), are examining the mummy of Imhotep, a high priest, and a sealed box (complete with curse) which was buried with him. Despite Dr. Muller's misgivings, young Norton opens the box, reads from the sacred scroll of Thoth inside, and resurrects the mummy. Years later, Frank Whemple (son of Sir Joseph, played by David Manners) is on his own expedition when Ardath Bey (who is really Imhotep) turns up and points out the burial place of Princess Anck-es-en-Amon. We next meet Helen Grosvenor (Zita Johann), who bears an uncanny resemblance to the dead Princess, Imhotep's lost love. Frank and Helen are attracted to each other and Ardath Bey struggles to reawaken the spirit of Anck-es-en-Amon in her. Helen finally yields to Bey and her own memories. But before he can ritually murder her and turn her into a mummy like himself, Frank and Dr. Muller burst in, emboldening Helen to beseech Isis for deliverance. Isis responds by incinerating Bey and the scroll together.

Miss Johann wins one of my two Best Actress Oscars; as Helen Grosvenor/Anck-es-en-Amon—she is superb! Her dual portrayal of the confused young modern woman and the doomed princess is spellbinding. We must always hold it against Universal that they cut her reincarnation scenes. Our first glimpse of her as she gazes out over Cairo, thoughts centuries away, is unforgettable. She intrigues us immediately with a timeless beauty that transcends type. And no one in the history of horror films—male or female—has ever portrayed hypnotic possession with more élan. Her expressions, when she rests on the divan after fainting at the museum, are fascinating to observe. It could almost be a study scene for Acting 101. And what incredible chemistry between Miss Grosvenor and Ardath Bey when they first meet! Poor Frank Whemple just doesn't stand a chance. David Manners, who in this writer's opinion is always good, is clearly overmatched by Miss Johann. She is too powerful for him. It just doesn't work in the film because we easily understand his

Zita Johann as Helen Grosvenor/Anck-es-en-Amon in *The Mummy*

attraction to her but not vice versa. (Maybe because he's the only male in the film who isn't dead, insane, or too old for her!) Mr. Manners only equals her when he tells her that she can't laugh at him—but the strength of that moment doesn't last. Later when she's trying to persuade the nurse to let her go to Imhotep, her body language is surprisingly seductive as she lies on her side and exposes one shoulder. Her best scene is after she does go to Imhotep. The now entirely awakened Anck-es-en-Amon acknowledges that this man has suffered the tortures of the damned for her and, with provocatively bent knee, reaches out to him exhorting, "...and now that the gods have forgiven us..." Her Anck-es-en-Amon is like Helen and, yet, unlike her—quite an achievement! It is indeed a loss that she disappeared from films. Other actresses would do well to emulate her.

King Kong, (1933) — Fay Wray

Carl Denham (Robert Armstrong) finds down-and-out Ann Darrow (Fay Wray) and persuades her to star in a movie to be shot on location on Skull Island. During the sea voyage, Ann and First Mate Jack Driscoll (Bruce Cabot) fall in love. King Kong carries off Ann, the men try to rescue her and battle an assortment of prehistoric dinosaurs. They capture Kong and return with him to New York. While being exhibited on stage, the ape breaks loose and once again grabs Ann. He is chased to the top of the Empire State Building, where airplanes do him in and he falls to his death. Ann, who is unhurt, is reunited with Jack.

Miss Wray is quite exceptionally lovely but simply cannot act. Her timing is always off. She anticipates every action and seems to be taking Betty Boop as her model in some bizarre way. Her scene with Robert Armstrong in the coffee shop illustrates my point; she cannot keep her eyes or mouth still. It is nearly impossible to sit through her passages with leading man Bruce Cabot, who does his macho thing while she coquettes. Robert Armstrong, Frank Reicher, King Kong, and assorted dinosaurs provide welcome relief from these two. Fortunately for us, Ann Darrow does not have many dialogue scenes but spends most of the film writhing in fear and screaming—both of which she handles aptly. Thankfully, her lack of artistry cannot spoil *King Kong*. Besides, I have to admit that Ann and Kong make a cute couple.

The Black Cat, (1934) — Jacqueline Wells

This superb film opens with newlyweds Joan (Jacqueline Wells) and Peter (David Manners) Alison, taking a train. They meet up with Dr. Vitus Werdegast (Bela Lugosi). A torrential downpour causes the bus to crash—killing the driver and injuring Joan. Werdegast takes the Alisons with him to Hjalmar Poelzig's (Boris Karloff) home, which is nearby. Unknown to the Alisons, Poelzig is a Satanist who betrayed his own side during the last war, married and murdered Werdegast's wife, married Werdegast's daughter (Karen, played by Lucille Lund), and intends to use Joan as his next sacrificial victim. Werdegast attempts to save Joan from Poelzig by playing chess for her, but loses. Werdegast rescues Joan from Poelzig and takes her to the basement, where Karen lies lifeless. Werdegast attacks Poelzig, gets the better of him, hangs him on the embalming rack, and proceeds to skin him alive. Peter rushes in, misjudging the doctor who is trying to help Joan, and shoots him. Werdegast orders the Alisons to leave, pulling "the red switch," which blows up the house.

From the beginning, even though affecting some stock, coy 1930s' heroine tricks such as posing for the camera, widened eyes and giggles, Miss Wells makes something special out of a role that could easily have been quite dreary. Well-matched with David Manners, they play off each other in a jazzy, F. Scott Fitzgerald manner which is a lot of fun. This couple seems to enjoy each other's company. She has a refreshing take-what-comes attitude and a completely captivating brunette prettiness that gets the audience on her side right away. After the accident, when she sashays in during the light conversation her husband is having with Poelzig and Werdegast, the actress displays her versatility by showing us an entirely different Joan than we saw at the start. She lowers her voice, undulates suggestively, and almost disdainfully asks Werdegast if he is "frightened." Not finished yet, she rakishly tilts her eyebrows at her Satanic host with something less than wide-eyed

Jacqueline Wells as Joan Alison in *The Black Cat*

heard of "Satanism" and she opens her eyes, forming a frightened, soundless "no" with her lips. This is entirely too cutesy and should have been fixed by director Edgar J. Ulmer. But she does not let us down in her climactic scene with Karen as she tells the poor girl that her father is alive and has come for her. After Poelzig forces Karen into the next room, Joan, with her back to us, listens silently, stiffens visibly, and slowly clenches her hand. Then she grips the banisters in despair, powerless to stop the horror taking place within. After she narrowly escapes being sacrificial fodder for the Satanists, she almost spits at Werdegast that Karen is alive and is Poelzig's wife. Her face is a veritable tangle of emotions; no whey-faced heroine here! She's also priceless in the embalming rack sequence, when she's unable to resist a good look at the grisly goings-on before letting out a last scream.

innocence and gives Peter a doozie of a kiss that prompts him to hastily bid good-night. The next morning, she doesn't seem to remember anything after the bus crash but instinctively protects herself from Poelzig's wandering eyes. In the Joan/Werdegast scene when he reveals that Poelzig murdered his wife, she responds with, "and you let him live," uttered forcefully with hardened lower lip, giving us a clear picture of just what Mrs. Alison would do if confronted with a similar situation. This young woman is definitely not a model of turn-the-other-cheek Christian forgiveness. There is one unfortunate moment in this scene, though, when Werdegast asks if she's ever

Bride of Frankenstein, (1935)—Valerie Hobson

The second film in the *Frankenstein* series starts off with Mary (Elsa Lanchester) and Percy Bysshe Shelley (Douglas Walton) discussing Mary's novel with their compatriot, Lord Byron (Gavin Gordon). As the windmill (from *Frankenstein*) burns, the Monster reappears, murdering the parents of little Maria (the girl he drowned in the first film). The injured Henry Frankenstein (Colin Clive) is brought home to Elizabeth (Valerie Hobson), where the weird Dr. Pretorius (Ernest Thesiger) visits them. Things progress rapidly from bad to worse—Pretorius uses the Monster to kidnap Elizabeth, thus forcing Frankenstein to create a female Monster. The resulting creature (Elsa Lanchester again)

Valerie Hobson as Elizabeth in *Bride of Frankenstein*

spurns her intended mate, who blows the laboratory to bits, allowing Frankenstein and Elizabeth to escape.

It was too bad that Mae Clarke did not reprise her role in the sequel to *Frankenstein*—her replacement, Valerie Hobson, is just not in the same league. Fortunately, the Elizabeth role is smaller this time and so is not the major liability it might have been. Another problem is that she and Colin Clive have absolutely no chemistry together. Her first line, "Oh heaven, what is this?" delivered in overbaked pseudo-Shakespearean style, indicates what is in store for us. Her soliloquy about the figure of death coming for Henry is ridiculous in the extreme. The unmotivated hysterics inspire laughter rather than foreboding. She does have a few redeeming moments when she stands her ground and tells off Dr. Pretorius, and later when she has a scene with Minnie (Una O'Connor) in the bedroom, but the overall effect is uneven. She does not create a real character with whom the viewer can empathize. In addition, it's hard not to compare her with Elsa Lanchester and Una O'Connor, who are both at the top of their form in this film.

Mark of the Vampire, (1935)—Elizabeth Allan

Mark of the Vampire begins with singing Gypsies, and a witch in a graveyard, none of whom are ever seen again. That same evening, Irena's (Elizabeth Allan) father, Sir Karell Borotyn (Holmes Herbert), is killed. Her fiancé Fedor (Henry Wadsworth) fades in and out of the picture, as we are led to believe that Sir Karell was murdered by vampire Count Mora (Bela Lugosi) and his daughter Luna (Carroll Borland). As the film rolls along, we discover that a family friend, Baron Otto (Jean Hersholt), killed Sir Karell in order to marry Irena himself, and the supposed vampires are really actors.

Insipidity may have suited David Copperfield's mother, but further debilitates this already flawed film. Miss Allan gives us no clue about Irena Borotyn and seems to take Helen Chandler's Mina as her model, but she fails. She matches her leading man, Henry Wadsworth, who is a complete washout and makes us long for David Manners. When Fedor comes stumbling into the room, obviously incoherent and injured, Irena shows about as much concern as she would for a cut finger. She recycles the same blank expression later when she spies Luna on

Elizabeth Allen poses for a publicity photo promoting *Mark of the Vampire*

the terrace. Miss Allan also has a tedious, all-purpose gesture of clutching at her throat in moments of distress or fear. This actress lacks spontaneity. She is so forced and unnatural that she would be well-suited for a spoof of Victorian melodramas. When she breaks down and says she cannot continue the deception any longer, she finally demonstrates some real ability. What a pity that this was the exception rather than the rule.

The Black Room, (1935)—Marian Marsh

A curse on the de Berghmans states that as their family began with twins (the younger murdering the older in the black room), so will it end. Years pass and Baron Anton (Boris Karloff) leaves home because his older brother, Baron Gregor (also Boris Karloff), cannot seem to forget the curse. Anton finally returns and learns that the local populace blame his brother for the disappearance of many women. While spending the evening with a family friend Colonel Hassel (Thurston Hall) and his niece Thea (Marian Marsh), we learn that Gregor is having an affair with their serving maid Mashka (Katherine DeMille) and also has designs on Thea—who loves Lieutenant Lussan (Robert Allen). Gregor murders Mashka, renounces his title to Anton, murders Anton (in the black room), impersonates Anton, becomes Thea's fiancé, murders Colonel Hassel, and attempts to marry Thea. His reign of terror is ended when Anton's faithful dog Thor ("Von") exposes Gregor's true identity and chases him to the black room where the evil baron falls on the knife held in Anton's dead hand.

Visually, Miss Marsh is ideal as the damsel in distress in this dark fairy-tale. Her character, though, is undeveloped and her performance uneven. Katherine De Mille makes a stronger showing in a smaller role. We are never in doubt what her character Mashka wants. Marsh was decidedly better in other films, notably *Five Star Final*. I am convinced that her portrayal of Thea Hassel was hampered to a great extent by the ineptitude of her leading man, Robert Allen, who is about as wooden and pompous as can be. Her scenes with him are tedious and artificial, except for the last one when he comes to her before her wedding, where the emotion is tender and affecting Thea's friendliness to Anton and genuine fear of Gregor are tangible. No other actress could weep as convincingly; her tears go straight to our hearts. She is particularly good in the courtroom scene and later with Gregor masquerading as Anton in the cemetery.

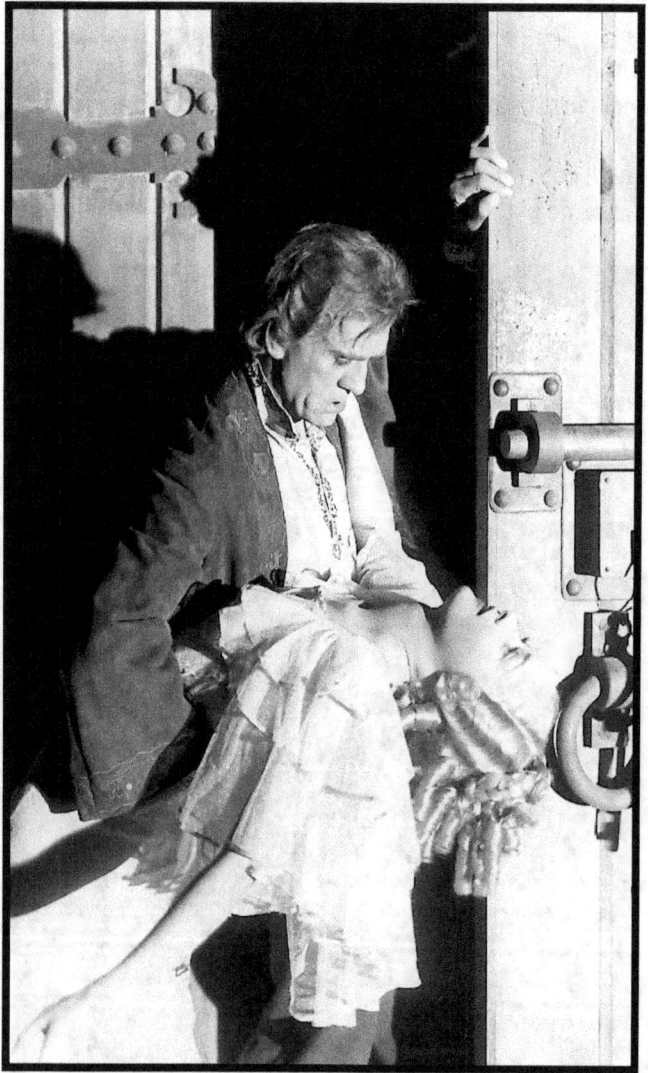

Boris Karloff and Marian Marsh in *The Black Room*

The Raven, (1935)—Irene Ware

The Raven opens with leading lady Jean Thatcher (Irene Ware) injured in a car accident and rushed to a hospital, where her fiancé Jerry Halden (Lester Matthews) and other surgeons try to save her. Jean's father Judge Thatcher (Samuel S. Hinds) begs brilliant, Poe-obsessed Dr. Richard Vollin (Bela Lugosi) to help his daughter. Jean survives and Vollin, who has fallen in love with her, tells Judge Thatcher that he wants the girl sent to him. The father refuses and Vollin swears vengeance. Edmund Bateman (Boris Karloff), an escaped criminal, seeks out Vollin and begs him to change his face. Vollin mutilates Bateman and forces him to become his henchman. Then he invites Judge Thatcher, Jean, Jerry and others to a weekend party at his house. Bateman seizes the judge and shackles him to Vollin's working model of *The Pit and the Pendulum*. Then he lowers Jean's bedroom into the basement. Jerry follows and Dr. Vollin makes both of them enter a room which crushes those inside it. Bateman, unable to let Jean die, frees the

Irene Ware as Jean in *The Raven*

couple. Vollin shoots him, but Bateman drags him into the room instead, where he is killed. Bateman dies and Jean and Jerry save Judge Thatcher.

When we first see our heroine, she sports a ridiculous hat and lounges indolently on Dr. Vollin's sofa as he soulfully serenades her on the organ. She deadpans her line, "Extraordinary man—you're almost not a man," so much that it falls completely flat; only Bela, the moody firelight, and the somber organ music save the scene. Her dance sequence, which may or may not have been done by the actress herself, is uninspired. Next, she tops even that with her coyly affected line, "Oh darling, isn't it wonderful, I can dance again." This special little moment between the two lovebirds is nauseating. When she and Jerry are driving in the car on the way to Vollin's shindig, she cannot manage lighthearted banter without being lead-footed. Miss Ware smirks and fiddles around with her mouth so much that it is distracting. She would have done well to have observed Zita Johann. Later, when the party is in full swing, her manner is so forced and self-conscious that she doesn't even appear to be having a good time. It gets worse. She grimaces and whimpers to her father, "Oh Dad, I'm so glad you're here... I just had a terrible fright." The line is not the best anyway and her delivery of it doesn't help. Our heroine has one good moment in the entire film as she apologizes to Bateman and appears genuinely sorry. But after this, it's downhill all the way. She tells her father that Dr. Vollin is "...not going to cut our throats while we're asleep," all the while continuing to simper and sidle up to her absurd fiancé. Then when a tree smashes her window and she sees Bateman coming up through the floor, she runs to Jerry, announcing her fear with an especially irritating little girl voice followed by a distasteful pout and swallow. We do not experience her fear nor do we feel any empathy for this woman. Jean Thatcher is a doll in a silly wig—not a living, breathing person. No actress worth her salt would gulp and whine her way through as many lines as Miss Ware does in this film. It is particularly evident on "I guess Daddy was right after all, we probably should have gone home," spoken with all the charm and grace of a spoiled brat. Fortunately, for the remainder of the film, we are too occupied with Vollin and Bateman to pay much attention to the judge's daughter. I have to confess, though, when the walls are closing in on Jean and Jerry I am not in a hurry for them to be saved. The cop-out ending has her preening and simpering to Jerry again as she accuses him of being "...the big bad Raven." Katherine De Mille or Francis Drake would have been infinitely better in this role. Irene Ware and Lester Matthews are the primary reasons *The Raven* is *not* a better film.

The Invisible Ray, (1935)—Frances Drake

This fascinating blend of horror and science fiction introduces us to Dr. Janos Rukh (Boris Karloff) and his wife Diana (Frances Drake). Dr. Rukh has found a centuries-old meteor which contains an element more powerful than radium. Awed by this discovery, fellow scientists Dr. Felix Benet (Bela Lugosi), Sir Francis Stevens (Walter Kingsford), Stevens' wife and nephew Ronald, and Diana Rukh, travel to Africa in search of the mysterious element. Diana and Ronald fall in love and Rukh finds his element—which poisons him. Benet, taken into Rukh's confidence, develops a counteractive for the effects of the poison. Rukh goes back to his laboratory home and cures his mother's blindness. The rest of them return to Paris and plan to use Rukh's discovery for good. Rukh, hopelessly poisoned and insane, follows. He then fakes his death. Diana marries Ronald Drake. Rukh decides to eliminate all five members of his African expedition. He murders

Frances Drake as Diana Rukh in *The Invisible Ray*

Sir Francis Stevens and his wife first. Later, when Benet lures Rukh out of hiding, he kills him as well. Rukh cannot kill Diana but decides that Drake must die. Rukh's mother finds him, knocks the counteractive out of his hand, and the tormented scientist dies—consumed by flames.

Miss Drake, to my mind one of the loveliest leading ladies ever, is a class act straight through. Her bright smile when she tells Janos that his visitors are arriving is appealing and shows us that she is truly fond of her husband. I am annoyed that Diana ends up with Ronald Drake, a pip-squeak of a juvenile if there ever was one, instead of the intense, far handsomer Janos Rukh. There appears to be a kind of chemistry between Diana and Ronald at first, but if you watch closely you'll notice that it's all coming from her! The heartbreaking scene when Janos cannot let Diana see him because of the poisoning is proof that the concentration should have been skewed in favor of that relationship rather than the one with Ronald Drake. Rukh's tension and Diana's pain are palpable. I also hate the crude juxtaposition of Diana's grief over Rukh's "death" one minute with wedding bells the next. Miss Drake's lustrous eyes speak volumes in the scene when Janos cannot bring himself to kill her. Boris Karloff's speech to her was cut, but two magnificent actors create one of the more memorable moments in the film, even without it. It's a pity that her career didn't last longer.

The Man Who Lived Again, (1936)
(aka *The Man Who Changed His Mind*)—Anna Lee

This witty, well-acted movie starts off with no-nonsense surgeon Claire Wyatt (Anna Lee), who plans to do research with the pioneering but not-quite-sane Dr. Laurience (Boris Karloff). Her boyfriend Dick Haslewood (John Loder) and Dr. Laurience's crippled companion, Clayton (Donald Calthrop), oppose this arrangement. Dr. Laurience eventually shows Claire the means to switch the brains of two chimpanzees. Claire is astounded but balks when Laurience announces his intention of trying the experiment with humans. Dick's father, publishing giant Lord Haslewood (Frank Cellier), tempts the unbalanced scientist to his empire with promises of a fully equipped laboratory and unlimited funds. After a hand-picked experts reject Laurience's ideas, Haslewood drops him. In retaliation, Laurience switches Haslewood's brain with that of Clayton. Haslewood expires and Clayton becomes the publisher. Laurience murders Clayton and changes minds with young Haslewood so he can have Claire and implicate Dick (now in Laurience's body) in his father's death. Dick, as Laurience, is mortally wounded while trying to escape the police. Claire races to the laboratory and reverses the procedure. Laurience dies.

Dr. Claire Wyatt and Dr. Laurience would be the perfect couple if she were crazier and he a little less so. Anna Lee plays her role with energy, humor and wit. I like her much more in this film than in the better known *Bedlam*, where she is just a trifle too arch for my taste. She is well matched with John Loder as Dick Haslewood, and is tender but firm when he tries to stop her from working with Dr. Laurience. Her rapport with Dr. Laurience himself is even better. Their offscreen camaraderie definitely works to their advantage onscreen. The relationship is one of mutual affection and respect. When Clayton declares that he is the only one who understands Laurience, Claire insists, "*I* understand him." Strong as she is, Miss Lee's Dr. Wyatt can also

Anna Lee in *The Man Who Changed His Mind*

his neck, urges Frankenstein to help his "friend." Wolf eagerly agrees but does not succeed in reviving his father's creation. After several murders in the village and Peter's stories of seeing a "giant" in his room, Wolf panics and realizes that Ygor has been using the Monster for his own private vengeance. Wolf shoots Ygor in self-defense and the Monster retaliates by kidnapping Peter. Wolf and Krogh pursue the Monster to the ruined laboratory and, without harming his son, Wolf knocks the Monster into the sulfur pit below.

Miss Hutchinson gets extra credit for having to deal with the child that all monster fans wish would go away—Donnie Dunagan. As Baroness Elsa, the wife of Basil Rathbone's elegantly neurotic Baron Wolf von Frankenstein, Miss Hutchinson proves herself more than up to the task. Her interactions with Basil Rathbone and be totally disarming, as evidenced by her giddy smile when Dr. Laurience brings the first chimpanzee into the laboratory. Miss Lee is powerfully eloquent when she urges her colleague to accept Lord Haslewood's offer, convinced that it is the best thing he could do. She also deftly gains the upper hand with Laurience when he begs her to help him with his experiments, saying it will be impossible without her. The actress delivers her brief response, "I know," without a hint of sarcasm. It is a memorable scene. She lives up to our expectations right to the end, where she leaps right in and saves her leading man, seemingly glad of an excuse to perform Laurience's experiment herself.

Son of Frankenstein, (1939)—Josephine Hutchinson

Film number three in this series starts with Frankenstein's son Baron Wolf von Frankenstein (Basil Rathbone), his wife Elsa (Josephine Hutchinson), and son Peter (Donnie Dunagan) returning to the village of Frankenstein to live in the ancestral castle. The villagers are openly hostile, but Inspector Krogh (Lionel Atwill) promises his protection. Wolf, wandering into his father's laboratory, finds Ygor, a blacksmith (Bela Lugosi), who steers him to the comatose body of the Frankenstein Monster. Ygor, who survived hanging some years before and whose mind is more twisted than

Donnie Dunagan and Josephine Hutchinson pose for a studio portrait for *Son of Frankenstein*.

Lionel Atwill are nicely shaded throughout. As one of the few completely sane people around, Elsa tries hard to hide her growing apprehensions but is unable to do so. She reacts splendidly to the famous line, "If the house is filled with dread, place the beds at head to head," her facial expression subtly changing from polite interest to mild anxiety. The role of Elsa is somewhat sketchy, but she makes the most of every opportunity. One of her many effective scenes is when she tells Wolf how hard she's tried not to be afraid. It would have been easy to overact, but Miss Hutchinson's skill makes us believe everything she says. She is similar to Gloria Stuart in that she knows when to step back and allow the others to take center stage.

The Wolf Man, (1941)—Evelyn Ankers

As the film opens, Lawrence Talbot (Lon Chaney, Jr.), son of Sir John Talbot (Claude Rains), returns to the family estate. Spying pretty Gwen Conliffe (Evelyn Ankers) through his father's telescope, Larry finds her father's antique shop, purchases a silver-headed wolf's head cane, and asks her out for that evening. Gwen does go but brings along her friend Jenny Williams (Fay Helm) and all three visit a Gypsy camp to have their fortunes told. Bela (Bela Lugosi), a lycanthropic Gypsy, sees that Jenny will be his next victim and tells her to go away. Hearing screams, Larry rushes to the scene and is attacked by a large wolf, which he kills with his silver-headed cane. Oddly enough, though, police find Bela's dead body rather than the wolf's, and Larry is uninjured. Feeling guilty over Bela's death, Larry goes to his burial place and finds the Gypsy's mother, Maleva (Maria Ouspenskaya), who tells him that he will also become a werewolf during the next full moon. Larry, now a werewolf, kills a man. Telling Gwen that he intends to leave town, he sees the sign of the pentagram in her palm—which means that she will be his next victim—and runs away. No one in his father's circle believes Larry's story, and Sir John hopes to end this foolishness by tying his son to a chair before helping to hunt the marauding wolf. Larry, transformed once again by the full moon, pursues Gwen and is finally killed by Sir John with Larry's silver-headed cane.

Evelyn Ankers as Gwen Conliffe has better chemistry with Lon Chaney, Jr. than anyone else. She manages to convey her interest in Larry Talbot as well as her confusion over the attraction he holds for her. It's marvelous how she interjects a world of meaning into just one word "no"—when Larry asks her if they came out to "...listen in on Jenny." The look in her eyes is a skillful blend of innocence and awareness. She answers his next question by looking at him and then simply taking his arm. Miss Ankers is completely winning in this scene and throughout the film. There's also an effective contrast in how she reacts to her dull but solid fiancé Frank Andrews (perfectly played by Patric Knowles), and the lycanthropic but fascinating Larry Talbot. Gwen tries hard to look lovingly at Frank, but the spark just isn't there. Evelyn Ankers in this film proves, beyond a doubt, that she has an impressive range and can glide effortlessly from humor and flirtatiousness to fear and tragedy. When she begs Larry to take her with him, we are incredibly moved. She injects an intriguing seed of doubt into the final clinch by murmuring Larry's name even while turning to Frank for solace. Miss Ankers gets an additional boost by the fact that *The Wolf Man* is a near perfect film. Ralph Bellamy, well cast for once, is not annoying, and even the minor characters have verve. Maria Ouspenskaya's Maleva is peerless. I love when Gwen implores her to help after Bela attacks Larry. She climbs down from her wagon, hand on hip,

Evelyn Ankers poses in a studio publicity shot for *The Wolf Man*.

and matter-of-factly inquires, "What happened to him?" Oddly enough, the Wolf Man himself sounds one of the very few false notes. In the initial transformation scene, he pulls off his sock, only to find hair growing on his leg and foot. He makes a futile, jerky motion with his arm and fist, almost as if to say, "Darn it all—hair growing there!"

Cat People, (1942)—Jane Randolph

Cat People tells the story of Irena Dubrovna (Simone Simon) who is afflicted with an strange curse—she turns

Alice (Jane Randolph) takes her frightening swim in *Cat People*.

into a leopard whenever her passions are aroused. Oliver Reed (Kent Smith) falls hard for Irena and marries her. Fearing the curse, Irena sleeps alone, which causes Oliver to turn to his office friend, Alice Moore (Jane Randolph), for consolation. Alice suggests that Irena should see a psychiatrist, Dr. Judd (Tom Conway), for her problem. Alice admits that she loves Oliver herself. Irena, sensing her husband's shifting affections, stalks Alice, but the other woman escapes. Oliver tells Irena that he wants a divorce because he now loves Alice. Panther Irena threatens Alice and Oliver at their office, but is driven away at the sign of the cross. Irena, herself again, returns home, finding Dr. Judd waiting for her. When he kisses her, she changes back into a cat. He injures her with his sword cane, but she kills him. Transformed once again, she goes to the zoo, opens the panther's cage, and allows it to finish her off.

Jane Randolph plays Alice so convincingly that I dislike her! This woman is calculating and selfish. She knows she wants Oliver Reed, that she will eventually get him, and doesn't let any obstacle (such as a wife) get in her way. Alice smiles at Irena even while she's plotting to take her husband from her. At the wedding reception, she blows cigarette smoke right over Irena's head with a gesture that plainly indicates she wishes it were in Irena's face instead! She goads Oliver into discussing his marital problems with her and that, understandably enough, infuriates Irena when she finds out about it. Alice is clever, too; she knows exactly when to break down in tears and reveal her love for Oliver. Miss Randolph is adept throughout but is particularly unpleasant in the museum scene when, with her usual false smile, she tells Oliver that it must be dull for Irena. Notice how she doesn't bother to ask Irena if she'd rather look at something else. Another example is when Alice, Oliver and Dr. Judd, another self-serving creep, discuss what they should do about Irena. It's obvious that Alice would prefer the good doctor's second option of annulment and commitment. However, when Oliver refuses to agree to the annulment and says that he should take care of Irena, she realizes she can score more points by supportively stating, "It's the only right thing to do, Ollie." Alice is definitely the survivor. Besides her less admirable traits, she is courageous and resourceful. Poor Irena, enchantingly played by Simone Simon, also has courage but is powerless to fight something stronger than she is. In a way, Alice and Oliver deserve each other. Each of them believes that life should be clear sailing, with no unhappiness. Both of them think they're decent people, which they are not. Oliver harasses Irena until she marries him, tells her she can have "all the time in the world" to consummate their union, and then, at the first sign of rough waters, dispassionately discusses his wife with another woman and eventually dumps her. Miss Randolph is so good that her character is completely alive. Kudos to this actress for daring to make Alice the nasty piece of work that she is.

The Ghost of Frankenstein —Evelyn Ankers

Ygor (Bela Lugosi), who apparently survived after being shot in *Son of Frankenstein*, finds his friend the Monster (Lon Chaney, Jr.) in the old sulfur pit. Ygor takes him to brain surgeon Ludwig Frankenstein (Sir Cedric Hardwicke), who is Wolf's brother. Along the way, the Monster befriends little Cloestine Hussman (Janet Ann Gallow) and kills a villager. Taken into custody, the Monster seems to recognize Ludwig, who agrees to examine him. The Monster escapes, rejoins Ygor, arrives at Ludwig's home, and kills the doctor's assistant. Ludwig's daughter Elsa (Evelyn Ankers), engaged to Erik Ernst (Ralph Bellamy) and blissfully unaware of

Evelyn Ankers as Elsa in *The Ghost of Frankenstein*

her father's tainted lineage up until now, is horrified and wants the Monster destroyed. Dr. Frankenstein at first wants the same thing, but his colleague Dr. Bohmer (Lionel Atwill) calls it murder, and Ludwig himself decides to change his father's creation forever by giving the creature the brain of his murdered assistant. Ygor easily persuades Bohmer, who would be Frankenstein's superior if not for a botched operation, to use his brain for the Monster instead. The scheme backfires because their blood types are not compatible, and the Monster goes blind. The maddened creature kills Bohmer and sets the laboratory on fire. Elsa and Erik escape, leaving behind Dr. Frankenstein and the Monster.

Again, Miss Ankers, as Elsa Frankenstein, is her usual polished, charming self in this fourth film of the Frankenstein series. Her assignment is a little tougher this time around because she's paired with Ralph Bellamy, whose sense of self-importance and officiousness do not work here. Her scenes with her father, expertly underplayed by Sir Cedric Hardwicke, are much more animated than those with her beau. The actress also generates more warmth with Janet Ann Gallow than does Lon Chaney, Jr.

Night Monster, (1942)—Irene Hervey

At lonely Ingston Towers, Margaret Ingston (Fay Helm) has seen and heard so many strange things that she questions her own sanity and sends for Dr. Lynn Harper, a noted psychiatrist (Irene Hervey). The Ingstons' maid quits, but returns for her possessions and is murdered. Dr. Harper, whose car has broken down on the way to Ingston Towers, hears screams and thinks she sees the killer. Walking in the dark, she is picked up by mystery writer Dick Baldwin (Don Porter), who is also going to Ingston Towers. In the meantime, Margaret's brother Kurt (Ralph Morgan) has summoned the three doctors who failed to prevent him from becoming a helpless cripple. All three, along with the chauffeur, are eventually found murdered. Spooky housekeeper Sarah Judd (Doris Lloyd) tries to keep Lynn and Dick from leaving. Margaret and Judd tangle, Lynn and Dick escape, and Margaret sets the house on fire. Outside, they are attacked by the mystery killer Kurt Ingston who, bent on revenge for his pitiful physical state, was able to temporarily restore his useless limbs by mental control. Ingston's teacher, mystic Agor Singh (Nils Asther), arrives just in time and shoots his pupil.

Irene Hervey as Dr. Lynn Harper is a crisply professional, yet caring and empathetic psychiatrist. She's a strong woman, but is noticeably unnerved about the weird occurrences at the Towers. Miss Hervey and Don Porter, as mystery writer Dick Baldwin, complement each other well. The actress relates suitably to Doris Lloyd as Sarah Judd and Fay Helm as her supposed

patient Margaret Ingston. Her confrontation scenes with Miss Judd are subtle jousts that she does not always win. Miss Hervey presents us with a lifelike image of a successful woman whose strength and vulnerabilities together are considerably appealing. It does not hurt that *Night Monster* is a well crafted, suspenseful film with no weak performances.

Frankenstein Meets the Wolf Man, (1943) —Ilona Massey

Larry Talbot (Lon Chaney, Jr.), resurrected by graverobbers, is on the prowl again in this film. A

confused Larry finds himself in a hospital and tells his unbelievable story to physician Frank Mannering (Patric Knowles) and a policeman. The same evening, Larry changes back into the Wolf Man and breaks out of the hospital. Another murder makes poor Larry long for death himself, and he seeks out Maleva (Maria Ouspenskaya) so that they can find Dr. Frankenstein. Unfortunately for Lawrence Talbot, the doctor is dead. The Wolf Man kills again that evening, and is chased to the Frankenstein ruins by the villagers. Himself once again, Larry discovers the Monster (Bela Lugosi) frozen in a subterranean cave. Talbot revives the creature and searches for the Frankenstein diary but cannot find it. Larry, pretending to be interested in buying the Frankenstein property, tries to obtain the diary from the doctor's daughter Elsa (Ilona Massey), but she insists she does not know where it is. Both of them are guests of honor at the wine festival that evening where Dr. Mannering also turns up and accuses his former patient of being a murderer. The Monster conveniently arrives, and he and Talbot return to the castle. Elsa accompanies Frank to the castle where he attempts to cure Talbot and deactivate the Monster. But like all the Frankenstein scientists before him, Mannering cannot resist seeing the Monster at his full power. The Monster clashes with the Wolf Man (full moon—again), and Elsa and Frank escape as one of the villagers dynamites a dam, drowning the two adversaries.

This lady flashes a more beguiling smile than any other horror movie heroine, but she disappoints us after the first few scenes. In lighter moments, Miss Massey is captivating and illuminates the screen. She must have been quite a hit in the many operettas that she did. However, she can't handle the drama. The actress comes off as pretentious and phony when she positions herself for the best angles. Her Baroness Elsa Frankenstein is unintentionally humorous when she tells Dr. Frank Mannering that she will take him to the ruins of her father's castle and then beams at him as if they're going on a picnic! But in a more positive light, Miss Massey is naturally elegant and poised so at least she is never exasperating. Plus she has an easy rapport with Patric Knowles.

Phantom of the Opera, (1943)—Susanna Foster

After losing his job in the Paris Opera Orchestra, violinist Erique Claudin (Claude Rains), who is virtually penniless from secretly paying for soprano Christine Dubois' (Susanna Foster) voice lessons, attempts to have his life's work—a concerto—published. Hearing his piece being played, he believes the publisher to be a thief and murders him. The publisher's assistant flings caustic chemicals in Claudin's face. Claudin, mutilated for life, escapes from the police by hiding in the sewers. Coinciding neatly with the violinist's disappearance, a mysterious ghost seems to be haunting the Opera House. Understudy Christine takes over for sick prima donna Madame Biancarolli (Jane Farrar). Suspicious over her sudden illness, the singer accuses baritone Anatole Garron of trying to kill her in order to advance Christine's career. The Phantom murders Biancarolli and her maid the next evening. After that, he's on the rampage—crashing an enormous chandelier down on the audience and taking Christine down to the sewers. Christine unmasks the Phantom while he plays the organ for her. Christine's suitor Garron joins forces with her other suitor, Inspector Raoul Daubert (Edgar Barrier), and together they destroy the Phantom and rescue Christine.

This film was served up with all the trimmings— gorgeous color, costumes, scenery—the works. So it's even more of a shame that the leading lady is a simpering fool. When we are first introduced to Christine DuBois, she is gloating in the wings over the attention being paid her by baritone, Anatole Garron. Moments later, yet

The Phantom of the Opera (Claude Rains) tries to take Christine (Susanna Foster) into his underground lair.

another suitor, Inspector Daubert, is dancing attendance on her as well. Miss Foster falls flat on her face in this sequence. She is saccharine and speaks with a baby doll voice which is extremely unappealing. Most of the time, she seems to be struggling to pronounce her words properly. This Christine has only one unaffected moment when she comes across Claudin in the hallway before he's dismissed from the opera. Miss Foster gives Mr. Rains the only heartfelt smile she has to offer in the entire film. One particularly galling scene has Christine singing a lullaby from her hometown, with Anatole, when Raoul comes to speak to her about Claudin. Raoul states that he knows nothing about opera and Christine replies, "It's not from an opera, Raoul, it's a lullaby." In the middle of her line, she treats us to an extra adorable blink of her eyes. So much praise has been heaped on Miss Foster's voice that, as a singer, I offer my opinion as well. She possesses an unremarkable coloratura soprano that is small and lacks any distinctive color. Her top notes are squeaky and her high C is just barely on pitch. The film would be unwatchable but for the technical perfection and the on-target characterizations of Claude Rains as Erique Claudin/The Phantom, Jane Farrar as the prima donna Madame Biancarolli, and a lovely cameo by Fritz Leiber as Franz Liszt.

The Seventh Victim, (1943) — Kim Hunter

The scene is Highcliffe Academy where Mary Gibson (Kim Hunter) is told that her sister Jacqueline (Jean Brooks) has stopped paying Mary's tuition. She sets out in search of her sister, after rejecting an offer to teach at the school. Mary immediately goes to La Sagesse, Jacqueline's cosmetic company, where a sinister Mrs. Redi (Mary Newton) informs the girl that she herself is the new owner. Determined to find Jacqueline, Mary discovers that her sister rents an empty apartment containing a noose with a chair beneath it but does not live there. At her next stop, the Missing Persons Bureau, a private investigator, Irving August (Lou Lubin), offers his help, which Mary initially rejects. Mary, acting on a tip from August, visits the morgue and is told to see Gregory Ward (Hugh Beaumont), who later turns out to be Jacqueline's husband. Mary and Irving August break into La Sagesse and August is knifed by an unseen assailant. Fleeing to a subway, Mary spies two men supporting the late Irving August between them. Mary now has three men helping her — Gregory Ward, Jason Hoag (Erford Gage) a poet she met at one of Jacqueline's hangouts, and psychiatrist Dr. Judd (Tom Conway). Judd does arrange a short meeting between the sisters and, afterwards, Mary learns that her much loved sister belonged to a cult of the devil, left them, and is now sentenced to death for breaking their pact of secrecy. Back with the cult, Jacqueline is about to drink the poison they urge on her, when one of their members pushes it away from her. On her own again, Jacqueline is hunted by the cult's assassin, but escapes to her apartment with the noose in it. Mary and Gregory acknowledge their love for each other and, back at the apartment, we hear the sound of a chair falling over.

Mary Gibson is a rather odd ingenue. She seems guileless enough, but before the film is half over, she has visited the Missing Persons Bureau and the morgue, has helped break into a cosmetics company after hours, has been indirectly responsible for a man's death, and has fallen in love with her sister's husband. Kim Hunter has exactly the right look for this role. This actress is so appealing that one would never suspect her inner strength and determination. She reminds me of Teresa Wright in *Shadow of a Doubt*. When we first meet her, we know that she will find her sister because, like Alice in *Cat People*, Mary is a Lewton survivor. Miss Hunter

Kim Hunter as Mary in *The Seventh Victim*

gives us a finely etched portrait of a sheltered young girl who valiantly faces situations that she probably never dreamed of before. She's terrific when she and Irving August break into La Sagesse after hours and, with wide, innocent eyes, she urges him to go down the forbidding hallway and check the locked room. (By the way, Lou Lubin is topnotch as Irving August. He's a seedy sort of private investigator but has enough heart that he decides to offer his help to Mary even after she rebuffs him. His pronunciation of La Sagesse is priceless!) Miss Hunter also manages to exude charm even though saddled with the charmless TV father of *Leave it to Beaver* (Hugh Beaumont) as a leading man. We feel that she would definitely be better off with Jason Hoag! Mary is the only person whom Jacqueline truly loves and we feel their attachment to each other. Winning as she is, through no fault of her own, she does not capture our hearts. After the film is over, the only person we care about is her luckless sister, Jacqueline.

Son of Dracula, (1943) — Louise Allbritton

Katherine (Kay) Caldwell, a Southern heiress (Louise Allbritton), has invited a Count Alucard (Lon Chaney, Jr.) to visit her father's plantation. After he arrives, Kay's father is found dead. Engaged to childhood sweetheart, Frank Stanley (Robert Paige), Katherine inexplicably marries the Count. Frank shoots at Alucard, kills Kay instead, and winds up in jail. Family friend Dr. Brewster (Frank Craven) suggests that Count Alucard is really Count Dracula and that Kay deliberately enlisted his aid in becoming a vampire so that she and Frank could be together for eternity. Frank makes a getaway and burns Alucard's coffin, causing the vampire to die in the sunlight. Frank returns to the plantation and sets fire to Kay's body, thereby freeing her soul.

Callous, sinister and yet ethereally beautiful, Louise Allbritton is the only anti-heroine in this survey. Evelyn Ankers, cast as her sister Claire, is more the conventional heroine type, but her role is too small to be considered that of a leading lady. Miss Allbritton has often been criticized for not turning in a good performance, but I disagree. She is focused throughout and creates a disturbing image, impossible to forget after the final reel. To say that Katherine lacks warmth is putting it mildly. This contrast is especially marked when she is onscreen with the sympathetic Claire. Miss Allbritton's eyes are hard, glittering and ice cold, and her mysterious little smiles, coupled with those eyes, are grim indeed. When the Count murders her father and she dispassionately examines the puncture wounds on his neck, she registers no emotion whatsoever. One of her best scenes is after Frank mistakenly shoots her and yet she appears sitting up in bed and smiling. Miss Allbritton employs a dry, broken voice, eerily suggesting death and the grave.

Louise Allbritton and Lon Chaney in *Son of Dracula*

This moment loses none of its shock value with repeated viewings. Another fine moment is when she visits Frank in his jail cell and stops him from using the "v" word, saying, "Don't use that word, we don't like it." Later, he objects to joining her unnatural existence. She replies, "I've already told you; you have no choice." A fine cast supports the actress, particularly Robert Paige as her loving fiancé. Mr. Paige's cry of "Kay, Kay my darling" as he sees her lying in the casket is absolutely heartrending. The only thing working against this macabre jewel of a film is Lon Chaney, Jr. as Count Alucard/Dracula. He makes a sincere effort and comes off rather well when using his physical power, but he lacks the elegance and unearthliness that Bela Lugosi would have provided.

House of Frankenstein, (1944)—
Anne Gwynne; Elena Verdugo

Yet another *Frankenstein* film, this one begins with Dr. Gustav Niemann (Boris Karloff) who tried to transplant a man's brain into a dog's skull, and Daniel, a hunchback (J. Carrol Naish), in Neustadt Prison. Freed by a fierce storm, the two men join Professor Bruno Lampini's (George Zucco) Chamber of Horrors caravan. Niemann orders Daniel to strangle Lampini and his driver and they are on their way to wreak vengeance on the men who put the unorthodox doctor in prison. One of them, Burgomaster Hussman (Sig Ruman), attends their midnight horror show with his grandson Carl (Peter Coe) and his wife Rita (Anne Gwynne). Dr. Niemann pulls the stake from Count Dracula's skeleton and blackmails him into murdering the Burgomaster. Count Dracula (John Carradine) tries to take Rita with him to his "world," but Niemann betrays him and tosses his coffin out into the dawn's light. Continuing on to the village of Frankenstein, Niemann and Daniel stop at a Gypsy camp, where the hunchback falls madly in love with Ilonka (Elena Verdugo), whom he saves from a vicious whipping. Taking her with them, the doctor and Daniel free the Monster (Glenn Strange) and the Wolfman (Lon Chaney, Jr.) from the ice. Ilonka and Larry fall in love, and Daniel eliminates two more men for Niemann, who tries to revive the Monster. Daniel, in return for services rendered, wants Talbot's body so that Ilonka will love him. Ilonka, meanwhile, has discovered the truth about Larry and shoots him with a silver bullet after Larry (once again the Wolf Man) fatally wounds her. Daniel, distraught over Ilonka's death, turns on Niemann, but the Monster kills Daniel and drags Niemann off, where doctor and monster both go down in the quicksand.

This movie has two leading ladies. Miss Gwynne has a rather limited role, but she does a credible job all the same. She's vivacious and playful in her opening scenes and matches delightfully with Peter Coe; then she subtly gives us a hint of what is to come by her morbid fascination with Count Dracula's skeleton. After the Count himself mesmerizes her, she lowers the pitch of her bubbly voice and unleashes a velvety sensuous quality—quite different from what we've seen before.

Anne Gwynne in a sexy publicity pose for *House of Frankenstein*

Elena Verdugo, marvelous all the way through, earns my second Best Actress Oscar (although in Hollywood lingo, it probably would have been Best Supporting Actress). Her dancing is assured and lively, with her artless pride in her skill truly touching. On the other hand, she can cause sparks to fly when necessary. The Gypsy leader is no match for her and has to resort to physical violence to subdue her. Her first moment with Daniel is a multifaceted gem; Verdugo reveals to us so many different hues that it is difficult keeping pace with her. One nice touch is when Ilonka peers over her mug at Daniel. She is both provocative and innocent as she asks, "Did you like me?" Her Ilonka has a chemistry with Larry Talbot only eclipsed by Evelyn Ankers. Her growing attachment to the gloom-haunted lycanthrope is gently expressive. She's just sensational when she lashes full throttle into

The Wolf Man (Chaney) threatens Elena Verdugo as Ilonka (left) in *House of Frankenstein*

62

poor Daniel with her corker of a line, "You're mean and you're ugly—I hate you!" She suffuses every flicker of her eyes and each infinitesimal movement with meaning. Miss Verdugo creates an exciting, unforgettable portrait of a woman who dies for the man she loves. I remember weeping the first time I saw her slowly crawl to Larry as she dies. My husband, Steven, a very tough critic, happened in on my *House of Frankenstein* viewing and remarked, "She's really good." Indeed she is.

House of Dracula, (1945) — Martha O'Driscoll

Picking up where *House of Frankenstein* left off, we see Count Dracula (John Carradine) apparently not destroyed in the previous film — visiting Dr. Edelmann (Onslow Stevens) and asking to be cured of his vampirism. However, the Count is only using Edelmann to get to one of his nurses, Miliza (Martha O'Driscoll). Larry Talbot (Lon Chaney, Jr.) also turns up at the doctor's house and he and Miliza fall in love. Talbot attempts suicide by jumping into the sea; Edelmann rescues him and finds the Frankenstein Monster. Edelmann catches on to Dracula's real intentions, but not before the vampire has infected him with his own blood. Edelmann does manage to cure Talbot, but Edelmann, now a Jekyll/Hyde vampiric killer, resuscitates the Monster and strangles his other nurse, Nina (Jane Adams), who is in love with him. Talbot kills Edelmann, starts a fire in the laboratory, and escapes with Miliza.

Like Anne Gwynne before her, this actress plays yet another of Dracula's love interests. The big difference here is that she can't act and is a distinct liability in this already flawed film. She has a breathless, little girl voice (that reminds me of Susanna Foster) and a nearly expressionless face. After Miliza meets Larry for the first time, the camera zooms in on her face for a close-up and, instead of appearing puzzled yet interested, she looks like a Revlon ad. In spite of the best efforts of the lush background music, she has zero chemistry with the luckless Larry. Her scenes with Jane Adams only serve to magnify her inadequacies because the contrast between her self-conscious artificiality and Miss Adams'

Martha O'Driscoll as Miliza is threatened by Dracula (John Carradine) in *House of Dracula*.

simple sincerity almost hurts. Miss Adams, even with disfiguring hump, is still lovelier than Miss O'Driscoll. O'Driscoll spoils the *Moonlight Sonata* scene with Count Dracula (thinly disguised as Baron Latos), which could have been one of the most compelling scenes in the movie, by her blank staring eyes and mask-like face. (Not in a hypnotic trance; just mindless...) A fabulous acting opportunity totally wasted — in complete contrast to John Carradine's virtuoso manner.

From taking the heroine-centric view of vintage horror films, some common problems arise again and again. As in a dance, the gentleman usually leads and the lady follows. It is liberating when the role allows the actress to break free from this mold. We have Zita Johann as Helen/Anck-es-en-Amon, the Ilonka of Elena Verdugo, and Anna Lee's Dr. Claire Wyatt. But generally the role required the actress to be decorative. She does not destroy the monster; she does not make the fight-or-flight decision. But none of this diminishes the importance of the actress' craft.

Universal's horror factory, during the 1940s, literally became a factory mass-producing competent B films and sequels to their more ambitious A productions of the 1930s. The reincarnation and mysticism theme of Karl Freund's *The Mummy* became simplified into western/serial star Tom Tyler's revenge motif in *The Mummy's Hand*. The dark fairy-tale universe of James Whale's *Bride of Frankenstein*, pitting beloved Outsider against Conformist, also became transformed into the standard revenge tale as madman Ygor plots to have his brain inserted into the all-powerful Frankenstein Monster in the thrill-a-minute *The Ghost of Frankenstein*. Amidst these reinventions of the original iconic monsters and horror romps, the films soon deteriorated into the comic book plotted and almost characterless monster rally films of the 1940s: *Frankenstein Meets the Wolf Man, House of Frankenstein*, and *House of Dracula*. In a single decade — of course, under new studio management and new directors/writers — Universal transformed inspired art into kiddie-oriented formula. The continuing reign of the studio's copyrighted monsters became an "end" product rather than the means to instigate creativity and new ideas into an anemic genre.

Empowered Women in the Val Lewton Canon

by Gary J. Svehla

While the 1930s artistically belonged to Universal (to this day the creators of the most inspired horror film cinema ever devised), the time was ripe by the early 1940s for a new kid on the block to breathe fresh life and creativity into product-driven horror cinema.

Enter Val Lewton, assigned to run the B unit of RKO pictures during the early 1940s, a man who was given gaudy titles first and then required to come up with scripts and movies based upon those titles. A lesser artist would have probably studied the Universal trend and made copycat imitations of the high-grossing Universal B monster films. But Lewton, thank Heaven, believed in a more adult approach to horror, trying to fill the gap that Universal had created when it moved from the A movies of the 1930s to the B programmers of the 1940s. Even though Lewton was not given much money with which to work, his concept was not to base his horror on monsters (with expensive makeup and effects) but to keep his horror movies character-driven, instilling psychological motives for the actions of his primary inhabitants in his horror universe. His movies would reek with low-lit mood and the atmosphere of horror better left unseen. Edmund Bansak's excellent book, *Fearing the Dark* (McFarland, 1994), tells the entire production history and Val Lewton biography, as does Joel Siegel's *Val Lewton, The Reality of Terror*. These books come recommended for those who wish to learn more about the films of Val Lewton and the Lewton influences in more modern horror movies.

But our thesis here is to explore six of Lewton's nine horror movies, the six that either feature women in leading roles or portray a vision of women as being dominant in a film genre usually characterized by women who are thinly developed (outside of their makeup, costumes and sex appeal), or relegated to being either defenseless victims, screamers, or window dressing to draw in the predominantly male audience.

This chapter will focus upon the empowered women revealed in Lewton's *Cat People, I Walked with a Zombie, The Leopard Man, The Seventh Victim, The Curse of the Cat People,* and *Bedlam*, supporting the premise that one of Val Lewton's more important contributions to budget-minded moviemaking was the depth of character instilled into females within his movies.

Most analyses of Val Lewton movies fail to emphasize Lewton's reliance upon resolutely written and even stronger acted feminine roles, roles which either are revealed as pivotal characters in the movie or outright star performances. When Lewton produced his first movie, *Cat People* in 1942, scripted by DeWitt Bodeen, the *femme fatale* and manipulative woman of film noir had yet to emerge, but Lewton's female characters (and I stress the phrase "Lewton's female characters" because he had hands-on control of his scripts, even co-writing several under the pseudonym of Carlos Keith) were often virtuous and determined explorers into worlds of hidden evil, while others emerged as tainted, corrupted and sometimes even defeated—but his women were

Val Lewton

never weak. While many critics feel that strong-willed females did not emerge into the horror film genre until much later, Val Lewton and his thought-provoking horror factory dispel that myth instantly by creating women who are three-dimensional, sometimes self-assured, sometimes world-weary, but always flesh and blood human beings imbued with both the strengths and flaws that make people true-to-life—and *interesting*.

Of the four major characters that populate *Cat People*, two are cleverly developed and two are stereotypes: Interestingly enough, both lead male characters are the stereotypes.

First we have the bland hero, Oliver Reed, portrayed by Kent Smith. Reed is a by-the-books male—good-hearted, no surprises, and dominated by logic without harboring any sense of imagination. His job reflects him totally: He's an architect whose tools of the trade include a T-square and clear-cut blueprints. While it is obvious how easily he is able to fall in love with sensual foreigner Irena (Simone Simon), a sexy feline of a child/woman, he makes a rather shallow commitment to his marriage as things develop. Immediately after seeing Irena sketch the panther at the zoo, Oliver announces, "I've never known an artist." Of course he is literally referring to a woman with a drawing pad in hand, but figuratively, he is referring to the personality on the other side of the coin from "architect"—he the small-minded man of common sense, she the captivating creation of imagination. Later, after marrying Irena and marital troubles intervene into Oliver's perfect little world ("I've never been unhappy before"), he is fast to recommend that his wife see a psychiatrist, a doctor of logic and reason. Oliver reprimands his wife by telling her, "It's not the stories—it's that *you* believe them. You need help!" In Oliver's world, every problem has a clear-cut solution and Oliver depends upon other professionals to solve his.

Second, the other pivotal male lead is the psychiatrist Dr. Judd (Tom Conway), an oily male lech, a doctor not above using his professional position to seduce the troubled and innocent Irena. "You believe if your husband were to kiss you, that you would turn into a beast. Suppose I were to kiss you..."

Irena pleads, "I need your help!"

Judd asserts his power by coldly threatening, "I could have you put away for observation... you're *that* close to insanity!"

Judd, played to the hilt of arrogance and just-below-the-surface perversity by perennial cad actor Tom Conway, becomes immediately the film's true villain, unlikable from the first office visit. We too blatantly see his intentions of sexual conquest, his not-so-hidden agenda of seduction by maintaining power over his patient. Judd's pretense of helping Irena never disguises the seething lust he feels toward her. While well-played, Conway's character is also stereotyped.

However, Simone Simon's Irena is multi-faceted—creating many layers of reality in her brooding characterization. First, Irena is sexually arousing, a flirt who enjoys the attention she attracts. When she meets Oliver and invites him back to her apartment, she coos: "I've never had anyone here... You might be my first real friend." As the relationship develops, Oliver and Irena fall in love, but she pulls back because of her fear of the "curse," which her village says will turn her into a beast

Kent Smith is the bland hero while Simone Simon and Jane Randolph provide the strong and complex women in *Cat People*.

Irena (Simone Simon) is overcome with sadness at being unable to give herself completely to her husband in *Cat People*.

once her passions are aroused: "I stayed away from people... I lived alone. I didn't want this to happen!"

Irena even allows her spiritual love to reign when she agrees to share marriage vows with Oliver, but she keeps her physical love in check, hoping to work out a compromise which will allow her marriage to survive. "I want to be Mrs. Reed... really want to be *everything* that name means. But I can't! Oliver, be kind, be patient. Let me have time to get over that feeling that there's evil in me!" The passion in her movement, the lust in her face, but also that deadening emptiness and loneliness in her eyes reflect this paradox: She truly loves Oliver with all her heart and soul, but physically having sex with the man of her dreams, she believes, will transform her into a savage beast that will slay Oliver. She understands that a man will wait only so long to have his physical needs satisfied, but she does not know what to do. She dares not give in to her instincts, but how will she make bland, unimaginative Oliver understand why she cannot submit to these passions? While she tries to be everything to Oliver, even accepting his present of a cat that recoils in anger against her, wisely suggesting to Oliver to exchange it for another pet (unfortunately, a defenseless bird in a cage that dies from fright as Irena playfully sticks her hand inside, attempting to grab the bird), Irena is constantly reminded that she exists within a no-win world.

Two scenes quietly convey the infinite sadness dwelling deeply within Irena. After voicing her frustration at being unable to satisfy her husband sexually, she runs into the bedroom, sinks down on her knees, huddled dejectedly by the bedroom door, snow falling outside observable through her rear bedroom window. The subtle symbolism of falling snow anchors the sadness of the sequence. In another scene, the depressed Irena undresses for her bath, clutching her arms around her curled-up knees and legs while sitting in the tub, crying alone, a figure of desperate solitude.

The fourth character, the enigmatic Alice Moore (Jane Randolph), becomes such a flesh and blood character that audiences are not sure how to react to her. First of all, she's Oliver's "buddy" at work, a friend who stands by him. At the wedding, Alice encourages the relationship: "Irena's a grand girl. Oliver and her will be very happy together." Yet when Alice is first viewed at work, C.R. Cooper Ship and Barge Construction Company, she becomes the female director barking orders: "A little more to the left... just a hair." Always portraying the good sport, Alice early on tells Oliver, "If *you* like her, *she's* okay with me."

However, while many observers view Alice as the decent friend who is ready and willing to stand by another friend in need, innocently falling in love with Oliver as she observes his pain, she can also be seen in a much more manipulative and unsympathetic manner. It is Alice who suggests that Irena see Dr. Judd (perhaps even knowing him to be the lecherous doctor he most certainly is), and when Oliver tells Irena that he told Alice about Irena seeing the doctor, Irena is justifiably angry (one of the rare times she displays anger toward her husband): "How could you discuss such intimate things! There are certain things a woman doesn't want other women to know." Alice and Oliver openly speak of Oliver's marital problems at work, and the manipulative Alice uses every advantage to pry their marriage a little further apart. Alice offers consolation, "It must make you very unhappy."

Oliver admits, "I don't know what to do about all this." Suddenly, laying all her cards on the table, Alice breaks down in tears and makes her play, "I can't bear to see you unhappy. I love you too darn much... Forget it, it's Irena, you're in love with her."

Oliver, his motives becoming a tad less decent, meets Alice's eyes head on: "I don't know if I'm in love with Irena."

Alice then turns on the passionate persuasion, always maintaining her air of decency and gosh-darn friendliness. "I know what love is. It's understanding. No self-torture, no self-doubt. Nothing can change us."

"That's the way I feel about Irena," Oliver admits honestly, the disappointment apparent on Alice's face.

Then Oliver sings a different tune, one that sparks up Alice's hope of winning her man. "In many ways we [Irena and I] are strangers. You and I—we'll never be strangers."

Alice's one pivotal line of dialogue sums her up totally: "I'm the new type of 'other woman.' That's why I'm so dangerous."

Alice's predatory nature from this stage onward is not so innocent, and her schemes to win the heart of Oliver make her character seem nastier and wilier, yet it almost seems a coincidence whenever she lowers the boom, always in a kindly and off-handed way. When the three of them are going to the Fletcher Museum to look at ship models, Alice immediately interjects, "I'm afraid this is dull for Irena," whom Oliver then sends away for an hour while Alice and he share some quality time together.

Alice (Jane Randolph) declares her love for Oliver (Kent Smith) in *Cat People*.

Soon Oliver breaks Irena's heart: Right after Irena proudly tells her husband that she has returned from seeing Dr. Judd for the second time and wants to be helped, Oliver states, "...things have changed. I love Alice, Irena. It's too late. I'll give you a divorce."

Thus the psychological motivation is well in place for *Cat People*'s major set pieces: Irena's silent pursuit of Alice as she walks through the park to catch her bus; Irena's stalking of Alice in the indoor apartment swimming pool, her bathrobe torn to ribbons; and Irena's allowing Dr. Judd to kiss her in his office, transforming her into the panther which kills Dr. Judd, but not before he buries his sword (from his cane) into Irena's back, soon leading to her death. Such a self-sacrificing, desperate move opens the way for Oliver (the man Irena still loves) and Alice to be together forever.

Val Lewton's second film, also directed by Jacques Tourneur, featured the exploitative title, *I Walked with a Zombie*. Once again the script, based upon an original story by Inez Wallace, written by Curt Siodmak (part of the Universal horror factory, no less) and Ardel Wray, features a strong lead female character, Betsy (Frances Dee), and another dominant secondary female character, Mrs. Rand (Edith Barrett).

The basic story concerns a young, unmarried nurse, Betsy Connell, working in Canada, who is hired by a sugar refining company to care for the wife of one of their most important sugar cane suppliers. This means Betsy's immediate relocation to the island of St. Sebastian in the West Indies, to live on the plantation owned by two half brothers: Paul Holland (Tom Conway) and Wesley Rand (James Ellison). The only strange question asked during her interview: "Do you believe in witchcraft?" But the $200 salary per month is not to be ignored and she accepts the position.

Since the urban romantic love triangle proved so successful in *Cat People* (without ever sinking to soap-operatic level), that same formula, though a tad more complex here, would be transplanted to the tropical locale. Interestingly enough, the two main male characters, the plantation owning brothers, are upon initial view seemingly opposing stereotypes, but in reality, their characters offer so much more subtlety. Frances Dee's liberated nurse offers nuances and complexities in her character which bring out underlying shadings in the men's characters as well.

On the small boat to her new island home, she meets the "Byronic," brooding Paul Holland, the more dominant brother and plantation owner. His sadness immediately interests Betsy: "No beauty here, just death and decay," Paul declares, recasting a romantic open-air boat ride under the calming blanket of stars into something deadly and disgusting. Holland states the small fish jump out of the water not for joy but out of fear because bigger fish are feeding on them... their decaying bodies become the sparkle on churning waves. Spotting a shooting star falling out of the sky, Holland continues, "Everything dies here, even the stars!"

Holland is an even colder fish when it comes to handing out instructions to his new nurse, telling her "this is not a position for someone easily frightened," which she most certainly was during her first night on the island wandering out alone to investigate the sobbing sounds she hears coming from the Tower, where she comes across the somnambulistic Jessica Holland (Christine Gordon), a literal sleepwalker whose dazed gaze signifies her detachment from the real world. Gordon, portraying Mrs. Holland in this brain dead state the entire movie, makes her more of a visual symbol rather than a human being. Later Holland reminds Betsy, "Please remember my wife is a mental case," without demonstrating any emotions toward how he feels about his wife other than approaching this entire predicament in a very business-like manner.

The overriding emotion at Fort Holland is quiet sadness. The sobbing that Betsy heard her first night was black servant Alma (Theresa Harris) crying over the birth of a newborn baby. These former slaves "weep when a child is born and laugh at funerals," reflecting the hellish life into which their slave ancestors had been born. Paul Holland becomes the character who most forcefully mirrors this sad sentiment throughout the movie.

Contrasted to this brooding, tortured and cold exterior is half-brother Wesley Rand, always a drink in hand, friendly, talkative and gentlemanly to a fault. Seeing Betsy scurry through the town during her day off, he too admits he has the day off and offers to show her the sights, stopping to have a drink at an outdoor establishment. Suddenly his happy-go-lucky nature dissipates when a wandering black minstrel (Sir Lancelot) sings a ballad about the Holland/Rand family and the skeletons in their closet: lyrics detailing Wesley's falling in love with his brother's wife and the cruel fate that awaited her. Wesley, both embarrassed and angered by the invasion of his privacy by the village Calypso singer, passes word via a waiter to have him stop singing immediately. The equally embarrassed singer formally apologizes as Wesley insults him.

Thus, we have a boldly inquisitive virgin nurse care for a virtually comatose patient, whose husband is brooding and abrupt, whose half-brother not-so-secretly loves his half-brother's wife, all such factors causing the expected tensions between plantation owner brothers. These are not the cartoon cut-outs of Universal B scripts of the 1940s.

Into this mix comes Wesley's mother, Mrs. Rand, who wisely opts to not live at the family estate, instead living at the establishment run by her late husband, the former island missionary. She is an elder woman of almost masculine authority, a woman who definitely knows what she wants in life and how to get it. "The fort needs a girl like you," Mrs. Rand tells Betsy. Rand quickly apologizes for not going to the fort to meet Betsy before now, but Mrs. Rand has heard wonderful reports stating that she is kind to Jessica and to her sons Paul and Wesley (who has passed out drunk and whom Betsy is unable to move). "Put him on a horse," his mother demands, shocking Betsy, who fears he might fall and hurt himself. Mrs. Rand is very disturbed about Wesley's drinking

Betsy Connell (Frances Drake) is attracted to the brooding Paul Holland (Tom Conway) in *I Walked with a Zombie*.

problem and asks Betsy to talk to Paul about removing the whiskey decanter from the dinner table. Betsy sheepishly responds that she has little influence over Mr. Holland, but Mrs. Rand responds, "You may have more influence than you think!" Thus, feminine power is asserted in a male-dominated culture.

Interestingly enough, when Betsy suggests such a move diplomatically to Paul, he becomes haughty and authoritative: "It's always been on the table," implying that whiskey on the table is a proud tradition. Seeming to be slightly upset, Holland barks, "I engaged you to take care of my wife, *not* my brother!" However, that evening at dinner, when Wesley notices the decanter has not been placed on the table, Paul tells him, "We'll try serving dinner without it," thus giving in to Betsy's demands after huffing and puffing that he would never consider breaking the tradition.

It becomes apparent in this mismatched romance that Betsy loves Paul, and that he too, even in his gruff manner, loves her (opposites attracting can be the *only* explanation). However, her self-sacrificing nature compels Betsy to make Paul happy by returning his wife to him in good health. First she convinces Paul to allow Dr. Maxwell (James Bell) to attempt shock treatment, but that scientific treatment is a failure. Soon Alma tells Betsy that the voodoo priest at the houmfort could cure Mrs. Holland, but that they will have to journey through the abandoned sugar cane fields at night to see the priest.

Of course such a scene establishes the lyrical poetry inherent in most Val Lewton productions. In this case, the cinematography of J. Roy Hunt, editing of future director Mark Robson, and the natural sound effects highlight the eerie midnight walk through the sugar cane fields, past the zombie sentry (Darby Jones), and directly through to the houmfort, following the sounds of voodoo drums and chanting. Surprisingly, once at the entranceway where Betsy bravely whispers her intentions, she is whisked quickly inside and there is confronted by Wesley's mother, Mrs. Rand. Inside, Mrs. Rand clearly states that Mrs. Holland cannot be cured.

However, Mrs. Rand's explanation of why she has become the voodoo priest when she is seemingly a Christian missionary is pivotal to understanding her strong feminine character. In order to help fight disease, she begged the village natives to boil water before drinking it, but they never took the authority of a woman seriously. After her husband died, the natives all disobeyed her commands. However, keenly understanding the woman's function within their primitive society, she got smart quickly. She told the natives that the gods would kill the evil spirits in the water if they boiled it, thus, "I let the gods do the speaking for me."

Betsy leads Jessica (Christine Gordon) the a houmfort to try to cure her in the famous Lewton walk scene in *I Walked with a Zombie*.

Unfortunately, the superstitious natives, reacting to the zombie-like Jessica Holland outside, stick a sword into her arm, and when she doesn't bleed, they declare her to be a zombie.

Paul, angered that Betsy would dare such a dangerous and stupid stunt with his wife, is met with romantic determination in Betsy's words: "I wanted to help you. You know why..." Paul always refers to Betsy's innocence, calling her the nurse who is afraid of the dark (and throughout the entire movie the courageous Betsy has been disproving that label), stating that she is "clean, decent thinking," naively thinking that "you think I want Jessica back." Soon, brother Wesley has gone to the authorities and accuses Paul of deliberately driving Jessica insane, the same half-brother who earlier admitted to Betsy that when Paul learned of his wife's plans to run away with Wesley he stated, "I'll keep her here by force if necessary."

Holland emerges as the true brooding hero when he reveals that even if Betsy loves him, she must leave. Reminding her of when they first met at sea, "You were enchanted—but I had to destroy that enchantment, to make you see ugliness and cruelty."

Betsy responds, "You were trying to warn me."

To which Paul responds, "No, I was trying to hurt you. It was the same way with Jessica, that's why I want you to go. I'd rather not have that love then have it and destroy it!"

Then in the frenzied climax, while the natives are using voodoo ritual to lure the comatose Mrs. Holland to them, and while the authorities are putting heat on Paul Holland to confess to his hideous crime of destroying his wife's sanity, Mrs. Rand comes forth

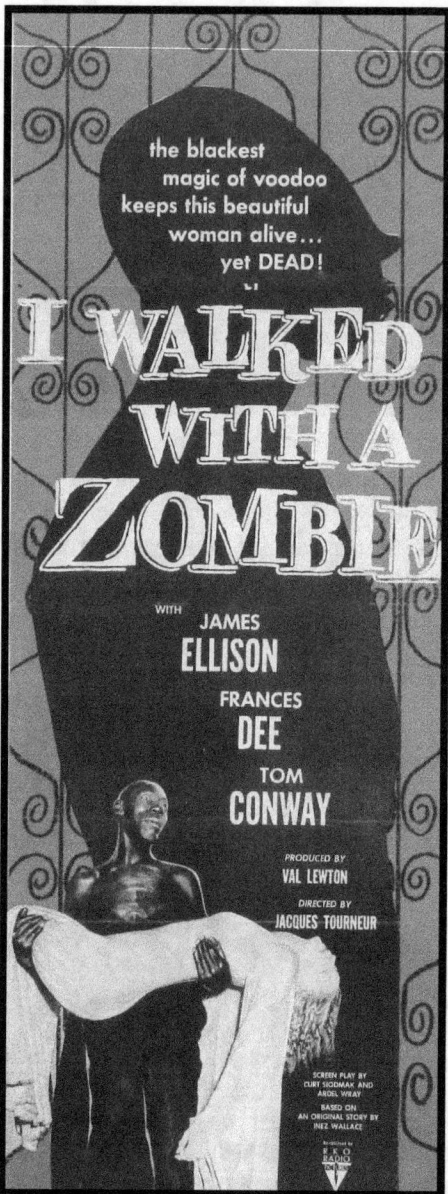

with the truth: "She is dead—living and dead!" To which Dr. Maxwell responds, "You're trying to tell me my patient is a zombie!"

Mrs. Rand's matriarchal power is all neatly explained. "That night she [Jessica] wanted to run away with Wesley, that night I went to the houmfort. She was beautiful enough to take my family in her hands and tear it apart. I kept seeing her face smiling because she was beautiful enough." Thus, knowing the evil lure that Jessica had become—married to one brother, in love with another—the only solution for a concerned mother to preserve her family was to literally destroy the free will of Jessica... by transforming the young enchantress into a zombie.

The only thing preventing Betsy and Paul from "getting together" is the presence of the not-quite-dead wife, Jessica. However, declaring that the woman of his desire, Jessica, "must be free," Wesley allows her out of the confines of Fort Holland, opening the gate as voodoo charms lure the somnambulistic woman away. Then, taking an arrow from the fountainhead, he stabs Jessica to death, carrying the corpse out to sea, the presence of Darby Jones not far behind. In a fairly transparent Hollywood plot—the wife gone, the alcoholic brother drowned—the young nurse and the rich Paul Holland are free to romantically involve themselves with one another.

Voiceover narration completes the film: "wicked woman and she was dead in her own life—dead in the selfishness in her spirit. And the man followed her—her steps led him down to evil."

Unfortunately, such a pat ending tends to weaken all the characters surviving such foolishness, but the character of Mrs. Rand, and perhaps less so Betsy, becomes a dominant female presence, one who breaks the stereotype of a dependent woman, a woman who is not afraid to do whatever it takes to preserve her family and also to serve the best interests of her tribal community. Betsy, at first the intruding young innocent, quickly demonstrates her courage and feistiness by daring to venture into places she best not go, commencing to fall in love with a married man, and yet is so pure in her commitment that she would rather bring his semi-dead wife back to him rather than steal him away from her. (Thus the obvious reference at movie's end, referring to the narration: Jessica was selfish and thus was evil; Betsy was self-sacrificing and thus was good.) The female complexity shatters stereotypical molds and the screenwriters create fairly well-drawn and very enigmatic female characters in this second Val Lewton production.

For the third Val Lewton production, *The Leopard Man*, the final one directed by Jacques Tourneur, women once again form the focus of the narrative, and while some do fit the category of victim, they all display varying degrees of courage and generally break the feminine moviemaking molds. The script was written by female Ardel Wray, who graduated from co-screenplay credit on *I Walked with a Zombie*.

The narrative cleverly comprises vignettes, focusing on a specific selection of characters that are intertwined by clever editing. For instance, the castanet-snapping Clo-Clo (Margo) walks down a deserted street at night, the aura of fear and dread slowly building. She passes an open window where a forceful mother prods her frightened teenage daughter Teresa (Margaret Landry) to venture out in the dark to get corn meal from the local grocery store before it closes. Clo-Clo keeps on walking, but the camera then goes inside the home and we follow this vignette through its conclusion. Mark Robson's editing, cleverly intertwining such subplots effortlessly, allows the narrative to be quick, concise and atmospheric.

The major opposing female characters include the already-mentioned Clo-Clo, the featured star performer, a dancer in the local small town nightclub. Appearing briefly from the big city comes newcomer Kiki (Jean Brooks) and her publicity agent Jerry (Dennis O'Keefe), who concocts an elaborate publicity stunt to draw attention to new talent Kiki. Making a dramatic entrance into the nightclub audience, Jerry pushes her: "You're onstage, they're all looking at *you*!" Dramatically appearing, Kiki enters the theater audience walking an

Clo-Clo (Margo) in another Lewton walk, this one in *The Leopard Man*.

actual leopard, led on a long leash. Dressed to the gills in basic black ("then I'll be just like him!"), her dramatic stunt draws immediate attention from the stage where star attraction Clo-Clo is performing. Without dread or without missing a beat, the enchanting Clo-Clo dramatically snaps her castanets at the wild beast, spooking it, and causing it to break free of its handler's grasp, the leopard running out of the nightclub into the unknown city streets. The unflustered Clo-Clo fires off to Jerry: "I don't need a leopard. I have talent, Mr. Publicity Man!" Thus, two hard-as-nails females lock horns in a demonstration of female willpower and superiority. Clo-Clo has obviously won the first round.

The rest of the movie goes to show the more human, less confident personalities of both women, at first establishing each as bitchy stereotypes, and then displaying their warm and fuzzy side.

For instance, Clo-Clo always consults a fortune-telling card reader Maria (Isabel Jewell), who appears in her dressing room, and whose shop she often visits for consultations. Throughout the movie, every time her fortune is read, the card reader draws an ace or other card that designates tragedy or death and tries desperately to hide the fact from Clo-Clo. The lack of fear in Clo-Clo as she walks to the nightclub, always alone, or worse yet, walking home, still alone in the dark (the village's fear of the runaway leopard ready to pounce out does not seem to faze her), reveals her inability to allow herself to become frightened

The film's most horrifying sequence, and one displaying the bravery of a female character, is the Teresa Delgado (Margaret Landry) sequence mentioned earlier whereby her parents force her to go to the store to purchase cornmeal. "Why do I have to go?" the teenager declares, but her complaining is not laziness

Arriving at the second store, the shopkeeper greets Teresa with, "I remember the little girl afraid of the dark." Once she orders her cornmeal and asks, "Pay you next time?", the owner agrees, saying, "We all pull together!" This becomes a pivotal line of dialogue, contrasted to the earlier store owner who refused to open up the store to help out the young girl, and it also reflects the subtle change in Kiki and Jerry's attitude as the movie unfolds.

Teresa (Margaret Landry), sister of Pedro (Bobby Spindola), is forced by their mother (Kate Drain Lawson) to go out into the dark night for cornmeal in *The Leopard Man*.

Returning home with her sack, poor Teresa returns into the darkness of the night, approaching the train trestles where ominous shadows swim over her and shimmy; two shiny eyes beam in the darkness as the sound of water plopping accents her increasing fear. Suddenly a train passes loudly overhead, and when exiting the tunnel, Teresa is met by the glassy-eyed presence of the escaped leopard. Running away, she drops the sack of cornmeal and runs to her house screaming, "Mama, let me in! It's coming closer, I can see it!" The mother, who must dislodge the bar on the door, can only hear scampering, growling and a scream. Slowly, blood begins to flow underneath the door, signifying the cruel fate of the dedicated and courageous teenager who did her best to accomplish her mother's demands. Even when viewed as the stalking victim, young Teresa represents a sense of fearlessness and dedication to one's family. Her mother's insensitivity seals her fate, but the young girl doesn't let her family down. Unfortunately, the same cannot be said about them.

but fear (of the escaped leopard). It is after dark and her mother rationalizes, "Did you ever meet one [a leopard] before going to the store!" Making one of the famous Val Lewton "walks," the young girl passes through dark streets and must enter a totally pitch black train trestle, only to sadly discover the first store is closed. She keeps banging on the window and door, waking up an elderly woman in a robe who declares it is "too much trouble" to open up for the young girl. "Once I'm closed, I'm closed." But since she has been told her home's front door will be locked until she returns with the cornmeal, she has to venture further out into the darkness, under the railroad tracks, to find another open grocery story. Passing under the trestles, the sound of the wind whips her into a frenzy as a tumbleweed bounces from out of the darkness into her path.

The scenery soon switches to another fresh-eyed young girl, Consuelo Contreras (Tula Parma), who uses the excuse of putting birthday flowers on her father's grave to meet her lover, Raoul (Richard Martin). She plans to meet him at 4 p.m. at the cemetery because the gates are locked tight at 6 p.m. Her mother knows why she is excited to leave, telling Consuelo that in her day a young girl introduced her boyfriend to the family and followed a rigid formality. But mother does understand the workings of love and allows her daughter to leave. Unfortunately, the girl arrives a tad late, finding cigarette butts thrown around the waiting area in the cemetery. However, she refuses to leave, waiting patiently for her lover to perhaps come back. Drifting half-asleep, Consuelo fails to heed the gatekeeper's whistle and finds herself locked inside after dark, the wind shaking the limbs of the trees above. The frightened girl looks upward wondering what animal may be lurking in the treetops there. Hearing a car start up (the sound first imitating the roar of the leopard), she finds a kindly man who offers to go for help to get her out. However, within the next few minutes, Consuelo becomes another casualty. While she is the victim of murder, she is a courageous one at that.

After all these subplots have been thrown out, we now return to the two feisty females, but they strangely appear slightly altered to us now. First the star, Clo-Clo, crows, "Sure, I'm a golddigger. May I never forget about money! Forget about Mama, the kids, the unpaid bills, the rent, and then marry some poor dope and get fat! Feelings don't buy houses, pay for rent, help bring up kids." The scene of Clo-Clo hustling an apparent rich old man for drinks is pathetic, but he gets the last laugh. Expecting to get a generous tip at the end of their chat, instead the sexy performer receives a matchbook from the smirking old gent. Arriving safety home after work, Clo-Clo desperately realizes she has lost the money paid her at work that night and ventures out into the foreboding darkness, only then to lose her life, another victim of murder (made to appear to be the work of the escaped leopard). However, Clo-Clo's motives have considerably softened—being seen at home, a less than modest one at that, kissing her children—revealing the compassionate, human side of poverty.

Even the urbane Kiki reveals her tough exterior can be easily melted, for she too has a good heart. After Jerry describes the graveyard as "such a sad little place," Kiki reveals, "Maybe I want to feel badly. Maybe I'm tired of pretending that nothing bothers me, that all I care about is myself, myself and my 2x4 career." Melting further and declaring her feelings for Jerry, Kiki admits, "I'm a softie." Since her nightclub engagement is over, the obvious thing for Kiki and Jerry to do is catch the first train out of town, but Kiki cries out, "We're gonna stay right here and catch a murderer. I want the town to be safe and happy again." Ironically, the couple is broke, having given their share of the entertainment profits to both grieving families out of sympathy.

As kindly old Dr. Galbraith (James Bell), curator of the village's little museum, turns out to be one of the screen's first psychopathic murderers (he hunted the leopard down, skinned it, declawed it, and used the animal's natural weapons as his murder weapons), Kiki bravely puts herself in imminent danger (Jerry in close pursuit) as a lure to reveal Galbraith as the fiend.

Echoing the words of the second shopkeeper, "We all pull together," Kiki and Jerry embody that philosophy.

The women who populate this small New Mexican village are sometimes viewed as independent and in full control of their destiny (Clo-Clo), but even they too are vulnerable, sensitive, and sometimes cruelly murdered. Even hard-as-nails manipulative women such as Kiki are ultimately revealed to be "softies," admitting that they care about the things and people around them, even willing to put their lives on the line to help others. Other women may be foolhardy, bravely submitting to romantic yearnings (Consuelo's graveyard rendezvous with her lover), while others may only be brave victims (such as the obedient and courageous Teresa). However, all the women featured in *The Leopard Man* are multifaceted characters who are always challenging and hold the

Consuelo (Tula Parma) meets her lover Raoul (Richard Martin) at the graveyard in *The Leopard Man*.

viewer's interest. The women of *The Leopard Man* may be slightly closer to stereotypes than in earlier Lewton movies, but the Lewton factory's emphasis on female characters here, presenting many different strong-willed women in one movie, cleverly reveals their complexities and emotional depth.

Mark Robson graduated from editor to director for the next Lewton production, one that many people consider to be the team's finest production, *The Seventh Victim*, written by Charles O'Neal and DeWitt Bodeen. This dark and morbid fable qualifies as one of the most depressing movies ever made and it comes closest of any Lewton production to intercepting the emerging film noir style (interestingly enough, Ardel Wray's script for *The Leopard Man* was based upon a novel by Cornell Woolrich, one of the most eminent hard-boiled/

Kiki (Jean Brooks) walks a leopard as her publicity agent (Dennis O'Keefe) looks on in The Leopard Man.

noir authors of his day). And as usual, the main female characters are well-developed, complex flesh-and-blood human beings, characters who are challenged by their environments, characters who fight against strong odds to win their survival, or nobly opt to "check out" by their own terms. Without hesitation, while only technically a horror film, *The Seventh Victim* illustrates the horrors of modern existence becoming existential in theme and quite adult in nature.

The two major women are sisters, seemingly quite the opposite of one another character-wise, but upon closer examination, these differences almost congeal, making the two dominant women much closer in personality than originally thought.

The first sister, Mary Gibson (Kim Hunter), has led a sheltered, protected life in a private boarding school. Checks arrive every month to pay her tuition; all that Mary has to worry about is earning good grades and getting along with the people at her school. Unfortunately, at the film's beginning, the older sister Jacqueline (Jean Brooks) has disappeared and has not paid her sister's tuition in over six months. Jacqueline, who owns La Sagesse Cosmetics, can usually be contacted by the plant's manager Mrs. Redi (Mary Newton), but even she has lost contact with the enigmatic woman. The headmistress of the school offers Mary a job as an assistant teacher to pay her board. But Mary is concerned about her sister and states she must go to New York to find her.

After leaving the room Mary is approached by another young woman who implores her, "Mary, don't come back! My parents died. I left, then came back. I didn't have courage. One must have courage to live in the world. I came back."

Thus the film presents Mary symbolically as the butterfly emerging from the womb-like cocoon, not quite ready to face the horrors of the actual world, but courageous and daring and willing to try. The young innocent is not about to become the seventh victim of the title, for that title is saved for someone much more tainted, corrupted and worldly—her own sister!

For the majority of the picture, *The Seventh Victim* becomes a mystery concerning Mary's attempt to find her sister. At first journeying to see Mrs. Redi at the cosmetics plant, Mary learns from Redi that Jacqueline sold Redi the company six months ago, but it is later learned that Jacqueline willed her the business, literally giving it to her. Redi does not know Jacqueline's whereabouts, claiming, "Her friends are not my friends." However, one of the factory workers reveals Mary's sister was here one week ago and rents a small apartment, #7, above a little Italian restaurant called Dante's—but she is never there. Later examining the room, Mary is shocked to find one chair in the living room positioned under a hangman's noose which dangles from the ceiling. This image alone is chilling.

Investigating further, Mary becomes involved with a well-gone-dry poet Jason Hoag (Erford Gage) who runs in Jacqueline's circle and who wishes to help the kindly Mary. Mary also engages the oddball private detective Irvin August (Lou Lubin), who claims he can find her sister in 48 hours (even though a big goon tries to scare him off the case immediately). Finally, Mary meets Jacqueline's husband Gregory Ward (Hugh Beaumont) who claims he loves her sister, stating there's "something exciting, unforgettable, something you never quite get hold of, something that keeps a man following after

The sisters, Jacqueline (Jean Brooks) and Mary (Kim Hunter), represent darkness and light in *The Seventh Victim*.

her." Oddly, Ward expresses Jacqueline's philosophy of life: that life is "not worth living unless one could end it." The stark image of the hangman's noose and chair waiting in Jacqueline's apartment is immediately remembered. The bottom line is that Mary is devoted and valiant in her quest to find her missing sister, willing to traverse the insidious horrors of urban existence.

Jacqueline Gibson, on the other hand, is secretive, eccentric, irresponsible and reckless, yet, she is also strong-willed, focused and a fighter. Having joined a group of urban devil worshipers called Palladists who are sworn to keep their cult a secret (Mrs. Redi inaugurated her into the sinister group), Jacqueline has broken her oath by telling her psychiatrist, Dr. Judd (Tom Conway once again), of the cult's activities. According to the sect's rules, she is the seventh violator of secrecy and she must be the seventh victim to die. However, since the cult is pledged to nonviolence, the followers only coax Jacqueline to take her own life by drinking poison, which she refuses to do. (To her, remember, life is not worth living unless one has the opportunity to end it—but by *her own* terms!) The cult keeps her locked up in a deserted room at the cosmetics factory, and in her delusion and paranoia, she uses a pair of scissors to kill the snooping private investigator Mr. August, thinking he was hired to kill her!

Now free and on the run, Jacqueline becomes a ghost-like presence, even momentarily appearing before Mary at the hotel door and, just as suddenly, disappearing again into the night. Her only message to her sister is a desperate plea: "He left me to meet them alone. I can't stay here!" Her psychiatrist, Dr. Judd, comes to Ward to ask for money, claiming Jacqueline needs $100 cash, but her husband only has $45. Judd often states that Jacqueline is dangerously close to insanity.

Jacqueline demonstrates her courage and cleverness by evading a hired killer (armed with a switchblade) who follows her through the city's darkened streets. One step ahead of her stalker, Jacqueline stops, listens, hides in the shadows, darts across the street, always holding her fate in her hands, never succumbing to dramatics or hysterics. She even merges with a drunken troupe of theater performers who take their break in the local saloon, but Jacqueline, who could enter for added protection, stands at the door and walks on.

The film's bleak ending once again involves a chance encounter between two world-weary females, Jacqueline and Mimi (Elizabeth Russell). Successfully evading the stalker, Jacqueline returns to her room above Dante's and there passes the dreadfully ill Mimi: "I'm Mimi. I'm dying. I've been quiet, ever so quiet. I never move. I rest and rest and still I'm dying."

Jacqueline penetrates the lethargic gaze of Mimi, and by speaking to this other person, she, in fact, is speaking to herself. "And you don't want to die... I've always wanted to die. Always!"

Mimi responds, "I'm afraid and I'm tired of being afraid... waiting."

Jacqueline then offers the tough solution, "Why wait?"

In other words, by accepting the finality and inevitability of death, one need no longer fear the ultimate outcome of existence. Knowing that death

Jacqueline refuses to be pushed into drinking poison, although the cult tries to convince her to do so, in *The Seventh Victim*.

can come at any second and that one can control the circumstance of one's death makes living for Jacqueline worthwhile. By showing Mimi that she herself holds her mortality in her own hands, that she can take her life whenever she chooses, death holds little power over the individual. Triumphantly, Mimi declares, "I'm not going to wait. I'm going out... to laugh and dance and do all the things I used to do."

Jacqueline does mutter, "You will die," but that's not reason enough to sit around and wait for the end, which may be a long time coming. As Mimi demonstrates at the movie's end, leaving her apartment, a smile on her face, all dressed up and ready to do the town, she will die eventually. Perhaps even sooner than later, but there's living to do now, and she plans to live her remaining life to the fullest. As she passes room #7, Jacqueline's apartment, the sound of a chair being knocked over is heard, the obvious sound of Jacqueline succumbing to that fated chair and hanging noose. But a death of her own choosing, one that is committed under her own control, in her own way. Suicide can be morbidly depressing, but as viewed in the Lewton universe, the character of Jacqueline acts out of strength. With the Palladists she has backed herself against the wall, but by refusing to take the poison or to simply give in to her stalker and let him stab her to death, she fights for her life. When she is ready, then, only then, does she take her own life. Her actions are hardly illogical, desperate though they may be, but her demise is clearly viewed as one of deliberate action, a clear demonstration of female strength.

Our fifth film in the Lewton oeuvre is *The Curse of the Cat People*, not actually a sequel so much as a picture with different themes and a drastically altered tone from the original, which just happens to feature many of the same characters (and performers) from the original *Cat People*. The debuting director, Robert Wise (co-credited with the replaced Gunther Von Fritsch), changed the focus of this 1944 entry (written by DeWitt Bodeen) from the investigation of a deteriorating relationship/marriage to the importance of childhood fantasy and imagination in the mind of a six-year-old who is told by her Daddy (a morbid man who never got over his wife's death) that her vivid imagination equals lying and deceit.

Once again husband Ollie (Kent Smith), now "happily" married to that new kind of "other woman" Alice (Jane Randolph), is the father of a precious six-year-old daughter Amy (Ann Carter), a child who is psychologically punished by her father because of her strong belief in imagination and fancy, elements which became self-destructive to his former wife Irena (Simone Simon). Ollie feels he must save his own child from such unhealthy flights of imagination. He becomes the dominant male in this light fantasy, yet he is definitely cast as the weakest character in the movie. The only other substantial male character is Edward the servant (Sir Lancelot) who is literally told to do this or that, mostly by Alice.

"Amy has too many 'fancies' and too few friends," Oliver mutters aloud as the parents are called in to meet Amy's teacher when Amy slaps one of the boys in her class (for killing her "friend," a harmless butterfly).

Later when looking at Amy's drawing displayed with other children's art on the wall outside the classroom, Alice responds, "I wonder if you don't resent that [her imagination and creativity] in her."

Oliver responds, "I'm sure I don't. It's something moody, sickly—it's almost as if she is Irena's child." Of course Irena's inability to enter a sexual relationship with Oliver, even after the wedding night, became one of the chief causes why Ollie, in utter frustration, fell in love with the "swell" girl at his office, Alice. His guilt over both his sexless marriage and the tragic death of his first wife makes daughter Amy a symbol of such failings and frustrations. Oliver blames his daughter for his own failings, with mother Alice frequently coming to the daughter's defense. "You think too much about Irena, blame yourself too much for her death!" To which Ollie replies, "It's because I knew what can begin to happen when people begin to lie to themselves, imagine things."

Most importantly here, Ollie makes the comment that a child's fantasy life of vivid imagination constitutes deliberate lying. Yet during casual card games with friends, Ollie sometimes seems a thousand miles away, he still keeps photographs of his dead wife in a living room desk that is accessible to daughter Amy and her probing questions. Ollie even escapes into the fantasy of building miniature ship models, supposedly as presents for daughter Amy, when it is apparent that building these ships is an imaginary escape for Ollie himself.

Ollie's inability to accept the curse of the Cat People, the truth of Irena's fears and frustrations, his inability to help her when she desperately pleaded to him to be understanding, and his inability to accept the reality of her death from the first film (she was literally slain by the psychiatrist who attempted to seduce her instead of curing her obsessions) cause him to psychically self-destruct. As Ollie explains to Amy's teacher Miss Callahan (Eve March): "My first wife Irena... you don't know what happened to her, just because she told lies to herself and believed them. I tried to stop it. In the end, she went completely mad. She killed a man and she killed herself." Ollie, by failing to come to terms with Irena's and his own reality, is now the one telling stories and believing them. And daughter Amy, like first wife Irena, becomes the happily alone artistic type, the type of off-kilter individual that immediately frightens Ollie.

The small yet pivotal supporting role of Eve March as Amy's teacher Miss Callahan demonstrates the establishment of balance within the healthy (female) individual in this movie. At film's start, taking her Tarrytown school children on a field trip to share with them the Legend of Sleepy Hollow, she tells her children that this rustic area might seem like any old little valley, but here is where songs, stories and legends were created. She then encourages the children to run and play for 15 minutes. Her imaginative and fantasy encouragements (tied directly to the creation of literature and great art) are the dominant aspects that make Amy like her teacher. Yet later, when the young teacher speaks to Ollie concerning the problems with his daughter, Ollie

The apparently happy family, Amy (Ann Carter), Ollie (Kent Smith) and Alice (Jane Randolph) on *The Curse of the Cat People*.

castigates her because she does not have children of her own. She quickly retaliates by telling Ollie that she has "studied" children and frequently quotes from behavioral science books she has read, as well as literature, to make her points forcefully. "Amy's not lying to you... it's an 'unseen companion' [referring at first to Stevenson's poem]," with the teacher stating when Oliver becomes his daughter's "friend," then her unseen companion will disappear. The teacher, another strong female character, is a blend of the artistic/imaginative/literary and the scientific/well-educated personality that provides a perfect role model for Amy.

Interestingly enough, a parallel relationship exists in the story's subplot, with daughter Amy's daring visits to see the senile, aging actress Julia Farren (Julia Dean), an old woman who lived her life of imagination and fantasy out on the stages across the world. The old woman first beckons the child into the garden, throwing her a special ring tied to a handkerchief. The child is startled by Mrs. Farren's ferret-faced daughter Barbara (Elizabeth Russell), who demands, "Give me that," referring to the handkerchief.

The elder thespian takes delight in performing little reenactments for the wide-eyed audience of one, Amy. Whenever Amy visits, either alone or with servant Edward, Barbara answers the door without saying a word, not-so-politely positions herself to listen in on everything, and slowly walks away seemingly floating downstairs, her eyes always locked upon the delicate young Amy or her mother. "She's always spying on me. She creeps into the room—she lives here—that woman is an impostor, a liar and a cheat," Mrs. Ferren declares. In both relationships (mother and daughter Barbara and father and daughter Amy), the parent accuses the child of lying when such is not the case.

Fireworks start when the child exits, leaving Mrs. Ferren and daughter Barbara alone to talk. "A liar! An impostor! Your own daughter. You called me that, yet you're sweet and kind to the little girl, a stranger. Look at me, I'm your daughter!" Barbara demands. Apparently, the elderly mother, a victim of dementia, looks upon her own daughter as an intruder and unkindly rejects Barbara. "My daughter Barbara died when she was six! That was long ago. You're only the woman who takes care of me—you're an impostor!" Therefore, in her senility, Mrs. Ferren believes that her daughter died at age six, exactly Amy's age—and Amy becomes her *de facto* daughter, Ferren rejecting the real daughter who lives in her own home.

Even during Christmas time, Amy buys Mrs. Farren a 25-cent present, a ring, that she delivers to the Ferren home accompanied by Edward. Amy immediately notices an unopened present in the Ferren household. The old lady squawks, "That's from her, *that* woman! It's been so long since I received a Christmas present." After the visitors leave, Barbara, obviously hurt, questions, "You didn't even open my present, and I'm your daughter!" To which Mrs. Ferren responds, "My daughter died... long ago." Tears in her eyes, bringing her hands up to her face, Barbara slowly vanishes down her staircase, her heart obviously broken.

Mrs. Farren (Julia Dean) is drawn to little Amy in *The Curse of the Cat People.*

Later in the movie, on the snowy, stormy night Amy, after receiving her first spanking from her father, runs away from home, Barbara and her mother are watching the storm.

"I hate the storm," states Barbara.

Her mother responds, "I don't hate it. It blows beyond me. It was on a night like this that Barbara died."

"But I'm Barbara. I didn't die. Don't you understand! No, no! You were out of your mind. You didn't know anybody; you didn't remember anything. Look into my eyes, mother. Say that I'm Barbara," the haunted daughter pleads.

"Everything that you say is a lie. You're a poor, lost woman. You're not my Barbara."

"You're always worse when that little girl is here. If she comes here again, *I'll kill her!*"

Imagine Amy and her father Oliver 30 to 40 years from now, and they might pretty well become as Barbara and Mrs. Ferren are today! Mrs. Ferren, the deluded old woman, a pathetic mother who rejects her love-starved daughter, calling her pleadings lies, ignoring the child who lives in her own house, refusing to open her presents. In this vision of Christmas-Yet-To-Come, could Mrs. Ferren be Oliver, succumbing to his refusal to accept a world of off-kilter logic in a seemingly logical world? In his delusions, could Irena be alive and daughter Amy the poor victim who took her own life? Could all of Oliver's guilt and failure be transferred to a deteriorating relationship with his own daughter, who only wants to be Daddy's little girl and please him?

In the film's climax, personalities merge as Ollie gets one more chance to save his relationship with his daughter and to perhaps save his own fragile sanity. Amy suddenly appears at the Ferren house, coming out of the cold. Mrs. Ferren immediately fears for Amy's life, remembering the cold threats of daughter Barbara. "We can't hide you there... she knows every corner of that room!" The only solution is to hide Amy in a room above (since the typical image of Barbara is her slow descent below). In her frantic state, the old woman cannot stand the strain of climbing her stairs, but she must try for Amy. "I can't do it," she grimaces, and Mrs. Ferren collapses dead on the staircase. Moments later daughter Barbara ascends the staircase, the wind rustling from the open front door. A look of hatred in her eyes, she mutters, "Even my mother's last moments you've stolen from me!" Amy cries out the phrase "my friend" as the aggressive form of Barbara becomes superimposed with Irena's warm, comforting presence.

As Amy cautiously walks down the steps, half-smiling, pleading "my friend," Barbara's hands assume a clutching stance as the woman at first attempts to choke the innocent Amy to death. However, with Amy's outright trust and warm greeting, Barbara's hands suddenly loosen their grip of hatred as woman and child embrace warmly, and the rescue party is heard approaching. Barbara, one of the saddest characters in the history of movies, silently walks offscreen never to be seen again.

At film's end, with Amy again seeing Irena alone in the snow outside her home, her father admits, "I see her too, darling," declaring that the two of them "are going to be friends"; with this last statement, just as Mrs. Callahan promised would happen when Ollie becomes a friend to his daughter, the imaginary friend, Irena, slowly vanishes out of sight.

Irena (Simone Simon) comforts Amy in *The Curse of the Cat People*.

Interestingly enough, it takes the strength of courage and imagination within the women in this film to bring stability and mental health back to the ailing Oliver. Dejected daughter Barbara never once gives up trying to win back the recognition and love of her mother. Daughter Amy never once gives up on her Daddy who often sends out false signals (Ollie on one hand tells his daughter to quit lying by living her imaginary life, yet he tells her of a magic mailbox tree to which she delivers her birthday invitations and, of course, no one shows up at her party—and later at the party he encourages her to blow out the candles on her cake and that her wishes will come true, to which she proclaims, "But you said in the garden that wishes don't come true!"). And mother Alice and teacher Mrs. Callahan never give up trying to convince Ollie to be more tolerant and understanding of his daughter Amy. In *The Curse of the Cat People*, the male is troubled, frustrated, and confused and it takes the strong loving support of the women in his life to put him back together.

The final film in our discussion, and the final film in Val Lewton's RKO series, *Bedlam*, written by Lewton (under the name Carlos Keith) and director Mark Robson, featured perhaps the most formidable Lewton female of them all. Lewton is at his most preachy here, and *Bedlam*, strong on political and social reform, strong on character and dialogue, seems to ignore the glorious strengths of before: thrills, chills and sudden scares. But Anna Lee's starring performance as 23-year-old spitfire Nell Bowen delivers the goods in an exceptionally energetic performance that remains one of the strongest in any Lewton production.

Desperately trying to recreate England's Age of Reason in historically accurate detail, the subtlety of Lewton's script focuses upon the hypocrisy of the age and its wonderful dialogue brims with sarcasm and wit. Fortunately, as written and performed, the character of Nell Bowen transcends the one-dimensional preachiness into which this character could so easily fall and the complexity of character makes the performance all the richer.

Nell Bowen is the mistress of Lord Mortimer (Billy House), not in the sexual sense as much as she amuses the royal buffoon and becomes marvelous ornamental window dressing for English society. The film begins by showing Mortimer, Bowent and Bowen's pet cockatoo riding together in a carriage. Speaking of the marvelous entertaining "loonies" committed to St. Mary's of Bethlehem Asylum, or Bedlam, Mortimer jests "maybe they'll teach you some new tricks now!" To which the saucy Bowen responds, "I have no need of their wit to entertain you, my Lord." Mortimer, responding to the violent death of an "inmate" escaping from Bedlam, a very sane poet who had been commissioned to write poetry for Lord Mortimer, Mortimer angrily travels to question the asylum's director Master Sims (Boris Karloff) about the strange nature of the man's death. When Karloff uses the word "accident," Bowen, always by Mortimer's side, sarcastically adds, "Master Sims is writing a new dictionary. Are accidents contrived, plotted, executed?"

When Master Sims addresses Mortimer and Bowen as "My Lord and the Beloved of my Lord," Bowen puts her foot down, figuratively, in the small of Sims' back, with a stinging rebuttal: "I think you misunderstand... I am milord's protégé—I entertain him and he has no more freedom with me than any other man."

Clearly Nell Bowen is establishing both her equality and independence with the aristocratic lord; she makes very clear that she is not a sex toy but a protégé, a caustic and very self-assured woman of equal footing with the pompous lord.

Bowen, who slowly evolves to become sensitive to the needs of the criminally (and not so criminally) insane, is initially pictured as a woman who uses her intelligence, her beauty, and dominating personality to gain advantages in life often only offered to males. Interested by Lord Mortimer's descriptions of Bedlam, she voices "a curiosity to see the loonies in their cages" and rides to the asylum the very next day to pay for her tour. As she is admitted to the main ward, her eyes bug out as she hears cries and screams. Yet her response is a sensitive, humane one: "They're all so lonely... they're all *in* themselves and *by* themselves." Sims, entertained by her fear and shock, declares, "Theirs is a bestial world. They're animals." He speaks of the amusement he receives from their delusional behavior. In outrage Bowen speaks out, "Amusement... from that mad girl with those staring eyes—" and she lashes Sims across the face with her riding whip.

Later Nell's friend Hannay (Richard Fraser), a Quaker, admonishes her for slapping Sims. "You shouldn't have done that!" But Nell's response is one of pride and empowerment: "Do you think he could harm me?" But Hannay makes clear his criticism: "Thee are able enough. It's those poor ones in there I am thinking of. Sims will make them suffer for those blows!" In other words, Nell was taking those remarks to be a put-down of her womanhood, believing Hannay was implying that Nell was unable to take care of herself. But the Quaker's response was directed at the true victims of physical and mental abuse, the pathetic inmates of Bedlam.

After establishing Bowen's character as strong, sensitive and caring, a virtual Florence Nightingale, the script then expands to show the self-serving social goals which appear in Nell's grand plans. In other words, a sensitive, caring nature *does* exist within her, but her character is first established in less than altruistic and innocent light. "Pity, I had no such feelings [for the inmates]. Sir, I struck him [Sims] because I wanted to. Because he's an ugly thing in a pretty world." The superficiality of her words ring out when she then describes the inmates as "animals without souls!" Perhaps choosing to disguise her caring heart as the frailty of a woman, Nell hits hard verbally by rising above her womanly failings. "My heart is a flint, Sir. It may strike sparks but they're not warm enough to burn. I've no time to make a show of love and kindness before my fellow man, not in this life. I have too much laughing to do." Apparently she has been spending too much time around pomposity and social advantage (symbolized by Lord Mortimer) and feels that such harsh talk reflects her strength while empathy and concern for the unfortunate only reflect her weaknesses. But we have seen the glimmer of such a

Nell Bowen (Anna Lee) dares to take on the sadistic Master Sims (Boris Karloff) in *Bedlam*.

caring heart, and her journey from *saying* the right thing to *feeling* the right thing to ultimately *doing* the right thing is the trek that this movie makes through Nell Bowen, a character of immense subtlety and change.

Once she sees Bedlam and its inhabitants firsthand, Nell becomes a crusader for more humane treatment. The inmates at the asylum are used by Master Sims as cruel entertainment at a party held at Lord Mortimer's. There, a "Gilded Boy" (Glenn Vernon), painted in gold paint, works feverishly to deliver his rehearsed lines (literally beaten into him by Sims), but he slowly suffocates and dies because his clogged pores cannot "breathe." While the aristocracy laughs it up, the outraged Nell later states: "A boy died tonight. A boy who had no mind to guide his thoughts or deeds. Maybe there'll be some concern about that among the Whigs, certainly not the Tories." Nell goes on to ask her favor, that money be spent to improve the horrid conditions at Bedlam—"good beds, blankets, good food... good treatment." However Nell's impassioned words fall on deaf ears. "I asked you to do a good deed and you refuse because it's too expensive!"

Nell makes a grave mistake when she hits Sims while her friend Hannay (Richard Fraser) looks on in *Bedlam*.

Soon Nell publicly embarrasses both Lord Mortimer and Master Sims, and Sims pushes Mortimer to sign papers asking for Nell to have a sanity review. Nell's depth of character is revealed in this brief yet pivotal sequence. Her cockiness comes to the forefront when she enters the board chambers, head held high, and declares, "Well, gentlemen, here is your lunatic!" Sims, who is stacking the cards in his favor, makes Nell look bad, saying that she refused to sell her pet cockatoo for outrageous money and that she took a bite out of a 300-pound note. But Nell's intelligence and quick thinking are revealed when she mocks the questions asked her: "Oh, don't fool yourself... a merry answer does not make me a fool. Ask me a sensible question, and you will have a sensible answer." Finally, her vulnerability and utter despair is revealed when the board not only votes that she is insane, but agrees with Sims' recommendation that she be committed to Bedlam. At this point she screams out, sobs, falls to her knees and lapses into unconsciousness. This one sequence brings out all of Nell's strengths, but as in the best character portrayals, her strength can sometimes be contrasted with her weakness: her failure to realize that her public ridicule of important people can force those people to silence her by any means possible. Her ideals speak quite loudly and often overpower her practicality, better judgment, and common sense when it comes to safety and self-preservation. But if her enthusiasm sometimes gets the best of her, her compassion and deep will to help others ring out loud and strong.

While imprisoned against her will at Bedlam, her fear and hatred of the pathetic "loonies" surface first. "I'm terrified... these people are like beasts... they're dirty, savage, mindless, disgusting." She gradually begins to mix her fear with compassion and caring: "I still want to help them—but not *here*, where they're all about me!" Her self-serving superficiality is again reiterated when she begs Hannay for a trowel for protection. "Give me a weapon... anything. Would you have me maimed, scratched, scarred—my face... look at my face again, look close!" But soon she befriends the upper-class "loonies" who reign near the pillar, but even when Sims orders her to share quarters with an animalistic man locked in a cage, Nell overcomes her fear and willingly enters to quite literally soothe the savage beast. At first her talk is just that—talk, but as her sensitivity and empathy grow for these unfortunates, her willingness to put her life on the line for her cause shows

Nell's sanity is on trial as Sims has her committed to *Bedlam*.

her to have evolved beyond bluster and fist-waving. As her commitment to Bedlam illustrates, Nell Bowen now lives out her words, and her commitment to her asylum unfortunates finally becomes believable and genuine to the viewing audience.

Val Lewton certainly wasn't the first Hollywood producer to cast women in complex and demanding roles, but he did so consistently in the majority of the B productions he completed for RKO. Women always remain a focus of these six productions, illustrating quiet determination and inner strength, but none of these women thematically share very much in common with one another. It is far too simplistic to divide the women into two categories—survivors and victims—because victims such as Jacqueline Gibson in *The Seventh Victim* show overpowering determination to live out their lives on the cutting edge and then end their life on their own terms, by their own chosen method and time.

No, in Val Lewton productions even female victims show strength of character and assertiveness. Poor six-year-old Amy from *The Curse of the Cat People* desperately wants to become everything that Daddy wants her to be, yet the child is confused by his mixed signals, sometimes condoning make-believe and magic and other times punishing her for such fancies. But Amy's strength becomes her unwavering devotion to her imaginary life and her new friend, the ghostly Irena. She can *try* to please Daddy, but she first of all pleases her inner self and needs. Irena, from *Cat People*, is desperately haunted by her fear of a village curse, a curse which promises sexual indulgence will transform her into a panther that will destroy her lover and new husband. She desperately tries to please Oliver in whatever way she can, short of consenting to have sexual relations with him, pleading with him to be patient and understanding. But when Oliver drifts to Alice, an office co-worker and all around good gal, Irena's passions are fueled up anyway and her self-destructive urges lead to her own death. However, she possesses the power to choose the insidious Dr. Judd as her victim and realizes that her death will lead to Oliver's happiness, if she is out of the way to allow his new relationship with Alice to blossom. Even in self-destruction, Irena is in charge of her destiny and actions. Finally, Clo-Clo from *The Leopard Man* pretends to be hard-as-nails and unafraid of the dark, yet in her little hovel, with her mother's care and baby's needs depending entirely upon her, Clo-Clo becomes vulnerable and sympathetic and her hustling of men for money becomes simply a survival skill. As Bruce Springteen once sang, she walks in the darkness on the edge of town realizing the dangers, and while she becomes a victim of madness by a psychopathic killer, she understands the risks and dangers inherent in her lifestyle. Even the young and innocent Teresa Delgado, the ultimate victim in *The Leopard Man*, is brave and dutiful, obedient to her mother's wishes until the end. She conquers her fears and traverses the darkness inhabited by an escaped leopard; her death is more fairly attributed to the cruelty of her family than it is to any personal character shortcomings.

In Val Lewton's universe, female characters are typically written to be strong and independent, always resourceful using their womanly wiles to make existence easier in a society controlled by men. Mrs. Rand, from *I Walked with a Zombie*, is representative of both Christian and Voodoo religions, utilizing magic powers to control both the childlike natives and her dysfunctional family, a family threatened to be torn apart by the insidious Jessica. Mrs. Rand is resourceful and isn't afraid to play dirty to maintain those priorities which matter most in

other film genres, but the Val Lewton factory during the decade of the 1940s created a series of important films which portrayed a positive, forceful female image. Whether casting women in dominant, starring roles, or including complex characterization in supporting female performances (Mimi and Teresa Delgado), women in Val Lewton movies were never stereotypes nor simple window dressing. While Lewton women might be alluring and sexual, they were never only scream queens nor sex kittens (not even in *Cat People*). No, the women who populated Val Lewton's universe were well drawn in the initial script, well performed on the studio sound stage, and well remembered today as those performances resonate both in our rewatchings of the movies themselves and in the writings of film history of past, present and future.

her life. Nell Bowen, perhaps at first too young, too loud, and lacking common sense, gradually becomes transformed into a dedicated agent of social change, having to transcend both the prejudices and fears in her life. Mimi, from *The Seventh Victim*, at first frightened and defeated, finally emerges as a liberated woman unafraid of the cards fate has dealt her, dressing to the hilt and going out for a night on a town—on her terms. Kiki, very much like Nell Bowen, seems sarcastic, hardened and socially above all the inhabitants in the little town of *The Leopard Man*, yet her evolving sensitivity, concern and care for the hapless citizens cause her to invest her time and money to make the town safe once again. Betsy Connell, the dutiful nurse from *I Walked with a Zombie*, isn't afraid to venture into areas of danger (the first night she wanders into the Tower to investigate the sobbing), including a relationship with a married man, for whom she valiantly attempts to restore the mental health of his zombified wife—an altruistic act done out of unselfish love and strength of character.

Horror cinema seldom creates female characters as memorable as those inherent in film noir and

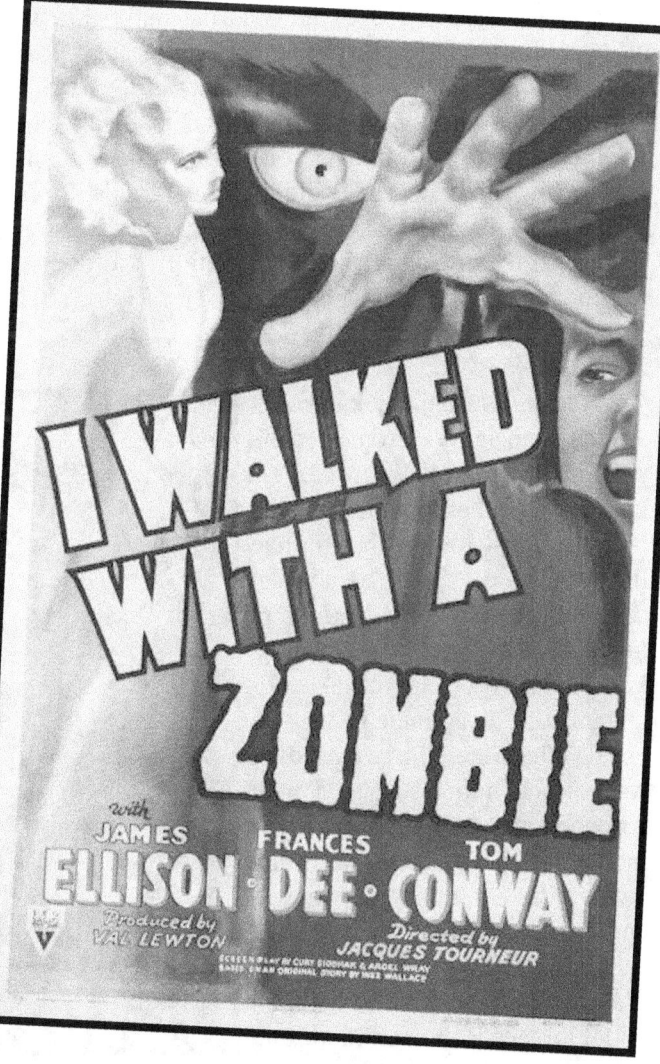

Bad Girls Meet Bad Ends

by John E. Parnum

A woman of the streets (Arlene Kazanjian), screaming as two ruffians fight over her, is spirited away in a carriage through the fog-shrouded streets by the mad Doctor Mirakle (Bela Lugosi) to a fate far worse than death. There, in his stark laboratory, he straps her half naked to a wooden cross and jabs a syringe into her bare arm as she moans in terror. "Hush. It will last only one more minute, and we will know if you are to be the Bride of Science." The whore continues to cry as Mirakle examines a slide under his microscope. Then, in a fury, he smashes the vials and shakes his fist at her. "Rotten blood! Your blood is rotten like your sins. You cheated me. Your beauty was a lie!" She faints, and a sinister assistant—Janos, the Black One (Noble Johnson)—drops her through a trap door into the river below. Later, when her lifeless body is pulled from the murky waters and taken to the morgue, the registrar unnecessarily asks an attendant the victim's profession, and the man answers knowingly, "Yes."

• • •

Actress Kazanjian, known as Arlene Francis by devotees of the popular quiz show *What's My Line?*, coaxed her father to let her mother take her West to seek her fortune in Hollywood. There, Universal cast her in their 1932 *Murders in the Rue Morgue* as a prostitute kidnapped by Doctor Mirakle for his hideous experiments with an ape. When the film wrapped, it was rushed into distribution with Arlene provocatively displayed in the poster art—strapped to that cross with her flimsy slip ripped and falling off her bare shoulder. As she related in *Arlene Francis: A Memoir* (written in collaboration with Florence Rome for Simon and Schuster, New York, 1978), she received the following urgent telegram from her father. "I Have Just Seen You Almost Nude In Front Of Loew's State And So Has Everyone Else. Come Home At Once!"

Some 55 years later, Michelle Bauer, portraying one of those infamous *Hollywood Chainsaw Hookers*, seductively strips for a john before cutting him to pieces with the tool of the title. In her book *Invasion of the B-Girls* (Eclipse Books, Forestville, CA, 1992), Bauer told author Jewel Shepard, "My mother loves these movies. She gets a big kick out of them." My, my. How times and attitudes change.

Let's face it, "soiled doves" have been around for a long time and were first referred to in horror films as early as 1918, when two versions of *Alraune* were released. In the German print, the beautiful but evil Alraune is conceived when a mad scientist collects the spilled sperm from a hanged man and inseminates a prostitute with it. The Austrian version that same year was directed by a young Michael Curtiz and varies somewhat by having the prostitute copulate with a mandrake root, which results in Alraune's conception. Two German remakes followed: one in 1928 (also called *Daughter of Destiny* and *Unholy Love*), and the other in 1930, under the alternate title *Daughter of Evil*. Both films starred Brigitte Helm as Alraune. Then, in 1952, Hildegard Neff assumed the role in a West German version released in America as *Unnatural*, with Erich von Stroheim as the scientist. And apparently prostitution will still be around in the year 2022, when the ladies of the evening will be known as furniture girls, as predicted in the 1973 science-fiction thriller *Soylent Green*.

The prostitute in horror films has been portrayed in many attitudes: neurotic, murderess, heroine, Frankenstein monster, vampire, zombie and mistress of her own fate. By far the most prevalent is her role as a victim, as illustrated in the prior excerpt from *Murders in the Rue Morgue*. But perhaps her prototype in this category is best illustrated as the music hall chippy, Ivy, in two adaptations of *Dr. Jekyll and Mr. Hyde*. These films have probably received more audience than Robert Louis Stevenson's novella, which made no reference to either Jekyll's fiancée or Hyde's mistress.

In the 1932 Paramount film, directed by Rouben Mamoulian, noble physician Henry Jekyll (Fredric March) rescues the tart Ivy Pearson (Miriam Hopkins) from a brute's savage attack. He carries her to her room where she shows him her bruises. The good doctor assures her they will disappear in a few days, but that she shouldn't wear her garter so tight. She rests his hand on her leg and tells him that he is "the kind a woman would do something for." She pulls up her skirt, kicks off her shoes, and mischievously throws a garter at him. When she is naked beneath the sheets, he examines her, and she kisses him passionately. Jekyll's companion, Dr. Lanyon (Holmes Herbert), looking for Henry, interrupts them. Ivy invites Jekyll to return as she swings her leg back and forth from the bed—an image that remains with both Henry and the audience for some time. Lanyon chastises Jekyll for his behavior, but Henry theorizes that if he could separate the good and evil natures in a person, he could cleanse not only his conduct but his innermost, forbidden thoughts and desires. As everyone knows, his experiments in this area are successful and result in his becoming the monster Edward Hyde, who seeks out Ivy at the local music hall. As she entertains a date by singing "Champagne Ivy is my name, good for any game at night, my boys; come and join me in a spree," Hyde requests her presence. She brings a bottle and two glasses to his table, but when she sees Hyde's ugly appearance, she tries to leave. He flatters her and says, "I'm no 'gentleman,'" a term she had used for Jekyll, "but I've got money," and sets her up as his mistress.

Cruelly mistreated by Hyde, Ivy goes to Jekyll for help, not realizing the two men are one and the same. He prescribes a lotion for the whip marks on her back, but she argues that a lotion won't help and pleads to him to let her work, slave and love him if he'll help her escape

Ivy Pearson (Miriam Hopkins) meets a sad end at the hands of the evil Dr. Jekyll in the 1932 version with Fredric March as Jekyll.

from Hyde. She refers to Henry as her angel. Since he has destroyed his formula, he assures Ivy that Hyde will never bother her again. But later, without the aid of the solution, Jekyll transforms into the beast and strangles the prostitute beneath a statue of an angel making love to a woman.

Nine years later, MGM bought the rights for the film from Paramount so they could produce their own version of *Dr. Jekyll and Mr. Hyde,* starring Spencer Tracy. MGM screenwriter John Lee Mahin basically used the 1931 script by Samuel Hoffenstein and Percy Heath, but had not reckoned with the 1934 Hays Office enforcement of the Motion Picture Production Code which, under Point 5 (the general heading of Sex), advised: "The methods and techniques of prostitution and white slavery shall never be presented in detail, nor shall the subjects be presented unless shown in contrast as such may not be shown."

Still, MGM and Director Victor Fleming were able to identify Ivy's profession in the mind of the audience. "I ain't no...," Ivy tells Jekyll as he carries her to her room, and Henry assures her, "No. I know you're not.

You're a girl with your heart just where it ought to be. Maybe just a little bit too generous, that's all." Ingrid Bergman, originally slated to play Jekyll's prim fiancée, convinced the studio to give her Ivy's role, while the sultry Lana Turner was switched to the virginal Beatrix. The ordinarily proper Bergman oozes sensuality in her attempt to fool the Hays Office. As James Robert Parish explains in *Prostitution in Hollywood Films* (McFarland & Company, Inc., Jefferson, NC, and London, 1992), producers developed conventions and ploys to clarify the world's oldest profession. "For instance, moviegoers were expected to 'know' that celluloid dance halls—in either big city or old West locals—were often covers for prostitution rings and that these ambiguously presented dance hall hostesses (aka taxi dancers, entertainers, etc.) were really whores." Despite these disguises, Joe Breen, guardian of the Hays Office, sent MGM a list of script changes to be made before he would approve the 1941 *Dr. Jekyll and Mr. Hyde*. These are described in Gerald Gardner's *The Censorship Papers* (Dodd Mead & Company, New York, 1987): "Page 33: Care will be needed with the characterization of the girl Ivy to avoid characterizing her as a prostitute... Page 38: The scene of the girl taking off her stocking must be done inoffensively and without any undue exposure... Page 39: This action of the girl falling back on the bed swinging her bare leg must be changed...."

Tracy's transformation to Hyde was accomplished with little makeup, his monster more Freudian than furry. His attendance at the dance hall is therefore more readily accepted than March's Neanderthal. But his comments to Ivy are as lascivious and cruel as ever: "Where did you get such a pretty voice?" he asks her. "Perhaps it's the pretty place it comes from," he leers. When she rebukes him, he has her fired and then instates her as his mistress. His transformations are accompanied by Dali-esque hallucinations: Hyde in a chariot whips two horses that become Ivy and Beatrix; Ivy sinks into a sea of mud; Beatrix is imprisoned in a Champagne bottle, but when it is uncorked Ivy comes exploding out like an orgasm against a fiery backdrop.

Hyde continues to mistreat Ivy, spitting grape seeds in her face as he mocks her lack of education: "Now, let's see. What shall we do? We could play cards. But you're probably tired of cards, aren't you? You might read to me. Yes, Milton's *Paradise Lost* would be nice. But we haven't the book, have we? And I don't suppose you know it from memory." Hyde's murder of the girl later comes almost as a welcome end to her torment, but in the eyes of Joe Breen, Ivy dies because sin must be punished and her death is as justifiable as Jekyll/Hyde dying for their crimes.

In the J&H films over the years, featured roles of hookers as victims have become more blatant. Marie O'Henry plays the streetwise prostitute with a heart of gold who listens to Dr. Pride (Bernie Casey) detail the death of his mother (who worked as a whorehouse maid) in the 1976 black exploitation film, *Dr. Black and Mr. Hyde* (aka *The Watts Monster*). Thirteen years later, Anthony Perkins assumed the dual role in the British *Edge of Sanity*, in which he slaughters the prostitutes in the infamous Whitechapel area.

Lana Turner is the good girl Beatrix and Ingrid Bergman the bad girl Ivy in this studio publicity art for the 1941 *Dr. Jekyll and Mr. Hyde*.

In the most recent version, *Mary Reilly* (1996), an unrecognizable Glenn Close (as you have never seen her before) is the heavily made-up, lipstick-smeared madam, Mrs. Farraday.

But most bizarre of all is the Hammer *Dr. Jekyll and Sister Hyde* (1971), in which the Doctor (Ralph Bates) transforms into Sister Hyde (Martine Beswicke). With both personalities falling for brother and sister tenants upstairs (and sometimes mistakenly romancing the opposite sexes), Jekyll realizes that his feminine alter ego is getting the better of him and so takes to the streets as Jack (Jekyll?) the Ripper to extract female hormones from the whores of Whitechaple to reinstate his masculinity.

Dr. Jekyll turns into the lovely Martine Beswicke in *Dr. Jekyll and Sister Hyde*.

The Ripper, of course, was an actual figure, terrorizing the East End of London in 1888, killing and dissecting prostitutes with such precision that he was thought to be a member of the medical profession. While Jack was never caught, films have taken great liberties at identifying the fiend. Marie Belloc-Loundes's 1913 novel, *The Lodger*, was the basis for Alfred Hitchcock's 1926 British film of the same name. Fox made two versions of the story, the first in 1944, with Laird Cregar in the title role, and the second in 1953 as *The Man in the Attic*, with Jack Palance as the Ripper. But because of the Motion Picture Code, the victims had to be classed as actresses and chorus girls—but we know what they really were, don't we? Promotional lines for *Man in the Attic* teased readers with the caption: "Haunted by the naughtiness of the Can-Can, he preys upon a backstage world!" beneath a photo of cabaret dancers hoisting their skirts. It wasn't until 1960, when the Code was relaxed a bit, that Jimmy Sangster could write a more sordid screenplay for *Jack the Ripper*, in which the notorious figure killed streetwalkers in his search for one particular prostitute named Mary Clarke. The most interesting feature of this black and white film occurs at the climax, when the Ripper is trapped at the bottom of an elevator shaft and is crushed by the descending car, with Technicolor blood oozing up through cracks in the floor.

More hookers were done away with in the 1971 Spanish/Italian entry *Jack, El Destripador De Londres*, with Paul Naschy. Then Klaus Kinski took a stab at it in Jess Franco's 1976 West German *Jack the Ripper—der Dirnenmorder von London*. In *Obsession: The Films of Jess Franco* by Lucas Balbo, Peter Blumenstock, and Christian Kessler (Grof Haufen and Frank Trebbin, Berlin, 1993), the authors praise Kinski for his persuasiveness and understated performance in this grisly film of explicit dismemberments: "The movie has nothing to counterbalance this outstanding performance, nor does it try to, relying solely on Kinski's genius, which perhaps was the intelligent choice, for Kinski *is* the Ripper."

Jack was a timely topic for Hammer films in 1971, for in addition to *Dr. Jekyll and Sister Hyde*, they also released *Hands of the Ripper* (they had touched on the subject in 1949 in *Room to Let*). In this departure, the Ripper's daughter Anna (Angharad Rees) is possessed by her father's spirit which is unleashed whenever she sees a glimmering object (like a knife blade) or has her passions fired up by a kiss. Anna disposes of a maid, a suitor, a whore named Long Liz (Linda Baron), a medium, and her shrink (Eric Porter).

These were not the first hookers to appear in Hammer Films. The studio loved to decorate their moody Gothic chillers with ladies of the evening. During the credits of *The Man Who Could Cheat Death* (1959), a shadowy figure cuts open a man he has just murdered. As he walks through the fog-shrouded streets, a woman standing against a streetlamp beckons to him. "Evening, dear." She is lucky. The killer, a doctor named Bonner (Anton Differing), has already extracted the gland he needs to extend his life. The prostitute he meets later at a low-class dive does not fare as well. Seeing Bonner, the chippy tells her drunken date, "Time is money, after all. My escort's here now." Bonner follows her down the foggy streets to a doorway. A cat screams as if in prelude of things to come. The hooker invites him in. The door closes, and another scream rends the night.

Those dark steps and alleys are witness to another murder in *The Curse of the Mummy's Tomb* (1964). Theatrical promoter Alexander King (Fred Clark) defies a curse by opening a sacred sarcophagus. As he walks home along the darkened streets, he passes a woman. "You in a hurry, Gov?" "What can I do for you?" he asks. "Nothing, deary. I wondered if there was anything I could do for you." The promoter is sad for her: "No, but no thanks." He reaches into his pocket for change. "Get a good night's sleep," he tells her. She is grateful and relieved: "God bless ya, Gov—you're a real gentleman!" and disappears into the fog. We wonder if something will happen to her; it does not. Instead, in the film's one truly frightening moment, King hears a deep hollow breathing from the top of a stone staircase—a sound from the depths of Hell. King's escaped mummy rewards his kindness to the prostitute by strangling the exhibitor.

Hammer's victimized hooker shows up in their 1961 *The Curse of the Werewolf.* Oliver Reed's Leon is a lycanthrope from birth, but his savagery is kept in tow through his stepfather (Clifford Evans) and the woman he adores (Catherine Feller). One night a friend lures him to an infamous tavern where one of the local prostitutes invites him to partake of her favors. Repulsed by the woman's advances and by the general low quality of the establishment (and, oh yes: There's also a full moon that evening), Leon becomes ill and goes outside for air. When the harlot follows him, he transforms into a werewolf and kills her; then, for good measure, he murders his companion also. Too bad Hammer didn't recreate the scene the way Guy Endore described it in his novel *Werewolf of Paris,* upon which the film was based—it could have been far more erotic. When Leon (Bertrand in the book) exhibits shyness in the whore's room, she suggests he remove her clothing without using his hands. He expresses puzzlement as to how to accomplish this. "You have teeth and toes, haven't you?" she instructs him. Unfortunately, as he pulls at her slip with his teeth, a bit of her skin gets caught in his mouth and he accidentally bites her: "A strange rage had overcome him.... She, feeling his hand strangling her cries, bit down for her part too, and fought wildly with her fists."

Not all hookers are victims of psychopathic fiends— some are victims of society and of themselves. Take Susan Webster (Ellen Drew) in the 1941 Paramount release *The Monster and the Girl*. She's a small town church-going gal lured by the promise of big-city excitement, despite the warnings of her devoted brother Scot (Phillip Terry). Once there, however, she finds jobs scarce and her money going fast. She meets smooth-talking Larry Reed (Robert Paige) at an employment agency, falls in love with him, and marries the rat. The small wedding ceremony, presided over by The Deacon (Joseph Calleia), is a sham, and when she wakes up the next morning, Larry is gone, and another gangster (Gerald Mohr) advises her, "One Larry more or less shouldn't upset a pretty girl like you... especially since I happen to know where there's a good job waiting. Not the highest class cabaret. Do a little drinking, a little dancing—make the yokels happy."

When Scot learns what has happened to his sister (because he knows, like we do, what cabaret dancers really are), he goes looking for Larry, but is set up on a murder rap by the gang who enslaved Susan. Scot is found guilty, despite his sister's heartrending courtroom confession of her fallen ways. She does win the sympathy of reporter Sam Daniels (Rod Cameron), who gets her off the streets and into the shelter of his home.

Now the first half of *The Monster and the Girl* unfolds like a typical '40s melodrama—perhaps a bit more daring than usual coming from Paramount who, like other big studios, avoided exposés depicting the horrors of hooking. But in the courtroom is a Doctor Parry (played by horror veteran George Zucco), who watches as Scot is led away shouting at the gangsters, "Somehow, somewhere, you'll get yours!" And sure enough, the night before the execution, Parry visits Scot and asks the condemned to will him his body: "I need the brain of a man, a strong healthy brain. Your help would be of infinite importance to the human race." "Help yourself!" Scot laughs hysterically.

Parry pops Scot's hate-filled brain into a gorilla who naturally escapes and goes on a rampage of revenge, eliminating all those involved in Scot's frame-up and Susan's sordid downfall. There is a kind of understanding between the woman and the ape, even though she is unaware that the creature is her brother. As the last gangster threatens her, she shouts at him, "It didn't matter what you did to me. I didn't count. But you killed Scot—made him die a hundred times waiting in that cell. Now you're waiting!" As the thug slaps her around, the gorilla breaks in and saves Susan who, we assume, will live out her redeemed life with her handsome reporter.

Ellen Drew makes a nice transition from hometown girl to hardened hooker to a woman who has overcome her illicit interlude. The film was promoted as a horror movie, and audiences were served a little extra for their money by the inclusion of the tame but then daring exploitation of a forbidden subject. David Hogan in *Dark Romance: Sexuality in the Horror Film* (McFarland & Company, Inc., Jefferson, NC, and London, 1986) summed up: "*The Monster and the Girl* is an odd, amusingly successful combination of that sort of simpleminded exploitation and the more legitimate horror genre. By today's standards, though, the circumstances of Ellen Drew's servitude seem mild.... But to audiences of the time, any sort of sexual misadventure was horrid and exciting." Perhaps if it were filmed today, say by Troma Productions, it might be titled *Harlot Heroine's Monster vs. White Slaver Slimeballs*.

So Paramount took a risk back there in 1941, and they took an even bigger one in 1964 when they released the most unpleasant, despicable movie up until that time to come out of a respected studio. In *Lady in a Cage*, an incapacitated socialite, Mrs. Hilyard (Olivia de Havilland), is trapped in her mansion's elevator over a Fourth of July weekend by three hoodlums led by a very young James Caan. It was filmed when all the grand dames of Hollywood, like Bette Davis, Joan Crawford, and Tallulah Bankhead, were coaxed out of retirement

Ann Sothern plays down and out hooker Sade who, with wino friend (Jeff Corey), breaks into Olivia de Havilland's mansion while she is trapped inside her elevator in *Lady in a Cage*.

and relegated to sick psychological horror thrillers. Ann Sothern, a versatile comedian in the *Maisie* series and veteran of her own TV show, was recruited to play Sade, a down and out prostitute who, with her alcoholic wino buddy (Jeff Corey), are the first to break into Mrs. Hilyard's plush digs. When the toughs arrive, they knock out the wino and force Sade to help them loot the house. And later, when she is locked in the wine cellar, it is symbolic of her being a prisoner of her profession, just as Mrs. Hilyard is a prisoner of her own wealth. While *Lady in a Cage* was condemned by most critics as a sickening example of just how far Hollywood had sunk, Ann Sothern's performance was noted as the film's only redeeming factor.

In 1957, when American International was releasing those C-grade science-fiction, horror, beach-party, and juvenile-delinquency double-bills to the delight of drive-in-going teenagers, Roger Corman wrote, produced and directed an unusual little thriller called *The Undead*, in which the focal role is played by Pamela Duncan as Diana Love, a sultry streetwalker. While the film was relatively devoid of sex, the idea was a bit daring for the audience for which it was intended, although it certainly would have satisfied the requirements of Joe Breen's watchdog group since the hooker is reformed at the end. An unorthodox psychotherapist named Quintus

Diana Love (Pamela Duncan) walks the streets in *The Undead*.

(Val Dufour) pays the prostitute Diana to participate in a regression experiment at the American Institute for Psychical Research. When he informs his mentor that through hypnosis he is going to take his patient back to a previous life, the astonished doctor asks, "Where will you find a subject weak and impressionable enough to arrive at the required state of trance?" Giving the stereotypical description of whores, Quintus answers, "Her type is the most easily influenced of basic character groups—almost devoid of willpower. That's why I chose her," as Diana waits in the other room rifling through the psychotherapist's coat pockets. Corman came up with the idea for the film to cash in on the hot topics of the day: Bridey Murphy and reincarnation.

As Diana reclines on the couch, the two men question her: "Do you have any difficulty getting up in the morning?" "I don't," she laughs. "I get up in the afternoon." This is about as racy and descriptive of Diana's activities as the film gets. Quintus places her in a trance: "No telling how many fathoms deeper we'll have to sink into that murky mind of hers before she wakes in another time, another place." At one point, the whore speaks French, but Quintus takes her deeper.

Diana rubs her wrist, trying to take off her bracelet, and we see that Diana is now Helena in a medieval prison cell, accused of witchcraft and trying to free herself from her shackles. When a guard enters, Diana's voice speaks to Helena, telling her that in order to escape she must pretend to make love to him—an idea that certainly would have never occurred to the chaste Helena unless someone like Diana had suggested it.

When this is accomplished, Helena escapes and climbs into gravedigger Smolkin's (Mel Welles) hearse and hides in a coffin under a corpse from her pursuers—another act which would have not bothered her future hooker incarnation. Back in the 20th century, Quintus realizes to his horror that because Diana has saved Helena, history has been changed and all of Helena's future reincarnations will cease to exist. So he must travel back to the past on Diana's brainwaves to assure that Helena's execution is carried out.

The Undead is quite imaginative and lots of fun, filled with good witches like Meg Maud (Dorothy Neumann) and evil ones like Livia (Allison Hayes in a medieval gown that reveals a 20th-century panty line), who quiets Scroop the tavern owner (Bruno Ve Soto) by exclaiming, "Rest thy corpulence!" Billy Barty is an imp and the bewitched Smolkin speaks philosophical nonsense and recites verse: "Hay diddle diddle, the rat and the fiddle, the corpse jumped over his tomb; the murderer laughed to see such a sight, as he strangled the girl in the gloom."

When Quintus arrives in the past, he is naked, since material things such as clothes can't travel on brainwaves. It is one of the film's many gaffes then to see this nude man wearing a watch. At the witches' Sabbath, presided over by Satan himself (Richard Devon), Quintus tries to persuade Helena to go through with her execution in order to save all her future lives, including Diana's. Meg Maud reiterates the difficult choice: "Death now, life after; life now, death everafter." When Helena asks Quintus what kind of woman Diana is, he replies, "Base and devoid of virtue—a wanton woman of the streets." But then Helena's other future reincarnations speak to her: "I am a poetess, give me life." "I'm a mother, give me life." "I'm a dancer, give me life." Finally, Diana the prostitute speaks to Helena: "I'm Diana. The wasted years of my past are done because I've lived in you. And the love and piety that fills your heart has cleansed mine." Helena makes her choice and loses her head to the block. Diana awakens on the couch, her life changed. But because he cannot travel back on Diana's/Helena's brainwaves, Quintus is trapped in the past, a servant of Satan. Hogan in his *Dark Sexuality* once again sums up: "Corman deserves credit for attempting to deal reasonably with the anomaly of time travel, a tricky premise which Hollywood usually explores with astonishing stupidity. Pamela Duncan... is well cast as the prostitute.... (who) is not made a point of derision or negative judgment. She is the film's heroine."

Director Brian De Palma delighted in casting hookers as heroines, especially if his then-wife Nancy Allen could fill the parts. In *Dressed to Kill* (1980), Allen plays high-priced call girl Liz Blake who is witness to nymphomaniac Kate Miller's (Angie Dickinson) brutal murder in an elevator. She is seen picking up the bloody razor by both the killer and a witness, so that not only does the killer want to silence her, but she becomes a prime suspect by the police. Liz, however, has a knack for staying alive; she is an intelligent hooker, setting up a date with her escort service on one phone while at the same time transacting business with her stockbroker on another. She aligns herself with Kate's brilliant teenage son Peter (Keith Gordon) and together they do their own sleuthing, much to the annoyance of Lieutenant Marino (Dennis Franz), who quips, "Hope you make a better hooker than you do a detective." Marino threatens to book Liz unless she breaks into the office of the victim's shrink, Dr. Robert Elliott (Michael Caine), to steal his appointment book, which might offer a clue to the killer. She sets up an appointment with Elliott and we see that she does indeed do her hooking well. "You're talking to an expert on bad," she tells the doctor. "Oh, really. Now what makes you such an expert?" he asks. "Cause I'm a hooker—I like to turn men on." "Do you ever have sex that's not paid for?" "Is that a proposal?" she inquires. "No. It's what we psychologists call a question," he answers as she removes her overcoat and stands before him in black bra, garterbelt and panties.

To reveal more would be not only indecent but would spoil the many surprises of *Dressed to Kill*. Allen's character is indeed intriguing in this De Palma homage to Alfred Hitchcock, but the plot has implausibilities, and is called by David Hogan in *Dark Sexuality* "a moralistic muddle." He further states: "It's a T and A show for uptown slaughter junkies. Kate... exists only to be punished by that curiously Puritan ethic informing nearly all slasher films. Kate may not be the world's most discreet wife, but her sexual urges are hardly capital crimes. Since our heroine Liz is a prostitute, the film indirectly proposes that sex for commerce is nobler than sex for its own sake."

Allen's second stint as a call girl was the following year in De Palma's *Blow Out*. Sally is hired to embarrass a governor and potential presidential candidate, but instead gets involved in murder when the tire of the car they are riding in is shot out, causing the vehicle to crash into a stream, with her client drowning. Independent horror-film sound recorder (John Travolta) captures the crash on tape and hooks up with the hooker to implicate high government officials in the assassination. Hampering their efforts is the psychopathic killer Burke (John Lithgow), who eagerly murders prostitutes as the Liberty Bell Strangler. In one of the film's more intense moments, Burke solicits a hooker in Philadelphia's 30th Street railroad station. When she goes to the ladies room to brush her teeth after fellating a sailor in a phone booth, Burke secretively follows her. The camera focuses on particular close-ups: toothpaste foam on the woman's lips, Burke leaning over a stall partition, the unraveling of a thin wire from his watch, the whore lowering her head to rinse and then lifting it again, the wire around her neck cutting into the flesh, and, finally, the hooker's feet swinging slowly, inches above a floor cluttered with rolls of toilet paper, a shoe, and her dropped toothbrush. It is an image so vivid that it was used as foreign poster art.

While De Palma loves to explore what neuroses dictate the actions of his villains and victims, especially in *Dressed to Kill*, his hookers seem to have it all together—their job is just a means to an end. Liz

Kathleen Turner and Anthony Perkins in *Crimes of Passion*

smartly turns her earnings over to a stockbroker instead of a pimp. Neither she nor Sally have any hang-ups about their profession. But this is not always the case. Take, for instance, Ken Russell's bizarre 1984 *Crimes of Passion,* in which Kathleen Turner plays a frigid fashion designer by day and a $50.00-a-trick hooker named China Blue by night. She can be graphically sexual when she describes to a john she is about to fellate how she practices playing the flute: "First I unwrap the case and then I take out the instrument, very carefully. And then I run my little hand all over it, up and down. And I like to lift it to my mouth and wrap my lips around it and then just wait for that sweet music to come pouring out." She can play the part of a woman being raped, and when the client asks if he was too rough, she laughs, "Don't worry, sweet Dick. I'm tough," wrapping the extra $10 bill he has given her around her bubble gum and throwing it in the wastebasket. She is witty when she assumes a stewardess role and tells her client, "I'm here to serve you. Please remember while we may run out of Pan Am coffee, we'll never run out of TWA tea." Despite the sordidness she sinks to, she also has her pride. When a man and wife hire her for a threesome in the back seat of their limousine, the woman scolds her husband for sticking his tongue in China's ear: "You never know where it's been." The insulted prostitute throws her payment down on the seat and leaps from the car. And, finally, she can be tender and sympathetic, as when a guilt-ridden wife buys her for her dying husband. It's a moving scene where China Blue breaks her cardinal rule by revealing her real name, Joanna Crane, when the invalid asks what he may call her.

All of the characters in *Crimes of Passion* are psychologically screwed up, but the most seriously disturbed is the combat-zone preacher played by Anthony Perkins. "I am the Reverend Peter Shayne. I know the plague that cripples you," he shouts at China Blue. "I have been sent by the Lord to save you and to rid the earth of that plague.... Do you recognize me, child?" Blue shoots back a snappy, "Sorry, I never forget a face, especially after I've sat on it." Later, his lust overcomes him, and he propositions her: "The Reverend Peter Shayne requests a few moments of repose upstairs in your holy of holys." He follows her to her hotel room where she tells him, "I make a great Joan of Arc, can't you tell?" To which he replies. "I imagine you do spend a good deal of time on your knees, my child." But these crude one-liners from Barry Sandler's screenplay soon become tiresome. Quips like "You wear your anger like a break-away chastity belt" and "Whores and metaphors don't mix," take away from the sinisterness of Perkins' character and serve only to show how clever Sandler and Russell think they are. There is more humor than horror when China Blue discovers a monstrous vibrator with a razor sharp edge in the preacher's black bag. "Who are you?" she screams at him. He leers back at her, "I'm you!" But the awful meaning of the phrase has been diluted by the off-color smut that preceded it.

The Reverend Peter Shayne is about as psychotic a character as Perkins has ever played, especially when he shouts "Last rites!" as he knocks China Blue unconscious, and then breaks into a hysterical wild-eyed version of "Come on along get happy; we're headin' for the judgment day." But unlike the psychiatric explanation of Norman Bates' neuroses at the end of *Psycho*, we never learn what causes the preacher's demons. China Blue, on the other hand, confesses to the one man with whom she could really settle down (John Laughlin) that her "hotel is the safest place in the world. I can do anything, feel anything because it's not me." As James Page explains in *Prostitution in Hollywood Films*, "...one learns eventually the Freudian basis for Joanna/China Blue's split life: Only in her guise of a prostitute does she feel safe and uninhibited, free to be anyone she wishes and do whatever appeals to her." He adds, however, that "it was difficult to take anything seriously with the blatant overacting of Anthony Perkins."

If Ken Russell's *Crimes of Passion* sounds excessive, wait until you see Frank Henenlotter's 1990 *Frankenhooker*. Fortunately this camp modern day send-up of *Bride of Frankenstein* is totally tongue-sewn-firmly-in-cheek, with lots of far out dialogue and clever situations. The story involves Jeffrey Franken (James Loring), whose girlfriend Elizabeth (Patty Mullen) is dismembered at an outdoor birthday party by a runaway lawnmower. Only able to salvage her head, this would-be Frankenstein places it on the dining room table and pours wine into its mouth, which leaks out of the severed neck onto the lace tablecloth. "How do you like the Beaujolais?" he asks, and then muses over where he can find parts to reconstruct his love. "If I need female parts, then I'll buy female parts. There's a place across the river where there are thousands of women anxious to sell their parts—no questions asked, of course—for the right amount of cash. I do have my Christmas club account." As he drives through Times Square he is exuberant: "This is like smorgasbord! What a buffet!"

Theorizing that crack is killing the prostitutes of New York City, he justifies his use of supercrack to get the job done faster. And sure enough, in a seedy hotel room, nine hookers explode from the stuff, sending Jeffrey back to Jersey with more parts than he needs. In reassembling Elizabeth, he calls a plate containing a large and small breast Mutt and Jeff; removes a shoe from a disembodied foot and discovers bunions which he files down. As the final touch, he places Elizabeth's head on the stitched-together body with its mismatched limbs. But after the creation sequence, the first words out of Elizabeth's twitching mouth are "Wanna date? Goin' out? Lookin' for some action? Need some company? Got any money?" When he answers "no" to her last question, she knocks him out and stomps out of the house on platform shoes. Catching the subway back to Times Square, she does the Frankenstein strut up Broadway to her pimp's hangout. However, when she resumes her trade and her johns invade her body, they are electrocuted and explode, with one grateful disembodied head sighing, "Ahhhhh, that was wonderful!"

Jeffrey rescues Frankenhooker from her sordid profession and whisks her back to New Jersey, but the

pimp follows them and knocks *Jeffrey's* head off. The pimp recognizes the various parts of his hookers that make up Elizabeth's body and calls them by name, which invites the unused parts in the deep freezer to escape and attack him. Since the blood Jeffrey needed for his experiments was estrogen-based, Elizabeth must use the remaining hooker parts to reassemble Jeffrey, and the film ends with the two hooker-stitched-together lovers gazing happily into each other's eyes

saying, "We're together again." As gruesome as all this sounds, *Frankenhooker* is really quite a hoot. *The Video Watchdog* (Number 2, 1990, page 11) reported that, "According to producer Edgar Levins, the MPAA initially declined to rate the film, explaining that they had no "S" rating for shit." Some folks have no sense of humor at all.

The clever idea of using hookers in the guise of a highly respected screen monster was not new. Back in 1979, three luscious vampire whores enticed their victims back to their mausoleum where they drained them of vital fluids, all under the watchful jaundiced eye of their vampire master Richmond Reed (John Carradine). The ads for *Vampire Hookers* stated: "Warm blood isn't all they suck!" which is also the title of the song sung during the closing credits. Carradine is the best thing about this Filipino/United States soft-core production directed by Cirio H. Santiago. Wearing a cape, white and hat and red bow tie, Carradine is in his element as he tosses out quotations at appropriate occasions: "It's time for you to shuffle off your mortal coil," he consoles one guest. And to his flatulent vampire-in-training assistant who has just brought him a sack of garlic: "Don't you read Shakespeare, you idiot? 'Eat no onions or garlic for we are to utter sweet breath.' Shakespeare was a vampire!"

The hookers, Cherish (Karen Stride), Suzy (Lenka Novak), and Marcy (Katie Dolan), all take turns seducing their victims before they dine, but the extended soft-core sex scenes are passionless in slow motion, interspersed for some reason with shots of gargoyles. These endless and sleep-provoking interludes do give us the opportunity to chuckle at the tan lines on these vampire women who would have ordinarily decomposed if exposed to the sun.

Far more impressive are the vampire hookers given major studio (Universal) distribution in the more recent *Bordello of Blood* (1996), in which Chris Sarandon plays the Evangelical preacher Reverend Jimmy Current, who resurrects Lilith (Angie Everhart), the "mother of all vampires" (as she's affectionately called), in order to rid the world of sin. But Lilith opens a whorehouse under a mortuary. The bordello scenes are the most amusing aspects of this rambling pseudo-erotic horror spoof (one vampire even has three breasts, another an 18-inch tongue), with the climax repeating the exploding hooker theme—this time brought about when the Reverend J.C. and seedy P.I. Rafe Guttman (Dennis Miller) squirt the "ladies" with a water pistol and super-soaker filled with holy water. The film is the second in the *Tales from the Crypt* feature-length series, and, with the major studio treatment and the popularity of the *Tales* television series, has not disappointed its intended audience. While *Bordello*'s newspaper ads contained such clever critic quotes as "It'll scare you stiff!!" (*Rotting Bone Magazine*) and "Two Thumbs Off!" (Joel C. Ghoul, *Good Groaning America*), *Vampire Hookers* deliberately depended upon misleading bogus warning statements to entice its public: "Due to the unusual subject matter and explicit presentation of this motion picture, only mature adults should attend." Richard Meyers in *For One Week Only* (New Century Publishers, Inc., Piscataway, NJ, 1982) warns about such deceit: "There are certain criteria by which the major studios work. These criteria include playing fairly straight with their audience. If the film doesn't live up to the promise of the advertising, the majors will lose money. The independent exploiters are not limited by this constraint. Their movies are so cheap that any means of acquiring money is not beneath them in some cases. Fact: Some will lie. Consumer beware."

I have avoided direct-to-video productions such as Hugh Gallagher's *Gore Whore* which features a laboratory-revived zombie named Dawn, the Undead (Audrey Street).

Hollywood Chainsaw Hookers is probably the most requested video of director Fred Olen Ray, seeing 35-mm theatrical release in 1988. The prolific Ray is a true lover of the genre and has probably done more to re-introduce retired actors to a new generation of audiences than any other director.

Ray begins *Hollywood Chainsaw Hookers* with a disclaimer: "The *chainsaws* used in this Motion Picture are *real* and *dangerous*. They are handled here by *seasoned professionals*. The makers of the Motion Picture advise strongly against anyone attempting to perform these stunts at home. Especially if you are *naked* and about to engage in strenuous *sex*. My conscience is clear." And well it should be, since in the first scene hooker Mercedes (Michelle Bauer—at that time, Michelle McClellan) picks up a trick at a bar and invites him back to her apartment. After stripping seductively for him, she tells him to close his eyes, then dons a showercap and covers her portrait of Elvis with plastic. "Take me to heaven," the john begs. "Your wish is my demand!" she snarls, revving up her chainsaw. Blood and body parts fly across the room and Mercedes calmly removes a severed hand from her breast. Seems Mercedes and her fellow hookers belong to an ancient chainsaw worshipping cult who believe the "blade of the saw purifies evil flesh and makes it holy to please our God." When Detective Jack Chandler (Jay Richardson) confronts one of these "Cuisinart queens," he asks, "What do you do? Pray to Black and Decker?" Chandler is led to the hookers while trying to locate runaway Samantha Kelso (Linnea Quigley—referred to by James O'Neil in his book *Terror on Tape* as the Goldie Hawn of Gore) who has infiltrated the cult.

Fred Olen Ray's 1988 camp cult classic *Hollywood Chainsaw Hookers* stars Michelle Bauer.

James Parish remarks in *Prostitution in Hollywood Films*, "With its wild mixture of film noir, splatter flicks, soft-core pornography, and detective capers, nothing is sacred in *Hollywood Chainsaw Hookers*. The attempted puns and double entendres fly fast and furious." And this is precisely what dilutes the extreme blood and gore—the introduction of wisecracks and hilarious bits, such as when Mercedes's chainsaw runs out of gas as she is about to slice open Jack, and another hooker chides her with, "You idiot! I told you to stop at Texaco." And Jack has to wonder "if we let our religious freedom go too far in this country." The actresses give their all to the film, especially Dawn Wildesmith (Ray's ex) who also did the makeup designs, and pert Linnea Quigley performing the virgin dance of the double chainsaws. Richardson is droll as the wise-cracking Chandler, but Gunnar Hansen as the cult honcho is a major disappointment. John McCarty in *The Official Splatter Movie Guide* (St. Martin's Press, New York, 1989) hits the nailgun on the head when he says, "Hansen's deft handling of his dialogue shows why, as Leatherface, he wasn't given any in *Texas Chainsaw Massacre*." But this is what makes Fred Olen Ray's films so pleasing to his fans. They're fun.

You may have noticed in this discussion that hookers have made the transition over the years from put-upon victims in the serious horror films of the '30s and '40s to aggressive but fun-loving "monsters" in the horror farces of the '80s and '90s. And perhaps it is best in these days of drugs and disease that these ladies of the night stay light-hearted in their sleaziness—that they develop a comedic character in their profession. *Bordello of Blood* vampire harlot Angie Everhart told Steve Newton in his *Fangoria* article "The Best Little Bordello of Blood" (Number 150, March 1996, page 21) that her "character is absolutely fabulous.... She's strong, she's powerful, she's a woman in every sense of the word. She gets to be sexy and intelligent and love life and be happy and fun. Just very happy to be alive." Co-writer and producer A.L. Katz follows up a few paragraphs later (page 22): "She's a wonderful villain and we have a lot of fun with her. Angie plays her wonderfully, so we're able to have beauty and humor and horror wrapped up in the same scene."

So filmmakers now view the sordid subject of prostitution as entertaining and light—even in horror films. It's a far cry from when Arlene Francis moaned in fear and pain on that wooden cross in one of Lugosi's cruelest and unsettling scenes. *The Monster and the Girl* only hints at the sociological and psychological damage the streets might have ravaged upon the female star. Ken Russell in his follow-up to *Crimes of Passion*, the 1991 *Whore*, gets a little closer to the truth—makes us see that sex for sale is degrading (and perhaps that's why the film did poorly). Deep down in our hearts we want our hookers and our horror humorous—not horrible. Like Michelle Bauer's mom, we want to get "a big kick out of them."

95

Attack of the Alien Women from Outer Space!

by James Singer

For the past three decades, alleged UFO abductees under hypnosis have described their hosts as pale, large-eyed beings that resemble taller, thinner versions of the Pillsbury Dough Boy, an image adapted by Spielberg for his *Close Encounters of the Third Kind*. Nothing could be further from the truth.

Hypnotize any one of several low-budget Hollywood producers of the 1950s or '60s and scrutinize their UFO encounters. From such minds, researchers have learned what extraterrestrials really look like: tall, brilliant, and beautiful women adept at blasting mutants, managing nuclear fusion labs, and piloting space ships, all the while performing these exacting duties while dressed in body-hugging swimsuits, ultra miniskirts and high heels. In short, centerfolds for *Scientific American*.

Despite claims of the government and scientific communities with their billion dollar, yet flawed, space probes, it's well known that our solar system is inhabited by various Amazonian super civilizations. For the serious student of cinematic history, this should come as no surprise. In fact, these revelations were fully documented over 30 years ago by such movie studios as Astor and Universal.

The concept of a society inhabited by attractive and seemingly available women is itself a myth as old as mankind and the message within this myth is that the female of the species is more deadly than the male. In Greek and Roman mythology, the Sirens, actually part woman and part bird, lured sailors to a watery death by seducing them with ethereal singing. In Greek mythology, the Amazons were a race of tough female warriors who removed one breast to improve their archery skills. The Amazon river in South America was named by the Spaniards who believed that such women lived near its shores; the word amazon derived from *a* (without) *mazos* (breast).

Whatever the myriad variations on men entering an isolated colony of females, it's basically the stuff of age-old male sexual fantasies (which skin mag publishers Hugh Hefner and Bob Guccione created and fulfilled in real life). It was only natural that these wet-dreams and essentially adolescent fantasies would transfer well from lost islands, hidden jungles, ancient cultures and uncharted lands to the planets and moons in our solar system as a subject for pulp fantasy publications, men's adventure mags, paperbacks (with their lushly drawn cover paintings) and motion pictures. Women don't make movies or write books about all-male societies discovered by female explorers and they probably never will.

Many of the "good-girl" pin-up artists of the 1940s and 1950s were heavily enamored of the otherworldly images of beautiful young girls from other planets or from the future, and their work can be seen in scores of men's mags, particularly during the '50s and early '60s, the dawn of true space exploration. The renowned Alberto Vargas of *Esquire* and later *Playboy* fame drew the set sketches and designed the futuristic cocktail-style dresses worn by the women of a post-nuclear war colony for *World Without End* (Allied Artists, 1956), a handsomely produced sci-fi adventure written and directed by Edward Bernds.

During the late 1940s and early 1950s, the flying saucer

craze erupted. Outside the boundaries of serious investigation were UFO devotees who, like 20th-century descendants of the Baron Munchausen, told of trips in saucers to other planets and encounters, some sexual, with erotically exotic female aliens. Several of these claimants, George Adamski for one, became "stars" on the UFO lecture circuit. A few even developed a cult core of believers, several of which remain in existence today, especially in South America.

Of course, these "true adventures" sounded not unlike the storylines from scores of science fiction/weird fantasy magazines and comic books. They were irritating to professional UFO researchers, but fascinating to enthusiasts of the fantastic, UFO/strange phenomena publications and books sold well.

Predictably, these interplanetary recounts fell into the capable, if trembling, hands of numerous movie producers, ever on the lookout for way-out, exploitable subject matter that fit into that crowd-pleasing "spicy" realm. Stories of beautiful, scantily clad women living on distant worlds were a natural to fulfill their own box-office dreams. So where are the absent male inhabitants of these societies in some of these films? Who knows? Who cares? The audience put their money down to see sexy outer space gals running around in revealing outfits with lots of leg showing, and maybe a cat fight or two thrown into the plot. If they were lucky.

While earlier comic strips and movies about the adventures of Flash Gordon and Buck Rogers invariably featured space sirens, the most memorable being Ming's daughter Princess Aura (Priscilla Lawson) in the Gordon shows, it wasn't until the post-War years that the space babe concept really went into full swing.

In *Flight to Mars* (Monogram, 1951), filmed in the two-strip Cinecolor process, an American rocket crew that included Arthur Franz and Cameron Mitchell discovered an advanced race of Martians. While the men of Mars were boring corporate types concerned with the dwindling of their natural resource, Corium, Martian babe scientist Marguerite Chapman, bothered not with protective work uniforms when aiding Franz in his rocket repairs. Instead she and the producers preferred the revealing micro-dress popular that year on the Red Planet. Far from being the imperious female alien who would

Alberto Vargas designed the male ideal of futuristic costumes for the women in *World Without End*.

surface shortly in upcoming films, Marguerite's a regular Martian girl-next-door who, of course, falls for Franz and helps him and his team return to Earth.

A big year for all-female space societies was 1953. Moviegoers saw *Abbott and Costello Go to Mars* (Universal-International), although Bud and Lou actually bypassed Mars for an encounter with actress Mari Blanchard, the stunning Queen Allura of Venus, and her society of decoratively garbed Venusians. Blanchard was perfectly cast; in her heyday she had the face, form and bearing of a goddess.

Abbott and Costello explore more than the terrain in *A&C Go to Mars*.

That same year, the *Cat-Women of the Moon* (Astor) used their paranormal feline powers to make life difficult for somnolent Sonny Tufts and tough guy Victor Jory. Originally shot in 3D, and later retitled *Rocket to the Moon* for television, this entry has an affectionate following. Wearing black bodysuits and tight wigs, the Cat-Women Alpha (Carol Brewster), Zeta (Susanne Alexander), Lambda (Susan Morrow), and the Hollywood Cover Girls hypnotically controlled the already tigerish Earthwoman Marie Windsor, who was usually made of tougher stuff in her trenchcoat and bullet movies.

Living beneath the lunar landscape with some badly overweight spiders, the Cat-Women use their abundance of gold deposits as bait to knife one dollar-minded crewman. This not being a Universal production, budgetary

Bud takes an all-too-brief recess from slapping his partner around to explore some social possibilities with the many starlets cast, among them eight Miss Universe contestants including Miss USA, Jackie Loughery, and Miss Sweden, Anita Ekberg, who was seven years away from wading in a Roman fountain with Marcello. Allura takes a jealous shine to Lou, preferring his brand of chubby virility to Abbott's mustachioed sleaze. Costello naturally must botch things with his kid-in-a-candy-store roving eye, causing the hot-tempered Queen to throw the boys and their two moronic mobster companions out of Venus and back into space.

Though not one of the true classic A&C films, I feel that *...Go to Mars*, directed by series regular Charles Lamont, remains the most entertaining entry of the comedy team's '50s movies. The Venus-world section itself has a wonderfully surrealistic pulp paperback look in set and costume design due to Universal's highly talented craftspeople. The handsomely shot silvery movie would have been truly cotton candy for the eyes had it been photographed in color. Blanchard's regal crown weighed a mighty 14 pounds and caused her no small discomfort. Shop carpenters rigged up a rope-operated traction board to alleviate Mari's neck and back distress between takes, the gizmo resembling a cross between something out of a miniature gallows and a punishment device drawn by bondage artist Eric Stanton.

Mini-dresses and catsuits were the standard attire for alien women as worn in *Cat-Women of the Moon*.

constraints necessitated the use of office desk chairs and other cheapo substitutes for the rocket's control room set. *Cat-Women*'s hard-boiled dialogue, deadpan sincerity of its melodramatics, and overheated acting, especially by the always entertaining Jory, give the film a lively charm.

Long before the gagwriters at television's *Mystery Science Theater 3000* got their hands on movies like *Cat-Women*, the reviewers at *The Hollywood Reporter* and *Variety* gave it a straightforward thumbs-up.

"Imaginatively conceived and turned-out science fiction yarn should get a good play in the s-f and exploitation market," wrote Whit of *Daily Variety*.

It was at this time that English filmmakers also heeded the call of pseudo-science exotica. However, their space gal films lacked the bachelor pad, men's mag pin-up allure of their American cousins, and ultimately suffered from those interminable scenes of endless conversations in pubs and drawing rooms that were the trademark of dozens of British science fiction films.

Devil Girl from Mars (Spartan, 1954) featured the imperious Patricia Laffan and her refrigerator-shaped robot bodyguard menacing future Hammer/AIP heroine Hazel Court and co-stars amidst a placid Scottish countryside setting. In a fetishistic costume straight out of another Eric Stanton dominatrix illustration, *Devil Girl* flew in to capture males for breeding experiments, another sexual fantasy rife in alien abductee case histories of the past 30 years. One wonders how films like this may have influenced the people who seriously claim these bizarre experiences.

On the flip side of the platter, the *Fire Maidens of Outer Space* (Topaz, 1956) were demure, fragile English rose types. Descendants of Atlantis, they live on one of Jupiter's moons and are in need of manly protection from a lecherous monster roaming their lovely gardens. American actor Anthony Dexter (star of *Valentino*, 1951) and his flight crew provide this beefcake bodyguarding, saving heroine Susan Shaw and galpals by dumping the Jupiterian horndog into a flaming pit. Like *Devil Girl*, *Fire Maidens* was written and played dead-straight, without a stitch of humor.

During the heyday of British sexploitation film production, the Brits released the sci-fi comedy *Zeta One* (aka *The Love Factor,* aka *Alien Women,* 1969) in which a Bondian secret agent battled a society of alien beauties invading Earth to get men. Based on an adult comic strip, the rowdy *Zeta One* starred a bevy of Hammer Film beauties: Dawn Addams, the well-endowed Valerie Leon, Kirsten Betts, and Danish actress Yutte Stensgaard (Carmilla/Mircalla the vampire in *Lust for a Vampire*, 1970), who plays a round of strip poker with the spy-hero.

In charting the cinematic history of Amazonian alien cultures, one discovers that Bud and Lou's hijinks on planet Venus had apparently culminated in some type of political upheaval, for in *Queen of Outer Space* (Allied Artists, 1958), tough but fair Mari Blanchard is out as queen and superbad girl Laurie Mitchell is in, with scientist Zsa Zsa Gabor aiming to depose her. Shot

Patricia Laffan as the *Devil Girl from Mars*

in CinemaScope and luminous colors, *Queen* also has a stirring music score by Marlin Skiles that melds celestial sounds with military motifs and even some avant-garde jazz. The best known and most entertaining of all the wild, wild astro-bachelor/space girl pictures, the genesis of *Queen* has been attributed to a party joke by journalist Ben Hecht.

In an interview with Tom Weaver, director Edward Bernds (of Stooges/Bowery Boys fame) said that Hecht had written a 10-page outline, *Queen of the Universe*, which was brought to Allied by producer Walter Wanger. Hecht's basic idea, a planet controlled by women (he probably saw *A&C Go to Mars*), was turned into a working screenplay by the talented Charles Beaumont, later a stalwart for Rod Serling's *Twilight Zone*. Bernds and a co-writer spoofed up Beaumont's script. Giving a nod to *Go to Mars*, beauty queen contestants, notably Tania Velia, Miss Belgium, along with gorgeous actresses Lisa Davis and Barbara Darrow, were cast as Venusians.

Badly burned by radiation caused by the wars of Venusian males (a key plot device), Queen Yllana hides

99

The evil queen (Laurie Mitchell) has her masked torn off in *Queen of Outer Space*.

her disfigurement, but not her vicious temper, behind a mask. With her lovely miniskirted army—the plain-looking girls must be under house arrest or something—Yllana dreams of pulverizing Earth with the very shaky looking Beta Disintegrator, but not before putting her four male visitors through their paces.

Space trailboss Eric Fleming, sedentary scientist Paul Birch, wisecracker Dave Willock, and wolfish Patrick Waltz crash land courtesy of *World Without End* stock shots, are mugged by that always irritable big spider and are generally pushed around by the "Wicked Queen and her posse" before they overthrow her with the help of Gabor and her rebels. Mitchell is radiated to a horrible crisp by her own machine—strong stuff for its time—and the boys decide to hang with the Venusian vixens until whenever. Something of a pain in the ass to Bernds during filming, the annoying Gabor apparently is the only space lady in motion picture history to learn English by monitoring Hungarian radio waves.

When the guards in *Queen* stick their ray guns in the Earthmen's faces, they repeatedly bark out the order "Bachino!"—no doubt Venusian for "move it" or something like that, one would think. However, according to one dictionary of international "dirty" words, "bachino" is a regional Italian slang word for fellatio. Whatever the reason for using this particular word in the script, it does change the movie's perspective a bit.

A formidable figure in a glowing, skintight body suit, Shirley Kilpatrick as *The Astounding She-Monster* (AIP, 1958) killed off most of the cast and one fuzzy bear with her touch of radioactive death, an unusual approach for an alleged peace delegate from outer space. Wordy geologist Robert Clarke figures out how to terminate the shapely invader with the lightning bolt eyebrows in record time, since this is a 59-minute ultra-low-budget picture. One of the most fantastic looking alien femmes in movie history regardless of budget, the astounding Miss Kilpatrick was photographed walking backwards in several scenes to mask a split up the back of her second-skin costume.

A striptease dancer and nude model, Kilpatrick herself was not the model for the film's neat poster, intriguingly illustrated by the great Albert Kallis. Contemporary artist and psychotronic movie historian Jimmy Zero says that Madeleine Castle, once a *Playboy* centerfold, provided the actual inspiration of *The Astounding She-Monster*'s uniquely stylized poster pose.

Director of *She Demons*, one of the all-time favorite monster chiller horror programmers, Richard Cunha shot *Missile to the Moon* (Astor, 1959) in one week for $60,000. A remake of Astor's *Cat-Women* (with some alterations), made as a co-bill with Cunha's *Frankenstein's Daughter*, this quickie starred Cathy Downs, Nina Bara and eight—count 'em— "International Beauty Contest Winners," among them *Playboy*'s Marianne Gaba. It must have been like homecoming week for space bad girls Laurie Mitchell and Tania Velia, here billed as Miss Yugoslavia.

The crew now consists of two rocket scientists (no pun intended), one fiancée, and two juvenile delinquent stowaways. It wasn't the same prop as in *Cat-Women*, but that darn giant spider was still present, a performer who surely deserved his own SAG card after all those screen appearances. Gumby-like Rock Men now also roamed the Lunar surface, trolling for astronauts, although it's clear that a 95-year-old cat woman could easily outrun them. A clip of the rocking Rock Men going after those nice Earth people was edited into the compilation film *It Came from Hollywood* (Paramount, 1982).

Missile to the Moon had the two main requirements for 1950s sci-fi—a giant spider and a scantily clad alien.

Astor wanted a sexier look, so the cat-women's fashion sense had changed, abandoning their slinky black leotards for the interplanetary diaphanous look popular on Venus. The slanted eyebrows and tight wigs remained. They and their queen, now called the Lido, plot to leave the Moon in the Earth spaceship. As nasty as her predecessors, cat-woman Alpha knifes the Lido in the back. "The Lido has met with... an accident," she intones, clearly a student of the Costa Nostra school of do-it-yourself job promotion.

The violence quotient is raised in this version. The ubiquitous spider pounces on a screaming moon maiden and eats her, Alpha gets a knife in her chest by her own hand, and all the cat girls die in terror when the air is released from their underground headquarters by an explosion. The climactic scene in which an astronaut is fried to a skeletal crisp by the lunar sunlight was also fairly gruesome in its day and was later edited out of most television prints.

From Mexico came *La Nave De Los Monstruous/The Ship of the Monsters* (Prod. Sotomayor S.A., 1959), a wacky little oddity that made the rounds of those infamous kiddie matinees of the early 1960s in urban theaters that were flea pits long before they were converted to flea markets. Mexican movie sex symbols Ana Bertha Lepe and Lorena Velazquez blast off their all-female planet to rocket Earthward with a robot assistant in tow. Clad in the obligatory swim suits and high heels, the statuesque pair waylay a singing vacquero, played by Lalo "Piporro" Gonzalez.

Besides engaging in several musical numbers (excruciating even for a six-year-old, let alone an infantile adult) with Senor Piporro, the aliens also control a menagerie of Halloween-style creatures that display a pretty salacious interest in the two sexpots. Lorena becomes a vampire (!) and takes over the ship,

but winds up with a traditional stake through the heart while Piporro and Ana find romance. Now here's a picture with something for everyone. As in *Cat-Women* and *Missile*, the girls have Greek alphabet names (Gamma and Beta). Velazquez later went on to star in the knuckle sandwich series of Wrestling Women monster movies. *La Nave* is just as delirious as those gonzoid films and the Santo pictures she also appeared in. The surprisingly sleek, spacious

In the "you've got to be kidding" file, Alien scientists Dr. Puna and Prof. Tanga (Gloria Victor and Delores Reed) meet up with smutty comedians Bob Ball and Frankie Ray in *Invasion of the Star Creatures*.

design of the ship's bridge included an elevator tube, a spiral staircase, and large, gyroscopic "generators," a more impressive set than in any of the American films in this chapter.

The *Invasion of the Star Creatures* (AIP, 1962) was close to the end of the line for the glamour babes from space movies. Bruno VeSota, the family-sized character actor from a dozen Roger Corman features, directed *Star Creatures* with a mini-budget of $25,000. *Star Creatures'* original screenplay, written by Roger Corman regulars Dick Miller and Jonathan Haze (*Little Shop of Horrors*), had been initially rejected by Corman. The final screenplay credit went to Haze.

Definitely a guilty little pleasure but nothing to be ashamed over, *Star Creatures* was a static, extended burlesque skit, using the kind of comedy routines that exotic dancers and baggy-pants comics used to perform for groaning drunks in the strip joints. Blonde Gloria Victor and brunette Delores Reed, actresses of epic dimensions, played aliens-in-hotpants Dr. Puna and Prof. Tanga, a very unsubtle play on words. Their dubious plans for invasion included growing an army of plant creatures (Vega-men) in garden pots in a cave hideout near an army base.

As goldbricking soldiers, the leering, close to drooling comedy duo of Bob Ball and Frankie Ray trip up those plans between doing impressions of Lugosi and Cagney, and tossing smutty wisecracks at the superstacked Puna and Tanga. Barely tolerant of these little wiseguys, the film's end sees both formerly dominant alien scientists turn into trophy-babe girlfriends for the two idiots. Yes, in the movies, a scriptwriter's impossible dream can become a reality. Squeezed by the budget, VeSota's Vega-men costumes were made from tights and burlap sacks, and the make-do sets were totally threadbare. Yet Bruno was fortunate (extremely fortunate) in the casting of the physically impressive Victor and Reed.

Greta Thyssen is the fantasy woman in *Journey to the Seventh Planet*.

Our silver screen friend John Agar and his cosmo-companions made a *Journey to the Seventh Planet* (AIP, 1962) and found a group of alluring fantasy women (Greta Thyssen, Ann Smyrner, and friends) in settings reminding them of home; all were just mental illusions constructed by an enormous and pissed-off Uranian brain. The *Reptilicus* man, Sid Pink, shot this in Denmark, his then-base of operations. A picture that's been knocked around in print, some of *Journey's* plot devices would turn up on such science fiction shows as *Lost in Space* and *Star Trek* years later.

In 1968, Corman combined elements of the 1962 Russian sci-fi movie *Planet of Storms* (aka *Planeta Burg*) with beachside footage of clam-shell bikinied Mamie Van Doren and her all-female clan of psychic Venusians—directed by "Derek Thomas" (Peter Bogdanovich)—to form the cut-and-paste *Voyage to the Planet of Prehistoric Women* for AIP's television arm.

One would think that, over the years, the porn film world would have latched on to the idea of an all-women planet or female alien visitors and would have screwed the theme into the ground. Such entries are actually difficult to find with the exception of *Star Virgins* (VCX, 1979) and *Ultraflesh* (Collectors, 1980), starring Seka and Serena. One reason is that the pulpishly imaginative space girl fantasies were meant to tease and titillate and that's not the objective of hardcore pornography.

Softcore exploitation producer David F. Friedman, however, did knock off a cheap little number called *Space Thing* (EVI, 1968), directed by Byron Mabe and starring the aptly named "Paula Pleasure" as a fiercesome rocketship mistress who dallies with her female crewmates and male visitors. All of it is the dream of a bored husband.

In 1957 The Three Stooges featurette *Space Ship Sappy* (Columbia) brought the boys to a planet of alien jungle girls (with fangs yet), and Dolly Parton went off the wall in the *Saturday Night Live* TV skit, "Planet of the Gigantic Hooters." Spoofing up a genre that already contains a naturally inherent amount of tongue-in-cheek humor means going back to the source. *Amazon Women on the Moon* (Universal, 1987), a John Landis presentation, faithfully recreated the now superdated look, color scheme, style and corn of *Queen* in a brief, good-natured parody, with exotic action actresses Sybil Danning well-cast as Queen Lara and Lana Clarkson as her handmaiden Alpha Beta.

Edited among the various all-star vignettes and short films as a chopped-up, milkman's matinee TV movie, the *Amazon* segment had all the by-now cliched elements: string-held rocket model; dead-on stock music; leggy, spear-carrying moon maids; a granite-jawed hero; the Brooklynese joker à la Dave Willock; and location filming at good old Bronson Canyon. Directed by Robert K. Weiss, the *Amazon* movie clips are an affectionate tip of the hat to a departed fantasy genre that may have been chauvinistic in outlook regarding the role of the sexes, but was never mean-spirited or vulgar in execution. The same can't be said for the countless movies made over the last 20 years in which the female characters are either bikini bimbos, out to make money washing cars, screaming victims of male psychomaniacs, or car-washing bikini-bimbos graphically murdered by psychomaniacs.

Lana Clarkson as Alpha Beta in *Amazon Women on the Moon*.

And it remains a type of film that has yet to ever completely run out of steam. Unlike the conservative 1950s, the sexual elements can be pumped up today for direct to cable and DVD sales. The lame teen comedy *Dr. Alien* (aka *I Was a Teenage Sex Mutant*, 1989) casts busty, baby-dollish Judy Landers as an extraterrestrial posing as a biology teacher and using one of her students for sex experiments. Objective? You guessed it: the old breeding game. In Ted Bohus' *Vampire Vixens from Venus* (Shanachie, 1995), centerfolds/actresses J.J. North, Leslie Glass, and Therese Lynn play aliens who take shapely human shape to drain Earth boys of their sex energies. Bohus made the picture on a budget of only $200,000, which in these inflationary times is a brutally difficult feat to accomplish.

Personally, I look forward to the day when someone will remake *Queen of Outer Space* with the current hot starlet for $200 million. Nothing is impossible in Hollywood, where they keep watching the skies for heavenly inspiration.

103

Harlots, Hedonists and Heroines: The Women of Hammer Films

by Susan Svehla

Hammer Films had produced a wide variety of films, everything from adventures to musicals, for the British film-going public before striking red gold with *The Curse of Frankenstein* in 1957. The surprising success of the brilliantly Eastman-colored frightfest single-handedly led to a bloody resurrection of horror films, a resurgence that was boldly led by Hammer Films. Their glorious set decorations, stunning costumes, haunting musical scores, stark Technicolor, and unexpected charisma of Peter Cushing and Christopher Lee drove a stake deep into the heart of baby boomers everywhere. And their leading ladies, well—any horror film magazine worth its salt has had more than one article dedicated to the lovelies of Hammer.

Hammer Studios loved women... they loved to victimize them, rape them, undress them, exploit them, and basically use them as plot-furthering devices or attractive set decoration. Noted Hammerphile Dick Klemensen quotes Hammer producer Michael Carreras on Jeanne Roland's role in *The Curse of the Mummy's Tomb*: "I thought she was quite pretty. She had never acted in her life. I used her as an ornamental piece... That is all she was meant to be, more or less." This archaic attitude could be one of the reasons Hammer's continuing popularity is mostly male oriented, much like the testosterone-laden James Bond following.

Not to drag in the very tired Hammer versus Universal debate, but unlike the earlier Universal horror product, Hammer had gore galore (brought to vivid life by cinematographer Jack Asher in their beautifully utilized Technicolor), excessive dialogue, and many of their characters lacked the mystique or charisma of such Universal icons as Karloff and Lugosi. As for relating to the females of Hammer, well, that was as difficult for most female audience members as relating to the Universal heroines. None of these frightened female characterizations from either studio came close to portraying a real flesh and blood woman, a character easily related to by the audience. However, occasionally a few Hammer gems slipped in providing strong female leads not forced into the typical one-dimensional parts so prevalent in the studio's other horror films.

As scripted, most of Hammer's women's roles were rarely developed (although many of the stars were rather overdeveloped, if you know what I mean!). Except for the obligatory nightgown-clad, bosom-heaving scenes, women often served no purpose other than providing a lovely image for teenage boys with raging hormones, the most frequent customers of movie theaters and drive-ins. Like other film studios, Hammer knew sex sold, and they took full advantage of that fact by outfitting their heroines in diaphanous negligees and beautiful low-cut gowns that displayed their lovely stars to full advantage.

While the major male players of Hammer—Cushing, Lee, directors Francis and Fisher, character actors Michael Ripper and Andre Morell—are admired and frequently the subject of books and magazine articles, the Hammer women are the ones most fondly remembered and much discussed.

Jeanne Roland was "an ornamental piece" in *The Curse of the Mummy's Tomb*.

HARLOTS

"You're behaving like a common whore..."
—*Rasputin, the Mad Monk*

Often Hammer's screenwriters seemed to be preaching a bizarre sort of morality in their film productions. The aristocracy is usually portrayed as vile and decadent, causing misery and grief to the downtrodden masses before they meet a gruesome fate. Women who, to put it delicately, enjoyed life on the wild side, are usually dealt with in the same manner. It's ultra-conservative and out-of-date idea Hollywood would gleefully and profitably emulate in the slice-and-dice films of the 1970s and 1980s.

The Curse of Frankenstein (1957): Baron Frankenstein's (Peter Cushing) naive fiancée (Hazel Court) comments it has always been her deepest desire to marry Victor Frankenstein, just as it has always been his deepest desire to marry her. Elizabeth is living in a dream world, for her true love is not the kind and gentle fellow she deludes herself into thinking he is. (Giving scripter Jimmy Sangster the benefit of the doubt, perhaps he was just illustrating the fate of women in the actual time frame in which the film occurred; for women were looked upon as mere chattel and had to accept many unpleasant situations in their quest for security.) Immediately after Elizabeth utters this pitiful speech we see Frankenstein in a passionate embrace with pretty maid Justine (Valerie Gaunt). Justine, looking for any way to better her lot in life, threatens to expose Frankenstein's experiments to the authorities if he refuses to marry her. The woefully obtuse maid vows to find evidence to implicate him, never considering the frighteningly obsessed Frankenstein might try to stop her. That night (clad in a filmy nightgown, of course), Justine sneaks into the lab where the scheming Frankenstein sends her to her doom by locking her in with his ungodly creation.

Our first harlot bites the dust, while good girl Elizabeth finds romance with Frankenstein's honorable assistant.

The Revenge of Frankenstein (1958): A frisky young lady leaves her shy suitor in the bushes because "he won't get on with it." Soon she will meet a decidedly more demonstrative creature, becoming another scarlet victim for Frankenstein's monster.

Dracula Has Risen from the Grave (1968): Zena (Barbara Ewing), a buxom, randy barmaid, faces the same fate as many other brunettes in John Elder (a pseudonym for producer Anthony Hinds) screenplays, always being rejected for the innocent blondes. It's interesting to note this is an about face from films of the '30s and '40s where brunettes were usually the wives or good girls and blondes such as Jean Harlow, Mae West and Barbara Stanwyck were the bad girls or *other* women.

Dracula (Christopher Lee) shows his contempt for Zena (Barbara Ewing) in *Dracula Has Risen from the Grave.*

The characterization of Zena falls into the typical lusty Hammer bad girl category. While she is serving drinks in the pub where she works, a reveler gleefully informs her "your dumplings are boiling over," leering down her low-cut blouse. Not missing a beat, she laughs and responds, "Your fly is open."

The barmaid, once seduced by Dracula, becomes a willing servant of the evil Count (Christopher Lee). When summoned to his presence, she smiles rapturously clutching her neck. He orders her to bring Maria (Veronica Carlson) to him, causing Zena to demand jealously why he wants the blonde and virtuous Maria when he has the more than willing Zena at his beck and call. Dracula, enraged, knocks her to the ground. It's a scene oft repeated in Elder-scripted films.

Poor Zena! It seems Dracula, like most men—alive or undead—doesn't mind amusing himself with the bad girl, but it's the good girl he wants to take home to the

105

castle. Zena gazes with anticipation at the mesmerizing Count as he reaches for her until she realizes his true intent of ridding himself of this little annoyance.

The Hound of the Baskervilles (1959): One of the better Hammer productions, based on a Conan Doyle story, filled with lush colors and a remarkably understated Christopher Lee performance as Henry Baskerville, reprises the women as victim or evil seductress theme. As the film opens, the evil Lord Baskerville (an ancestor of the Lee character), with disgustingly lecherous intent, has the nubile young daughter of a servant imprisoned. He tortures her father and then tells his drunken friends they may have their way with the terrified and defenseless girl. Meanwhile, she manages to escape through a window and flees across the dark and dangerous moor. Baskerville, infuriated, lets loose the hounds, and then follows her to a ruined Abbey where he viciously kills her (in the novel she dies of fright). Thus the curse is brought down upon him and his hapless descendants.

Many years later Dr. Watson (Andre Morell) accompanies the new heir, Henry Baskerville (Lee), to Baskerville Hall. Henry meets Cecile Stapleton (Marla Landi), the daughter of a neighbor (Ewen Solon). He is instantly attracted to her. Cecile is portrayed as a wildly seductive Gypsy type (the novel describes the character as Stapleton's sister, not daughter, and we are told she has a perfect figure, a proud and finely cut face, and most elegant—certainly not a type with enough sex appeal for Hammer). Henry falls in love with Cecile and, despite the warning of Holmes (Peter Cushing) and Watson, allows her to lead him to the ruined Abbey. When he tries to kiss her, she slaps him and screams she is also a Baskerville, and after he is dead she and her father will get what they deserve. Stapleton loosens a frightening hound (his own animal that has been terrorizing the community, thereby fanning the flames of the legend) on Henry. Holmes shoots the dog; the wounded creature subsequently turns and mauls Stapleton. Cecile, trying to escape, falls into the mire and drowns.

Screenwriter Peter Bryan evidently felt the need to spice up the Conan Doyle novel by changing parts of the novel. Cecile (whose name was Beryl in the book) was really the wife of the villainous Stapleton. She tries to warn Henry of the danger throughout the narrative. After refusing to lead Henry to his doom, she is beaten by her enraged husband. The novel ends with Stapleton drowning in the mire and Henry taking an ocean voyage to overcome his experiences. In the novel, as in the film, Henry doesn't get the girl. Of course, in both film and book, he no longer wants her.

The Curse of the Werewolf (1961): As werewolf-in-waiting Oliver Reed and friend visit a local watering hole, a voluptuous prostitute, plying her seductive and wanton wiles, entices the innocent Reed to her boudoir, causing Reed to turn into a werewolf. The tarnished woman is torn to shreds for her wicked, wicked ways.

Rasputin, The Mad Monk (1966): Barbara Shelley seemed to present a unique problem to Hammer. With her auburn hair and sultry voice, she did not fit the typical Hammer Barbie doll mold. In *Rasputin*, Shelley portrays Sonia, a lady in waiting (a double entendre if I ever heard one) to the Czarina of Russia. While attending an elegant court ball with her friend Vanessa (Suzan Farmer) and their brothers, Sonia declares she is bored and convinces the men to take them to a bar where there is a little more excitement. At the bar Sonia disdains Champagne and orders vodka, which she knocks back with a gasp, emitting an unladylike belch. She and the surrounding patrons find this hilarious and carry on uproariously, disturbing the egotistical Rasputin (Christopher Lee) as he performs a Russian folk dance. Approaching her menacingly he says, "You will come to me and apologize."

Cecile (Marla Landi) tries to escape from Holmes in *Hound of the Baskervilles*.

Intrigued by the mysteriously dangerous man, she returns to the bar the next day, inquiring of the owner the whereabouts of Rasputin. The barkeep warns her to be careful. "I'm perfectly capable of taking care of myself," she replies, very sure of herself. Sonia locates Rasputin and offers her apology. He commands her to kneel before him, which she unquestioningly does. Rasputin slaps her viciously (John Elder again) before discovering she is the Czarina's lady in waiting. Learning this, he abruptly abandons violence for seduction. Elder asks us to readily accept that this feisty independent woman would fall under this evil man's spell as he takes her into his arms and her clothes fall into a heap about her feet.

As in *The Evil of Frankenstein* where screenwriter Elder expects us to believe women would flock to seek the professional services of the sadistic woman-hating Doctor Frankenstein, implying he could charm the pants off all women (literally) as they wait patiently for his attention (obviously a case of the very misguided theory whereby women fantasize about being taken forcibly), Elder has Sonia reject her entire life to become the willing slave of Rasputin. Elder also follows his tried and true trend of rejection and jealously when Rasputin becomes bored with dark-haired Sonia and expresses his desire for the lovely, innocent blonde Vanessa. Sonia, in a mad fit of rage, attempts to kill the two-timing villain. Rasputin glares into her eyes, cold-bloodedly convincing her to destroy herself. Her brother finds her lying in a pool of blood, her wrists slashed. Sonia pays a high price for her sexual abandon.

Hard to believe the feisty Sonia (Barbara Shelley) would fall under Rasputin's (Christopher Lee) spell in *Rasputin, The Mad Monk*.

The Gorgon (1964): A young woman, madly in love with her artist boyfriend, poses topless for him. She begs to know when they can be wed. The man tells her they must wait until he makes a name for himself in the art world. Informing him she is pregnant, she watches in amazement as he rushes from the house to see her father to "take responsibility for his obligation." The girl, in a panic, runs after her lover, warning him her father will kill him. We see her scream and the next day her body is found, turned to stone. Hammer and *The Gorgon* strike down another tart.

Vampire Circus (1972): The young daughter of the Burgomeister, bored with the local village talent, falls under the spell of the darkly seductive circus animal tamer, Emil. She meets a gruesome fate in the un-fun house of mirrors.

She (1965): Ursula Andress is Ayesha, She Who Waits, also known as She Who Must Be Obeyed (a title I find sort of appealing). She is waiting for the return of her long-dead lover, a man she jealously killed ages ago

Bette Davis as *The Nanny* loses her sanity because of her promiscuity in her younger days.

delightfully tears up the scenery as she tries to kill her young charge, Joey. We later learn the Nanny had an illegitimate child which she abandoned to care for other peoples' children. One day, she is called to her daughter's side as the girl lay dying, the victim of a botched abortion. She rushes to her daughter, leaving her young charges alone. The adorable little girl, Suzy, accidentally falls into the bathtub and subsequently drowns. Joey is blamed by Nanny for pushing the child into the tub. Both deaths drive the Nanny over the edge as she terrorizes Joey and later kills his aunt. Promiscuity doomed the Nanny to madness and her illegitimate daughter to death.

In *Die! Die! My Darling!* Tallulah Bankhead portrays a Bible-thumping lunatic who speaks to her dead son, almost as a lover, and tortures his fiancée, hoping she will repent her evil ways (her new relationship with a man) and be able to join her son Steven in heaven. At one point in the film she calmly tells Patricia (Stefanie Powers) she has the best of both worlds: She was married to Steven and can still die a virgin. In the deranged mind of Bankhead's character, Patricia, once engaged to Steven, is now *his* for life and there is nothing better than being married and not having to have sex. While Powers is tortured for her emerging libido, she is one of the very few sexually active Hammer women who actually manage to remain alive at the end of the film.

when she had found him with another woman. Quite a reasonable action, one may think. However, it never seems to have occurred to her he'd do the same thing again, and again, and again. For her evil actions, She experiences the worst fate Hammer could envision for a woman—aging—as she dies in the eternal flame. The film does not generally receive critical praise but Andress looked divine in the elaborate costumes by Jackie Cummins, and Peter Cushing was at his slyest best portraying a drunken letch at the beginning of the film.

Repressed and forbidden sexuality play a part in both *The Nanny* (1965) and *Die! Die! My Darling!* (1965). Both films are dominated by their forceful stars Bette Davis and Tallulah Bankhead (women who had reigned supreme on the silver screen in their younger days and gleefully do so once more in these films). While Hammer is to be commended for providing parts for these shining stars, except for their over-the-top performances there is little reason to recommend either of these films. Bette Davis as a stereotypical spinster governess in *The Nanny*

Stephanie Powers and Tallulah Bankhead in *Die! Die! My Darling!*

HEDONISTS
"Strange love..." —Lust for a Vampire

Countess Dracula (1970): Old age, often considered by society (both male and female) a fate worse than death, is given the Hammer treatment in *Countess Dracula*. It's difficult to decide if this film is so offensive because it's incredibly sexist or merely because it is such a god-awful movie. Its one saving grace is the performance of Ingrid Pitt, who has a field day constantly switching between depravity and madness and youthful exuberance.

Hammer Films was entering its declining years, as can be witnessed by *Countess Dracula*. The film has none of the lavishness of the earlier Hammer productions. The dull colors of brown and gray grimly match the mood of the film. Except for the innocent daughter, Ilona (a young Lesley Anne Down), all the characters are portrayed as decadent and detestable. The costumer appears to have grabbed all the available period clothing available, for the costumes feature a bizarre clash of European cultures with a few exotic dancing girls thrown in for good measure.

As the film opens, Countess Elizabeth (Pitt) has just buried her not-so-dearly departed husband. As the Countess prepares to bathe, a serving girl cuts herself, accidentally splashing blood into the face of the Countess. Elizabeth discovers the blood has made her younger and orders her nurse, Julie, to bring her the girl. The next morning the sobbing mother of the girl asks where her daughter could be. "Try the whorehouse," she is roughly advised.

The now young and beautiful Countess dances joyfully around the room. She orders the Captain of the Guard, Dobi (Nigel Green), to arrange for highwaymen to kidnap her daughter, planning to impersonate the girl. She takes the identity of her daughter and proceeds to seduce a young friend of her husband's, Imre (Sandor Eles). Ingrid Pitt laughingly told me how during the seduction scene in a barn, Eles lost his fake mustache down her low-cut dress, and how she proceeded to remove the offending object from her person.

The Countess, in a wildly erotic embrace with Imre, sees herself in the mirror. An aged face stares back. She has lost her youth and beauty and runs screaming from the room. Dobi tells her she can't go on this way; each time the blood wears off she gets uglier. Captain Dobi has long been in love with Elizabeth, not the aberration she has become, but the real Elizabeth. This time, it's the woman, rather than the man, who abandons a dedicated partner for a younger lover. Unfortunately Dobi, like any man who woefully falls under the spell of a vixen, will take all forms of humiliation Elizabeth doles out, and like a pathetic puppy, is glad for any bone she happens to toss him.

Countess Dracula (Ingrid Pitt) goes to any length to stay young and beautiful in *Countess Dracula*.

He and Imre celebrate the upcoming marriage of Elizabeth (pretending to be Ilona) and Imre by getting sloshed at the local pub. Dobi asks, "Why should a man be a slave to one woman when he can have the pick of many?" He pays a barmaid to accompany them back to the castle. The Countess has once again lost her comeliness and hysterically storms about her room. Dobi drags her to see Imre with "the cheapest whore in town." The Countess forces Dobi to bring the girl to her. As she bathes in the blood of the hapless harlot, the gruesome bath has no effect. They find a book in the library on blood sacrifices (something every well-equipped library has on the shelf) and discover the blood must be from a virgin.

The next day in the village, the Captain visits a slave market. He spies a plain girl sitting with a goat. Asking the slaver if she has ever been with a man, the slaver replies, "Who'd want her?" He tells Dobi he can have the girl for free but the goat must be paid for. The girl is barely shown, treated as undeserving of the audience's pity because she is not as desirable as the other victims.

Countess Dracula, like most films, was merely reflecting the mores of society at the time the film was produced. The late 1960s and early 1970s ushered in the worship of youth and beauty. The massive acceptance and trust placed in the visual media is greatly responsible for the disdain felt by the general population toward the average person. Unfortunately, many women, as well as men, have become equally shallow regarding appearance, although this thinking process seems to have grown most prevalent among obsessed scream queen fans who haunt conventions seeking to have their photos taken with silicone-laden untalented actresses who may have appeared in some low-budget horror film travesty. When hearing a female horror film star is appearing at a convention, the question first asked is, "What's she look like now?" While pursuit of beautiful people is basically a harmless amusement, it is not so harmless when these people contemptuously ignore all others of the opposite sex who don't approach the standards they so incorrectly embrace.

The Countess embodies this hedonistic worship of youth and beauty. She knows nothing of love, only desiring the shallowness of attractiveness in herself and her young lover. Ordering Dobi to bring her another virgin, she later has her nurse search the castle to make sure her wishes have been obeyed. At the top of the stairs nurse Julie finds the virgin, the Countess' own daughter, Ilona. As Countess Elizabeth ages during her wedding ceremony, she rushes for her daughter, madly in pursuit of the pure blood of the virginal Ilona. Imre saves Ilona but is stabbed by the deranged Elizabeth.

Prehistoric Women (1968), brought to us by director Michael Carreras and screenwriter Henry Younger (Carreras' pen name), gives new meaning to the term *bad*, although many reviews refer to the film as intentional camp. Martine Beswicke is wasted in a role that casts her as the evil leader of a group of nasty brunettes with bad hair who keep a group of sweet, lovable blondes as slaves. Our hero (Michael Latimer) is captured by natives and, after being forced to view a wildly seductive watusi, touches the immense horn of a stone rhinoceros (Freud would have a field day with this film) and travels back in time. He helps release the beautiful slave girls and their men (who for some reason are all old, dirty and ugly). Kari (Beswicke) lashes Latimer with a whip but he grabs it, pulls her toward him, and proclaims, "You will never rule me." Later, after falling instantly in love with generic blonde slave girl Saria (Edina Ronay), he agrees to be Kari's love slave only to help the hapless blondes escape. The evil brunettes force the innocent blondes to grovel on the ground for food.

When one objects, Kari faces her in a classically schlocky cat fight. Thrusting her ample chest forward, Kari impales the girl on a wooden shaft. Later the vicious Kari sacrifices Saria to the devils. Decked out in flowers and placed on the back of a giant stone rhino, Saria waits to meet her fate. All the sweet young blondes bow to her in farewell, which allows the audience to get a good look down their bikini tops and at their scantily covered rear ends. Latimer leads a revolt of the scruffy men who discover the devils are nothing more than horny neighbors. Kari meets her fate on the rhinoceros horn, one

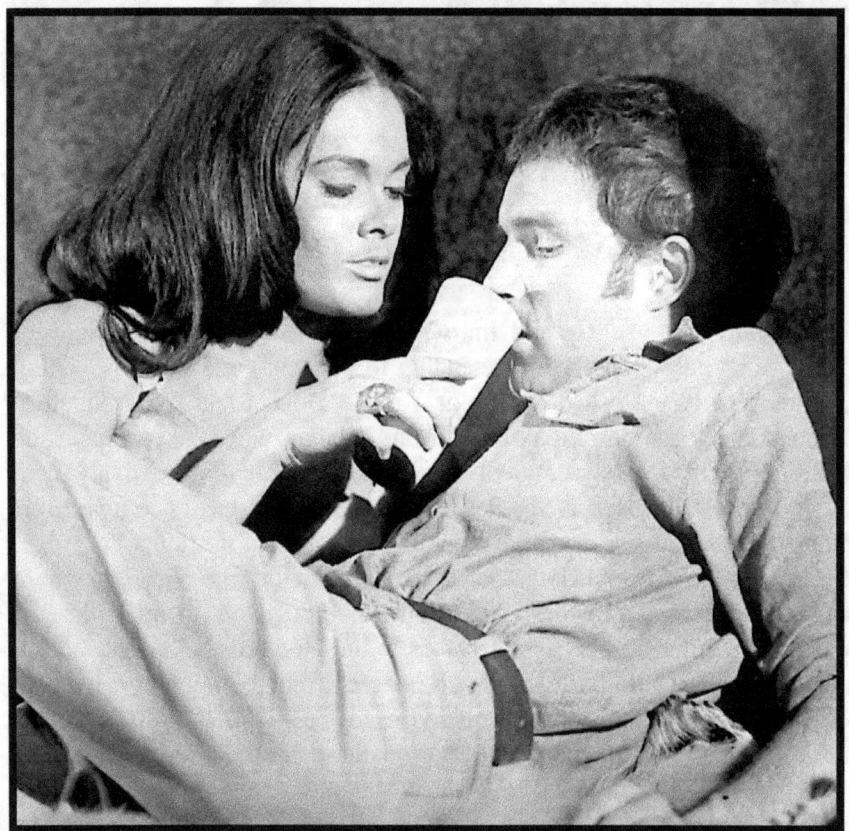

Kari (Martine Beswicke) tries to seduce Michael Latimer in *Prehistoric Women*.

of many chuckle-inspiring sexual innuendoes throughout the film.

Erotic, sensuous, arousing. These are all words used to describe the Karnstein series of *The Vampire Lovers*, *Lust for a Vampire*, and *Twins of Evil*. Perhaps pathetic, sexist, and boringly inept would be a better description.

The Vampire Lovers (1970) is perhaps the lesser of the three evils. Ingrid Pitt portrays Mircalla, the houseguest from Hell. She manages to move in with innocent Emma (Madeline Smith), who readily falls under the spell of the seductive vampire. After Emma becomes ill, Mircalla (really Carmilla) then seduces Emma's governess (a brunette) who falls victim to the Hammer curse of losing her lover to a younger, more beautiful woman, in this case Emma. Carmilla decides to take Emma away with her to her coffin when the governess (Kate O'Mara) jealously protests. Carmilla approaches the infatuated woman, who stares at her with quivering excitement, excitement that soon turns to terror as she is killed by the ferocious bite of the vampire.

Mircalla (Ingrid Pitt) seduces the innocent Emma (Madeline Smith) in *The Vampire Lovers*.

Little challenge is offered any cast members, especially the ladies who are only required to scream their lungs out, remove their clothes, and take seductive turns around the set.

Lust for a Vampire (1970) allowed even less character development than *Vampire Lovers*. The creatures inhabiting this Hammer universe are a pathetic group of whiners, perverts, shrews, and one annoyingly stupid male lead.

Mircalla, this time portrayed by wispish Yutte Stensgaard, is enrolled in an all-girls school. Our first glimpse of this citadel of higher education amply provides the viewer with an idea of where the rest of the film is headed. The front lawn of the school is filled with over-aged and over-endowed "schoolgirls" wearing flimsy gowns doing some form of ancient Greek dance.

Writer Richard LeStrange (Michael Johnson), desiring to inspire the young ladies, secures a position at the school. He immediately falls under the spell of nubile new student Mircalla. Meanwhile the fitness instructor, Janet Playfair (Suzanna Leigh), sets her sights on Richard.

Richard and his young lover manage to sneak some quality time together (these modern vampires seem quite at home in the daylight). He declares his undying devotion for her as they make love to the tacky pop tune, *Strange Love*. Heaven help us. This is possibly one of the dullest love scenes ever filmed.

Janet, who is what passes for a heroine in the film, is clueless about mysterious goings on at the school. She never realizes a police inspector sent to investigate the school is missing. Richard loses his lover when a beam falls on Mircalla at the finale, impaling her.

After viewing the above two films, even with aspirin, my pain threshold wasn't high enough to tolerate *Twins of Evil*. Hammer mirrored society's mores and were always careful to keep any of Dracula's attacks on male

victims glaringly asexual. But two beautiful women together, now that was a different story... double your pleasure, double your box-office.

Dr. Jekyll and Sister Hyde (1971) presented a promising premise of male/female duality that eventually fell into typical exploitation and mediocrity.

Jekyll (Ralph Bates), searching for an anti-virus, decides he will not live long enough to complete his research and vows to prolong his life for the good of humanity... no matter what the cost. The good doctor prolongs his life by injecting female hormones obtained from the bodies of prostitutes. However, as with all drugs there is one little side effect, although this side effect has a decidedly different bent—he turns into the bewitching Mrs. Hyde (Martine Beswicke), who introduces him/herself as Jekyll's sister.

The film begins with stylishly moody sets and beautifully detailed period costumes. Unfortunately, it soon deteriorates into a kill and kill again plot with Jekyll needing more hormones as Sister Hyde begins to gain dominance—perhaps a hidden statement about the emerging women's lib movement? In his voluptuous female form, Hyde is enthralled with her new body and sensuously rubs his/her hands over him/herself. One interesting, if kinky, subplot has Jekyll feeling the first stirrings of love for next door neighbor Susan (Susan Broderick), while Sister Hyde seduces Susan's brother, Howard (Lewis Flander). Much to her chagrin, Sister Hyde is usually frustrated in her amorous adventures, turning back into Jekyll at the most inconvenient times.

The film's screenwriter Brian Clemens missed a chance to show the trials and tribulations Sister Hyde faced acclimating herself to her new body (other than sexually) and the prejudice he would have faced as a woman in early London; instead Clemens went for pure schlock appeal. Beswicke had little to do other than caress her body and seduce men, which, I suppose, is not really bad work if you can get it.

Hammer's *Vampire Circus* (1972) introduces us to the selfishly hedonistic character portrayed by Adrienne Corri. As the film opens, the woman leads a young child into a castle, another tender morsel for the evil Count who resides there. He sucks the blood of the little girl as the woman ecstatically watches. In a nod to Universal, the villagers, led by the local schoolmaster, storm the castle. The naked, promiscuous woman turns out to be the wife of the straight-as-an-arrow schoolmaster. The villagers force her to watch as her undead lover is staked. She manages to escape, only to return many years later seeking her revenge.

The Gypsy woman (Corri is billed in the credits as such) is the mother from Hell as she abandons her husband and daughter early in the film for the sexual charms of the Count. She returns with the circus and her two incestuous vampire twins who attempt to lure her daughter (their half-sister) to her doom, using her blood to give life to their beloved Count. Corri is not a vampire, but she is used by them for chores they cannot accomplish, such as ripping the protective cross from her own daughter's neck. In the end, the woman cannot allow her daughter to be killed and meets her own death at the fangs of the vampires.

Vampire Circus also broke a long-standing cinema taboo by showing the murders of the little girl and later two young boys who are all bitten by the vampires. Strong stuff, even for the early 1970s.

Viewing this film today, one tends to ponder the differences between European and American audiences, both now and then. In the U.S., the nudity and sex were usually the scenes cut—these uncut versions are those most eagerly sought out by fans. However, in Britain, the sex and nudity is basically ho-hum stuff. It is the violence that is censored or given the "X" rating. I'm sure those are the uncut versions most desired by British fans. Which is more offensive or destructive? Why do American parents allow their children to watch unspeakable acts of violence but cringe when they see any form of nudity or sexuality? Almost 40 years later this controversy still rages with no clear answer in sight.

The Brides of Dracula (1960) introduces the ultimate Hammer hedonistic woman. She is not a decorative beauty like our other hedonists, but the mother who spawned an evil creature of the night. Martita Hunt turns in a chilling performance as a decadence-loving woman who encourages her equally degenerate son in his unending quest for thrills. This lifestyle backfires on her when the son is inflicted with the ultimate social disease... vampirism. She cannot bear to destroy her son, consequently chaining him in a suite of rooms, luring young girls to the chateau to feed his hunger. The Baroness meets her destruction when a silly girl (dinner for the Baron, played by David Peel) falls for this handsome man and releases him. He is not very happy with mother, viciously and incestuously turning her into a vampire.

Adrienne Corri as the Gypsy Woman is not a vampire but instead is the mother from Hell in *Vampire Circus*.

Van Helsing (Peter Cushing) discovers the remorseful Baroness at the chateau. She confesses she is to blame for the evil her son has done. Filled with regret, she tells him there is no escape for her, she must do her son's evil bidding for eternity. However, there is *one* escape—when the sun rises, Van Helsing drives a stake through her heart.

Hammer's hedonists, like their harlots, always met a bad end, even though some repented at the last minute: Carmilla, who really loved Richard in *Lust for a Vampire*, the mother in *Vampire Circus*, and the Baroness in *The Brides of Dracula*.

While the bad girls of Hammer were guaranteed a face-to-face meeting with the Grim Reaper, the good girls didn't have an easy time of it either.

Greta (Freda Jackson) finds the hedonistic Baroness Meinster (Martita Hunt) bitten by her vampire son, in *The Brides of Dracula*.

HEROINES
"...You've got a brain in that pretty little head of yours..." — *The Phantom of the Opera*

Good girls certainly had a rough go of it in Hammer films. The bad girls were always more fun and much more interesting characters, while the good girls were often used as an easy way to forward the plot, usually by doing something amazingly inane.

There could be two reasons for Hammer's treatment of women in its films: Either they were faithfully portraying women's lot in life during those times when women were merely an annoyance to society, facing a life of servitude whether to a father, husband or employer; or often they were proper ladies who were practically sold to prominent husbands, having no rights whatsoever. They could not have bank accounts, own property or vote. The current revival of interest in the novels of Jane Austen clearly illustrates this. Perhaps Hammer was ahead of its time. On the other hand, Hammer executives could have just been using their stable of Hammer beauties as surefire moneymakers.

Hazel Court is a lovely Elizabeth in *The Curse of Frankenstein* (1957). Unfortunately screenwriter Jimmy Sangster does not give her a great deal to work with storywise. Elizabeth elegantly floats from scene to scene in stunning gowns but has very little impact on the film.

At the beginning of the film, Victor Frankenstein and his aunt have just returned from his mother's funeral.

Paul (Robert Urquhart) tries to convince Elizabeth (Hazel Court) that she is in grave danger in *The Curse of Frankenstein*.

As he ushers her and the young Elizabeth (played by Court's real-life daughter) out, the aunt informs Victor her daughter is a good girl who will grow up to be a good wife, basically selling the young child.

Years later the grown Elizabeth, engaged for many years to Victor, arrives to await their wedding, naively believing Frankenstein loves her as he cavorts with his pretty maid. Frankenstein bemoans womanhood with "women, how cleverly they twist their words to meet their own ends."

Frankenstein's assistant, Paul (Robert Urquhart), tries to convince Elizabeth she is in grave danger but she, of course, refuses to listen.

The eve of the wedding she decides to investigate the lab, and hearing something on the roof, goes to see what it is. Not a very smart move, as the Monster grabs her. Frankenstein rushes to the roof, shoots at his creation, misses, and hits Elizabeth. (However, as obsessed as Frankenstein is, perhaps, he really *wanted* to hit the woman and save the Monster.)

Elizabeth recovers and Victor is imprisoned for killing the maid. Paul tells her Frankenstein is quite insane and there is no hope. Supposedly Paul will be the new benefactor of Elizabeth.

Eunice Gray as Margaret, heroine in *The Revenge of Frankenstein* (1958), as written by Jimmy Sangster, seems little more than an afterthought. She is a minister's daughter but shows up the first day in a beautiful red gown, something proper ladies would probably not do. Margaret does little else throughout the film other than free the Monster, setting up the climax.

Frankenstein (Peter Cushing) has set up a medical practice under the name Dr. Stein. His reception room is filled to overflowing with robust mothers and daughters, the script implying the patients have been seduced by Dr. Stein's charm. This is a little difficult to believe, since the man is as charming as a snake. A mother insists her voluptuous and obviously quite healthy daughter is so tired she is barely able to stand, and the mother urges Dr. Stein to listen to the girl's heart palpations. The young lady thrusts her lacily clad bodice toward the doctor. He tells the mother there is nothing he can do for the girl. The mother replies, "You are a man, doctor... you can do a great deal for her."

Frankenstein is amazed to find a minister's daughter, Margaret, has come to work in the charity ward he keeps. The mad doctor is using the hospital as a body parts shop for his new creation. A janitor informs Margaret the doctor cuts up his poor patients alive and one of his victims is at the top of the stairs. Margaret sneaks into the room where Carl, Frankenstein's latest work, is resting. He tells her the straps holding him are hurting him, and she compassionately loosens them, allowing him to escape and wreak havoc.

Katy Wild in *The Evil of Frankenstein* (1964), written by John Elder, has possibly one of the worst woman's roles in the entire Hammer catalog. In fact, Wild is listed in the credits as merely "Beggar Girl," portraying a homeless mute—no problem with learning her lines. Her main duty seems to be leading the Baron and his new assistant around, a device used to forward what little plot there is. Wild also does a little medieval housework as she sweeps up the castle and looks after the Monster. An evil hypnotist tries to rape her, but after tearing her blouse, decides he shouldn't be bothered with such trash.

When the girl sees the Monster in pain she gives him what she thinks is wine, hoping to ease his suffering. The Monster goes berserk, destroying himself, the lab, and Frankenstein (until the next film, that is).

The premise of a deformed woman who suddenly acquires beauty and the ability to take revenge on the men who have tormented her is an appealing thought. However, *Frankenstein Created Woman* (1966) never takes advantage of that idea and rapidly descends into just another man-controlling-woman tale.

Christina (Susan Denberg), daughter of the local innkeeper, has traumatically grown up with a damaged left side, her arm and leg virtually useless. A horrible scar mars her face. Christina tells her lover Hans (Robert Morris) her father was ashamed of her, never wanting to be seen with her when she was young.

Christina is constantly taunted by "three louts" with whom Hans has a fight. The louts stand outside her window and sing "fair Christina fair of face, you'll stay a virgin till you're dead," putting into crude words the supposed fate of unattractive woman, the same theory used in *Countess Dracula*. Hans wants to confront the troublemakers but Christina pulls him back saying desperately, "Love me, love me."

When the louts murder her father, Hans is accused and convicted. He is sentenced to die. Christina knows nothing of these events, having left for a doctor's appointment in another city. She returns by coach only to see Hans being guillotined. The distraught woman throws herself from a bridge. Her body is taken to Frankenstein (Peter Cushing) where he installs Hans' soul into her body. When the bandages are removed, the deformed dark-haired girl is now a stunningly healthy and beautiful blonde. If only it were that easy.

During the day, Christina is the picture of purity and innocence. However, once the sun goes down she turns into a seductress who leads the three louts to their deaths, a feat of which the audience heartily approves. Unfortunately, we are asked to believe Hans is controlling her and forcing her to commit these murders. After the final murder we hear Hans' voice saying, "You have done what you had to do, you may now rest." Christina, asking Frankenstein to forgive her, jumps into a raging river.

Poor Christina was not even allowed the satisfaction of destroying these killers herself, but had to be instructed by Hans. The tortured woman, seeking justice and revenge herself, would have made a much more interesting film.

Veronica Carlson turns in one of the best performances by a woman in any Hammer film as Anna

Anna (Veronica Carlson) and Karl (Simon Ward) are at the mercy of Dr. Frankenstein in *Frankenstein Must Be Destroyed*.

in *Frankenstein Must Be Destroyed* (1969), written by Bert Batt. Anna is a complex dual character—strong but also displaying moments of weakness.

Anna doesn't approve of her fiancé stealing drugs from the asylum where he works and selling them to help pay for Anna's mother's medical bills. However, they can think of no other way to get the money. Frankenstein (Peter Cushing) discovers what they are doing and blackmails them into helping him with his despicable plans. He treats Anna as a servant, often ordering her to bring him coffee.

The evil doctor kidnaps a scientist, removes his brain, and buries the body in Anna's backyard. Later he enters her bedroom, locks the door, and rapes her. Both Carlson and Cushing were upset about the filming and inclusion of this controversial scene. The scene was not necessary and made little sense. Frankenstein has always been basically an asexual character totally obsessed with his work. The scene was subsequently cut out of American prints, which in no way hurt the film.

Anna's stronger side is displayed when a water main breaks, exposing the grave of the victim. Sobbing, she drags the body through the spraying water and mud to hide it in the bushes before the public works men arrive. Later, the Monster approaches Anna for help; mistaking his intentions, she stabs him. He flees, and Frankenstein, discovering what Anna has done, murderers her.

Also turning in a nice performance as a resilient woman is Maxine Audley as Mrs. Brandt, the wife of the man Frankenstein has murdered. Although her husband has been in an asylum, she obviously still loves him and conducts a search for him when he disappears. Seeing Victor Frankenstein on the street, she follows him to Anna's home. Knocking on the door, she asks to see Frankenstein, who leads her to her husband who is heavily bandaged. Of course this is only her husband's brain in another man's body. When she returns the next day, they have disappeared. The creature returns to his home to explain to her, but she is unable to comprehend and reaches for a gun. He finally convinces the disbelieving woman and she goes to the police for help.

Screenwriter John Elder (Anthony Hinds), whose respect for women knows no bounds, could not have possibly thought of any further ways to traumatize poor Madeline Smith as Sarah in *Frankenstein and the Monster from Hell* (1974). She is an inmate in a mental institution, forced to visit the frightening patients, reluctantly performs surgery, is raped by her father, becomes the love object of a huge Monster, and is unable to speak.

The beatific Sarah is fondly called Angel by the inmates of the asylum. She cannot speak due to an earlier traumatic experience. When Frankenstein's newest assistant, Simon (Shane Briant), comments on Frankenstein's crude surgery, the Baron explains Sarah performed the operation since his hands were destroyed in a fire. He goes on to comment there is no physical reason Sarah cannot speak... her father had attempted to rape her; after this experience she never spoke again. Her father is the depraved head of the asylum. Frankenstein intends to mate Sarah with his new creation, a hulking Neanderthal. The Monster eventually kills Sarah's

father and is then torn to pieces by the inmates, who think that he means to do harm to their "angel." At the film's conclusion, Frankenstein is left hopelessly insane, muttering to himself and, hopefully, Sarah and Simon will live happily ever after.

Yvonne Furneaux as Isobel in *The Mummy* (1959), as written by Jimmy Sangster (who seemed to have a difficult time creating realistic women characters), contributes nothing more to the film than window dressing.

The Mummy is brought to England to avenge the desecration of his love's tomb and only halts his attack on John Banning (Peter Cushing) when the Mummy discovers that Banning's wife Isobel (Furneaux) resembles the princess of the tomb, his long lost love.

The Mummy's Shroud (1967) has two very interesting women's roles, probably due to the fact John Gilling both wrote and directed. Elizabeth Sellars portrays Barbara Preston, married to the vulgar and abrasive man who financed an archeological expedition. She is much like a typical Hitchcock heroine: beautiful, blonde and cold. Her attitude of quiet amusement as her husband frets over the deaths of members of the party who entered the tomb is chilling. Of course, he's not worried about saving anyone else's skin except his own, not even his son's. Maggie Kimberley is Claire (another cool blonde), a member of the expedition in love with Preston's son. Claire is the one who figures out the cause of the mysterious deaths and goes to the museum to ask the Mummy's forgiveness for desecrating his tomb.

Hammer's science fiction films, often overshadowed by the horror entries, are some of the best films Hammer ever made, and while their female characters are not given a great deal of screen time, they are all women who, rather than wringing their hands, take action, whether right or wrong.

Barbara Payton turns in a fine performance in *Four-Sided Triangle* (1953), directed and co-written by Terence Fisher. Lena (Payton) at first is described as hard and cynical, having failed at everything she has ever attempted. However, after she becomes assistant and mother-hen to her two brilliant childhood chums: "She became the most wonderful thing in the world, a woman who is also a companion and comrade to her men-folk."

The film is still original, even when viewed today, although the story is often talky and extremely slow-paced, with the look of a teleplay.

Two brilliant boyhood friends conduct experiments with a duplicating machine. Finally they succeed.

Claire (Maggie Kimberly) figures out the cause of the mysterious deaths in *The Mummy's Shroud*.

Robin (John Van Eyssen) and Lena announce they are to be married. Bill (Stephen Murray), the other friend, is devastated; he too is deeply in love with Lena. Bill perfects the machine so it can duplicate living beings, and persuades Lena to allow him to duplicate her, a copy of her for his very own. Lena, madly in love with Robin, still is a good friend to Bill and, hoping to ease his pain, agrees to his bizarre request.

The copy is made—an exact duplicate. Bill calls her Helen and they go away on holiday. At first everything is wonderful, but soon Helen is depressed and tries to commit suicide. What Bill and Lena did not realize is, Helen is exactly like Lena, even in her love for Robin. Bill begs Lena to help him erase Helen's memory. Before the equipment is placed around her head she tearfully whispers, "good-bye Robin." The lab catches fire—Bill and his duplicate do not survive the flames.

The Creeping Unknown (aka *The Quatermass Xperiment*, 1956) is basically a two man and one monster show. Rather than women being ignored, the lack of their presence seems more an indication of the time when women weren't involved in scientific work. At least we are spared the picture of the female scientist pouring coffee for the men doing the important work. The only woman, Margia Dean as Judith Carroon, portrays the

Barbara Judd (Barbara Shelley) is deeply affected by the aliens in *Five Million Years to Earth*.

wife of an astronaut who is slowly turning into a cosmic blob. Judith, fearing Quatermass's intentions toward her husband, hires a private investigator to help her kidnap him from the hospital. Carroon sucks the life from the P.I, and joins Judith outside where she puts him in the car. As she is driving she notices his hand, which is turning into an oozing plant-like mass. Judith screams, frightening Carroon away. Quatermass, hearing the news, says, "Stupid idiot trying to take the whole thing into her hands." She is found behind the wheel of the car staring at nothing. Once again we see the woman only used as a device to free the monster, but at least she took *some* action rather than wringing her hands..

Barbara Shelley turns in another fine performance for Hammer, this time in the third Quatermass entry, *Five Million Years to Earth* (aka *Quatermass and the Pit*, 1967). She portrays Barbara Judd, the assistant to Dr. Rooney. Rooney is the archaeologist investigating skeletons found while digging a new subway.

Barbara tramps through muck and mire with the men and never flinches when working with or photographing the grisly finds. She also helps Quatermass with his investigation of ghostly sightings, providing him with material and information. When presenting their information to the Minister of Defense, the man implies Barbara is a hysterical woman with a vivid imagination. Eventually, Barbara, like most residents of London, is affected by the alien signal.

Maureen Connell, like Barbara Shelley, plays a strong woman in Val Guest's *The Abominable Snowman* (1957). As Helen Rollason she helps her husband, John (Peter Cushing), collect botanical samples in a remote Himalayan village. Never complaining about the harsh conditions, she only protests when she learns her husband, recovering from a climbing injury, is planning to search for the Yeti.

Helen sees the guide return without her husband's party and goes to the High Lhama (Arnold Marle) for help. He tells her no one can help the group. She decides to go after them herself and arranges for a group to accompany her. When they camp for the night she awakens when she hears a strange cry. Running into the raging blizzard, she finds John propped against a slope.

Director John Gilling consistently provided some of the better women's roles in his films for Hammer.

The Reptile (1966), with its influences of a mysterious Eastern religion and secretive family, reminds one of a classic Sherlock Holmes story. Anthony Hinds (writing as John Elder) presents Valerie Spalding (Jennifer Daniel) as a courageous and sensible woman, although her compassionate side is also shown.

Harry Spalding (Ray Barrett) and his new wife Valerie have just moved to a cottage left to them by Harry's brother, who has died under mysterious circumstances. They are warned away by the local barkeep (Michael Ripper in an excellent performance). Harry tells Valerie they can leave but Valerie, showing she is not afraid, replies, "It's our home and we're staying."

One dark night a strange man taps at their window, startling the young couple. His face is black and swollen. Harry brings him inside while Valerie, displaying more backbone than other Hammer heroines, neither faints nor screams. She sets about seeing to the comfort of the dying man.

The couple are invited to dinner at the home of their mysterious neighbor, Dr. Franklyn. They are puzzled when the daughter Anna (Jacqueline Pearce) is not at supper; she is being punished, although the girl is allowed to join the party after dinner. She enters wearing a brilliant red sari and begins to play a sitar. Anna begins to play more intently, becoming more defiant with each pounding note. Her father, agitated, suddenly smashes the instrument.

Later Harry finds a note from Anna begging for help. He goes to the house and is attacked by a snake-like creature. Staggering home, he tells Valerie to get a knife and cut him on the neck. She quickly complies. Valerie makes Harry as comfortable as possible and then sets out across the moors for help. Once again the story shows the strength of this woman, making her one of the most realistic of Hammer's female characters. Later she finds the note and decides to go to the house to rescue the girl. A gutsy but not well thought out move. She enters through a window and follows Dr. Franklyn to the basement, where he struggles with a servant overturning a lamp, which causes a fire. Franklyn picks up a sword to kill the snake woman, his daughter Anna, when Valerie screams. Chasing her into the library, he locks them in.

Smoke begins coming under the door but Franklyn refuses to allow Valerie to leave. As Anna is about to attack Valerie, Tom (Ripper) breaks the window, causing Anna to die from the cold air. Harry leads Valerie outside as the house and its cursed family is engulfed in flames.

The character of Dr. Franklyn could be compared to the Baroness in *The Brides of Dracula* in his quest to go to any length to protect the monster his child has become. A little gem from Hammer.

Gilling also brought us *The Plague of the Zombies* (1966) written by Peter Bryan. The women, the focus of the film, are little more than attractive victims, kidnapped and turned into zombies by a decadent member of the aristocracy who is using the zombies as cheap and dispensable laborers for his mines. The film never explains why the two small women were chosen as victims rather than strong young men, other than as a Satanic sacrifice.

Jacqueline Pearce as Alice has little more to do than wander around pale and sickly. She is married to the local doctor, who writes to Sir James Forbes (Andre Morell) for help in combating a strange plague affecting the village. Forbes' daughter, Sylvia (Diane Clare), a friend of Alice, accompanies him. Sylvia realizes something is wrong and follows Alice. She loses sight of her and is surrounded by a group of rich thugs (another recurring theme in Hammer films), who take her to the home of Squire Hamilton (John Carson). They select cards, the winner to have Sylvia. (Hammer, to their credit, made rape a contemptible and vile act. Rapists were invariably, and horribly, punished.) Hamilton orders them to leave

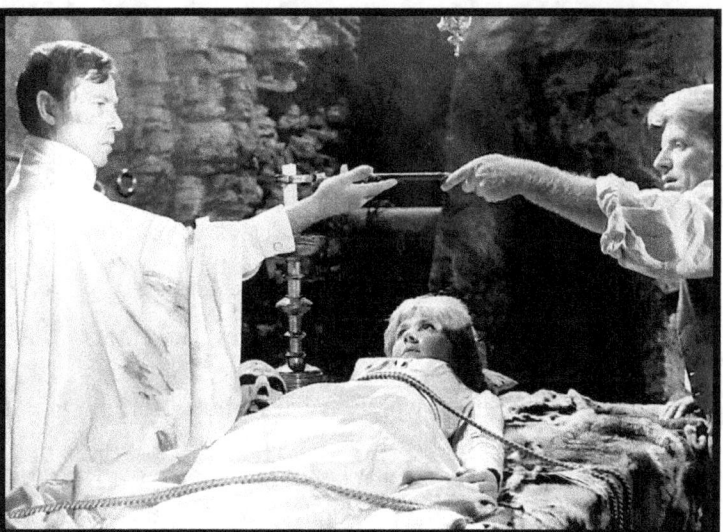

Sylvia (Diane Clare) is in a bind in *The Plague of the Zombies*.

119

Barbara Shelley as Carla in *The Gorgon*

and she indignantly requests he escort her home. He refuses. On the way back she runs into a zombie, who drops the dead Alice at her feet.

Hamilton psychically calls Sylvia to him during a Voodoo ceremony, forcing her to walk to an abandoned mine where a zombie picks her up and carries her to a sacrificial altar. She is saved by her father.

Gilling also contributed the screenplay to *The Gorgon,* which was directed by Terence Fisher. Barbara Shelley stars as Carla, a woman torn between her love of Paul, her duty to Dr. Namaroff, and her fear of the Gorgon. She is also haunted by an unknown terror.

The brother of a murdered artist is summoned by his father to help find answers to his brother's mysterious death. Carla, Dr. Namaroff's (Peter Cushing) assistant, is the only person to show any compassion to the murdered man's father at the inquest. The father is lured out of the villa by strange singing. He manages to write a letter to his son Paul (Richard Pasco) before completely turning to stone. Carla warns Paul the Gorgon is real and urges him to leave, or he'll be found like all the others.

Paul, in love with Carla, wants to take her away but she insists she cannot leave although she is unable to give him a reason for this decision. Professor Meister (Christopher Lee) arrives to help Paul solve this mystery, immediately suspecting Carla.

The lovers meet at an abandoned castle. Paul enters and spies a regal Carla sitting on a throne. She tells him she will leave town with him but it must be right away. This time Paul refuses to leave; he must find out the cause of the strange fate that befell his family. Carla sadly tells him later will be too late. We still do not know if Carla is aware she is possessed.

Paul and Namaroff battle under a full moon as the Gorgon looks on. Namaroff tries to cut off her head but instead gazes upon the aberration and is turned to stone. Paul sees her reflection in the mirror. Turning toward the creature, he watches in horror as Meister picks up a sword and cuts off her head. Paul slowly turns to stone as the head of the Gorgon turns into Carla.

The Gorgon definitely follows a different path than other Hammer offerings. Even in their grimmest films, the heroes usually survived; however, in *The Gorgon*, not only do our two lovers die, we witness the expiration of almost the entire cast!

Shelley also starred in *The Shadow of the Cat* (1961) as a young woman trying to locate her missing aunt. The aunt had been done in by her money-grubbing husband (Andre Morell) and her not-so-dedicated servants. Shelley is constantly being told by the men of the family they will take care of her—they plan on "taking care of her" all right—in the most nefarious sense of the phrase. A great little mystery directed by John Gilling and written by noted mystery writer George Baxt. *The Shadow of the Cat* is a delight and well worth tracking down.

The Viking Queen (1967) is a rarely seen Hammer film, and it hopefully will remain that way. Romans (with British accents) cruelly rule the downtrodden British villagers who are led by "The Viking Queen" (Carita, who speaks with an European accent). Hammer went for a bit of the S&M thing as the beautiful queen is publicly flogged, her dress torn off as she is beaten by the evil Roman leader, who takes advantage of the

Carita as *The Viking Queen*

fact that the good Roman leader The Viking Queen loves is off fighting Druids. The queen leads an army against the Romans, looking stunning in her designer armor. Meeting her lover on the battlefield, she kills herself rather than go to Rome for trial. Carita probably considered suicide during the first 20 minutes of filming this bomb.

The Curse of the Werewolf (1961) and screenwriter John Elder present four pitiful female characters used mercilessly to forward the story. One woman gives birth to the cursed child, two women love him (keeping the wolf at bay), and one's promiscuity turns him into a raging animal. Yvonne Romain portrays a jailkeeper's daughter, unable to speak, who is viciously raped by a beggar she had befriended. She is found in the woods and taken in by a kindly man, Alfredo (Clifford Evans). He and his servant Teresa (Hira Talfrey) care for the poor girl. A child is born on Christmas day—Leon, but the mother does not survive. Teresa loves the boy like a mother, even though she fears he is cursed, as indeed he is. His lycanthropy is kept in check by the love of Alfredo and Teresa. When he grows to manhood he leaves his loving family for a job at a winery. Leon (Oliver Reed) falls in love with the owner's daughter, Cristina (Catherine Feller). However, she cannot marry Leon because her father has arranged a marriage for her. She does not love this other man but must obey the wishes of her father. This drives Leon to a local bar and the arms of a lady of the evening. A night of drinking and debauchery causes him to turn into the werewolf, killing the woman he had picked up. When he returns, Cristina stays with him all night, nursing him. When he awakens he finds their love for each other has kept the curse at bay. She agrees to go away with him, but before she returns, he is arrested. Leon begs Cristina be allowed to stay with him, but the priest and Alfredo take her away. Cristina and Teresa watch in horror as Leon is chased over the rooftops by a mob of villagers trying to destroy him. Alfredo climbs a tower and shoots his beloved son as Cristina and Teresa stand in the street, alone with their grief. Another unhappy ending. As in *The Gorgon*, true love does not always conquer all.

The Devil's Bride (1968) looked wonderfully promising with a script by the great Richard Matheson, based on a novel by Dennis Wheatley, and directed by Terence Fisher. It was promising until the point in the film where the foursome fighting the evil Mocata (Charles Gray) are stupid enough to leave the couple's young daughter alone in her room while they are protected by a magical circle. Surprise! The daughter is kidnapped by the Devil worshipers. It is impossible to believe any mother would leave her child in such danger, a fact that basically destroys the validity of the entire film.

Vampires, and Dracula in particular, were given sex appeal by Hammer Studios who felt (correctly) women would not be able to resist a tall, dark stranger. They turned the heretofore fairly dull vampire's bite into a "vampire's kiss" filled with sexual intensity and innuendo. Our heroines were bewitched by the seductive vampire but usually managed to survive the experience.

Sweet and innocent Lucy (Carol Marsh) and happily married Mina (Melissa Stribling) succumb to the deadly charms of Dracula (Christopher Lee) in *Horror of Dracula* (1958), often cited as Hammer's best film.

Dracula desires Lucy for his new bride since her fiancé, Jonathan Harker, has recently destroyed his old one. Lucy, lying in bed growing weaker with each vampire's kiss, resembles the innocent Judy Garland in *The Wizard of Oz*. Her lovely dark hair is in braids and she wears a pale blue nightgown, her face a vision of purity. When her brother Arthur (Michael Gough) and sister-in-law Mina leave, Lucy rises, locks the door, opens the window, and removes the protective cross from around her neck. She breathes heavily as Dracula

Van Helsing (Cushing) tries to save Lucy's (Carol Marsh) soul in *Horror of Dracula*.

121

enters the room. Van Helsing (Peter Cushing) instructs the family to place garlic flowers in the room and keep the windows locked. Lucy begs a servant, Gerta, to take the flowers away for she cannot breathe. The next morning Lucy is dead.

Later, Gerta's little daughter, Tania, tells them she has seen Lucy in the woods. That night Lucy calls Tania to her, telling the child she is taking her someplace quiet to play. Arthur sees her leading the little girl to the cemetery. Lucy spies Arthur and says, "Come, let me kiss you," as the horrified Arthur watches his sister incestuously advance toward him. Van Helsing thrusts a cross in front of the fledgling vampire, burning the shape into her forehead. Lucy screams and runs back to her crypt. Van Helsing tenderly places his coat and a rosary around the little girl before entering the crypt and driving a stake into Lucy's heart. He forces Arthur to gaze upon Lucy; she has been released from the curse of the undead and is once again the innocent, beautiful girl she was before Dracula "spoiled" her.

Dracula, still needing a bride, lures Mina to a meeting. She enters an undertaker's shop thinking she is to meet Arthur. A coffin lid slowly moves aside.

The next morning she comes in holding a cloak tightly about her neck. Mina listens intently as Arthur and Van Helsing plot Dracula's demise. Her husband forces her to take a crucifix for protection. She gingerly takes it, screams, and faints. The cross leaves a burn mark in her palm.

Arthur and Van Helsing keep watch outside the house, convinced Dracula will come for Mina. She opens the bedroom door knowing Dracula will be there. He is standing at the bottom of the stairs. She steps back into the bedroom, her lips quivering. Dracula grasps her face and kisses her before nibbling on her neck. While Arthur and Van Helsing search for his coffin, Dracula carries Mina to his castle. He digs a grave, unceremoniously dumps her into it, and begins covering her with soil. Val Helsing eventually destroys the Count—as he dies the cross disappears from Mina's hand, which Arthur tenderly picks up and kisses.

Dracula, Prince of Darkness (1966) treats us to one of Barbara Shelley's best performances as Helen, a woman who appears forbidding and repressed, but loses her inhibitions when seduced by Dracula, echoing the "she only needs a good man" routine.

Two couples on a sightseeing trip are forced to stay in a strange castle when their coachman abandons them. The younger couple, Charles (Francis Matthews) and Diana (Suzan Farmer), appear happy and adventurous while the older brother is dull and stodgy. His wife Helen is stern and frightened, appearing quite unreasonable. Helen's personality, like her nightgown, is basically dull gray.

That evening her husband hears a noise and investigates. He is hung above the coffin of Dracula, his throat slashed. The blood pours into the coffin and once again Dracula rises from his grave. A servant goes to Helen's room, telling her something has happened to her husband. That's really an understatement. Ignoring her fear, she rushes downstairs. The stunned woman stares in horror at her husband's body as Dracula approaches her. Even by today's standards, this is a horrifying scene.

Helen, her long hair hanging free and nightgown flowing about her, approaches her sister-in-law. Diana demands to know where Charles is. "You don't need Charles now," Helen answers (a brief hint of the Hammer lesbian vampire films in the studio's future). The young couple manage to escape and are taken to a monastery by a kindly priest. Dracula, of course, is merely toying with Helen; he really desires Diana, the lovely young blonde. The priests find Helen hiding in a barn

The repressed Helen turns into a bold seductress when seduced by Dracula in *Dracula, Prince of Darkness*.

and take her to the monastery, where a stake is viciously driven into her heart. Once staked, Helen is at peace, a beautiful corpse, a common thread running through the Hammer vampire series.

Dracula kidnaps Diana and flees to his castle (another recurring theme). She is locked in Helen's coffin, managing to escape when the wildly careening carriage crashes, causing Dracula's coffin to slide across the ice. Charles, attempting to stake the vampire, waits too long and, as the sun sinks below the horizon, Dracula rises and attacks him. Diana, displaying remarkable backbone for a Hammer character, grabs a rifle from the priest, fires a shot, causing water to run near the feet of the struggling men. The priest takes the rifle back, shooting a circle into the ice. The running water surrounds Dracula, eventually forcing him into the water.

Marianne (Yvonne Monlaur) is threatened by her roommate (Andree Melly) in *Brides of Dracula*.

The Kiss of the Vampire (1963) critically receives high marks for originality. However, the film only progresses slightly faster than a snail's pace. A battle between good and evil is waged for the soul of Marianne as the evil Ravna tries to turn her into a vampire while her husband and a drunken professor use white magic to combat Ravna's power.

A young honeymoon couple are forced by a series of circumstances to stay at a remote village inn. The only other guest is an alcoholic professor. The couple is invited to dine at the mansion of Dr. Ravna (Noel Willman). Ravna is quite taken with Marianne (Jennifer Daniel) and invites the couple to a masked ball. At the ball Marianne is drugged and lured to a room where she is locked in with the evil doctor. He gains control of the young woman by gazing into her eyes. Marianne walks toward the bed and lies down, as Ravna approaches and kisses her. Meanwhile, her husband Gerald (Edward De Souza) is also drugged. A group of white-robed zealots gather as Ravna presents their newest member, Marianne.

Gerald returns to the inn and secures the help of the drunken professor (Clifford Evans). He explains Ravna is the leader of a decadent cult of vampires. In *The Kiss of the Vampire*, as in *The Brides of Dracula*, vampirism is considered a result of a hedonistic lifestyle.

Gerald goes to the chateau, finds Ravna and Marianne, only to have her gaze with rapture at Ravna, declaring her undying love for the vampire. When ordered to prove it she crosses the room to her husband and spits in his face. Gerald manages to escape with Marianne, and with the help of the professor, defeats the vampire cult.

Another Marianne is desired by a vampire in *The Brides of Dracula* (1960). This time Marianne is a young French student teacher traveling to a girls' school. She is left at a remote inn by her coachman. The Baroness Meinster (Martita Hunt) invites her to dinner.

Marianne is perhaps the most annoying female character Hammer ever created. While hired to teach French and deportment, she comes across as bitchy, spoiled and basically stupid. Leaning out the coach window, she rudely yells at the coachman for traveling too fast; she ignores the warning of her hostess regarding the Baron, snoops around the chateau, allows herself to fall under the spell of the evil Baron (David Peel), sets him free, and after seeing his effect on the mad servant and realizing the Baron has killed his mother, she still agrees to marry him! Van Helsing also seems a little smitten by this obtuse creature and manages to rescue her and destroy the Baron.

Maria (Veronica Carlson) is saved from Dracula (Christopher Lee) by the Monsignor (Rupert Davies) in *Dracula Has Risen from the Grave.*

Dracula Has Risen from the Grave (1968) stars Veronica Carlson as Maria, the beautiful niece of a Monsignor. Maria does not quite fit the typical Hammer good-girl mold, showing a welcome rebelliousness toward her ultra-religious family. Maria disobeys her mother and uncle when they command her to stop seeing Paul, her true love. She also seems quite at home in the pub where Paul works, but Maria exudes goodness and purity and to hammer that point home, she is mostly clad in white throughout the film.

The doors of Dracula's castle have been locked by a huge cross placed there by the Monsignor (Rupert Davies). Dracula (Christopher Lee) seeks his revenge on the priest by seducing his innocent niece Maria.

After Maria is ordered by her family to no longer see her boyfriend Paul, he gets roaring drunk and is comforted by barmaid Zena, who leads him upstairs and begins to unbutton his pants. Maria, having climbed out her window and traveled over the rooftops to Paul's room, demands to know what is going on, grabbing Zena's hand away from Paul.

Maria tucks blankets around the partially undressed man and kisses him; we see him caress her back. She leaves him around sunrise. Climbing in through her bedroom window she falls onto the bed and hugs her doll, a sign of her childlike innocence, although directly in contrast to the pervious scene.

That night, Maria stands at the window of her bedroom, pulling her robe closer. She covers her breasts, taking a step backward when Dracula appears. Staring into his eyes she lies back on the bed and pulls the white robe open. The vampire bends toward her, kissing her face and eyes as she raises her neck, willingly. We see her hand clutch the doll and release it in ecstasy. The doll falls to the floor, a symbol of Maria's lost innocence.

The next evening Maria rises and opens the window. She eagerly pulls her nightgown open, awaiting the deadly kiss of her dark lover. Her undead romantic tryst is interrupted by the Monsignor, who bursts into the room. Later, Dracula, after evading Paul, meets Maria on the rooftop, commenting, "Now my revenge is complete."

Maria, in her bare feet and white nightgown, rides by Dracula's side in the carriage as he races toward his castle. She follows him through the forest, a frail white ghost trailing in the wake of this dark menace. When they reach the top of the mountain, he throws her to the ground, demanding she remove the huge cross barring his way. She obeys, throwing the cross over the cliff. As Paul and Dracula struggle, the vampire falls over the cliff directly onto the cross.

The Phantom of the Opera (1962), written by John Elder from a story by Gaston Leroux, and directed by Terence Fisher, is so different from most Hammer entries, it is actually hard to believe it came from the same studio. It's a pity the film was not a financial success; its failure convinced Hammer of the fruitlessness of trying new ideas. Bernard Robinson, possibly the most important person ever employed by Hammer, outdid himself with his art direction for this film.

Heather Sears, as the ingenue opera star Christine Charles, does a fine job as the heroine. Talented, compassionate, independent and unafraid, she faces the frightening perils of the opera house with strength and courage.

When the opera's temperamental diva is frightened away, Christine auditions for the lead in *St. Joan*. Producer Harry Hunter (Edward De Souze, whose role is much more defined than other Hammer second-banana roles) is immediately charmed and hires her.

As Christine visits the dressing room, a deep voice tells her he will teach her to sing, but "only for me."

Lord Ambrose D'Arcy (Michael Gough in a wonderfully sleazy performance), the supposed composer of the opera, is also charmed by Christine and offers to give her "private lessons." He takes his new star to dinner, becomes quite drunk, and insists she accompany him to his home. "You're a delicious little thing. I'm going to enjoy teaching you." It's obvious Christine knows what this notorious letch plans on teaching her, but is not sure how to gracefully remove herself from his clutches and still keep her new job.

Spying Hunter entering the restaurant, she begs him to attend the "lesson" with her, pleading with her eyes; he understands her urgency. Hunter, always happy to annoy the pompous D'Arcy, readily agrees.

D'Arcy changes his mind and orders Christine to take a cab home. Harry, the perfect gentleman, escorts her home and during their carriage ride she tells him of the mysterious voice overheard in the dressing room, while he speaks of the mischief that has also occurred at the home of the opera. They return to the opera house and enter the dressing room. The lights slowly dim and a deep voice warns Hunter to go away, to leave Christine behind. Of course, Hunter refuses.

The next day D'Arcy sends a note to Christine, dismissing her and later fires Hunter.

Hunter goes to see Christine, explaining he too has been sacked and they are going to celebrate. While she is getting ready, her landlady tells Hunter of a boarder, Professor Petrie, who wrote beautiful music but was tragically killed in a fire. Hunter and Christine investigate, managing to fall in love along the way. Late that night Christine returns to her room, her heart full of joy. However, her happiness is short lived; she is kidnapped and taken to the underground lair of the Phantom.

The Phantom (Herbert Lom) beckons her closer. "I am going to teach you to sing, Christine. You will be the greatest singer the world has ever known." He rehearses her unmercifully, slapping her when she cries she cannot go on (remember John Elder adapted this).

Harry discovers Christine is missing and follows a trail through the sewers to the hidden lair. Entering the cavern, he tells the Phantom he knows the whole story. The Phantom, really Professor Petrie, begs Christine to allow him to teach her to sing. She does not have

Christine (Heather Sears) debuts as Joan of Arc thanks to the Phantom in *The Phantom of the Opera*.

to say a word. Her compassionate expression tells the Phantom, as well as the audience, her answer.

She debuts as Joan of Arc to a standing ovation, glancing with appreciation to the Phantom, watching from a box. He notices a piece of equipment falling toward Christine and, swinging onto the stage, he pushes her aside. The Phantom dies for her. While the makeup of the Phantom is perhaps the film's weakest link, the story and performances more than compensate for that complaint..

The following films do not readily fall into any specific categories, although some comparisons are immediately evident.

Jimmy Sangster seemed to have a difficult time creating roles for women, often downplaying their parts in the story. This is clearly evident in *The Curse of Frankenstein*, *The Revenge of Frankenstein*, and most notably in *The Mummy*. However, women are the central focus of *Horror of Dracula* and *The Brides of*

Helen (Maureen Connell) discovers her husband (Peter Cushing) in *The Abominable Snowman*.

Dracula. Sangster, along with co-writers Peter Bryan and Edward Percy, rates high marks for creating two of the best female character parts Hammer would ever see: the Baroness Meinster and Greta (the mad servant) in *The Brides of Dracula*. Kudos must also be given to actresses Martita Hunt as the Baroness and Freda Jackson as Greta. Director Terence Fisher equally deserves praise for the beautiful look of the scenes with Mina and especially Lucy in *Horror of Dracula*.

Writer Nigel Kneale and writer/director Val Guest had little use for any women in *The Creeping Unknown* and *Enemy from Space*. However, they then gave us two important woman's roles in their following films. Although the role of Helen Rollason is small in *The Abominable Snowman*, it is nevertheless quite an important part of the film. Barbara Judd in *Five Million Years to Earth* is an integral part of the story, and Barbara Shelley does the role proud.

Writer/director John Gilling's female characters tended to be strong and compassionate. Claire (Maggie Kimberly) in *The Mummy's Shroud* investigates the mysterious deaths plaguing the camp, while John Elder's script and Gilling's direction has Valerie administering to her husband and then trying to rescue poor Anna in *The Reptile*. Even though, like most Hammer heroines, she needed to be rescued in the end, her character was more assertive than most. Carla in *The Gorgon* is a sympathetic heroine/villainess who is terrified but does not know why, seeming to realize subconsciously she is the cause of the terror in the village. Even Sylvia in *Plague of the Zombies* (written by Peter Bryan) is adventurous and follows Alice into the forest, although Sylvia is the weakest character in the Gilling series.

Michael Carreras and Tudor Gates seemed to be merely exploiting the emerging sexual freedom of the time in their screenplays for *One Million Years B.C.*, *Prehistoric Women*, *The Vampire Lovers*, *Lust for a Vampire*, and *Twins of Evil*, although I must admit they are the films that still seem to capture fans' imaginations as well as their libidos.

Other writers occasionally contributed scripts to Hammer, never quite falling into any generalizations. Brian Clemens' *Dr. Jekyll and Sister Hyde*; Jeremy Paul's *Countess Dracula*; Richard Matheson's *The Devil's Bride* and *Die! Die! My Darling!*; Judson Kinberg's *Vampire Circus*; Peter Bryan's *The Hound of the Baskervilles* and *The Plague of the Zombies*; and Bert Batt's *Frankenstein Must Be Destroyed* were all different and original with diverse female characterizations, but in certain ways each film can still be easily recognized as a Hammer production.

Then there is John Elder, Anthony Hinds' pen name. He managed to write some of the very best as well as some of the very worst screenplays Hammer ever produced.

The Curse of the Werewolf; The Phantom of the Opera; Rasputin, the Mad Monk; The Reptile; and *Dracula Has Risen from the Grave* are all well received films with interesting female characters who usually manage to hold their own against the more assertive and better-defined male leads. Of course, he also wrote *The Kiss of the Vampire, The Evil of Frankenstein, Frankenstein Created Woman*, and *Frankenstein and the Monster from Hell,* which were not exactly the most stellar roles ever created for women. Even in his better films he had a tendency of allowing his heroines to be routinely beaten and raped. However, to his credit, this action may have been used to further illustrate the despicable quality of his villains.

Hammer may not have presented women in a realistic manner, but they certainly gave us something to talk about, while bringing spine-tingling chills to millions of moviegoers. Their unique forum of mayhem still thrives today, thanks to DVD releases and their reemergence in 2010 with the critical acclaimed *Let Me In*.

Queen Bitches of the Universe

by Susan Svehla

"Life's a bitch, now so am I."
—Catwoman, *Batman Returns*

BITCH: A spiteful or lewd woman.
A complaint. *A difficult or confounding problem.*
—*The American Heritage Dictionary*

Over the years, the word "bitch" has developed into a misnomer. Women earning their own way in the world, making snap decisions, and unfortunately acquiring the male ruthlessness gene are routinely referred to as bitches. Perhaps that is the correct word—for these women are definitely *a difficult or confounding problem* to those around them.

This chapter will take a look at some of my favorite bitches, women who are unmistakably an enigma to those near and not-so-dear, and their trials and tribulations from the 1920s to the 1990s. At times, the road's been rough but our versatile females transgressed it admirably. One can't help but admit it: Bitches are delightfully more fun than the typical hand-wringing namby-pamby heroines so prevalent in the movies.

"The Fearless Peerless Pearl White." In 1914 *The Perils of Pauline* turned Pearl White, an actress who starred in dramas and comedies for Pathé, into the queen of the silent serials. Pearl did most of her own stuntwork, gamely allowing her director to impose untold tortures upon her, all the while managing to outwit a myriad of nefarious villains trying to do away with our plucky heroine, Pauline.

Pauline was the ward of a kindly guardian whose deepest desire was for his son Harry and Pauline to wed. But Pauline is no ordinary girl; she wants to see the world and have great adventures before settling down. Pauline's guardian dies and his evil secretary, Koerner, has gained control over Pauline's fortune. The dastardly Koerner spends the remaining 20 chapters using guns, trains, avalanches, fire, arrows, knives, and any other form of malicious mayhem that crosses his evil little mind trying unsuccessfully to murder the adventurous Pauline.

Women were beginning to realize there was life beyond the kitchen... *The Perils of Pauline* helped point the way.

CATCH THIS WOMAN!
—Tricky Eyes, Dangerous Smile,
Exquisitely gowned, nimble fingers
—she's *Outside the Law,* 1921

The life of the party and HOW!
—Clara Bow in *The Wild Party*, 1929

The Seven Deadly Whims
New lips to kiss
Freedom from conventions
A new world for women
No more chaperones
Life with a kick in it
The single moral standard
Our own latchkeys
—Gloria Swanson in *Prodigal Daughters*, 1923

The 1920s—a swingin' time was had by all—especially at the movies. Douglas Fairbanks, Rudolph Valentiono and Ramon Novarro set women's hearts aflutter. Tom Mix, Buck Jones and Hoot Gibson provided authentic cowboy action, Lon Chaney gave patrons the shivers, *especially* when an unsuspecting Mary Philbin removed his mask in *The Phantom of the Opera*, old dark house mysteries such as *The Cat and the Canary* and *The Bat* were the rage, Our Gang, Buster Keaton, Charlie Chaplin and Charley Chase made people laugh, and Clara Bow, the "It" girl, was appearing in racily titled films such as *Dangerous Curves, The Wild Party, Rough House Rosie*, and *The Fleet's In*. Gloria Swanson, Billie Burke and Mary Pickford routinely saw their name over film titles. Pickford, Chaplin and Fairbanks would eventually form United Artists, and America's sweetheart, Mary Pickford, would retire a *very* wealthy woman.

In 1926 Fritz Lang would complete what is without a doubt his masterwork, *Metropolis*, a film that featured a saintly heroine and her robotic alter-ego, a depraved maniac who tries to lead the inhabitants of Metropolis to their doom. Lang and cinematographer Karl Freund created a terrifying glimpse of a future inhabited by haves and have-nots. The visionary set design and brilliant cinematography created an underground city populated by downtrodden workers and an aboveground paradise inhabited by a decadence-loving upper class. The lives of both the workers and elite are controlled by the machinery needed to run the complex futuristic city. Perhaps screenwriter Thea von Harbou (a real-life bitch in every sense of the word) consulted her crystal ball before completing the script for *Metropolis*—today, the have-nots far outnumber the haves, with the gap widening every day.

While the script is often cited as quite silly, we do get to watch Brigitte Helm ran a gamut of emotions in dual roles—from saint to sinner as Maria, leader of the underground workers, who pleads with them to await a mediator to help them communicate with the above-ground elite, and as the pleasure-loving robotic double created by evil scientist Rothwang (Rudolf Klein-Rogge). Helm has a field day rolling her eyes, frenetically dancing with the upper-class, cavorting, carousing, causing riots, and laughing hysterically as the hapless workers, realizing they have destroyed their children and homes (never considering they made an error, placing the full responsibility on the impostor Maria), burn her at the stake. She cackles with glee as the flames destroy the robot. Meanwhile, the real Maria and Freder (Gustav Froehlich) manage to save the children, evade Rothwang, and bring about a peace between the laborers and the above-grounders. With the Nazi influence growing in Germany, Lang would depart for the United States. Von Harbou would remain behind and become a good little Nazi.

The evil Maria (Brigitte Helm) imposter is burned at the stake in ***Metropolis.***

SHE WAS NOT ALIVE...NOR DEAD...
Just a *White Zombie*—1932

WARNING! The Monster demands a Mate!
—*Bride of Frankenstein*, 1935

Look Out! She'll Get You!
—*Dracula's Daughter*, 1936

The virtuous Maria would reflect the fast-approaching '30s. The party clothes were put away and the dress-down clothes brought out. The Depression was raging. A trip to the movie theater was a rare treat and not to be undertaken lightly. A visit to the local movie palace would probably be followed by a visit to the ice cream parlor for a 15-cent walnut sundae or a 5-cent lemon root beer. Film advertisements would be scrupulously inspected before the monumental selection of a film was made. Studios would indulge the public's desire to escape the despondent times—their taste for frivolity would lead to a plethora of escapist entertainment. Sophisticates were in vogue, on the silver screen that is. Nick and Nora Charles would begin their detecting career in *The Thin Man*, *Snow White* would capture the hearts of America, John Wayne would begin his domination of the Old West, and Shirley Temple, the tiniest of the Fox blondes, would become a box-office champ. Marlene Dietrich would slink her way through many a classic, Tarzan and his mate would swing across the theater screens, Mae West, with a twinkle in her eye, would invite audiences to come up and see her sometime, Fred and Ginger would dance their way into film history, Jean Harlow was the blonde bombshell, Bette Davis was a *Marked Woman*, Garbo talked, and laughed, and fell in love.

Laurel and Hardy inspired zany mayhem, Errol Flynn would swashbuckle his way into female affections, and 1939 would present a film list that even today sends film buffs into a state of nirvana: *Gone With the Wind, The Wizard of Oz, Son of Frankenstein, Stagecoach, Ninotchka, Dark Victory, Destry Rides Again, Goodbye Mr. Chips, The Little Princess, The Hunchback of Notre Dame, Mr. Smith Goes to Washington, Gunga Din, Love Affair,* and *Wuthering Heights.*

And then there was Universal—a Mecca to horror film fans. Universal made Hollywood history with legendary bogeyman Bela Lugosi as *Dracula* and then followed that amazing feat by introducing Boris Karloff in *Frankenstein*. The studio would dominate the horror field until doing a fast fade in the 1940s, but until that time they delighted, frightened, and swept audiences away from the terror of reality. The gruesome twosome of *Dracula* and *Frankenstein* would be followed by such glorious gems as *Murders in the Rue Morgue* and *The Mummy* (1932), *The Invisible Man* (1933), *The Black Cat* (1934), *The Raven, Werewolf of London,* and *Bride of Frankenstein* (1935), *The Invisible Ray, Dracula's Daughter* (1936), and *Son of Frankenstein* (1939).

Universal's success did not go unnoticed by the other majors. They contributed their own classics to horror film annals: Paramount delved into the decadent side of humanity in *Dr. Jekyll and Mr. Hyde* (1932), *Supernatural* (1933), *Island of Lost Souls* (1933), and the sadistic *Murders in the Zoo* (1933). RKO would weigh in with *King Kong* (1933) and *The Most Dangerous Game* (1932); Warner Bros. would wax poetic in *Mystery of the Wax Museum* (1933), and MGM would

Frances Drake with Peter Lorre in *Mad Love* faces the typical Golden Age terrors.

Dorothy Gale (Judy Garland) defeats the wicked witch in *The Wizard of Oz*.

tap their maverick filmmakers to bring us *The Mask of Fu Manchu* (1932), *Freaks* (1932), *Mark of the Vampire* (1935), and *Mad Love* (1935).

Universal heroines were standard issue—lovely delicate flowers terrified by monsters and rescued by manly protectors who would sweep them off their feet and take them away from all this terror. But the '30s also provided three of my favorite over-the-top examples of femininity, one feisty heroine, one deliciously decadent nymphomaniac, and one adventurous little girl.

Dorothy Gale (Judy Garland) in *The Wizard of Oz* has always been every little girl's favorite heroine. She faces mean old Miss Gulch (Margaret Hamilton) when Gulch tries to take Toto away ("You go away or I'll bite you myself, you wicked old witch!"). She slaps the lion on his snout when he threatens Toto (even before realizing he was a *cowardly* lion), and she leads her friends to the Witch's castle to retrieve the wicked old Witch's broomstick. We all shivered in our pj's as the Wicked Witch threatened Dorothy in the Munchkinland square, and gasped when she wrote, "SURRENDER DOROTHY" in the skies above the Emerald City. We hid our little moppet heads as the monkeys carried Dorothy through the skies to the castle and we cried as Dorothy said good-bye to the Scarecrow. Every little girl wanted to *be* Dorothy and travel over the rainbow, and now as adults we still dream about it. However, the real star was the wonderful Margaret Hamilton as The Wicked Witch of the West. She cackled wildly, frightened little children and small animals, and sent chills down our spines with every crack of her tongue ("I'll get you, and your little dog too!"). A simply sublime witch.

The *Mystery of the Wax Museum*'s publicity materials advertise Fay Wray and Lionel Atwill as its stars. But it is Glenda Farrell who steals the show, managing to hold her own with the flamboyant Atwill. Farrell would make her mark as a tough-talking blonde in the Jean Harlow mold. Before appearing in *Wax Museum* she had appeared in *I Am a Fugitive from a Chain Gang* and *Little Caesar*. The wise-cracking blonde would come into her own with the Torchy Blane series in 1938.

Farrell portrays mouthy reporter Florence Dempsey, roommate of the dull Charlotte Duncan (Wray). As Florence makes fun of Charlotte's boyfriend, she is chided for her frivolous ways. Florence embraces life while Charlotte hides behind it.

Charlotte: "I don't think you could have a real affair. I don't think you could care for anyone."

Florence: "I've been in love so many times my heart's callused. But I never hit one with dough. I'd rather die with an apoplectic heart from shaking cocktails and bankers than expire in a pan of dirty dishwater."

Lionel Atwill, as the demented Ivan Igor, has been masterminding the theft of bodies and using them to restock his wax museum. When Charlotte visits her artist boyfriend at the studio, Florence discovers an amazing resemblance between Joan of Arc and a missing body. She rushes to her newspaper office where she engages in snappy patter with despised editor, Jim (Frank McHugh).

Florence: "Hello, light of my life."

Jim: "Well, well, Prussic Acid."

Florence, visiting the exhibit with Charlotte, sneaks over to the Joan of Arc and scrapes a bit of wax from her foot then follows a henchman of Igor's to a deserted basement. She's accompanied by a rich young man, Winton (Gavin Gordon), she met the night before in the slammer. He is a little hesitant to get involved, having had enough interaction with the police. "OK, brother, then you can go to some nice warm place and I don't mean California." Florence climbs in a basement window and explores the area, scaring herself as she bumps into things. Unfortunately, Florence is not only adventurous, she tends to jump to conclusions, notably when she calls the cops convinced a body is in an oblong box she has discovered. The police burst into the room and approach the box with trepidation; however, it's not a murderer who inhabits the house, but bootleggers. Florence grabs a couple bottles as they leave.

Fay Wray (seated) and Glenda Farrell represent the typical 1930s virgin and bitch in *Mystery of the Wax Museum*.

In the car Winton professes his love for the daring Florence.

Winton: "I've only known you for 24 hours, but I'm in love with you."

Florence: "It doesn't usually take that long."

Florence heads back to the newspaper office where she tackles her considerably unhappy editor.

Florence: "Mitt me kid, I got a classic."

Jim: "...an evil spirit to mar my happiness."

Florence heads back to the museum where she is just in time to save the wretched Charlotte from a wax bath. Actually, she sensibly runs screaming for the police—a nice touch—rather than stay and put her pretty neck in jeopardy; she actually uses her head for something other than a hat rack.

Florence returns to the newsroom in glory, jovially accepting congratulations from her colleagues.

Florence: "Well, how about it poison ivy?"

Jim: "Rotten. You had a million dollars worth of luck with you."

Florence: "Could I possibly do anything that would meet with your approval?"

Jim: "Yeah. Cut out this crazy business, act like a lady, marry me."

Florence: "I'm gonna get even with you, you dirty stiff. I'll do it."

Will they live happily ever after? Maybe; however, we all know she'll be back in the newsroom before the honeymoon's over. And we're glad.

Farrell spiels forth her newswoman patter with the zeal of an early Rosalind Russell and is a welcome change from your comparable '30s scream queens.

Myrna Loy. Her name brings to mind the shaking of a cocktail mixer from *The Thin Man* or the aroma of fresh baked apple pie from *The Best Years of Our Lives*. But Loy, under contract to Warners, began her career playing mysterious Oriental women in *Crimson City* (1928) followed a year later with *The Desert Song*. She would eventually sign with MGM where she would enact her last Oriental role as the misanthropic sex-fiend Fah Lo See, daughter of Fu Manchu (Boris Karloff), in *The Mask of Fu Manchu*.

Much has been written about this campy delight, but this all-star queen of evilness is one of the highlights of this chapter. Every line she utters is dripping with honey-coated daggers (screenwriters Irene Kuhn, Edgar Allan Woolf and John Willard must have laughed with wicked glee while composing the dialogue). Loy's eyes brim with a silent mirth as she doles out Fah's vicious tortures and ludicrous speeches.

Fu Manchu is desperately seeking the sword and mask of Genghis Khan, which will give him the power to control the world! He kidnaps Dr. Barton (Lawrence Grant) who was to head the expedition. Fu calls Fah into the throne room. "My daughter, explain to this gentleman the rewards that might be his. Point out to him the delights of our lovely county, the promise of our beautiful women—even my daughter, even *that* for you." Loy manages to maintain a blank look on her face while Karloff delights in delivering his over-dramatic lines with gusto.

Myrna Loy has a field day as vampy Fah in *Mask of Fu Manchu*.

"For a white man, no. May I suggest, however, a slight delay in your customary procedure."

"You have further need of him?"

"I have. He shall still be the means of discovering for me where they have hidden the sword and mask."

"And for that purpose you will..." Fah asks, leaning forward in excitement.

"Precisely." Karloff lisps.

We're not sure exactly what Fu is going to do to Granville, but we know it won't be pretty.

Loy has no more amusing dialogue and disappears from the finale all together. Perhaps they were saving her for a sequel that never came about.

Like the thoroughly evil villainesses of Disney, Fah has no redeeming values—and that's why we love her.

"What I like about you is you're rock bottom... It's a great comfort for a girl to know she could not possibly sink any lower."—*The Big Steal*, 1949

"You know how to whistle, don't you, Steve? You just put your lips together and blow."
—*To Have and Have Not*, 1944

"Doesn't it ever enter a man's head that a woman can do without him?"—*Road House*, 1948

"Men like to see women cry. It makes them feel superior."
—*The Spiral Staircase*, 1946

Barton does not know the location of the artifacts and Fu holds him for ransom. The sword and mask are delivered by the virile Terrence Granville (Charles Starrett), true love of Grant's virtuous daughter. As Granville confidently strides into the throne room Fah smiles and catches her breath. When he removes the "sword" she again catches her breath and parts her hands in delight. Unfortunately for Granville, the sword is a fake. As he is led away, Fah smiles with enjoyment.

As Granville hangs by his hands Fah watches as his shirt is torn off. "The whip!" she yells. She watches in orgasmic ecstasy as they beat Granville, yelling "Faster, faster, faster, faster, faster!" Subtle? Not in the least, but perversely entertaining nonetheless.

Granville is taken to Fah's rooms and placed on a divan. She leans down to kiss him as her father enters. She looks up with a smile, leering, "He is not entirely unhandsome, is he, my father?"

The 1940s. The men were overseas, women were working in factories, and children huddled by heat registers during air-raid drills. Teenagers would visit the local cinemas to watch John Wayne and Gary Cooper shoot 'em up, Humphrey Bogart chase the stuff that dreams are made of, and Judy Garland, Gene Kelly and Fred Astaire make movie magic in MGM's glorious musicals. Screwball comedies reached their peak in the 1940s with films such as *The Philadelphia Story, My Favorite Wife,* and *His Girl Friday*. Hope and Crosby were on the road, Abbott and Costello joined the cinematic army, Orson Welles was obsessing over Rosebud, Jimmy Stewart was having a wonderful life, and Humphrey Bogart opened Rick's Place. Radio shows were the entertainment of the average folks, never missing Jack Benny and *The Shadow*. With men off to war, women were taking charge of their homes, their families, and their new-found responsibilities in the war factories.

The tough-talking dame would become a staple of an emerging film genre, noir. The men were scoundrels or easy pickings, the women cheap floozies looking for an easy ride to the good life. Hollywood actresses were in their glory as prime parts for women became standard operating procedure. Veronica Lake, Lauren Bacall, Lizabeth Scott and Barbara Stanwyck would become the beneficiaries of this dark trend.

Universal horror films were on a downward spiral, their crown as king of horror passing on to the unpretentious and unsuspecting RKO, whose resident geniuses—producer Val Lewton and directors Robert Wise, Jacques Tourneur and Mark Robson—would almost single-handedly save the struggling genre.

Shirley Temple with Gale Sondergaard as the sly Tylette in *The Blue Bird*.

Other than the intelligently drawn Lewton heroines, horror didn't offer much to actresses during this war-ravaged decade. One notable exception is Gale Sondergaard, who would have a feline field day as the sly Tylette, Shirley Temple's conniving cat in *The Blue Bird* (1940), and as Sherlock Holmes' nemesis in *The Spider Woman* (1944).

Holmes: "...Something uncanny about it, something monstrous and horrible. Something that drives these poor fellows to their so-called suicides... murders brilliantly conceived and executed. They're very near to being perfect crimes. Indubitably these murders are the work of a well organized gang and directing them is one of the most fiendishly clever minds in Europe today. I suspect a woman... Because the method is peculiarly subtle and cruel. Feline, not Canine... the bloke is driven to suicide and in that case it's murder."

Watson: "Driven. That sounds like a woman, doesn't it?"

The Spider Woman and Holmes verbally fence using the "I knew that you knew that I knew" routine. The best bit in the film has the notorious Spider Woman visit Holmes at 221B Baker Street with her young nephew. The kid is worth the price of admission for his hysterical imitation of a miniature Dwight Frye as he hops around catching flies.

As the 1950s approached, the survivors were home from the real horrors of the battlefield, women were safely ensconced in their kitchens once more, horror films were dead, and science fiction films would dominate the next decade.

"CRIMES OF PASSION PENT UP
IN HIS SAVAGE HEART!"
—*Creature from the Black Lagoon*, 1954

"A Beautiful Woman by Day—
A Lusting Queen Wasp by Night."
—*The Wasp Woman*, 1959

"Mankind's first fantastic flight to VENUS
—The Female Planet!"
—*Queen of Outer Space*, 1958

1950s. The black and white flickering of the tiny round television screen hypnotized a nation. Families lined up on the sofa to laugh with Uncle Miltie, Red Buttons, Amos 'n' Andy, Our Miss Brooks, Jack Benny, Red Skelton, Jackie Gleason and George Gobel. They waited eagerly for *Texaco Star Theater* on NBC as well as *Your Show of Shows, I Love Lucy, You Bet Your Life, Disneyland, The $64,000 Question, The Ed Sullivan Show, Gunsmoke, Wagon Train, Have Gun Will Travel*,

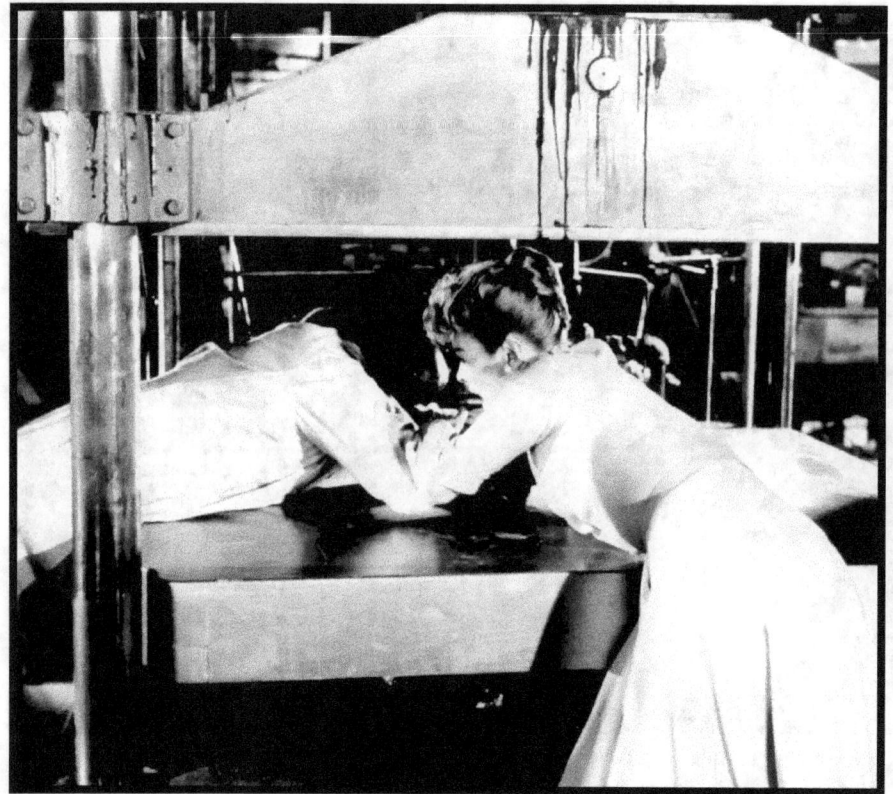
Patricia Owens as the brave wife who helps her doomed husband find peace in the 1958 *The Fly*.

and *The Rifleman*. The teens of the '40s were now heading to a place called Korea for a war they didn't understand; at home, family values reigned supreme.

In a rush to decrease their huge star salaries, Hollywood studio moguls brushed aside major stars like annoying dandruff. The studio system was dead and a decline could be seen in the Hollywood product. The studios frantically scrambled for gimmicks to combat the new technology of television. Glorious Technicolor, breathtaking Cinemascope, and Stereophonic sound along with Amazing 3-D were just a few rabbits pulled out of Hollywood's brown derby.

Bette Davis fastened her seat belt for a bumpy ride, Judy Garland was reborn as a star, Judy Holliday was *Born Yesterday*, Gloria Swanson was ready for her close-up, John Wayne was *The Quiet Man*, Spencer Tracy had a *Bad Day at Black Rock*, David Niven went *Around the World in 80 Days*, Maurice Chevalier was thanking heaven for little girls, Susan Hayward wanted to live, and Marilyn Monroe got serious at the *Bus Stop*.

Families, looking for cheap entertainment for the kiddies, packed some Kool-Aid and popcorn, put the kids in their jammies and headed for the local drive-in. Teenagers, looking for a little make-out time, headed there for the same reason, or to the local drive-in restaurant for burgers, fries and shakes.

Independent studios cranked out product for this new audience of fans who were more interested in the drive-in experience than in the movies shown—society's new-found fear of technology made science fiction films a perfect exploitative choice. Since women were back home where they supposedly belonged, the tough dames of the 1940s did a quick fade and Suzy Homemaker took her place.

Women did boldly go where no woman had gone before—outer space, but unfortunately they were just along for the ride, although they sure brewed a mean cup of coffee. They also appeared as sexy aliens in a list of *non*-Academy Award contenders such as *Cat-Women of the Moon, Fire Maidens of Outer Space, Devil Girl from Mars*, and *Queen of Outer Space* starring that well-known thesp, Zsa Zsa Gabor.

The Fly (1958) was a notable exception to the rule. Patricia Owens turns in a thoughtful performance as the wife of a scientist who manages to turn himself into an overgrown insect. Owens bravely destroys her creepy-crawler husband in a printing press before being arrested for his murder. Positively one of the most original sci-fi films of the decade with a great female lead role.

She Devil (1957), a not-so-great film but a drive-in delight, has one of the bitchiest women this side of PMSville. Mari Blanchard stars in this overly talky sci-fi/horror yarn as a destitute dying woman who is given a new serum by a duo of kindly scientists. Miraculously, the serum saves her life and in the process makes her indestructible—she's even able to change her hair color at will, which comes in handy as she sets out to get everything she's always wanted and woe to anyone who stands in her way. Needing new clothes, she whacks some poor schnook over the head with a glass ashtray in a ritzy clothing store, hides in a dressing room, her hair turns blonde, and she merrily saunters out, free as a bird—*vulture* that is. Kyra (Blanchard) seduces gullible scientist Dr. Scott (Jack Kelly), convincing him not to

The 1960s. Was there ever a more bizarre decade of American history? Mini-dresses and go-go boots were the rage. Kids tuned out and turned on, Vietnam was a stone around everyone's neck, and movies left behind the innocence of the past. Families were still hypnotized by the flickering tube spending quality time watching *The Real McCoys, Bonanza, Hazel, Candid Camera,* and *The Dick Van Dyke Show*.

At the movies Shirley MacLaine visited *The Apartment*, Shirley Jones seduced *Elmer Gantry*, Paul Newman was *The Hustler*, Natalie Wood and Warren Beatty enjoyed a little *Splendor in the Grass*, Mrs. Robinson put the moves on Dustin Hoffman, Rosemary had a baby, and William Holden rode with the *Wild Bunch*... It was truly a *Mad Mad Mad Mad World*. Hip British comedies were the rage, but like modern art, nobody really understood them—however everyone pretended to, while in the U.S. Peter Sellers confounded audiences in *Dr. Strangelove*.

Horror films took a decidedly grisly turn with the mother-obsessed Norman Bates in *Psycho*, the wacko Bette Davis in *What Ever Happened to Baby Jane?*, the flesh-eating zombies from *Night of the Living Dead*, the pre-slasher slasher flicks *Homicidal*, *Strait-Jacket*, and *Repulsion*—and the putridly disgusting *Blood Feast*. Sci-fi went big-budget with the A productions *2001: A Space Odyssey* and *Planet of the Apes*.

Women's roles weren't even as good as they had been in the 1950s, for now horror displayed a truly nasty side as women became victims of axes, knives and psychos, or were cast as bimbos providing handy diversions for James Bond. The queen of the 1960s

search for an antidote, then decides she wants to marry an obnoxious millionaire; she strangles his wife (in her brunette disguise), marries the dolt, and then kills him by forcing their car over a cliff. Of course, she emerges from the wreckage little the worse for wear. Dr. Scott and Dr. Bach (Albert Dekker) knock her unconscious by using carbon monoxide and then operate, turning her back into the pathetic creature she once was. Of course, during those days the murderess could not be allowed to survive, and Kyra promptly returns to her previous condition and dies of tuberculosis.

Patricia Neal managed to control Gort in *The Day the Earth Stood Still* (1951) but for the most part, women were relegated to the background providing enough screams and sex appeal for 1950s' audiences. There was one place women dominated—poster art for sci-fi posters. No self-respecting poster debuted without some scantily clad babe being carried away by a hulking monster.

> "Who gives up the pill? Who takes sex to outer space? Who's the girl of the 21st Century? Who nearly dies of pleasure?"—*Barbarella*, 1968

From the Academy Awards to B-horror—Joan Crawford in *Strait-Jacket*

bimbos was without a doubt *Barbarella* (1968). Jane Fonda and then-husband Roger Vadim are responsible for this adaptation of a hip French comic... like much of the 1960s, the film makes little sense and failed to rocket Fonda to the sex kitten fame Vadim was seeking for her. Thankfully Fonda had talent and managed to put this turkey in her past and sink her teeth into some real roles rather than the outer space hunks she met up with in *Barbarella*. One exception to the nymphet 1960s was the Mexican film *Wrestling Women vs. the Aztec Mummy* (1962). Two wrestling Amazon beauties, Loretta Venus and The Golden Ruby, help an archeologist battle an evil Oriental mastermind, the Black Dragon, and after he is done away with by the mummy, they take on the dusty old fiend himself. Use the fast forward button on your DVD to skip everything but the women's fight scenes. They're great as the wrestling Amazons take on gangs of thugs, beating them to a pulp again and again and again. The follow-up is *Wrestling Women vs. the Aztec Ape*. The 1970s were quickly approaching, although most aging hippies failed to notice. The mid-1970s would provide a bizarre alien bitch whose amazing cult following will never fade—yes, I'm speaking about Frank-n-Furter, the bitchy, decadent, perverse, murdering mad doctor from *The Rocky Horror Picture Show* (1975). While technically not a woman, Frank is absolutely a queen bitch of the universe as he slinks about in his black corset and fishnet stockings—"I've been making a man, with blonde hair and a tan, and he's good for relieving my tension; I'm just a sweet transvestite from transsexual Transylvania." Tim Curry as Frank simpers, seduces, and shocks as he cavorts through this perverse tribute to horror films. As his world crumbles about him, he pathetically proclaims, "It's not easy having a good time."

"A NEW HOPE"—*Star Wars*, 1977

"In space no one can hear you scream."—*Alien*, 1979

"Be afraid. Be very afraid."—*The Fly*, 1986

It was the best of times, it was the worst of times. Television really was becoming the "boob tube," music was bland, and films were dark and depressing or on the flip side, fluffy and moronic. These are the decades of alternate universes. In one ghastly universe, women were dragged kicking and screaming into the gory 1970s, 1980s and 1990s. In the other universe women became the heroes, fighting side by side with men for truth, justice and the Galactic way. These intrepid women fiercely waged battles with evil dark forces, bloodthirsty vampires, chest-bursting aliens, robots from the future, flesh-eating zombies, and even the evilest villains of them all, Nazis. They are the typical Hitchcock hero, regular gals placed in extraordinary circumstances who manage to survive their incredible journey.

The first universe is inhabited by psycho slashers who prey mainly on teenagers, preferring nubile young ladies, especially the promiscuous ones. The virgin always manages to survive. The sexual liberation of the 1960s never seemed to have an effect on horror filmmakers, who chose to have their heroine/victims remain pristine examples of purity. An archaic attitude obvious to almost everyone except said filmmakers and some Republicans.

Any geek with a video camera began to make movies featuring inane scripts, horribly bad acting, gratuitous T&A, and eager "scream queens" who happily remove their clothes at the drop of a clapper.

Jane Fonda in *Barbarella*, which was directed by her then-husband Roger Vadim.

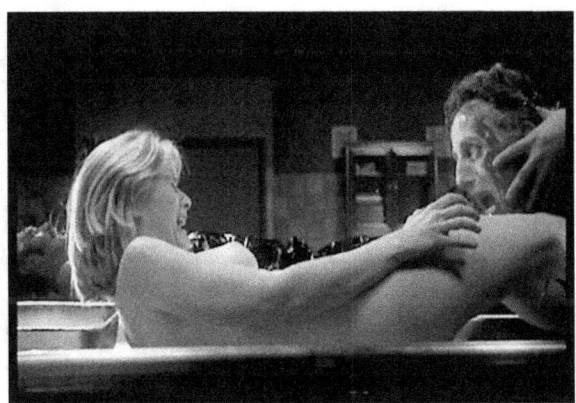
Maybe it's me, but unlike most male critics, I never found this rape scene from *Re-Animator* amusing.

Women were chainsawed, dismembered, terrorized, brutally raped, butchered and mangled. We prayed the psycho would finally do in that annoying screaming girl in *Texas Chainsaw Massacre*, grew disgusted with the sequelitis and resurrection of fiends from Jason to the Shape, and don't even get me started on Freddy, whose bloody antics forced me to leave the theater. *Re-Animator* repulsed women with its gross sex scene between a restrained woman and a decapitated head. Please people, let's show *some* restraint. This universe deserves to be swallowed by a black hole and bloodily spit out on the other side of the galaxy.

The other universe is the meat and potatoes of this chapter. In 1977, a long time ago in a galaxy far, far away, a Star Destroyer majestically flew across theater screens. Audiences gasped and cinematic history was made by George Lucas, a weird assortment of aliens, a crack special effects team, and a relatively unknown cast consisting of the naive Luke Skywalker (Mark Hamill), the dashing Han Solo (Harrison Ford), and the feisty Princess Leia Organa (Carrie Fisher). *STAR WARS*. Today, as the first note of the Academy Award–winning score (by John Williams) sounds, my heart beats a little faster and I begin to feel the same adrenaline rush I felt back in 1977. Forget Dorothy and Oz, I wanted to *be* Princess Leia, fighting to save the galaxy from the evil Darth Vader and the Empire. Being chased by Harrison Ford wouldn't be bad either.

For anyone living in a cave, the Galaxy is ruled by the evil Empire who are building a giant Death Star they plan to use to finally defeat the rebel alliance. Young Luke Skywalker and his mentor Obi Wan Kenobi along with pilot Han Solo and Chewbacca set out to return a set of plans for the Death Star to Princess Leia. Leia has been captured by Darth Vader.

Leia is one tough cookie as she is taken before Grand Moff Tarkin (Peter Cushing). Six hefty stormtroopers surround the diminutive Princess as she confronts Vader.

"Governor Tarkin. I should have expected to find you holding Vader's leash. I recognized your foul stench when I was brought on board."

"Charming to the last."

The Princess is rescued by Luke and Han, sort of. She ends up doing most of the rescuing as she grabs a blaster from Han and fires into a wall ordering Han, "Into the garbage chute, fly boy."

Luke is smitten with the Princess, but then so is Han. "I'm either going to kill her or I'm starting to like her."

Leia, Luke and Han escape and lead the rebels in a successful attack on the Death Star.

On the *Star Wars Trilogy* deluxe laser disc box set, George Lucas discusses the casting of Princess Leia: "I wanted somebody teenager like. So it was finding somebody who could hold their own against strong actors and still be the Princess that she needed to be and still be the authority figure she needed to be, and make her believable."

Princess Leia gave little girls a much needed role model, a strong independent woman willing to risk everything to save her people, but also a woman who remained virginal and feminine to the last (throughout *Star Wars* she is clad in flowing white robes; her attire would change throughout the series as her character matured).

The Empire Strikes Back (1980) and the Princess is right in the midst of the battle, commanding troops, bantering with Han Solo, and escaping the evil Vader in the City in the Clouds.

The sexual electricity between Leia and Han heats up to boiling as their delightful repartee provides a welcome relief from the darkness encompassing the sequel to *Star Wars*. They are a cosmic Tracy and Hepburn as they bicker their way across the galaxy.

The rebels, based on the ice planet Hoth, are under attack from the Empire. They are preparing to abandon the planet. Han and Leia argue about Han's plan to leave.

"Han."

"Yes, your highness."

"I thought you had decided to stay. Han, we need you."

"We need?"

"Yes."

"What about *you* need?"

Star Wars gave little girls a strong but still feminine female role model in Princess Leia (Carrie Fisher).

"*I need*? I don't know what you're talking about."

"You probably don't. ...afraid I was going to leave without giving you a good-bye kiss?"

"I'd just as soon kiss a wookie!"

"I can arrange that."

Leia must be pulled from the command station as the Stormtroopers break through. Han, Chewy, C3PO and Leia escape on the Millennium Falcon, evading a star destroyer in an asteroid field.

As they make repairs, Han tries once again to break through Leia's tough exterior.

"Come on, admit it. Sometimes you think I'm all right."

"Occasionally. Maybe. When you're not acting like a scoundrel."

"Scoundrel! Scoundrel. I like the sound of that... there aren't enough scoundrels in your life."

"I happen to like nice men."

"I'm a nice man."

Leia, along with most female audience members, is melting fast. But she never lets her guard down enough to allow love to interfere with her main goal of defeating the Empire.

Leia, Han and Chewy are captured by the Empire in the City in the Clouds and tortured. They are being used as bait to lure Luke to a confrontation with Darth Vader. Han is frozen in carbonite and given to Boba Fett, the bounty hunter. Their good-bye kiss in a orange backlit scene is worthy of *Gone With the Wind*. As Han is lowered into the freezing chamber, Leia proclaims, "I love you." "I know." Leia and Chewy are on their way to Vader's ship when they escape, but it is too late to save Han. As they take off, Leia hears Luke calling to her and they race back, barely in time to save him.

1983 saw *The Return of the Jedi*. Leia, masquerading as a bounty hunter, leads Chewy into the nefarious den of Jabba the Hutt, a huge slug-like creature who proudly displays the frozen Han Solo on his wall. As Leia releases Han from the carbonite, they are discovered. Han is thrown into a dungeon and Leia is made a slave of Jabba, wearing the tiniest of slave girl costumes. My, she had matured. Luke shows up, they all escape and lead an attack to shut down a force field protecting the new death star which is orbiting the forest moon of Endor, a planet inhabited by a cuddly race of little bear-like creatures. The rebels are having a difficult time keeping the Stormtroopers at bay while trying to enter the fortress controlling the force field. Leia, covering Han as he tries to hot-wire the door, is hit in the shoulder by a laser blast. They are trapped and ordered to surrender by the Stormtroopers. Leia secretly shows Han a blaster she is holding. "I love you," he says with relief. "I know," she answers.

Of course the Empire is destroyed thanks to Luke and his converted father, Darth Vader. Everybody lives happily ever after.

Princess Leia would pave the way for a new cinematic heroine. No longer would women be plot devices or lovely victims of monsters. They were the focal point of some of the largest money-making films of all time. Princess Leia toppled more than one empire.

Star Wars would be followed the next year by *Superman* (1978) starring Christopher Reeve and Margot Kidder as Lois Lane. The Lois Lane character has always been annoying, especially so in this adaptation. Lois Lane never manages realistically to carry off the strong woman guise, perhaps because she is always involved in stupidly dangerous stunts, forcing Superman to spend most of his valuable time rescuing her.

In 1979 the U.S. was invaded by *Alien,* as the grizzled and weary crew of the freighter Nostromo returns to Earth with a valuable cargo. Virtually a remake of *It! The Terror from Beyond Space*, both films had two female crewmembers, but the women onboard the Nostromo were not the "get me a cup of coffee" type of gals. Lambert (Veronica Cartwright) was a whiny complainer, and when cited for it, she replies, "I like to complain." Ripley (Sigourney Weaver) is the third in command and refuses to unquarantine Dallas, Lambert and Kane when they try to re-enter the ship after Kane is attacked by the mysterious egg creature. Android Ash (Ian Holm) disobeys her and opens the door.

Ripley is a woman of many talents: she knows the ship backward and forward, is a pilot, and has no qualms about taking charge after Dallas disappears.

Rapidly losing crew members to the deadly alien, Ripley decides on a drastic course of action. "We're going to blow up the ship. We'll take our chances in the shuttle." The only chink in Ripley's armor is the cat that accompanies the crew. The three remaining members split up. Ripley hears screaming and rushes toward the sound; Lambert and Parker (Yaphet Kotto) have both become victims of the alien. Ripley sets the self destruct activator and enters the shuttle. The alien, realizing her plan, blocks the door of the shuttle. Ripley rushes back to try to stop the self-destruct but is too late. She screams at the computer (which the crew called Mother): "You bitch!"

Ripley takes a flame-thrower and heads back toward the shuttle. The alien is nowhere to be found. She straps

Ripley (Sigourney Weaver) in *Alien* and its squeals is one of the great roles for women in sci-fi films.

in, having only seconds to get out of there before the ship blows. "I got you, you son of a bitch." Of course, it wasn't quite that easy. The alien is on the shuttle. Ripley manages to put on a spacesuit and blow the bastard into space.

Leia led the way—but Ripley was the real queen bitch of outer space. The idea of a woman surviving—let alone destroying the monster herself—with no help from anyone (re: men) was a refreshing concept whose time had come. Audiences were amazed and astounded, and loved it, propelling *Alien* to a coveted position as a top moneymaker for 1979. *Alien* had no romance, no sex, no beauty. It was a down and dirty adventure film that took no liberties with its female characters (except for the tiny underwear Weaver wore in the film—how anybody could do any actual work in those things is anybody's guess).

Outside of *Star Wars*, most sequels are emphatically inferior to the original film. *Aliens* (1986) director James Cameron had his hands full when the studio decided to visit a planet full of the viciously intelligent aliens. Cameron is one of today's hottest directors, a director who has a remarkable track record when it comes to female characters. Perhaps he was influenced by producer (and wife at the time) Gale Anne Hurd. *Aliens* develops Ripley as a heartbreakingly complex character who sadly regrets leaving behind a child on Earth while she worked in space.

Found floating in space 57 years after winning her battle with the alien, things are not all sugar and spice for Ripley. The Company, not happy she blew up a 42 million dollar ship, declares her unfit to hold a license as a commercial flight officer. She is released on psychometric probation. Ripley is forced to work on a loading dock. Until...the Company has sent terraformers to planet LV426, the home of the face-hugging alien monsters. There has been no communication from the settlers and the Company approaches Ripley to go with a squad of Marines to find out what happened. She refuses, but cannot live with the nightmares that haunt her, so she finally agrees.

The Marines are some tough hombres and they are loaded for bear. The squad has its share of women, notably Vasquez (Jenette Goldstein), who makes Ripley look like Shirley Temple.

The Marines find no one alive except a terrified little girl, Newt (Carrie Henn), who takes a liking to Ripley. Ripley becomes a mother figure to Newt, a much needed sign of humanity in the hard-as-nails character. When the Marines stumble into the lair of the aliens, the slaughter is wholesale. The green commander Lt. Gorman (William Hope) falls apart and Ripley must drive to the regiment's rescue. The most frightening countenance of *Aliens* is the failure of the Marines. The idea that this superior fighting group cannot defeat the aliens is doubly terrifying, forcing the audience to face the conclusion there may be no hope. The remaining Marines shakily plot a course of action.

Ripley: "I say we take off and nuke the entire site from orbit."

Burke: "This installation has a substantial dollar value attached to it."

Ripley: "They can bill me."

The rag-tag band tries to escape, Vasquez bringing up the rear. She is trapped by an alien and shoots it in the head. The creatures acid-blood splatters over her. Lt. Gorman goes back for Vasquez and, when trapped, sets off a grenade; Vasquez clutches his hand before the explosion. Meanwhile, Newt has been taken by an alien.

Ripley, Cpl. Hicks (Michael Biehn), and Bishop (Lance Henriksen) reach the shuttle. Ripley duct tapes (the best invention since sliced bread) two weapons together and has 19 minutes to find Newt before the entire complex explodes.

Newt, in the alien's lair partially cocooned, cries out for Ripley. Ripley grabs Newt and runs right into the nastiest mother in the universe, the alien Queen. Making it known she will torch the eggs if attacked, the alien allows Ripley and Newt to back out of the lair. Giving the creature an "I lied" look, Ripley turns the flamethrower on the eggs.

The shuttle reaches the safety of the ship orbiting the planet, but their worries are not over—the Queen has gotten a free ride on the shuttle and is mighty annoyed with Ripley.

Ripley climbs into a cargo mover and the two very pissed off mothers battle to the death; eventually Ripley manages to maneuver the alien into outer space. Weaver was nominated for an Academy Award for her portrayal of Ripley.

Ripley is more ferocious in this film, but any mother can turn into a beast when protecting her child, in this case Newt.

The follow up, *Alien 3*, totally alienated audiences in the first five minutes when scripters killed off Hicks and Newt before the story even began. And then they killed off Ripley! Talk about ticked off audiences.

Returning to the past, 1936 to be exact, George Lucas, Steven Spielberg and Karen Allen brought Marion Ravenwood to vivid life in *Raiders of the Lost Ark* (1981). A decidedly updated version of the serial heroine, Marion doesn't take crap from *anybody*.

Indiana Jones (Harrison Ford), seeking a medallion owned by Prof. Ravenwood, travels to Nepal where he finds Marion, Ravenwood's daughter, who has just completed a shot-drinking contest with the locals—she's still standing, but you should see the other guy.

"Indiana Jones. I always knew someday you'd come walking back through my door. I never doubted that. Something made it inevitable. So what are you doing here in Nepal?"

When he starts to answer, she hauls off and gives him a right to the jaw. Their previous relationship didn't exactly end on a happy note.

Nazis show up, and Jones and Marion desperately fight for their lives. Marion takes a break from the frenzy of battle to gulp from a stream of whisky flowing from a bullet-ridden barrel before conking a bad guy over the head. As the villains run for the hills and her bar burns to the ground, she picks herself up, commenting, "Well, Jones, you still haven't forgotten how to show a lady a good time."

Marion sticks with Indy, hoping to get the money he promised her for the medallion. She's kidnapped in a market, tied to a pole, seduced by the evil Belloq (Paul Freeman) (who doesn't get far when she drunkenly pulls

Marion Ravenwood (Karen Allen) and friend in *Raiders of the Lost Ark*

Darryl Hannah as Pris in *Blade Runner*

a knife on him), gets thrown into a snake-infested pit, and kidnapped again from a ship she and Indy are using to try to get the Lost Ark to safety. The women taking Marion's place in the following two sequels couldn't hold a candle to Allen.

Blade Runner (1982), Ridley Scott's stylish sci-fi noir, featured three women... Sean Young as Rachael, the beautiful replicant Deckard (Harrison Ford) falls for, and two of the nastiest female villains this side of the Milky Way, Pris and Zhora.

A group of escaped replicants have returned to Earth hoping to find their creator and prolong their short life span. Deckard is hot on their trail. Zhora (Joanna Cassidy)—"off world kick murder squad, talk about beauty and the beast, she's both"—is working in a dumpy club as an exotic dancer. Deckard, pretending to be a nerdy government official, questions her only to be elbowed in the stomach, punched in the face, and strangled with his own necktie. Zhora is interrupted before she can finish off the gasping detective and flees through the rain-drenched streets. Deckard chases her, firing; she is shot and crashes through a series of plate glass windows.

Pris (Darryl Hannah)—"a basic pleasure model, a standard item for military clubs in the outer colonies"—poses as a life-size doll when Deckard investigates the apartment where she is hiding. As he pulls a veil from her head, she kicks him before doing a series of flips that would make a gymnast envious, and lands on his shoulders, her legs crushing his head between her thighs. She viciously smashes his face between her hands before backing up for another series of flips. Deckard shoots her. Like any typical noir, *Blade Runner's* characters are neither totally good nor totally evil. Pris and Zhora die horrible deaths for merely wanting to live, although they might have gone about it in a kinder, gentler way.

1984 was a banner year for sci-fi fanatics. *Dune* debuted to less than raves, but Lady Jessica (Francesca Annis) was a worthy character going to great lengths to protect her son Paul (Kyle MacLachlan) from the evil Harkonnens, even jeopardizing the life of her unborn daughter.

2010, the sequel to *2001: A Space Odyssey* didn't inspire the awe and wonder the original did, but it did have something the earlier film didn't—female crew members. In fact, Helen Mirren captained the Russian ship.

Night of the Comet is a quirky sci-fi comedy with two Valley Girl heroines (who just happen to have had an artillery-loving father who taught them the pleasures of automatic weapons) taking on the zombies the comet has created. What to do when your entire world has been destroyed: that's right, go shopping! The girls (Catherine Mary Stewart and Kelli Maroney) manage to avoid the flesh-eating zombies and a group of deranged scientists before settling down with nice guy Hector (Robert Beltran) and two kids they saved from the scientists' lab. As the film closes Samantha (Maroney) happily finds another survivor, who is young an hunky, and they drive off into the sunset.

Two years before *Aliens*, James Cameron and Gale Anne Hurd struck cinematic gold with a little film that took the country by storm and made a mega-star of Arnold Schwarzenegger: *The Terminator*.

Sarah Conner (Linda Hamilton) is your average American girl: small apartment, lousy job, and an indestructible robot from the future out to murder her before she can become the mother of a rebel leader. Rebel soldier Kyle Reese (Michael Biehn) arrives from the future to protect Sarah, who is slow to believe his wild story.

"Do I look like the mother of the future? Am I tough, organized? I can't even balance my checkbook."

The unrelenting terminator chases Sarah and Kyle to a factory. Sarah and a severely injured Kyle break in, an explosion kills Kyle. Sarah manages to crush the indestructible cyborg in a press.

Later, a very pregnant Sarah (she and Kyle did find a little time together) drives into the mountains with a German shepherd, a gun, and the courage to face an unknown future.

Sarah, like Ripley, was an average Jane who through extraordinary circumstances became something of a superwoman, a thing everyone hopes they could do if faced with similar threats.

In *Terminator 2: Judgment Day* (1991), Sarah has turned into a hardcore commando, committed to a mental institution for her belief in the coming apocalypse. Her son John (Edward Furlong) is now a teenager who hooks up with Arnold Schwarzenegger, this time playing the good terminator.

Linda Hamilton as Sarah Conner, who turns from frightened woman to kick-ass heroine as she tries to protect her son in *Terminator* and sequels.

"She'd shack up with anybody she could learn from so she could teach me to be this great military leader."

They rescue Sarah from the institute and set out to kill Dyson, the man responsible for creating Skynet, the computer that will destroy the world. Armed to the teeth, Sarah fires into the man's home, bursts into the house, but finds she cannot kill him in cold blood. Arnold and John arrive and they convince Dyson (Joe Morton) to help them destroy the project he is working on as well as the chip from the earlier terminator destroyed in the first film. Throughout the entire film they have been fleeing a new terminator, the T-1000, an indestructible creature of liquid metal. Sarah and Morton manage to destroy the lab, Morton giving his life to save the world, and the group escapes followed by the T-1000. He is eventually melted in the bubbling vat of molten metal at a steel mill.

Sarah is not only a mother figure protecting her son, but the future of humanity as well.

In the remake of *The Fly* (1986), a courageous heroine is born this time in the statuesque form of Geena Davis who, as the lover of the mutating Jeff Goldblum, embraces the suffering, oozing creature, perhaps one of the most tender and truly heroic moments ever filmed. True love really does conquer all. As in the original film, she helps the pathetic creature she loves destroy himself.

Star Trek IV: The Voyage Home also debuted in 1986. *Star Trek* never had really strong female leads, although Uhura was always along for the ride. However, Catherine Hicks as Dr. Gillian Taylor outwits the Enterprise crew by hitching a ride to the future to care for her beloved humpback whales.

Millennium (1989) has heroine-from-the-future Louise Baltimore (Cheryl Ladd) traveling into the past trying to stop time paradoxes from destroying the future. Louise leads teams to the past where they remove the victims of disasters before the event happens. These people are taken to the future where they are society's last hope for saving the human race; the current inhabitants of the future are sterile, sickly creatures destroyed by harsh chemical pollution.

Science fiction as a genre has always been ahead of its time in its portrayal of characters and social conditions. *Millennium* is no exception. Based on a novel by John Varley, *Millennium* fell victim to bad casting and a confusing time travel story. However, Louise Baltimore was a strong female who was willing to go to any lengths to ensure the future of mankind.

The Abyss (1989) was a cursed project from day one. The shoot was way behind schedule and over budget because of the difficulty in filming in the huge underwater tank. Also, James Cameron and Gale Anne Hurd were quietly separating, a fact that didn't surface until after the film publicity tours were over. Whatever the problems, Mary Elizabeth Mastrantonio as Lindsey Brigman is exceptional. As the film opens, a military plane discharges its passengers. A sea of army boots descends followed by a pair of shapely legs in high heels.

"Oh no, look who's with them. Queen bitch of the universe."

Lindsay is not happy her project is being turned over to the "goon squad."

"Man, if Bud goes along with this, they're going to have to shoot her with a tranquilizer gun."

Bud Brigman, foreman of the underwater drilling rig Lindsey has designed, is contacted by the crew above and warned of an approaching hurricane, Fred.

" I don't know man. I think hurricanes should be named after women, don't you?" The tech laughs as papers begin to blow around and Lindsey, a walking hurricane, enters from outside. She speaks to Bud, miles below.

"Virgil, you wiener, you never could stand up to a fight."

Virgil, Bud's real name, comments to a shipmate, "God, I hate that bitch."

"Probably shouldn't have married her then, huh?"

A nuclear sub has been destroyed and rests on the edge of a deep abyss. A team of Navy Seals is sent down to the drilling rig to recover the warheads. Lindsey addresses the Seals on the dangers of the deep.

"We're been fully briefed, Mrs. Brigman."

"Just don't call me that. I hate that."

"All right. Well, what would you like us to call you, sir?"

Lindsey is the first to have contact with the aliens who reside in the abyss. Learning of the nuclear warhead the Seals have snuck on board the rig, she pounds on their door with a fire extinguisher until they open the door. Lt. Coffey (Michael Biehn) is affected by the depth and is rapidly losing control. He climbs into a minisub trying to destroy the aliens, chased by Bud and Lindsey in another sub. Coffey damages their sub, which rapidly fills with water. The sub contains only one diving suit.

Bud: "You're smart, think of something."

Lindsey: "I've got a plan."

"What's the plan?"

"I drown and you tow me back to the rig."

Bud holds Lindsey close as she allows herself to drown in one frightening and touching scene. The sight of water beginning to fill the sub and Lindsey gasping for breath is chilling.

The crew manages to revive Lindsey and Bud decides to go over the edge of the abyss to retrieve the warhead. Lindsay keeps Bud focused as he dives further than any human being.

"It's not easy being a cast iron bitch. It takes discipline and years of training. A lot of people don't appreciate that."

Bud grins. The aliens save him and halt their attack on humanity because of the love between Bud and Lindsey. They still have some hope for the human race.

Now we come to everyone's favorite anti-heroine, Michelle Pfeiffer, feline, feisty and ferocious as Catwoman in *Batman Returns* (1992). In a grotesque version of *Cinderella*, Selina Kyle is the mousy secretary to bad guy Max Shreck (Christopher Walken). At a business meeting Selina timidly speaks up, "I have a suggestion—well, actually, really more like a question."

"We haven't properly housebroken Miss Kyle, I'm afraid. In the plus column though, she makes a hell of a cup of coffee." Walken is bad to the bone and plays his evil part for all it's worth. Pfeiffer is outstanding as the confused Selina and vindictive Catwoman; she is one mean cat.

Bud (Ed Harris) has a plan to save his wife Lindsey (Mary Elizabeth Mastrantonio) but it's not a pleasant one in *Abyss*.

When the Penguin attacks, Selina is grabbed by a clown. Batman (Michael Keaton) comes to her rescue; Selina gives the clown a kick for good measure.

"Wow. The Batman. Or is it just Batman? Your choice of course."

Batman stalks silently away.

"Well, that was very brief, just like all the men in my life. What men?" She looks at the fallen clown. "Then again there's you, but you need therapy."

Selina soon discovers the evil Shreck is up to no good.

"...Go ahead, intimidate me, bully me if it makes you feel big. I mean it's not like you can just kill me."

"Actually, it's a lot like that."

Shreck pushes Selina out a window, her broken body falls into the snow. Cats surround her and her eyes pop open. Stumbling home to her lonely apartment, she automatically listens to the messages on her answering machine—one sends her over the brink she has been tottering on.

"Hello, Selina Kyle. We're just calling to make sure you try Gotham Lady perfume. One whiff of this at the office and your boss will be asking you to stay after work for a candlelight staff meeting for two."

Selina trashes her apartment, smashes her pink neon sign that read "HELLO THERE" to now read "HELL HERE." She grabs a black leather coat from the closet, opens her sewing machine, and emerges as Catwoman.

As a goon attacks a woman in an alley a shadow looms.

"I just love a big strong man who's not afraid to show it with someone half his size."

The goon approaches her menacingly. Catwoman stands legs apart, exuding confidence, power and sensuality.

"Be gentle, it's my first time."

She kicks him four times before those deadly claws pop out. Catwoman hisses and slashes his face—tic-tac-toe—before the claws find his eyes.

The girl smiles, "...thanks..."

Catwoman grabs her face. "You make it so easy, don't you? Always waiting for some Batman to save you. I am Catwoman, hear me roar!"

The next day, Selina shows up at the office, much to Shreck's surprise. "Who'd have thought she had a brain to damage? She tries to blackmail me, I'll drop her out a higher window."

Catwoman breaks into Shreck's department store happily playing with her new cat toy, a bullwhip. She skips rope and snaps the heads of mannequins before two guards spot her.

Michelle Pfeiffer has a grand old time playing the delightful Catwoman in *Batman Returns*.

"I don't know whether to open fire or fall in love."

"You poor guys, always confusing your pistols with your privates."

"Don't hurt us lady, our take home's less than $300."

"You're overpaid, hit the road."

Catwoman places explosive devices in the store. Batman climbs after her to a roof where he tries to avoid hitting her, but finally has no other choice.

"How could you, I'm a woman!"

He approaches, "I'm sorry. I..." She kicks him in the stomach; using her whip she forces him over the side of the building.

Batman and Catwoman practice a bizarre courting ritual much like two little kids on a playground, punching each other in the arm. However, their playground is the rooftops over Gotham City and they never stop punching each other in the arm. Catwoman slashes Batman's side while he napalms her arm. These two make your average S&M practitioner look normal.

Meanwhile, Selina and Bruce Wayne are engaging in their own courtship ritual. "It's the so-called normal guys who always let you down. Sickos never scare me—at least they're committed."

Later Catwoman sits on the chest of a stunned Batman who had been gunned down by the police.

"You're catnip to a girl like me—handsome, dazed and to die for."

Catwoman finally corners Shreck in the underground hideout of the Penguin. Batman/Bruce tries to convince her to go away with him, "Let's just take him to the police then we can go home together."

Luna (Evanna Lynch), Heromine (Emma Watson) and Cho (Katie Leung) are three of the strong and bewitching female characters from the Harry Potter series.

there to emphasize the story, not *be* the story. But for fans who think film history starts with *Star Wars*, there are movies where the women are as awesome as the men. We have the *X-Men* (and women), Scully in *The X-Files*, the women in *The Descent*, that really creepy woman in *Audition*, plus the other Asian films such as *The Ring*. *Avatar* provides us with many brave women, although they are blue and not really women, Sookie in *True Blood*, Kate Beckinsale in numerous vampire and werewolf films—well the list could go on and on. The thing is, those movies don't really resonate with me like *Star Wars* did. But there is one heroine that I think will be included with the other unforgettable kick-ass heroines in fantastic films—Hermoine Granger (Emma Watson) and the other little witches in the Harry Potter series. Now there is a true movie heroine and role model for the modern girl.

One can't really get too intellectually serious about any of these films; after all, *it's only a movie!* and nothing could be duller than long treatises on the feminine, social, anti-social, homosexual, violence, blah, blah, blah... aspects of films. To me there is no better film than one that can transport you to another time and another place, wiping away the harsh realities of life for a couple of hours. Like the saying goes—if you want to send a message, call Western Union.

I adore these female characters. They're fun, outrageous, daring and dynamic—wouldn't it be nice to have just a *little* of their chutzpah? Scream queens and hand-wringing maidens are rapidly fading into oblivion being replaced with sword-wielding, martial-art experts taking on vampires and werewolves. Which makes me thankful bitches will continue to reign supreme at the box-office.

"Bruce, I would love to live with you in your castle forever just like in a fairy tale." She slashes him, "I just couldn't live with myself, so don't pretend this is a happy ending."

Shreck taking all this in can only think of one thing. "Selina Kyle, you're fired."

Shreck shoots Batman and then fires at Selina, but like all cats she has nine lives and uses the last one to electrocute Shreck.

Bruce Wayne rides through the lonely snow-covered streets of Gotham. Is that a shadow or a sequel?

Most current films coming out of Hollywood have strong females, but the movies seem so bland and forgettable. I guess I'm just becoming a grumpy old fart, but I do like an actual story with my movies and think special effects should be

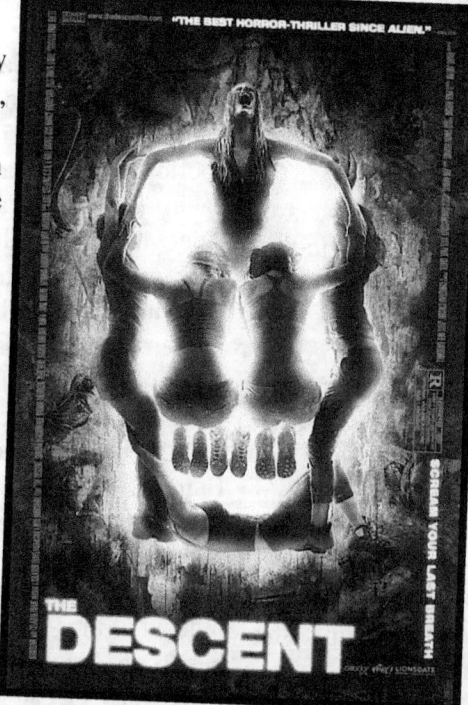

Scream and Scream Again! Horror's Honor List of Scream Queens

Julia Adams: *Creature from the Black Lagoon* (1954)
The film is most noteworthy for those shimmering, sharp underwater sequences that depict the long and leggy Julia Adams, in her white swim suit, almost operatically swimming on or near the surface of the water while the Gill Man silently (yet intensely) watches her, swimming almost in synch with her, further underneath the surface. Filmed almost as a ritualistic mating water ballet, the film never gets better than these scenes. The wavering light shining through the water sequence when Adams treads water, her legs and feet dangling within inches of the creature's playful grope, her feet shaking off the tickling sensation she feels when the Gill Man is inches away from her toes, remains an iconic moment in horror cinema.—Gary J. Svehla

Ramsey Ames: *The Mummy's Ghost* (1943)
The most praiseworthy addition is not necessarily the performance by Ramsey Ames as the heroine (she is rather lackluster and pretty in an odd sense) but the manner in which the audience is told that she is the reincarnation of the Princess Ananka by the ever-increasing white streak in her hair. By the time Carradine has her tied down in his railroad shack and is ready to inject her with the herbs to make her immortal, her hair is all white. When Kharis carries her beneath the swamp water, not only is her hair white, but her face has become mummified and wrinkled.—Gary J. Svehla

Drew Barrymore: *Scream* (1996)
Scream's best sequence is probably its pre-title one starring Drew Barrymore as a young innocent, at home alone, waiting for her boyfriend, popping popcorn as the stillness of the house gets to her. Soon the phone rings and a threatening voice on the other line spooks her. Barrymore remains relatively unfazed until the voice tells her to look outside and she sees her boyfriend tied to a chair on the patio. Soon the fiend who wears a distinctive Halloween ghost mask attacks, killing her and her boyfriend in grisly fashion, stabbing Barrymore repeatedly and then violating her body after she dies. It is a classic slasher sequence and is intense to behold.—Gary J. Svehla

Julia Adams and that famous white swimsuit in this publicity shot for *Creature from the Black Lagoon*.

Kate Beckinsale in *Underworld*

Kate Beckinsale: *Underworld* (2003)
In her first kick-ass action role, Beckinsdale portrays Selene, a strong, but still sexy Vampire who hunts down werewolves with automatic weapons and sometimes her bare hands. The intriguing story concerns two races that have evolved by remaining deeply hidden within human culture—the aristocratic, sophisticated Vampires, and the brutal, feral Lycans (werewolves). To humanity, their existence is no more than a whisper of a myth. But to each other, they are lifelong mortal rivals, sworn to wage a secret war until only one race is left standing.

"I would love to have done an action movie years ago, but usually you just want to play the boy's part," said Beckinsale, who also got involved in the action in the 2004 Universal release *Van Helsing*. "The girls in action movies are usually...on the plane making the phone call. I don't want to be that in *Die Hard*. I wanted to be blowing up the elevator shaft, and you never get to do that."

"I really feel like there's not really been [a female action star] since Sarah Connor [in *Terminator 2*] and *Alien* and *La Femme Nikita*. There's not really been a good serious female action hero for a long time, and when there is, they tend to be winking a bit at the camera."

There is no winking on Beckinsale's part in this film. No campy humor. No *Charlie's Angels* references—none of that. It is all quite serious. There is also no real nudity in the film, although some would expect it from an action genre movie that features a female lead.

"It was quite important to me to do a female action flick that was done in a certain tone," said Len Wiseman, Beckinsale's director and husband. "Because I do think that people push it over the edge and it's become kind of cheesy and corny to have to just play up the sex appeal way too much. And, I wanted to approach Selene's character as if it could have been a male. And, really, I think the best way to do a female action hero in a role like this is to really look at the script and say at the end of the day, 'should it be a guy? Should it be a girl? Let's make it a girl.' And really, not do much more than that. You know, she's already in a tight liquid latex leather thing, anyway. That completely does it. All the guys will be happy. She's sexy right from the beginning. Anything that we do above and beyond that, I think just tips it over the fence."

A fact Beckinsale tends to agree with. "I find the sort of latex suit and very shiny bottom takes care of it okay," Beckinsale smiled. "I think there was an issue in a scene where [my character] got in the shower, which I think is fairly early on. I just feel [that in films such as] *Die Hard*, you don't get the kind of shot where Bruce Willis is licking his armpit, so why do we have to have it?"

It's also one of the reasons why Beckinsale, who has a 12-year-old daughter, Lily, wouldn't care to take on an eye-candy role such as a Bond girl. "No," said Beckinsale emphatically, "I wouldn't want to be a Bond girl. No."

But then again, this is a girl who wants to be in the thick of the action. Not just lying in the background looking pretty. Although she was recently voted "The Most Beautiful Woman in England," don't expect her to rest on that title, or her laurels.
—Sam Borowski

Virginia Bruce: *The Invisible Woman* (1940)
The Invisible Woman features a fading John Barrymore and Virginia Bruce as the title character. Bruce is just right as the perky Kitty, but even her nude sequence

behind the screen fails to sizzle. John Barrymore, reduced to ham-fisted roles in less spectacular movie projects, is really quite good in this underplayed heavily made-up performance. He plays the wacky scientist whose projects are undermined by the son of a wealthy patron who has just gone broke from financial excess. Instead of being able to offer a volunteer $3,000 to be turned invisible, Professor Gibbs (Barrymore) can only offer the thrill but no compensation. But that's enough for Kitty, who wants to use her momentary invisibility to gain revenge on the nasty boss who fired her from her modeling job for speaking her mind.

The movie, light on comedy, special effects and plot, ends with a newborn baby suddenly turning invisible. Perhaps the best performance in the movie belongs to the fading John Barrymore, whose professor is warm, zany and comical when needed to be. However, when compared to the other movies, this A. Edward Sutherland–directed B production is bare bones at best. Not even a supporting role by Margaret Hamilton can save this non-entity.—Gary J. Svehla

Virginia Christine: *The Mummy's Curse* (1944)
It seems the swamp where Kharis took his Princess Ananka at the conclusion of *The Mummy's Ghost* floated way, way down south. In the film's best sequence, heroine Virginia Christine slowly emerges from the sun-baked clay and pulls herself out of her burial bog to slowly and quite eerily walk to a nearby pond where she can wash the clay, dirt and age off. After she emerges from the swampy earth mummified, a little water changes her into a beautiful young woman.—Gary J. Svehla

Susan Clark: *Skullduggery* (1969)
Clark's presence graced high-profile films (*Madigan* [1968], *Coogan's Bluff* [1968], *Porky's* [1981]), unsung gems (*Skin Game* [1971], *Night Moves* [1975]) and superior genre efforts (*Colossus: The Forbin Project* [1970], *Murder by Decree* [1979]), but—like Blythe Danner and Candice Bergen—she never achieved the film stardom she deserved. Is her performance here that great? Consider: Is there any other reason to watch *Skullduggery*?—Anthony Ambrogio

Hazel Court: *Doctor Blood's Coffin* (1961)
A 1950s aliens-attack film, several Gothic Edgar Allan Poe pictures, Hammer films, a British ghost story—Court did it all. And as screamer, love interest, villainess or tough, competent heroine (as here, doing an early version of the horror heroine later encountered in the late '70s and '80s), Court did it all with believability, iconic power, a superb speaking voice and a smoldering sexuality. One of the best of the horror heroines, this fine actress deserves greater recognition and attention.—James J.J. Janis

Jamie Lee Curtis: *Halloween* (1978)
One of horror's great heroines, Curtis distilled all that had gone before and created one of modern horror's few iconic female characters. Curtis runs away, seeks help, screams, uses clothes hangers as weapons and fights madly when cornered... doing whatever's necessary to survive the onslaught of Michael Myers. Sadly this template would soon be distorted beyond recognition.—James J.J. Janis

Jamie Lee Curtis: *Halloween: H20* (1998)
In the wake of the resurrected slasher picture, now an item of cinematic nostalgia, comes the return of Jamie Lee Curtis, 20 years later, to the franchise that made her a star. And interestingly enough, her character as developed by scriptwriters Robert Zappia and Matt Greenberg, working from a 14-page treatment by wunderkind Kevin Williamson (who claimed he was too busy working on *Dawson's Creek* to write another horror film script), contains some real grit: Laurie is reincarnated as an alcoholic single mother, driven to delusions of seeing Michael Myers anywhere/anytime, who has changed her name to escape her past, becoming headmistress of a private high school. Just the type of job cut out for alcoholic, delusional, identity-changing survivors.

But one important thing was forgotten, perhaps two: original director John Carpenter and an imaginative script!

Remember, most of the success of the original *Halloween* was due to director John Carpenter's subtlety:(his subjective point of view from the Shape/Michael Myers' point of view, thus avoiding graphic stabbing shots; his intensity of building up scares that truly delivered their intended shock; his careful development of Laurie's (Jamie Lee Curtis) character as a sheltered, virginal teen in contrast to her peers, etc. Here we have horror director hack Steve Miner, whose idea of a good scare is turning up the musical track (they do reuse Carpenter's original theme; remember, he composed the score for the first film as well) and have someone slide into frame entering from the left or right.

Besides having the reestablishment of Jamie Lee Curtis in a lead role (with mother Janet Leigh as her private school secretary in a performance that amounts to little more than a cameo), what about the plot? Once again, it's nothing more than another body count movie, and with such a slim cast, a brief one.

The final meeting between Laurie and Michael is cathartic and dramatic and it does show why Laurie has remained a survivor. But the last confrontation as the crushed Michael extends his fingers and Laurie extends hers to touch his, and then the quick flash of the ax resulting in Michael's head rolling, doesn't seem final enough.—Gary J. Svehla

Josette Day: *Beauty and the Beast* (1946)
Day, though perhaps a bit old for the part of Beauty (she was 32), is elegant, inspired, forthright and compelling.

Josette Day is Beauty and Jean Marais is the Beast in Cocteau's *Beauty and the Beast*, 1946.

She must have been the role model for June Cleaver—she even wears pearls while doing the laundry. Her transference of her infatuation with Avenant to a love of the Beast, and *his* transformation as a result of that love was developed in a storyline that defied most conventional filmmaking techniques.—Wolf Forrest

Faith Domergue: *The Atomic Man* (1955)
Domergue has never received the credit she deserves in the development of the horror/sci-fi heroine. Combining aspects of the competent Lorna Gray type with the Fay Wray screamer, Domergue created characters who were more than able to function in a world of monsters and horror while still being recognizably human to the audience.—James J.J. Janis

Sarah Douglas: *Superman II* (1980)
While the name was changed (from Faora to Ursa), Douglas plays comicdom's most fearsome female serial killer, incorporating all of the characteristics displayed by the witches in *Eastwick* and showing their logical, inevitable results here. A practitioner of sexual genocide and a child murderer, Ursa is powerful, a flirt, clever, cold blooded and deadly. An iconic, classic performance. —James J.J. Janis

Shelley Duvall: *The Shining* (1980)
No, it's not the novel, but it's still one of the most brilliant ghost movies ever filmed... and Duvall's performance helps to get it there. Throughout the film, Duvall must play Wendy as an apparently ditzy and mousy housewife, a terrified mother/potential victim, and finally as a resourceful survivor who saves both herself and her son from her axe-toting husband. Usually overlooked in favor of Nicholson (and nominated for Worst Actress by the 1980 Golden Raspberries), Duvall nevertheless turns in a terrific performance in a role requiring tremendous range.—Cindy Collins Smith

Glenda Farrell: *Mystery of the Wax Museum* (1933)
It is Farrell's hard-as-nails reporter (the counterpart to Lee Tracy's similar role in *Doctor X*) that grates, especially her interaction with her editor, with whom she reluctantly admits she has fallen in love. Farrell is feisty and fun, but her blonde hardness makes her difficult on the eyes and ears after a while. Original horror scream queen *King Kong* (1933) star Fay Wray is her typical delightful self, but her role becomes secondary to Farrell's and Wray seems to have less to do here.—Gary J. Svehla

Sally Field: *Kiss Me Goodbye* (1982)

Yes, I like her; I really like her! This American remake/rethink of the Brazilian *Dona Flor and Her Two Husbands* (1978) replaces that film's erotic *amour fou* and stupid macho double standard with screwball comedy (just like McCarey used to make). Field delights as a Carole Lombard/Irene Dunne-ish "Topper" whose new romance is complicated by the return of her dead husband (a ghost whom only she can see).—Anthony Ambrogio

Lorna Gray: *Captain America* (1944)

Gray (aka Adrian Booth) had a fine career in serials as an action adventuress long before any warrior princess leapt shrieking across the TV screen. Gray plays Captain America's assistant in this serial, and it represents her sublime moment. Cool, competent and with no agenda axe to grind, Gray—when faced with a challenge—uses her brains and is more than ready to start blasting away with the stylish snub-nose revolver that she keeps in her handbag. No speeches. No outrage. Just hot lead.—James J.J. Janis

Virginia Grey: *Target Earth* (1954)

In *Target Earth*, the eerily deserted city of Los Angeles stars as Any City, U.S.A. where a massive and mysterious evacuation has occurred. Only people rendered unconscious, either by heavy sleeping pills or violence, remain to face the alien invaders rampaging and killing all human life. *Target Earth*, a very low-budget sci-fi programmer, features comic relief with the "eat, drink and be merry; tomorrow we die" hedonist couple Jim Wilson (Richard Reeves) and Vicki Harris (Grey). Early initial sequences highlight deserted city streets and show the way that these left-of-center humans face their fate (Grey and Reeves deciding to raid every juke joint between here and the ocean, partying until the day of doom). Heroic Virginia Grey stands up to the gunman and takes two shots at close range, allowing Denning to overpower the criminal (although Denning still takes a shot to the shoulder) before irate Richard Reeves strangles the formerly tough gunman to death.—Gary J. Svehla

Brigitte Helm: *Metropolis* (1927)

Brigitte Helm's dual performance as Maria the liberator and the insidious and subversive robot turned human is brilliantly impressive. The initial images, almost religious in a brightly lit Joan of Arc sort of way, introduce perhaps the most innocent visage of Helm's underground leader who seeks to organize the workers for a better, richer way of life. In contrast, once the female robot has been

Gloria Holden as *Dracula's Daughter*

made human in the image of Brigitte Helm, she now features a snarling, curling lip, blackened eyes and an aura of manipulative evil that never could radiate from the formerly religious martyr. Without speaking a word of dialogue, the dual-character contrast within Brigitte Helm is cinematic acting of the highest order.—Gary J. Svehla

Gloria Holden: *Dracula's Daughter* (1936)

Gary J. Svehla in MidMar 65 notes, "Gloria Holden does a magnificent job as Countess Zaleska, Dracula's daughter, a woman who tries to escape the morbid addiction of vampirism. Holden's performance is best when it is internal, her eyes, face and mannerisms conveying the internal conflict between her attempt for a normal life vs. the curse of her blood relative."

Countess Zaleska is not in the pantheon of Classic Universal Monsters. She's never been a *Famous Monsters* covergirl or an Aurora model kit, which is a shame. Zaleska is a great, tragic character, and Holden gives a haunting performance as the tormented woman torn between her humanity and her vampiric heritage.—Brian Smith

Zita Johann: *The Mummy* (1932)

Wearing a very skimpy costume by movie's end (I wonder if the censors would have allowed the costume

if her breasts had been larger), Johann submits a quite eccentric performance, one of the better female leads of any Universal production by virtue of the fact that Johann has the opportunity to create a well-defined character, one who has lived through the ages via reincarnation. As her memory is jogged and she begins to remember her past lives and ultimately accepts the power of Egyptian god Isis, Johann turns from typical horror heroine to a rather morbidly developed character of depth.—Gary J. Svehla

Nastassja Kinski: *Cat People* (1982)
While Kinski lacks the feline quality of Simone Simon, she brings a fierce carnality to the role. Kinski is fascinating to watch in an otherwise uninspired remake.—Brian Smith

Catherine Lacey: *The Sorcerers* (1967)
In this little-seen film, Boris Karloff plays a downtrodden hypnotist who is on the verge of perfecting a thought-transference process. All goes swimmingly until his wife becomes obsessed with experiencing the good things in life. Lacey is splendid as the bitter, determined woman whose marital relationship deteriorates into a lethal battle of wills.—Steven Thornton

Laura La Plante: *The Cat and the Canary* (1927)
As heiress Annabelle, La Plante is youthful yet surprisingly matronly and very proper. She does a fine job when required to be suspicious or terrified. When the lawyer asks to see Annabelle alone, he offers to give her the envelope of the man who inherits everything if Annabelle is deemed insane. The lawyer tells her that the letter has been opened and that the person named within already knows he/she is second in line and could cause grave danger to Annabelle. As the lawyer speaks, in the background, the library shelf is slowly pushed forward, as a fiend emerges from the panel in back, his cat-clawed hand slowly reaching out for the lawyer's neck. "The name is..." the lawyer declares, as he is grabbed from

behind and forced into the panel that suddenly closes. At the film's climax, after attacking the hero in his underground lair and knocking him unconscious, the Cat sneaks back into the house proper and, creeping slowly up behind Annabelle, once again his cat-like hand lingers in the air above and behind her for an infinite period of time.—Gary J. Svehla

Julie London: *Nabonga* (1944)
Nabonga was London's first film. Apparently her career never took off. One cannot see why from this film. She plays the childlike yet vaguely amoral Doreen as very likable, yet she is capable of saying to the cringing Gorman, "Samson won't hurt you unless I tell him too," as if she were asking him if he would like sprinkles on his banana cream pie.—J.J. Janis

Barbara Payton: *Bride of the Gorilla* (1951)
Payton, looking more than a little like Elisha Cuthbert (the dim-witted Kim on TV's finest series, *24*), smolders as the temptress doomed to always marry the wrong man, her latest husband being Barney. We know something is very amiss when the smoldering Payton invites Barney to their bed on the wedding night, and he nervously opines that he needs to take a walk in the jungle and that he'll be back soon.—Gary J. Svehla

Jane Randolph: *Cat People* (1942).
Much has been written about Simone Simon's performance as Irena in RKO's *Cat People,* but this writer finds Jane Randolph's role in that same film to be equally impressive. Sexy and self-assured without sacrificing any of her vulnerability, Randolph transforms her role as the film's "other woman" into a very real, and most likable, character.—Steven Thornton

Edith Scob and Alida Valli: *Eyes Without a Face* (1960)
Alida Valli, soon to be known a generation later for her appearances in Italian horror movies, is interesting in an almost silent role as assistant (her face also reconstructed... a scar on her neck hidden by necklaces) to Genessier (it is always apparent she loves the doctor and will do anything for him), who silently waits unseen in cars on crowded Paris streets, attempting to find the right young girl with the proper facial features to become the latest medical guinea pig. In other sequences, she becomes almost like a mother to the disturbed Christiane, comforting the girl and giving her strength and faith that her father will be able to restore her face. Valli's is a supporting role, but it is one that lingers.

But perhaps the most interesting performance is that of Edith Scob as the hauntingly beautiful Christiane, the girl who wears an ivory white face mask that only reveals her hair and eyes, making her face as rigid yet as beautiful as any statue crafted by an Italian artist. Christiane is often viewed curled up in a fetal position on the couch. Her wide, sad eyes are a mirror to her soul, revealing a young woman lost in hopelessness. Even after her face is restored and the mask is gone, her actual facial features do not appear much different than when she was wearing the mask, but her short-term hope is lost as her face slowly deteriorates, captured in a series of still photographs shot over the course of almost one week. Earlier, from a subjective focus, the audience caught a blurred shot of Christiane's mask-less face as she stared at the face of the victim-to-be lying helpless on the operating table. Christiane's depression is caused by the fact that even if the operation is successful, her success means the disfigurement or even death of an innocent girl, much like herself. At the movie's climax she releases the wild dogs, who attack and maul the face of the unsuspecting Dr. Genessier, and the doves, whose white presence in the dark night is more an image of beauty on which to end the film rather than a logical plot resolution. *Eyes Without a Face* ends on a note of quiet, intense beauty, allowing such imagery to create a dramatic conclusion.

Many of us first encountered *Eyes Without a Face* in its butchered and dubbed American release, 1963's *The Horror Chamber of Dr. Faustus*, serving as the other half

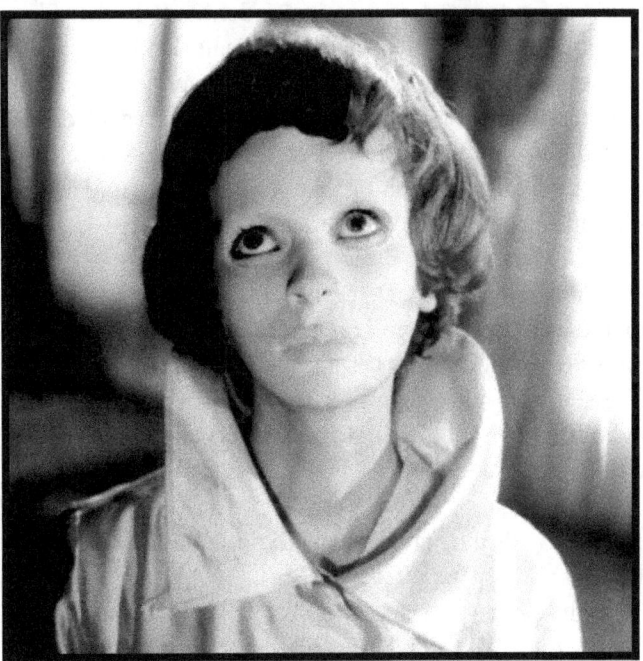

Edith Scob as Christiane in *Eyes Without a Face*

of a double-bill with *The Manster*. But that bastardized version is nothing like witnessing Franju's original vision. The movie's stark black and white photography by Eugen Schufftan (aka Shuftan) is among the eeriest ever concocted for a horror film classic, showcasing naked corpses in trench coats being dumped into a river, dank kennels with raging dogs in cages, the no-frills operating room, the cold police station, the darkly lit morgue and the gloomy mausoleum, each establishing set pieces of morbid and depressed horror. *Eyes Without a Face* is not a black and white movie; it is best described as black and gray.

Eyes Without a Face lies in my top-25 horror film favorites.—Gary J. Svehla

Venita Stevenson: *City of the Dead* (1960)
The lovely Venetia Stevenson, portraying the doomed college researcher Nan, creates the right tone of vulnerability, shock and screaming terror as she investigates the supposed reanimation of witchcraft in the quaint hamlet of Whitewood, a New England village appearing to have remained in the timeless image of the era of the Salem witch trials (thus allowing the production to be modern with its mod academic image in half the scenes and period Gothic with its fog-shrouded timelessness during the other half).—Gary J. Svehla

Gloria Talbott: *I Married a Monster from Outer Space* (1958)
Here's a performance so good that, even though it's often cited as underrated, it remains underrated! In this film, Talbot creates a fully realized female lead character, something practically unheard of for a genre film of this vintage. Her thoughtful, convincing portrayal—fearful but determined, feminine but headstrong—is one of the principal strengths of this gem of a movie. Hers is the finest female leading performance in a 1950s sci-fi film.—Mark Clark
The film's strength tries to be the sensitive characterizations of the just-married Tom Tryon and Gloria Talbott, and this may very well be Talbott's finest performance. She plays the sensitive wife who is a sexually frustrated woman who tries to light a sexual spark in Tryon's trousers, yet fails.—Gary J. Svehla

Sigourney Weaver and Wionna Ryder: *Alien Resurrection* (1997)
The alien was reduced to a background role as Ripley (Sigourney Weaver) came to the forefront: Her body, now alien-infested, forces Ripley to come to terms with motherhood, monsters and mortality.

Winona Ryder, a virtual babe-in-arms amongst the most cold-blooded renegades of the universe, comes across as a wimp, not a badass. However, borrowing an idea from the first two entries, she is surprisingly revealed to be an android who manages to return from the dead.

Unwisely following the lead and major flaw of the third installment, none of the cast is sympathetic, as everyone is either pro-alien, stupid, cold-blooded or blindly militaristic. Even the character of Ripley is compromised for the first time in the series: She is reduced to delivering one-liners such as "She'll breed. You'll die!" or "Was it everything you expected!" Since Ripley has been cloned and contains alien genes, she is superhuman (her newfound strength and agility) and supercold (her aloof personality and attitude). Instead of remaining the human anchor in a sea of hardware, monsters and technology, she is reduced to sticking her rifle through the rotting human corpse of an alien victim and blowing off the head of an alien predator sniffing around. She fails to connect emotionally with any other character and she seems more intent on survival then on maintaining any semblance of humanity. The loss of Ripley's soul is the greatest disservice this movie commits.—Gary J. Svehla

She (1935)/*The Mummy* (1932)
Haggard's novel *She*, like *The Mummy*, juxtaposes an ancient romance with a modern one in which one person survives from the past and the other has been reincarnated in a new body. In ancient Egypt, Kallikrates was a priest of Isis who committed sacrilege, breaking his vow of celibacy by loving the Princess Amenartas. After the two fled from Egypt, they crossed paths with Ayesha (known to the natives she rules as She-who-must-be-obeyed). Ayesha fell in love with Kallikrates but, because he loved another, she killed him in a fit of jealous anger. Amenartas then escaped with Kallikrates's child. Because Ayesha gained immortality by bathing in a mysterious flame, she lived on, awaiting the return of her beloved. And return he does, 2,000 years later, in the form of Leo Vincey, the descendant and, in a sense, the reincarnation of Kallikrates.

By blending Amenartas and Ayesha into a single character and then reversing the lovers' sexes, *Mummy* screenwriter John Balderston turned this situation into the forbidden love of Princess Anckesenamon, a priestess of Isis who broke her vows as a vestal virgin, and Imhotep, High Priest of the Temple of the Sun at Karnak. No jealousy is involved in this situation, however, and Anckesenamon, unlike Kallikrates, died of natural causes. At her death, Imhotep compounded his sacrilege by stealing the Scroll of Thoth from the temple and trying to use it to return her to life. Interrupted, he is punished by being buried alive, but 3,700 years later he is accidentally revived and sets out to regain his lost love. Thus, whereas Ayesha remained alive over the centuries, suffering solitude as her love endured, Imhotep's suffering was more immediate and physical, but also more temporary. Their basic needs and goals, however, are the same.

Before Ayesha can be reunited with Kallikrates-in-Leo, he must undergo a process of death and rebirth by bathing in the eternal flame, thus becoming immortal, like her. As a first step, she destroys Kallikrates's preserved body, which she has kept through the centuries. Similarly, Imhotep tells Anckesenamon-in-Helen that they may not love "until the great change," which involves killing Helen, mummifying her body, and then using the scroll to revive it to eternal life. First, though, he burns Anckesenamon's mummy. "I destroy this lifeless thing," he tells Helen. "Thou shalt take its place but for a few moments, and then rise again even as I have risen... For thy sake I was buried alive. I ask of thee only a moment of agony. Only so can we be united." In another link between *The Mummy* and *She*, both Imhotep and Ayesha reveal to others images of the past in the surface of a pool of water.

Although Ayesha is beautiful and Imhotep is certainly not handsome, the two characters share a similar mixture of attraction and repulsion, of malevolence and suffering. Each, too, is (in Haggard's words) "a being who, unconstrained by human law, is also absolutely unshackled by a moral sense of right and wrong." They are passionately devoted to their goals, to satisfying the long-denied need to be with their beloveds.

In Haggard's novel, a conflict arises because a native girl, Ustane, has fallen in love with Leo. Ayesha, who can "slay with mine eyes and by the power of my will," kills her new rival: "Ayesha said nothing, she made no sound, she only drew herself up, stretched out her arm, and... appeared to look fixedly at her victim. Even as she did so Ustane put her hands to her head, uttered one piercing scream, turned round twice, and then fell backward with a thud—prone upon the floor." Both Ayesha's method and her casual ruthlessness ("she stood between me and thee, and therefore have I removed her") are transferred to Imhotep, who does not even need to be in his victim's

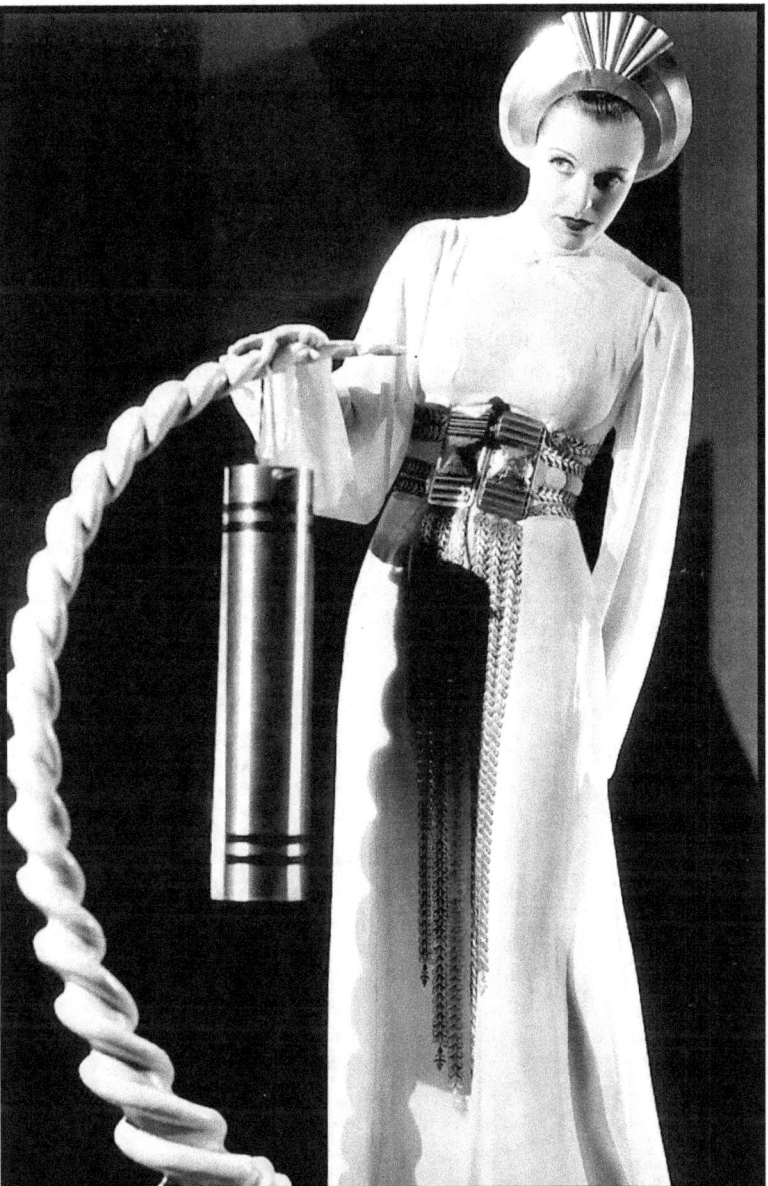

Helen Gahagan as Ayesha in Merian C. Cooper's 1935 *She*.

presence to cause his death and who attempts to destroy Frank Whemple (David Manners), "that boy for whom love is creeping into your heart. Love that would keep you from myself."

In the 1935 film, *She*, Ustane becomes the more articulate Tanya, who tells Ayesha that she has a stronger hold on Leo "because I'm human and you're not, because I'm young and you know love belongs to the young. Your magic makes you seem young, but in your heart you're old, old. You were young once, like me, but now you're old and it's too late for love forever." This change in the character may have originated in Balderston's script of *She*, because Tanya here sounds very much like Anckesenamon-as-Helen who, in *The Mummy*'s climax, tells Imhotep, "I'm alive! I'm young! I won't die! I

155

loved you once, but now you belong with the dead. I am Anckesenamon—but I—I'm somebody else, too. I want to live, even in this strange new world."

All of this material from *She* takes on a new identity when placed in the context of Egypt, and it certainly gives *The Mummy* the emotional substance and dramatic power that cannot even be glimpsed in the *Cagliostro* plot summary. But in adapting these elements to their new form, Balderston drew on still another influence to flesh out the relationships and develop the plot. That influence was his own stage and screen adaptations of *Dracula*. Thus, both films present an un-dead creature who seductively threatens the heroine with death, while offering a kind of eternal life, thereby endangering both her life and her soul. In each case, the creature's manner is reserved, mixing politeness with irony, and he can influence others with a hypnotic force. Combatting him are the young man who loves the heroine and an older expert in the occult (played in both films by David Manners and Edward Van Sloan, respectively). Each film even includes a pivotal scene in which the expert tests his suspicions, using a mirror in *Dracula* and a photograph in *The Mummy*, which prompts the creature to drop his pose of civility. In both cases, too, a talisman offers protection from the creature's power, with a figure of Isis serving this function in *The Mummy* instead of a crucifix.

Germanic in concept is the emphasis placed in *The Mummy* on the force of Imhotep's will, which can summon or kill across considerable distance. A good example can be seen in Murnau's *Nosferatu* (1922, photographed by Fritz Arno Wagner), in which similar intercutting evokes the fact that the heroine senses the vampire's approach and is drawn to watch for his ship's arrival. Another, more immediate, influence was probably a sequence in *Svengali* (Warner Bros., 1931), in which the title character (John Barrymore) summons Trilby (Marian Marsh) to him, as director Archie Mayo moves his camera from Svengali's face, across the city's rooftops, to Trilby's bedroom—an approach similar to the moment in *The Mummy* when the camera sweeps across Cairo to connect Imhotep to Helen.

In the original script, Imhotep had shown Helen only Anckesenamon's death, her burial, and his interrupted attempt to revive her at the pool in his house. Then, in the final sequence at the museum, he used a mirror to reflect her five prior lives as she sees herself reject a young gallant in 18th-century France, bid farewell to 13th-century crusaders, commit suicide in an 8th-century Saxon stockade, become a Christian martyr in ancient Rome, and embrace Imhotep in the sanctuary of Isis. After that, he finally showed his own burial alive. Wisely, the extraneous material on Helen's lives was dropped and the footage of Imhotep's fate moved to the scene at the pool, so that the flashback tale is told all at once. This renders the film more compact, while making Imhotep's statement by the pool about his suffering for her more comprehensible.
— By Paul M. Jensen

Gloria Venus: *Doctor of Doom* (1963)
Doctor of Doom involves our old reliable mad scientist who is working out the bugs on

female brain transplants. The dubbing is ridiculously funny, featuring those dramatic deadpan voices sputtering forth the most inane dialogue. At first the doctor feels his female experiments die because he needs to operate on more intelligent women, so he kidnaps one, transfers her brain and she too dies. Thus, he figures it out—he needs to use physically stronger women as his experiments, so he eyes up the female wrestling champion, Gloria Venus, as his intended victim. However, Gloria Venus and wrestling partner Golden Rubi generally kick the butt of the Doctor of Doom and his henchmen, even when the good doctor employs his secret weapon Gomar, the blatantly silly offspring of the first successful male/gorilla brain transplant, a human of enormous physical strength. But whenever the villains attack, the wrestling tag-team spins into action, making *Doctor of Doom* look like a South of the Border Republic serial.—Gary J. Svehla

Fay Wray: *Black Moon* (1934)
Usually dismissed as "just" a scream queen, Wray was anything but. In all of her genre films, Wray gave intelligent, thoughtful performances of average women with average desires and dreams who, when suddenly confronted with the horrific, do what *any* normal woman would do: scream in abject terror. It was through Wray that the audience, few of whom were expert in the ways of monsters, could relate to and comprehend what they were witnessing. Wray grounded these classic films in reality.—James J.J. Janis

Maris Wrixon: *White Pongo* (1945)
If *White Pongo* belongs to anyone, it belongs to Maris Wrixon as Pamela Bragdon. Until Kroegert makes his move, the story hinges on the Pamela character. She has come to Africa for excitement and she is going to get it. As Bishop observes, she does not really care about anyone except herself and a significant portion of the film's running time is devoted to a PRC version of a Von Sternberg/Dietrich movie, with Pamela gaily toying with and manipulating the men around her. And Wrixon is more than up to the task. As she relaxes languidly in

Maris Wrixon and *White Pongo*

a canoe, her mouth moving in an unsettling manner and her eyes gazing hungrily at poor Bishop as if he were a slab of prime beef, Wrixon's expressions speak volumes about the character that Schrock probably did not intend. Pamela is not some helpless female. She is constantly taking charge of her situation and driving the action. Even after the story becomes more action-oriented, she never waits to be rescued, using any opportunity to take some type of action. *White Pongo* is simply a Maris Wrixon movie.

Wrixon's acting resume lists her as having uncredited parts in such fine pictures as *Each Dawn I Die* (1939) and *High Sierra* (1941). Some of her other work includes Karloff's *British Intelligence* (1940) and the provocatively titled *Women in Bondage* (1943). Her only other horror credit is Karloff's *The Ape* (1940), also with Ray Corrigan.
—James J.J. Janis

Women to Die for—1960s Onward
Midmar Readers Have Their Say...

The short-lived MidMar magazine *Movie Mystique* asked writers and readers to send us their five favorite horror, fantasy or sci-fi female actresses/characters from the 1960s through today. As usual they came through with interesting and insightful choices.
Our favorite kick-ass heroines from 2002/3 were:
Jennifer Garner (*Daredevil*)
Angelina Jolie (*Lara Croft: Tomb Raider: The Cradle of Life*)
Natalie Portman (*Star Wars Episode II: Attack of the Clones*)
Halle Berry (*Gothika*)
Jada Pinkett Smith (*The Matrix Reloaded*)
Carrie-Anne Moss (*The Matrix Reloaded*).

1. Gaylen Ross from *Dawn of the Dead*
2. Jamie Lee Curtis from *Halloween*
3. Daria Nicolodi from *Opera*
4. Toni Collette from *The Sixth Sense*
5. Julie Christie from *Don't Look Now*
Gasp—Sigourney Weaver is not on the list for *Alien*? Tough choice but I'll live with it.
—Robert Tinnell

1. Sigourney Weaver in the *Alien* series (women kicked butt).
2. Jamie Lee Curtis in *Halloween* (perhaps set up the cliché of good girl surviving, but her performance and character grew in the series, and her tragic end was the only decent thing in the latest in the series).
3. The Blair Witch—this character influenced the look of many a horror film (both good and bad) since its premiere.
4. *Species*—tied with *Lifeforce*—sexy women can be deadly—alluring as a snake seducing its victims.
5. Linnea Quigley—the quintessential scream queen (with special mention to Michelle Bauer, Debbie Rochon and Brinke Stevens).
   One must not neglect the writing talents that contributed so much to fantasy—namely J.K. Rowling (*Harry Potter*) and Anne Rice (the Lestat stories).
—Kevin Shinnick

1. Sigourney Weaver - *Alien*
2. Linda Hamilton - *Terminator 2*
3. Carrie Fisher - *Star Wars*
4. Jamie Lee Curtis - *Halloween*
5. Heather Donahue - *The Blair Witch Project* (thought I'd throw you a curve...)
—Craig Hoffman

1. The *Alien* films with Sigourney Weaver
2. *The Fog* with Adrienne Barbeau
3. *The Others* with Nicole Kidman
4. *Star Wars* with Carrie Fisher
5. *Halloween* with Jamie Lee Curtis
—Gary Rhodes

1. Jamie Lee Curtis—for her unforgettable screams and verve in *Halloween*
2. Salma Hayek—for her dance in *From Dusk Til Dawn*
3. Jane Seymour—for being the ultimate princess in *Sinbad and the Eye of the Tiger*
4. Milla Jovovich—for being "perfect" as the Supreme Being in *The Fifth Element*
5. Natasha Henstridge—for being my all-time favorite demonic alien in *Species*
—Scott Essman

1. Barbara Shelley
2. Susan Farmer

3. Veronica Carlson
4. Pam Grier
5. Jamie Lee Curtis
—L.L. Spikessr

1. Vulnavia (Virginia North) in *The Abominable Dr. Phibes* (1971). She is the sexiest (and most efficient) assistant a mad doctor ever hired—or did the automatonic genius Dr. Anton Phibes (Vincent Price) build her? Certain elements of the film suggest that Vulnavia is an artificial being, and although the final release print does not contain any references to Vulnavia's human or android status, early drafts of the script indicated the beautiful but deadly sidekick was indeed some kind of robot. Human or not, Vulnavia is a key player in the greatest horror-comedy of the 1970s.

2. Edwina Lionheart (Diana Rigg) in *Theatre of Blood* (1973). The fanatically devoted daughter of crazed actor Edward Lionheart (Vincent Price again) is absolutely necessary to her father's deranged schemes, and Rigg makes Edwina's loyalty to her dad seem logical, not just the kink of the scriptwriters. *Theatre of Blood* stumbles a bit by expecting us to believe Rigg in male drag for most of the picture—her voice is a dead giveaway from the first line that "he" is a "she"—but the performance itself is keenly realized and a crucial contribution to the second greatest horror-comedy of the 1970s.

3. Lady Sylvia Marsh (Amanda Donohoe) in *The Lair of the White Worm* (1988). Ken Russell's sexy, campy take on Bram Stoker's last novel is another delightful mix of screams and guffaws, and the picture's success can largely be credited to Amanda Donohoe's wonderfully vampy take on the leading role. Donohoe seems to be channeling old school horror heroines like Barbara Steele and Ingrid Pitt with her performance (although, to be fair, neither Steele nor Pitt ever ran around threatening ingenues with gigantic strap-ons). A great piece of work from an actress who, alas, makes too few screen appearances lately.

4. Catwoman/Selina Kyle (Michelle Pfeiffer) in *Batman Returns* (1992). She may not be your father's Catwoman, but Michelle Pfeiffer is both sexy and tragic as the Caped Crusader's greatest femme fatale—and most obviously perfect romantic match. No other adaptation of DC's most popular villainess has captured the complicated, even schizophrenic nature of the relationship Catwoman has with Batman. Many people hate this cockeyed masterpiece, but even the cruelest critics recognize the charm and energy Pfeiffer brings to the role.

5. Marla Singer (Helena Bonham Carter) in *Fight Club* (1999). Yeah, yeah, I hear your protests, fanboy—you say *Fight Club* isn't a "horror film." Well, it is definitely a modern Gothic, and without giving the major plot twist away to the uninitiated, let's just say this picture has just as serious an identity crisis at its center as a certain Hitchcock classic involving an alienated young man and his horrible mother. If you don't recognize male anxiety about masculine identity, desire and relevance

Dianna Rigg as Edwina Lionheart in *Theatre of Blood*

in an increasingly materialistic world of oft-feminized conformity, you obviously haven't been dragging a penis around lately. "If I had a tumor, I'd name it Marla," the Narrator (Edward Norton) says about this flaky, profane, possibly crazy but ferociously sexy Goth chick—the only woman he can relate to, and even then only because they are equally marginalized by the world. It's tough to be attracted to somebody you find repulsive, and it's even harder to make such a conflicted person seem real. Helena Bonham Carter pulls it off; too bad *Fight Club*'s apocalyptic finale seems to prohibit any hope of a sequel.
—Jonathan Lampley

Sigourney Weaver turns up the heat in *Ghostbusters*.

1. Ripley (Sigourney Weaver), *Alien* & sequels
2. Laurie Strode (Jamie Lee Curtis) from *Halloween*
3. Dee Wallace Stone from any number of horror/sci-fi films (*ET, The Howling, Critters, Cujo*...)
4. Sarah Connor (Linda Hamilton) from the *Terminator* films
5. Any of the Girls from *Ghostwatcher* (sorry, shameless plug for our own film!)

    I almost forgot, Sigourney Weaver from *Ghostbusters* I and II. She should be on your list for both *Aliens* and *Ghostbusters*
—Jason Contino

1. Sarah Douglas—Stunning, dark eyes and a beautiful complexion made her anything but a victim in fantasy films. Often she victimized. She was a total vamp as Ursa in *Superman II*—still the most powerful female in fantasy film history. She was dignified and evil also in *Conan the Destroyer* and gave good performances in many other films such as *People that Time Forgot*, *Return of the Swamp Thing* and *Solarbabies*.
2. Sigourney Weaver—Great in *Alien*, *Aliens* and *Ghostbusters*. She was a perfect hero just as Harrison Ford was as Indiana Jones.
3. Lynda Carter—*Wonder Woman* was every man's and boy's fantasy. She will always be great for her defining that character.

    I know many fans wish they could read more about these amazing, pioneering sci-fi women, who set the stage for the strong, physical heroines and villainesses we see today.
Thank you and good luck,
—Kenny Strong

1. From the '70s on, movies are very restrictive, as most of the women's parts/characters after this were just refinements on archetypes from earlier movies. Probably the only exception to this is Sigourney Weaver's character in the *Alien* series of the extremely strongwilled, almost masculine yet very human space (wo)man. This character is somewhat unique and is reflective of the gender social equality sentiments of the end of the last century.
2. A very good blend (view it as a maturing fusion) of a woman as nurturer, scientist, explorer, equal is the character of Beverly Crusher on *Star Trek: The Next Generation* as played by Gates McFadden. She cares and so you care with her.
3. Prior to the '70s, a few interesting women's parts appeared that were sort of the best examples of the genesis of the types of roles/parts/characters that would follow. The female leads in *Rocky Jones* were dressed and scripted to have a very button-down sensuality (allure in the future—one can get away with a lot in the future—the replicators on the original Enterprise must have worked overtime making all those black stockings...they certainly were not overtaxed making cloth for the women).
4. Similarly Anne Francis' character in *Forbidden Planet* has an innocence that allowed the plot to focus on a human story. No matter how incredible the technology, even in the far future our stories and our needs will be emotional...her innocence and "needs" motivate a large part of the story.
5. Maria from *Metropolis*.... SHE from *She*... the *Bride of Frankenstein*...all more interesting and fresh than '70s plus, where most of the characters were just these gone to excess.

—Hope this helps...in great haste...Best, Buc

Narrowing this down was a tough business. I mean, who can fail to recognize Princess Leia Organa (Carrie Fisher), the tomboy princess, from the original *Star Wars* trilogy or the resourceful Ripley (Sigourney Weaver) from the *Alien* film series? Nor is it easy to omit Clarice Starling (Jodie Foster), the FBI agent who is condescended to by her superiors and male agents and who must confront fear-filled memories of her past while attempting to manipulate criminal mastermind Hannibal Lecter to get his aid in solving a case. Or how can I bypass Cameron Diaz who was so delightful not only as Lotte Schwartz in *Being John Malkovich*, but also as Princess Fiona in *Shrek*, a delightful parody of Michelle Pfeiffer's plight in *Ladyhawk*? And what red-blooded male wouldn't want to have a laboratory assistant like Teri Garr's Inga from *Young Frankenstein*, so compassionate, so curvaceous, so compellingly giving of herself to complete the work at hand? If the criterion was most frightening female, then surely I would have picked Evelyn Draper (Jessica Walter) from *Play Misty for Me*, or Annie Wilkes (Kathy Bates) from *Misery* or even Catherine Tramell (Sharon Stone) from *Basic Instinct*. But the key word is "favorite," so my five picks are as follows:

Teri Garr as Inga in *Young Frankenstein*

1. Chihiro (Daveigh Chase in the American version) from *Spirited Away* is a terrific heroine, and one of the most memorable from any fantasy film. She's only nine years old, she's moving to a new place with her parents, and she is resentful and fearful. Through her experiences in Mizayaki's marvelous story, she learns many things including lessons on courage, resourcefulness, loyalty, responsibility, and even love.

2. Jen Yu (Xion Long in English version, played by Ziyi Zhang) from *Crouching Tiger, Hidden Dragon*: Here is a very romantic albeit exciting character. I truly love the subplot where she chases after a Mongol bandit who has stolen her comb, only to wind up falling in love with him as he continues to treat her with kindness and respect. In one exciting sequence, she is disguised as a boy whom some thugs attempt to recruit, only to take on a squadron of them and defeat them soundly

Ziyi Zhang in *Crouching Tiger, Hidden Dragon*

with her martial arts prowess. Her family tries to marry her off in a politically advantageous marriage, but she rejects the traditional role and wins Master Bai's admiration, creating a desire within him to have her as a worthy student of his own martial arts knowledge.

3. Buttercup (Robin Wright Penn) from *The Princess Bride*: Ms. Penn has to embody the world's most beautiful princess who is taken away by Prince Charming (Chris Sarandon) only to discover that he is truly a son-of-a-bitch. Never fear, her true love Wesley (Cary Elwes) is soon in pursuit to rescue her from marriage and death. Seen by some as a send-up of fairy tales, Goldman on the contrary is quite sincere in his depiction of mythic perfection while indulging in some delightful twists of fairy tale clichés.

4. Grace (Nicole Kidman) from *The Others*: This is a surprisingly good performance by Kidman as the mother of two children whose rare skin condition keeps them from the rays of the sun. The role requires a pitched sense of hysteria that increases with the spooky goings-on that invites comparison with Deborah Kerr's brilliant performance in *The Innocents*. And for once, the final twist proves truly chilling.

5. Edna McCauley (Ellen Burstyn) from *Resurrection*: This is one of the great female character studies essayed by one of our finest female actresses. It would have been easy to select Burstyn's Chris MacNeil from *The Exorcist* instead—a mother facing her worst nightmare as her cherubic child transforms into a foul-mouth monster whom medical science is powerless to help—but her Edna, though a much quieter performance, is equally skillful and much more in need of some attention. Edna has an accident that causes her to gain some healing powers. While a true miracle worker, because she does not invoke the name of God in her healing, she becomes suspect under the eyes of her boyfriend and others in the community.

—Dennis Fischer

1. Sigourney Weaver in *Alien* (1979). If you look at this film with fresh eyes, you will be surprised all over again by the subtle way that Ripley begins just as one of the crew. She isn't particularly likable at first. But slowly, the character moves to the foreground of the film and, in the process, Ridley Scott redefines how women could be portrayed in horror movies in particular and in movies in general. This is groundbreaking all the way round.

2. Jamie Lee Curtis in *Halloween* (1978). Another obvious choice but once again, try to look at it anew. Curtis' character is terrified but strong and resourceful. She refuses to give up. The clichés were once new, weren't they?

3. Madeline Kahn in *Young Frankenstein* (1974). Was any actress since Carole Lombard this funny and sexy? At the same time? "Ah sweet mystery of life, at last I've found you."

4. Ellen Burstyn in *The Exorcist* (1973). Although the movie is perhaps overrated, Burstyn is wonderful as the mother facing every parent's worst nightmare. Her 12-year-old child has suddenly become possessed by the Devil and is not quite herself. Can we remember when American movies actually had leading roles for grown-up women? Just watch Burstyn in this and the much better *Alice Doesn't Live Here Anymore* and you'll wonder what happened to the movies and to us, the audience.

5. Reba McEntire in *Tremors* (1990). OK, this is an odd choice, but Reba steals every scene she's in from a gang of scene stealing character actors. She's tough, resourceful and much smarter than her paranoid, gun-wielding husband. She's also very funny.

—Stan Campbell

1. Sadako from the *Ring* trilogy
2. Melanie Ballard from *Ghosts of Mars*
3. Laura Palmer from *Twin Peaks* (I know she's not onscreen much, but she's still the central figure).
—Jim Harper

Five female characters, hmmm...
1. Ellen Ripley (Sigourney Weaver from *Alien* series) "OK, we're here, let's kill all the monsters."

Country superstar Reba McEntire in *Tremors*

2. Clarice Starling in the Hannibal Lecter series (I preferred Julianne Moore over Jodie Foster).
3. CCH Pounder (Fran Ambrose) from *Psycho IV*, radio talk show hostess discussing matricide who receives the ultimate ratings-boosting phone call.
4. Sil (Natasha Henstridge) from *Species*—homina, homina, homina
5. Mrs. Blaylock (Billie Whitelaw) from *The Omen*
—Gary Billings

I'm mentioning lesser-known, some just in U.S., actresses. During the '60s and '70s, N.J. kids could get warped by fab TV in English and Spanish!
1. Julissa, who starred in *The Snake People* (1968) with Boris Karloff.
2. Spanish star Amparo Rivelles of (1963) *Dona Macabra*, a horror soap opera about an elderly lady with an "unusual" family. Amparo was a big star in a slew of Mex productions I have yet to discover. She also appeared in the soap *Hyena* (1973) as a murderess.
3. Simone Simon, so feminine in Val Lewton's *Cat People* (1942) and its sequel. A contrast to the tomboyish female roles of WWII.
4. Zoe Tamerlis in *Ms. 45* (1981). Female *Death Wish*. Wrecking vengeance on the scum of the night; and who can forget her in that stylish nun outfit? Mike Manikowski, Chiller Theatre's photographer, met her at Chiller, and said she was nice but had a lost, lonely look. A month later she was dead of a drug overdose.
5. Emily Perkins appeared with Farrah Fawcett in the shocking true-crime film *Small Sacrifices* and more recently *Ginger Snaps* (2001). She is the movie.
6. Jodie Foster starred with Martin Sheen and Scott Jacoby (who also starred in the weird TV movie *Bad Ronald*) in *The Little Girl Who Lives Down the Lane* (1976).
7. Mimi Rogers. When she cries, I cry...you forget she's acting. She's good in the religiously bizarre film *The Rapture* (1991). She also starred in an unforgettable episode of *Tales of the Crypt*, where an angry model, tired of not succeeding, bumps off her roommate and shows up to the beauty pageant in her place...not quite aware of what the winner gets! BWWAAAHAHAHA!!
—Rose Solar

1. Lynda Carter in *The New Adventures of Wonder Woman* (1976). The Golden Age Wonder Woman (1941-48) is complex, filled with far more quirks and contradictions than it is possible to describe. To even consider bringing the character to life accurately beggars the imagination. Yet, for the pilot film for the later series, somehow Lynda Carter caught magic in a bottle "roping" the Amazon Princess—though in a still ever slightly watered down fashion. Sadly for the program itself, the magic was lost. Carter, the program and *Wonder Woman* became mediocrity in red and blue tights. Ahhh but that first movie!!!
2. Erin Gray as Wilma Deering in *Buck Rogers in the 25th Century* (1979). As Wilma Deering, Gray was competence and sexiness personified in an utterly believable and human spandex package. So perfect a fit was Gray in the role that this writer has to concentrate not to refer to the program as *The Adventures of Wilma Deering and her Sidekick Buck*.
3. Jamie Lee Curtis as Laurie Strode in the *Halloween* series. As simply one of the greatest heroines in the history of the genre, Curtis created a strong female character who did not substitute intelligence for anger nor humanity for ideology. What is more Curtis maintained the character's integrity through four separate appearances. A sharp contrast to the destruction of Sigourney Weaver's Ripley.
4. Misato Tanaka as the revenge-obsessed military officer determined to destroy Godzilla to avenge the death of her commander in *Godzilla vs. Megaguiras*. Non-super powered heroines in action-oriented genre films are notoriously difficult to do right. If not unbelievable then they end up just being irritating.
5. Anita Mui as Wonder Woman in *The Heroic Trio*. As the straight arrow member of the female super team, Mui easily overcomes the difficulties that such a role entails, making the

character not only regal but tough as nails, exotic yet intimate. Instead of being dull, Mui dominates the film...no easy task with the likes of Maggie Cheung and Michelle Yeoh in the flashier parts.

6. Maryam D'abo in *The Living Daylights*. The last good Bond girl before the PC rot began to set in. No cutting remarks. No anger. No sudden super powers. No overcompensation. No asinine speeches telling Bond off. Just a real woman caught up in a situation beyond her comprehension and coping. Just a real woman in the first (and last) genuinely romantic relationship with Bond in (for) a very long time. Oh, and she has a cello.
—James J.J. Janis

1. Ripley (Sigourney Weaver) from *Alien* and its sequels is perhaps the most obvious. She blazed a trail and undeniably set the tone for so many of the take-charge women who populate more and more horror, sci-fi and fantasy films.

2. While Hammer's female vampires of the '70s were able to take advantage of the new-found freedoms of the time, the standout among lady vampires for me would be Countess Bathory (Delphine Seyrig) in *Le Rouge Aux Le'Vres* (*Daughters of Darkness*); dressed and lit like a latter-day Dietrich, she remains one of the more compelling of deadly dames.

Delphine Seyrig in *Daughters of Darkness*

3. A favorite Hammer female fiend would be Miss Hyde (Martine Beswicke) in *Dr. Jekyll & Sister Hyde*. While some say the movie didn't explore all the possibilities, what was there was an entertaining view of what it would be like in some ways for a man to adjust to *being* a woman.

4. In Ken Russell's *Lair of the White Worm*, Lady Sylvia Marsh (Amanda Donahoe) was playful, witty, stylish, sexy, crafty, very much in charge and decidedly deadly. One of the great femmes fatales in an offbeat and perverse gem.

5. And representing the elders, there's Vera Cosgrove (Elizabeth Moody), dear old Mum from director Peter Jackson's dark comic splatter fest *Braindead* (aka *Dead Alive*). The mother from hell, she wouldn't let something like living death and decomposing interfere with her ambition to climb the social ladder...until she realized during the course of her disgusting transformation that she could simply *eat* the social ladder and anyone on it!

Well, there you have them! I jotted down many more, but these are among the favorites I could think of. —Joe Winters

Here are my choices for the 5 female characters I like/ think are the best from the 1970s and on:

1. Carrie White as portrayed by actress Sissy Spacek in the 1976 Brian De Palma film classic *Carrie*. No movie captures the brilliance of teenage torment better than this thriller.

2. Laurie Strode as played by Jamie Lee Curtis in the John Carpenter classic *Halloween*. Laurie Strode struck a blow for all strong female horror characters in this slasher classic. *Still* one of the best female characters in a horror film from 1970 on.

3. Officer Ellen Ripley as played by actress Sigourney Weaver in the four *Alien* films (1979-1997). Ripley revolutionized and changed the way females looked and acted in horror/sci-fi films from that point on. She could be tough, gutsy, demanding and courageous and yet be gentle and caring (like with the little girl Newt in *Aliens)*. She could also take care of herself as well as others (like kicking ass with the guns and beating the alien queen at the climax)!

4. Regan McNeil as played by Linda Blair in the possession classic *The Exorcist*. She created such an impact with her role and performance in this shocker that she was nominated for an Oscar, had nightmares later on because of her participation and also received death threats. Watching this little girl turn into a vile vomit-spewing demon-possessed being and witnessing the ramifications of the possession and exorcism is a very intense cinematic and acting experience, indeed!

5. Evelyn Draper as played by Jessica Walter in Clint Eastwood's directorial debut, *Play Misty For Me*. As Evelyn, Jessica Walter really gets the goosebumps standing on end, as slowly, she becomes possessive and

eventually totally psychotic. As time goes on she attacks his maid, kills a cop, goes after his girlfriend and eventually tries to kill Dave himself before being thrown off a cliff to her death!!! Hope these picks help out!
—Dan B.

1. *Christine*—That's right, my favorite female character in horror/sci-fi was this bright red 1958 Plymouth Fury; the title character in the 1983 John Carpenter film, based on a Stephen King novel. And what a fury it was. After all, hell hath no fury... like Christine. But this machine loved her male owners so much *she* would kill for them. She would also kill them rather than see them with someone else. Now that's true love! She also had an appreciation for classic '50s music. After all, that's all her radio would play. What a woman!

2. Laurie Strode—This Jamie Lee Curtis character from the *Halloween* movies is another one of my top faves. Curtis was terrific as the terrified teen in the role that literally made her a star. I also liked the way the character morphed from victim in the first one, to victim fighting back in the second film, to heroine in *Halloween H20* (yes, I have to admit I saw this). She is the quintessential heroine/teen target in the slasher genre.

3. Sally—Nancy Allen portrayed the prostitute who helped John Travolta solve the mystery of the dead politician in the 1980 Brian De Palma film, *Blowout*. It broke my heart to see her perish in the final battle with the killer played by John Lithgow. But her performance was top notch.

4. Gale Weathers—Courteney Cox-Arquette plays the pushy newswoman with the heart of gold in the *Scream* trilogy. Talk about a character arc: In the first one, we don't know if Gale's ruthlessly out for a story, or even a possible suspect at one point in the first film, but by the third film, she is getting married to the lovable sap, Dewey, played by then real-life husband David Arquette. I felt that the Gale character was well-written and not just one-dimensional and really added something to the trilogy that resurrected the horror genre in the mid-nineties.

5. Ripley—This wouldn't be a real list without Sigourney Weaver's defining character from the *Alien* series. Perhaps one of the strongest female characters in any genre, she could just as easily be No. 1, and chances are she will top most people's lists. What can you say about this character that hasn't already been said? This was an all-time role, and Weaver certainly played it well and got the most out of it. When you think *Alien*, you think Ripley.
—Sam Borowski

Despite a scarcity of well-written female characters in science fiction, horror and fantasy films, there are dozens of candidates to choose from among those who contributed laudable portrayals. The field can be narrowed further by limiting the choices from among those women depicted as authentic and symbolic saviors of humanity.

Our finalists, though trapped by the limitations of living and working in "a man's world," not only suffer, survive and persevere, they shatter the "glass ceiling" holding them back. These women represent the finest examples of compassion, self-sacrifice and nobility found in the human spirit.

165

1. Sarah Connor (Linda Hamilton in the first two *Terminator* movies). Sarah is a nowhere gal living in a nowhere world with a nowhere job. She becomes the surrogate mother of the future human race. Her resourcefulness, intellect and determination will save civilization from the brink of destruction and its own shortsightedness.

2. Lindsey Brigman (Mary Elizabeth Mastrantonio in *The Abyss*). Lindsey is the "queen bitch of the universe." She has forsaken marriage, motherhood and manners to acquire respect, appreciation and acceptance. Bud Brigman mouths the audience's own sentiments to his estranged wife when things start to go wrong: "I'm really glad you're here." Lindsey must undergo a figurative and literal rebirth before her rekindled love delivers the world from annihilation by visiting aliens.

3. Ellen Ripley (Sigourney Weaver in the *Alien* series). Ripley faces the greatest nightmare ever to face mankind. It is her brains, brawn and beauty that win the day in these horror stories set in the future. Though she becomes a kick-ass crusader, she never loses her sensuality, witticism and maternal charm.

4. Evelyn Carnahan (Rachel Weisz in *The Mummy* and its sequel). Director Stephen Sommers wrote an aside in his initial script about Evie—"We're going to fall in love with her"—and he kept his promise. She is confident in her abilities, proud to be a librarian and ambitious in her desire to outshine the Pembroke scholars. Evie's knowledge, fortitude and intuition are instrumental in preventing the ancient evil from devastating the planet. (Though her curiosity unleashed the terror of Imhotep, it was the Medjai who created the hom-dai in the first place.)

5. The Knight Sabers (Sylia, Priss, Linna and Nene from *Bubble Gum Crisis*). The final favorite is not a single individual, but a femme force of four. These lady mercenaries, equipped with advanced "Hard Suits," would make Marvel Comics' Tony Stark's superhero persona (Iron Man) proud. These original video animation shorts are loaded with guns, gals and gratuitous violence/nudity. Our quartet of liberated women not only fight for themselves, but protect humanity from rampaging replicants (combat boomers).

—Joseph Higgins

Attack of the Movie Poster Pin-Up Girls

by Gary J. Svehla

The ballyhoo and advertising campaign is oftentimes the secret of a movie's success, as typically embodied by the magnificent movie posters which adorn theater lobbies. Today such glossy posters are printed double-sided so they can be illuminated in backlit movie marquee poster cases— ofttimes such spectacular graphic design is far more creative than the movie. But one common factor has remained true to the art of the movie poster, and that is the depiction of the female as a dominant focus of the layout and design. It doesn't matter if the female is a victim, a seductress, a predator, a heroine or the kick-ass queen of outer space, females and movie poster art are inseparable, and the success of a movie's publicity campaign depends, in large part, on how effectively the female form is displayed.

This survey begins at the dawn of the classic horror movie cycle and explores the progression of the female in horror, science fiction and fantasy film poster art from the silent 1920s through our current Dolby Digital era. While it would prove impossible to detail every movie poster issued through the 1990s, we have selected a representative sampling to make our case of demonstrating the importance that females have assumed in fantasy movie posters throughout the ages and in selling these movies to the public.

Perhaps our survey should begin with the classic 1933 *King Kong*, the poster featuring our giant angry ape gripping the scantily clad original screaming heroine, Fay Wray, firmly in his paw. In this simple yet effective painting, the huge ape, obviously a male, demonstrates the primeval power the male of the specifies holds over the powerless female. As every adolescent male in the audience fantasizes, male brute force can indeed conquer the resistance of the lovely lady.

Turning momentarily away from 1930s mainstream productions, we can revel in the delirious and sordid poster art favored by independents, such as 1930's *Ingagi*, showing a normal-sized gorilla overpowering a female jungle native, effortlessly fondling her breasts as he forcefully carries her away. What the poster art of *King Kong* only hinted at, *Ingagi* shows us without censorship or pretense.

A few years earlier Fritz Lang's German silent movie masterpiece, *Metropolis* (1926), often featured poster art depicting the futuristic female robot portrayed by Brigitte Helm. Curiously, the robot conforms to a woman's curvature and of course large breasts drive home the point that this automaton is distinctly female and naked (as any robot would be).

Perhaps the most impressive poster of the 1930s (and still the most expensive movie poster ever sold at auction)

is Universal's *The Mummy* (1932) featuring Boris Karloff as Imhotep, the Egyptian priest reanimated 3,700 years after his death, and the sultry full-bodied sensuality of his reincarnated princess, as depicted by Zita Johann. Here the female is proudly displayed before an Egyptian tablet, her arms spread, wearing a red cocktail dress, oozing both power and sexuality. Johann is no one's victim and her image is a powerful one.

The decade of the 1940s carried on the same traditions. Posters for *Captive Wild Woman* (1943) showed an irate circus gorilla carrying off the horrified Martha MacVicar as other circus animals howl in the background. And to get even more Neanderthal, *One Million B.C.* (1940) shows caveman Victor Mature slinging his blonde mate Carole Landis up and over his shoulder, she almost posing seductively with her right leg held high. However, to contrast this image of woman as victim, we have Simone Simon from Val Lewton's *Cat People* (1942) looking both sultry and empowered hovering over the poster as a powerful human feline, able to stare anyone or anything down.

The decade of the 1950s becomes a pivotal one for the depiction of females, who are even more focused in the poster art. In fact, this decade should be noted for evolving the female from a supporting position on the poster art, mostly a secondary figure, to the main spotlight focus, such as Zsa Zsa Gabor's leggy sprawl as the focal point for the film *Queen of Outer Space* (1958). Likewise, women become predatory alien invaders as depicted on the poster of *Terror from the Year 5,000* (1958), resembling an almost human spider creeping, floating from one dimension to another.

Perhaps the most iconic female poster of the decade is Allison Hayes as the busty and leggy giant vixen who straddles the elevated superhighway (cars crashing below with men exiting their cars and looking skyward at her well-toned legs) from *Attack of the 50 Foot Woman* (1958), a poster that outshines its movie.

Another classic image is that of Robby the Robot carrying an unconscious blonde whose bare arms and legs dangle, creating a classic motif for the sci-fi classic *Forbidden Planet* (1956). Just the image of the metallic robot, painted from low-angle to make his monstrous bulk appear more threatening, carrying the fainting female, is an extenuation of similar poster art showing females fainting dead-away in the arms of gorillas and apes from earlier decades. The robot has become the gorilla of the sci-fi age. Just look at the similar shot of robot Gort holding the squirming yet powerless blonde beauty from the poster of *The Day the Earth Stood Still* (1951). To emphasize the robot's power, a laser deathray shines from his visor while he holds his female. To recapture that primal relationship between men and women, *The Neanderthal Man* (1953) features a modern-era caveman

literally attacking a woman wearing a low-cut dress who is being forced backwards into a supine position.

Curiously, Margaret Sheridan, the featured female in Howard Hawks' *The Thing... From Another World* (1951) in truth plays a small supporting role; however, she is plastered all over the poster showing her being kissed by star Kenneth Tobey and cowering in fear protected by Tobey in three different sequences. *The Thing* is basically a science fiction variation on *Frankenstein*, featuring a cast of isolated military types and pale and frail scientists, but to see the poster art, Sheridan's independent female character is reduced to a raven-haired beauty in need of male protection.

One of the first alien invasion movies, admittedly photographed with Gothic overtones, is *The Man from Planet X* (1951), whose poster art features a space-suited green alien extending his gloved arms toward the fully dressed yet pointy-bra-sweater-wearing Margaret Fields. Thrusting out her chest because of her rigid posture, her hands and arms bent behind her for support, she appears to be showing off her womanly wiles for her alien captor. In a reverse image, *Devil Girl from Mars* (1954) features a leather-clad cape-wearing female alien, the subtly labeled "devil girl," who dominates the entire left side of the poster art, even having the artist depict her spinning-top flying saucer as wielding power secondary to hers.

Cat-Women of the Moon (1953), featuring "Hollywood Cover Girls" as the Cat-women, boasts a fairly insignificant poster showing women wearing catlike black tights holding their hands as claws over their shoulders, to demonstrate their feline predatory nature.

Monster from the Ocean Floor (1954) features one of the first instances of a common poster theme, a phallic-like tentacled monster whose slimy probes wrap themselves around the legs, arms and stomach of, in this case, a blonde wearing a white bathing suit.

Another classic movie image from the 1950s is the archetype little green men from Mars image from *Invasion of the Saucer Men* (1957), where the chief alien is holding a half-nude, unconscious blonde in his left arm. The other arm is extended outward, as though the evil-eyed fiend is saying, she is mine so don't even think about taking her away.

Equally dynamic is the startling image of a semi-naked buxomy blonde beauty, attempting to climb a dangling rope to safety, as the claws of a giant crab threaten to crush her to death, from the poster for *Attack of the Crab Monsters* (1957). Also, the not-too-subtle poster for the unsubtly titled *The Woman Eater* (1957) shows a skimpily-clad redhead squirming and trying to escape from the clutches of a people-eating plant whose creeping green tentacles grope her legs, her shoulder and her lower stomach regions.

American International always played up the juvenile sex appeal in their posters, especially in movies such as *Day the World Ended* (1956), where the atomic bomb-created three-eyed mutant lusts after the negligee-clad beauty who cowers in terror, as the poster proclaims "human emotions stripped raw."

Perhaps the classic female-in-peril poster from the decade belongs to *Creature from the Black Lagoon* (1954), where the underwater amphibian creature has eyes only for the leggy and white bathing-suited Julie Adams, who swims away in fear, looking over her shoulder, the image of innocence about to be violated by a hell-spawn of nature.

The movie poster advertising campaign of the decade of the 1960s did not produce such a consistent and recognizable style as that of the 1950s, but with the era of loosening censorship and the rise of exploitation cinema, the role of women in poster art became even rawer.

The Last Woman on Earth (1960) featured the image of two men fighting to the death as a secondary image,

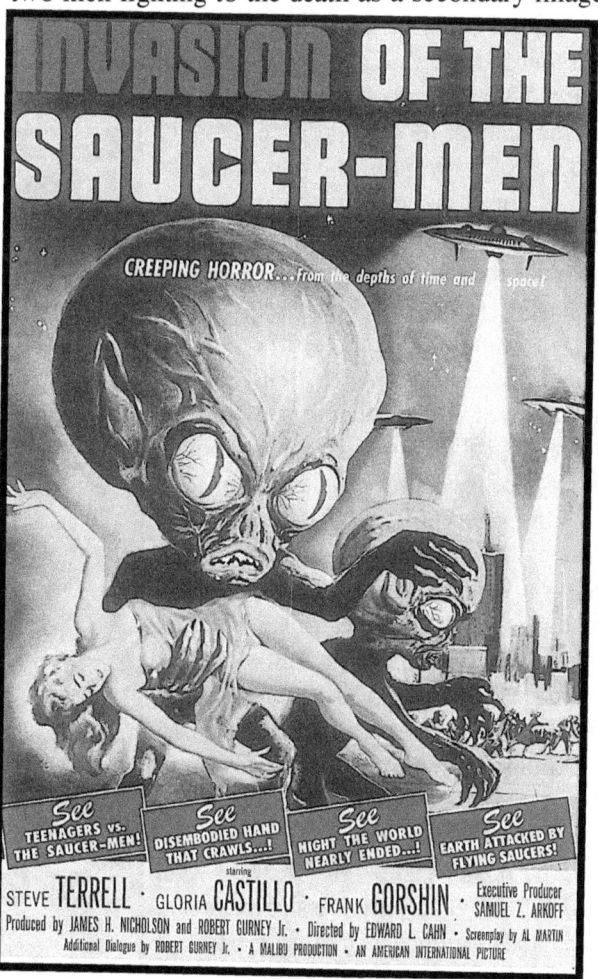

but the main image filling the poster was that of a partially naked woman, her breasts covered by her long flowing hair, discreetly protected by a white sheet. The poster explicitly demonstrates how men would kill themselves for an evening with this last woman. The poster proclaims, "They fought for the ultimate prize."

A disembodied head sits on a laboratory table in total fear, as a human brain with an eyeball looks on in the background, in *The Brain that Wouldn't Die* (1962), an image of a new variety of female victim, disfigured as well.

Hammer's remake of *One Million Years B.C.* (1966) featured the iconic shot of newly emerging star Raquel Welch posing in her fur bikini, standing in front of a menagerie of dinosaurs and prehistoric monsters; obviously this woman was ready to take on all the horrors of such a primitive world.

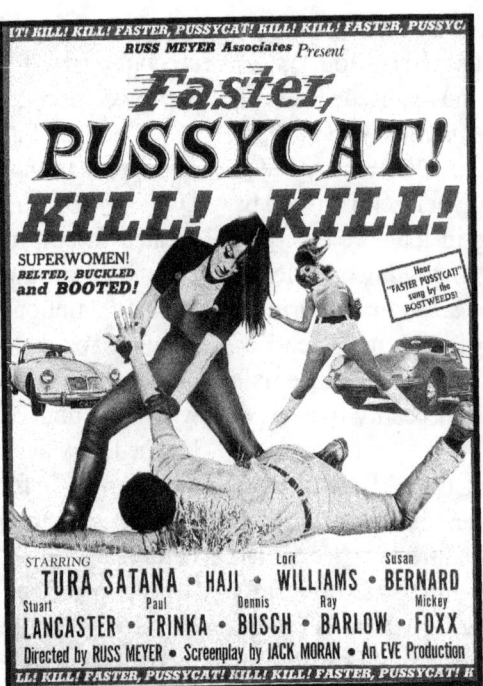

Equally sexual and empowered, the posters for *Frankenstein Created Woman* (1967) show erotically charged Susan Denberg, her leg shackled, barely dressed, but that intense look on her face screams, don't mess with me! She represents the new era of Frankenstein monsters.

One of the most impressive posters of the era is the bathtub poster art of Sharon Tate being savagely taken in her bath by the vile vampire king Ferdy Mayne from *The Fearless Vampire Killers* (1967), an image that immediately sums up the sexual appeal of vampirism, even though Tate's face registers complete surprise.

One of exploitation cinema's true classics, *Two Thousand Maniacs* (1964), shows a woman stripped to her bra with her hands tied behind her, rope stretching around her stomach, as she halfway turns around with a look of complete fear on her lips and eyes. This poster returns the image of woman to terrified and unprotected victim, an image less likely to be found in this decade.

The poster campaign for *The Green Slime* (1968) features a classic image of a sexy babe wearing a form-fitting spacesuit

and helmet, being grabbed by the huge green tentacle of the giant one-eyed slime monster which grabs and gropes her upper thigh area in a very suggestive image.

The low-budget *Dementia 13* (1963) features a poster showing a blonde woman crawling in shallow water, showing lots of cleavage, as a bestial hand grabs her head, most likely about to force her head underwater.

In another classic poster for a mediocre film, American International created an intense color-rich poster for *Blood Bath* (1966), showing females in the background chained to a stone wall, as a beautiful young blonde, caught in a rope net, is slowly lowered into a boiling vat of blood, a terrifying fate for any human of either sex.

Another foreign import, *Horrors of Spider Island* (1965), features the horrifying image of man turned into spider creature (an actual giant spider in his web hangs over the man's head to drive home the point) whose claws surround a frightened girl's head. To further drive home the point, the poster states: "He strangles his victims with his mammoth claws!"

In a change of pace, the Russ Meyer exploitation classic *Faster, Pussycat! Kill! Kill!* (1965) features the buxomy Tura Satana (described on the poster as "Superwoman! Belted, Buckled and Booted!") twisting the arm of the flat-on-his-belly male aggressor.

But perhaps the most memorable image of the 1960s female poster girl (besides Raquel Welch in her prehistoric bikini) is that of Jane Fonda as *Barbarella* (1968) wielding a raygun, sporting metallic boots and wearing a variation of a chain-mail bikini, making the female warrior appear as queen of the universe, ushering in a new era of kick-ass heroines.

The 1970s and 1980s evolved in both creating the poster art imagery of the empowered, strong woman and of the female victim (sometimes merging the image of both at the same time). Surprisingly, the American poster for Hammer's *The Vampire Lovers* (1970), having nothing to do with the movie, features an aggressive female vampire about to tear up an almost naked beefcake male who, in role reversal, is chained to the castle wall.

Yet the same studio's poster for *The Incredible 2-Headed Transplant* (1971) features the ridiculous image of a two-headed man carrying an almost nude woman in his/their arms, her bare legs posed provocatively and her chest thrust forward for maximum cleavage appeal.

Female victims seemed to suffer more in the emerging 1970s. The poster for *Satan's Slave* (1976) shows a totally nude blonde (cleverly, the smoke from a burning candle covers her private areas, as the "S" in the title covers one nipple) tied spread eagle, being readied for human sacrifice (a silhouetted male with a huge dagger stands over her).

The original poster for the classic *The Texas Chain Saw Massacre* (1974) is almost subtle, yet its dominant image is that of the suffering female victim. In the foreground we see Leatherface wielding his chainsaw, while partially hidden behind him is the image of a female victim, hanging from a meat hook, her mouth wide open in pain and terror, as her powerless arms vainly attempt to pull herself off the hook. In a very interesting poster, Hammer's *Blood from the Mummy's Tomb* (1972) shows a severed hand choking the throat of Valerie Leon, who is fully dressed, even wearing a cape, her gigantically portioned cleavage popping out, which makes her out to be the most buxom Hammer heroine ever.

Foreign import *Lady Frankenstein* (1971) spawned a fabulous poster featuring the almost totally naked Frankenstein monster, lying on the operating table, while a whip-carrying mistress, dressed in a formal gown, stands erect over his prostrate form.

Perhaps the definitive female movie poster of the 1970s is *I Spit on Your Grave* (1978) which shows the rear image of a sweaty female, her blouse literally ripped off her back exposing cuts and bruises, her tiny shorts ripped and revealing a bloodied left buttock, but she carries a dagger in her right hand, as she traipses through the woods. The poster declares: "This woman has just cut, chipped, broken and burned five men beyond recognition... an act of revenge!" Here we merge the images of one woman as both victim and predator.

The beautifully designed poster for *Slave of the Cannibal God* (1978) features a blonde woman, her transparent blouse literally melting from her body, as she is bound upright with rope, and a giant snake crawls over her upper thigh turning to attack, huge fangs bared. The era of the original sexy scream queens was ushered in by movies such as *Hollywood Chainsaw Hookers* (1988) featuring a scantily dressed Michelle Bauer, her face twisted with rage, wielding the largest chainsaw ever imaged. Equally impressive is the poster for *Sorority Babes in the Slimeball Bowl-O-Rama* (1988), which features the image of three hot babes straddling two men, tied and bound, strutting their stuff on the bowling alley lanes, white bowling pins in the background.

The poster campaign for *A Nightmare on Elm Street* (1984) is interestingly depicted, showing an obviously naked in-bed teenager pulling the covers up around her breasts as she is awakened from her sleep by the nightmare image of Freddy Krueger and his knives-as-fingers imagery of horror.

One of the most innovative and startling poster images of the era was that of sexy and bold Nastassia Kinski from *Cat People* (1982), simply showing the rain-soaked female, her green eyes half

a female stripped to her underwear being bent backwards, forced down on her knees, as a giant cockroach mounts her chest and stomach, strangling her, looking as though this movie is all about insect/human mating. Poster art for *The Slumber Party Massacre* is equally intense and well-staged. The photographic poster design, shot in low-angle from behind and underneath the fiend's widespread legs, shows the absolute fear of the four females, wearing their most intimate lingerie, who fall to the floor in terror. The man is holding an electric drill in his left hand, and the drill must feature the world's longest (and definitely most phallic) drill bit. A very cleverly designed poster, indeed.

Moving into the era of the 1990s and beyond, the role of the woman in science fiction, horror and fantasy movie art has not changed as much as it has been redesigned and refocused, sometimes imaginatively, other times shockingly blandly.

Even before its status as a hip and popular TV series, the original theatrical release of *Buffy The Vampire Slayer* (1992) features a determined and intense Buffy holding a wooden stake in her hand, as a terrified male cowers in fear hiding behind her.

One of the more interesting posters, a variation on the 1950s classic, is a stunningly updated *Attack of the 60 Foot Centerfolds* (1996), featuring firemen on an extended hook-and-ladder vehicle climbing up toward the crotch

closed and her pouting ruby-red lips slightly spread, her shoulders bare, looking seductively straight ahead. Hers is the image of a woman sexy and strong. Traci Lords, who graduated from underage hardcore porn, looks downright sleek and eloquent in her black dress that she wore to showcase her first mainstream movie, *Not of This Earth* (1988).

Poster art for *The Evil Dead* (1982) highlights a woman straining to prevent herself from being dragged underground—her right arm is stretched skyward, as a corpse tightens its grip upon her throat.

The beauty and the beast image enters the modern era in the poster for *Swamp Thing* (1982), where the shapely figure of Adrienne Barbeau is carried off into the swamp by the ugly and brutish (yet profoundly sad looking) Swamp Thing.

Perhaps the two most outstanding female posters of the era, besides Sigourney Weaver in *Aliens*, are *The Nest* (1988) and *The Slumber Party Massacre* (1982). Played for kinky sex appeal, *The Nest* features stark imagery of

of the giant beauty and impotently shooting their hoses at her. The centerfold's gleaming blonde hair, white teeth and rapidly disintegrating white outfit make her the vision of both beauty and female strength.

Humor entered the realm of horror movie poster art with *Scary Movie* (2000), featuring the cast sitting in movie theater seats, sharing popcorn with the *Scream*-type fiend, as each star demonstrates a variation on registering fear. Most interestingly, in the front row, one brunette is ready to scream as she holds a cell phone up to her ear, the bane of every movie theater-goer.

In a parallel take, the poster art for *Scream* (1996) shows the wide-eyed close-up of a female face, her hand pressed against her mouth and cheeks, registering intense panic, without any hint of humor. What that face registers is what director Wes Craven desires his audience to experience.

While not as classic as the poster for *Aliens*, the poster for *Alien 3* (1992) shows a decidedly unsexy Sigourney Weaver, her buzz-cut making her look like a chemo patient, stripping her of her commanding power and authority, although her intense facial features show not a trace of weakness.

During the past 20 years, besides the standard one-sheet movie poster, many mainstream, potential blockbuster movies featured personality posters that emphasized one of the major stars isolated from the rest of the cast. The beautiful yet intense Nicole Kidman from *Batman Forever* (1995) emphasizes the importance of female starring roles in genre movies.

Recent modern horror movies such as *I Know What You Did Last Summer* (1997) feature poster graphics showing four darkly lit blue-tinged faces of four guilty teens, the most prominent face being that of a brunette, her eyes darting guiltily across the poster. These teens are predators, not victims, and their steely gaze only demonstrates cold-blooded intentions.

Halloween: 20 Years Later (1998) is similar, but in this instance the five faces, Jamie Lee Curtis being most prominent, do not register the same emotions. Near the back of the group, we can see fear and nervousness, but as we approach the two dominant women in the foreground, the expressions are those of strong-willed determination.

While the roles women played in films have generally fallen into similar stereotypes—the predator, the victim, the heroine and the warrior—the depiction of women playing variations of the same themes in movie poster art has drastically changed decade by decade. Sometimes such graphic designers opt for imagination and cleverness, other times they opt for copycat repetitiveness. Exploitation cinema sometimes forces poster artists to employ quirky and even shocking graphics; other times offbeat humor and playfulness become the operant tone. Often the poster is superior to the movie, and sometimes hardly any correlation exists between the graphic poster design and the film. So it may be best to judge a poster by the visceral and emotional effect it exerts over the movie fan who passes by that lighted movie poster case inside the theater lobby. As we can easily observe, sometimes the financial success of the movie is related to the superiority of its posters, and in 80 years, this simple fact has never changed.

Middle Earth's Heroines

By Susan Svehla

Pages have been written on the Peter Jackson masterpiece trilogy *Lord of the Rings*. But, with such an incredible slate of characters, the women of *LOTR* seem to have been overlooked by the media. True, Tolkien did not have the knack of creating vibrant female characters, but screenwriter Fran Walsh managed to flesh out three amazing creatures, adding to their story from the novel's Appendices.

Some naysayers may think women can't script or direct cutting-edge horror because they aren't visionary (or disturbed?) enough. But I think, looking at Fran Walsh's first two films, that point is effectively proven obsolete. Peter Jackson and Fran Walsh are one of the most successful husband/wife genre filmmaking teams working today. The couple married in 1987, and their first film together was the low-budget *Meet the Feebles* (1990), which Walsh scripted and Jackson directed, produced and co-wrote. Their next film was *Dead Alive* (1992), supposedly the bloodiest film ever made, which Walsh again wrote as well as cast. In 1995 Walsh and Jackson received their first Academy Award nominations for *Heavenly Creatures*, after which Walsh moved on to writing and producing with 1996's *The Frighteners*.

Walsh and Jackson wouldn't win an Academy Award until 2004 when they pretty much swept the Oscars for *The Lord of the Rings: The Return of the King* (2003). Walsh not only co-wrote and co-produced the film, she also co-wrote the Oscar-winning song "Into the West."

Walsh is a notoriously private person and happily works behind the scenes, leaving the PR to Jackson. Writer Sarah Catherall interviewed Phillipa Boyens (another talented woman who co-wrote and produced the *LOTR* trilogy), who said of Walsh and Jackson's work together, "There was an implicit trust between Peter and Fran and the level of understanding between the two—I've never seen that before. They were just incredible. They meshed brilliantly and in terms of their professional relationship, they were so in sync. Fran could answer something on Peter's behalf and vice-versa. They trust each other and listen to each other." Boyens added that Walsh attended all the rushes from *LOTR* and often directed second-unit filming.

Liv Tyler as Arwen in *The Lord of the Rings*

Walsh wrote the *LOTR* screenplay based on the novel and also produced the film. Peter Jackson worked closely with Walsh and Philippa Boyens as they brought Tolkien's vision to vivid life in the wilds of New Zealand. In adapting the characters Walsh notes, "It is the humanity of the characters that rewards the reader. And we hope we've been able to translate that for the film audience... In a sense *The Fellowship of the Ring* is about understanding that in spite of our differences there is value in standing together." Boyens states, "The more time you spend in Tolkien's world, the more complex it grows. It was all there for us, but the scope was tremendous."

Of the three female characters in *LOTR*, two are introduced in the first film, *The Fellowship of the Ring*. The beautiful Arwen (Liv Tyler), lover of Aragorn, is introduced earlier in the film

Galadriel (Cate Blanchett) presents special gifts to the Fellowship of the Ring, including Frodo (Elija Wood).

than in the novel. In the film Arwen is sent by the elves to help the Hobbits reach Rivendale. She carries Frodo on the back of her white horse, fleeing from the Black Riders across the ford where the water washes the demons downstream. In the novel Frodo makes the terrifying ride alone on an Elven horse.

Tyler was drawn to Arwen, the immortal Elven princess. "To me, Arwen brings a real touch of femininity to the tale of Middle Earth," says Tyler. "In the midst of a war, she has fallen in love, and become the backbone and motivation for Aragorn's fight."

Arwen must make a choice for love and mortality or an immortal life with the elves. Tyler remarks, "It's about mortality versus immortality. Those are the difficulties of Arwen and Aragorn being together. But they can't say good-bye."

Liv Tyler made an auspicious film debut with the leading role in *Silent Fall*, directed by Bruce Beresford. Tyler also starred in cult favorite *Empire Records*. She then appeared in Bernardo Bertolucci's *Stealing Beauty* and *Inventing the Abbotts*. Tyler turned in a heart-wrenching performance as the daughter of Bruce Willis in *Armageddon*. She worked with Robert Altman in *Dr. T and the Women*. Liv Tyler's next film casts her opposite Jennifer Lopez and reunites her with *Armageddon* co-star Ben Affleck in Kevin Smith's comedy *Jersey Girl*. For her role in *The Lord of the Rings: The Fellowship of the Ring*, Tyler and the rest of the principal cast were nominated for Outstanding Performance by the Cast of a Theatrical Motion Picture by the Screen Actors Guild.

Cate Blanchett was cast as the mysterious elf queen Galadriel, whom the company met after Gandalf fell in Moria. Galadriel presents special gifts to the Fellowship, gifts which play an important part in the third film. She also gains the love and devotion of the cynical dwarf Gimli. Cate Blanchett was drawn to her character's fascinating strength. "I loved playing Galadriel because she is so iconic. She is the one in *The Fellowship of the Ring* who truly tests Frodo," says Blanchett. "I also think she has a profound message to give about taking responsibility for ourselves and our actions. And, yes, I have to admit I have always wanted to have pointy ears!"

Blanchett was astonished by how completely the world of Middle Earth and its many cultures had been

Eowyn (Miranda Otto) impersonates a man so she can join the army and fight the darkness covering the land.

explored by the filmmakers. "By the time I started working, there was such a strong and real-life sense of the various cultures, their histories and their hopes for the future," she notes. "It was really like becoming part of a whole different universe. I've never experienced anything like it before."

In 1998, Blanchett portrayed Queen Elizabeth I in the critically acclaimed *Elizabeth*, directed by Shekhar Kapur, for which she received a Golden Globe Award for Best Actress in a Drama and a BAFTA for Best Actress in a Leading Role, as well as Best Actress Awards from The Chicago Film Critics Association, The London Film Critics Association, On-line Film Critics, Variety Critics and UK Empire Award. She also received a Best Actress nomination from the Screen Actors Guild and the Academy of Motion Picture Arts & Sciences. In 2003 Blanchett earned critical praise for her performance in *Veronica Guerin*.

Miranda Otto portrays Eowyn, the third female and only human woman in *LOTR*. Eowyn falls in love with Aragorn, but although he believes he has lost Arwen, he remains true to her. Although Eowyn is introduced in the second film, it is in the third film that she truly shines as she impersonates a man and takes up a sword in the fight to save Middle Earth. Otto comments, "There are very few women in *The Lord of the Rings*. Eowyn is the first real human female character. Galadriel and Arwen, who are both Elves, were introduced in the first film. But the second film takes you into the world of human beings. It's a very difficult time in Rohan and she has had to watch the whole house deteriorate, the whole lineage decline. She wants to spur Theoden into action, but she is powerless to do that to her king. Generally, in the myths and legends we hear as young girls, we're given Sleeping Beauty. We're given Cinderella. They're all stories about women who are in difficult situations who are then saved by men. But Eowyn is a character who is in a difficult situation and must become empowered or lose everything. Here is this amazing man, Aragorn, who represents everything that she wants to happen again. And yet she knows she must find the strength within to save herself and her people."

Otto recently completed the Australian romantic comedy *Danny and the Deckchair*, in which she is reteamed with Rhys Ifans. She was last seen onscreen with Ifans alongside Tim Robbins and Patricia Arquette in Charlie Kaufman's next feature after *Being John Malkovich*, *Human Nature*. The dark comedy, directed by Michel Gondry, premiered at both the 2001 Cannes Film Festival and the 2002 Sundance Film Festival and was released in April 2002.

A graduate of the prestigious Australian theatrical school NIDA, which also boasts such alumnae as Mel

Arwen gives up everything to be with Aragorn (Viggo Mortensen).

Gibson, Judy Davis and Cate Blanchett, Otto has been honored with Australian Film Institute award nominations for her work in *In The Winter Dark*, *The Well*, *Daydream Believer*, and *The Last Days of Chez Nous*. She has also appeared in Robert Zemekis' *What Lies Beneath*, with Harrison Ford and Michelle Pfeiffer; Terence Malick's *The Thin Red Line*; *Kin*; *Dead Letter Office*; *Doing Time for Patsy Cline*; *True Love and Chaos*, and *Jack Bull*, opposite John Cusack, for HBO.

Costume designer Ngila Dickson went for a new ethereal aesthetic for the female characters. For the two Elven leading ladies, Cate Blanchett and Liv Tyler, Dickson took their otherworldly qualities to create an alluring race who are "the angels of the story," as Dickson puts it. "The Elves are tall, slender and elegant. They have a floating image to their costumes, using colors and fabric that are light and semi-shimmery." For Eowyn (Miranda Otto), Dickson designed and hand-made several wardrobe changes to reflect the changes taking place in her culture. "There is always this dichotomy in her character," says Dickson. "Her natural bent is to be fiery and passionate about her people, but caught by the strictures of the society which demand that you wear woman's clothes and behave like a lady." Ngila Dickson,

Fran Walsh, Peter Jackson and Philippa Boyens pose with their Academy Award statues.

born in Dunedin, New Zealand, was nominated for an Academy Award and a British Academy of Film and Television Arts award, among other accolades, for her work on *The Lord of the Rings: The Fellowship of the Ring*. She also designed the costumes for Edward Zwick's *The Last Samurai*, starring Tom Cruise.

For her work on *Xena: Warrior Princess*, Dickson garnered the Best Costume Award at the 4th International Cult TV Awards. Dickson's film credits as a costume designer include Peter Jackson's *Heavenly Creatures*. For television, Dickson has designed for the series *Hercules*, *Xena, Warrior Princess* and the *Ray Bradbury Series*.

The soundtrack to *The Fellowship of the Ring* features two original songs by acclaimed musical artist Enya, a longtime fan of the trilogy. Jackson, likewise a fan of Enya's music, invited her to New Zealand to meet with him and watch footage from the film. Among the tracks Enya contributed are the songs "Aniron," which accompanies an intimate sequence between Arwen and Aragorn; and "May It Be," which is heard during the end titles of the film. Although other artists provided the songs for the second and third entries, Enya remains the voice of *Lord of the Rings*.

Thankfully we can alwasy visit our Middle Earth friends via DVD—although we will meet Galadriel once again in *The Hobbit*, which is set to be released December 2012.

Deadly Delights—Movies Featuring Our Favorite Queens of Evil

Abbott and Costello Meet Frankenstein (1948)

Dr. Mornay (Lenore Aubert) is both a femme fatale *and* a mad scientist, but she's no match for Dr. Lejos/Dracula (Bela Lugosi). She balks at performing the brain operation on the Monster (Glenn Strange), foolishly thinking that she has the upper hand over Dr. Lejos. Lejos commands her to look into his eyes. She attempts to resist, but cannot. Dr. Mornay is utterly helpless before Dr. Lejos. After he vampirizes her, Dr. Mornay is suitably subservient to her master.—Brian Smith

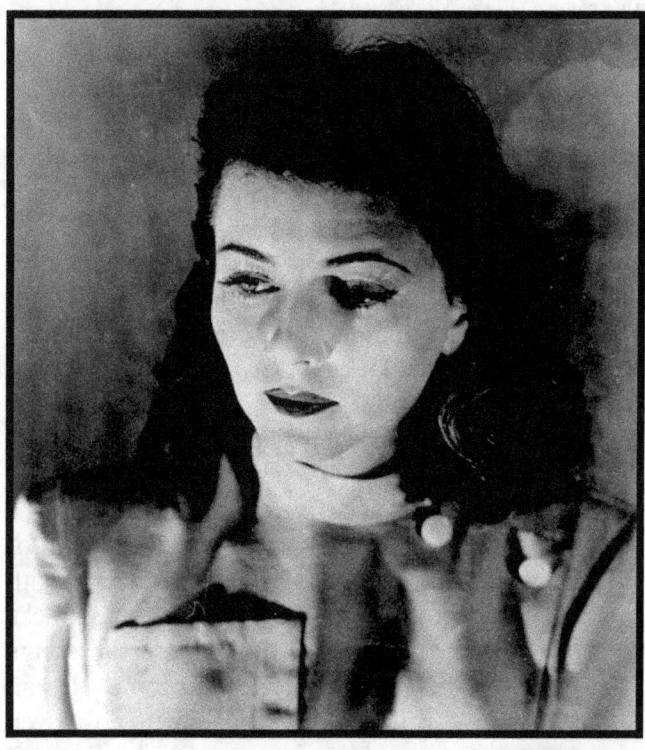

Lenore Aubert as the evil Dr. Mornay in *A&C Meet Frankenstein*

The Astounding She-Monster (1958)

Ronnie Ashcroft's hoot of a female-alien flick suffers from all of the usual quirks that hallmarked the heyday of the notorious B movie: the mandatory voice-over narration at the beginning, static direction (Ashcroft's camera stays put while the actors simply move from one part of the set/location to another), wooden script (morose-looking Robert Clarke mumbles most of his lines, well out of microphone range), abysmal special effects (the alien's spaceship is the magnified head of a lighted match, and the "man-in-a-bear suit" scene is terrible), erratic continuity and "let's just go through the motions" acting. But what more can you expect on a budget of $18,000, with none other than Edward D. Wood Jr. as a consultant? Two gangsters and their moll kidnap a blonde Beverly Hills socialite (the attractive Marilyn Harvey), take her to the woods and break into a log cabin where geologist Clarke happens to be on vacation. Unbeknownst to the squabbling characters in the cabin, Shirley Kilpatrick arrives on the scene, photographed mostly out-of-focus to accentuate her shimmering, one-piece spandex spacesuit, not to mention her ample figure, and prowls the dark woods, searching for human contact. After she has killed one of the gangsters and Clarke's dog with her deadly radioactive touch, and the other gangster with his moll have perished, it is left to hero Clarke, left on his own with the freed socialite, to throw an acid bomb at the alien as she enters his cabin. She fades to nothingness, leaving behind a medallion which contains a message: The female was an emissary sent to Earth from The Council of Planets on a mission of goodwill. Earth has been monitored from space for decades and the aliens (whoever they may be) wish to eliminate our planet's problems. Clarke and Harvey wonder whether or not another emissary will be sent. "But would it come to bring us goodwill or simply avenge her death?" ponders a bemused Clarke as the end credits roll. We will never know! German composer Guenther Kauer wrote the odd soundtrack, which rattles along in a series of shattering highs and burbling lows in the background, bearing no resemblance whatsoever to the images unfolding before us on the big screen, and at one point in the proceedings, Kilpatrick's costume split at the back, requiring the actress to walk backwards in some shots as there was no time to repair it. Glorious schlock, all of it, and at 62 minutes long, Ashcroft's ludicrous sci-fi outing certainly doesn't outstay its welcome. Just sit there and revel in its tackiness!—Barry Atkinson

Batman and Robin (1997)

While most fans think this is one of the worst in the series, they just don't get it. This is a classic Poverty Row horror programmer complete with a seductive mad scientist/villainess and a bitter mad doctor trying to reanimate his beloved dead wife. The quirky Uma Thurman does wonders transforming from the mousy nerd to the sensual Poison Ivy, whose kisses spell death. Her fight with the equally dishy Batgirl (Alicia Silverstone) is campy classic comic book fun. True, *Batman and Robin* is fluff, but it is inspired, fun, emotionally involving and features two superb portrayals of villainy.—Susan Svehla

Black Sunday (1960)/Barbara Steele

Some things in life demand our gaze with particular urgency: a dynamited high-rise as it sinks to the earth; a funnel cloud; Arizona's meteor crater; home video of a helicopter crash. And the face of Barbara Steele.

For more than 40 years, Steele's magnificent features and the intensity of talent that animates them have haunted the dreams of countless filmgoers and television watchers. She is, in a word, singular: tall and slender, with long raven hair and enormous, piercing eyes that suggest willfulness and intellect. Her cheekbones are pronounced, her mouth full and expressive. A strong chin dominates a square jaw. She is considerably more than merely pretty, yet is not beautiful in the traditional sense. Without question, Steele is ferociously compelling. When she deigns to exhibit the spider's gaze she mastered years ago, we see perfection and imperfection, heat and chill, the intensity of life and the eternal darkness of the grave.

From her first starring film, *La Maschera del Demonio* (*The Mask of the Demon*; U.S. title, *Black Sunday*, 1960), in which she played a vengeful witch and the witch's innocent descendant, Steele has been typecast as a dark goddess, a stunningly beautiful yet malevolent creature capable of doling out pleasure and pain in equal measure.

Black Sunday was the first of many horror films Steele made in Italy. She took dual roles more than once, and even when she played but a single character, her persona suggested the extremes of female sexuality. Male viewers yearn for her even as some are intimidated. Females envy her power.

Paradoxically, Steele's ability to intimidate compounds her desirability. By the standards of Western society, where female sexuality is feared as strongly as it is desired, Steele is the *ne plus ultra* of the Eternal Feminine. Onscreen, she is a creature of wild extremes, the breathtaking beauty who inspires rapture and desire but whose price often is the immolation of the worshipper's body and soul.

The real Barbara Steele is not a dark goddess, and for many years she refused to discuss that aspect of her screen persona. Although she has worked with Fellini and Schlondorff, only the horror pictures interest most of those who came to interview her. These are films Steele made very quickly, sometimes simultaneously with others when she was very young. They helped her to learn her craft, but because their themes and aesthetics are weighted in favor of director and cinematographer, the films also frustrated her and left her feeling unfulfilled and even abused. So it is that this erudite, poetic woman came to be viewed as a completely different sort of creature, one quite inimical to the actress' true nature. And yet for all this, Barbara Steele's dark persona seems true; it certainly is meaningful, as it tells us volumes about our ambivalent regard for women and female sexuality.

Because the horror films Steele made in Italy revolve around archetypes—unprincipled scientist, victimized wife, malevolent succubus, stalwart hero— and rigid, codified settings and situations—dank castles, shadowed corridors, thunderstorms, torture, nightmares, death, resurrection, revenge—almost no one except the director, art director and cinematographer got to have fun. Less actors than symbols, the onscreen participants in *Nightmare Castle*—the dubbed, American-release version of the 1965 Italian thriller *Gli Amanti d'Oltre*

Barbara Steele in *Nightmare Castle*

Princess Vajda (Barbara Steele) with Javuto (Arturo Dominici) in *Black Sunday*

Tomba (*Lovers from Beyond the Tomb*)—and similar thrillers were forced to perform within strict boundaries and conventions. Even Steele, who at least was able to exhibit wide ranges of emotion in her horror films, was asked to run through the same range in picture after picture. It was what audiences expected and, all the worse for Steele, it was a trick, an actor's stunt, at which she happened to be very skilled. Because she was young and wanted to work, she agreed to do the trick over and over again.

Barbara Steele was the last person signed as a contract player by the Rank Organisation, Britain's dominant filmmaker/distributor for a quarter of a century. Steele was given small roles in such trifles as *Bachelor of Hearts* (1958) and *Upstairs and Downstairs* (1959) before her contract was sold to 20th Century-Fox in 1960. She was subsequently assigned to co-star in a Don Siegel/Elvis Presley Western, *Flaming Star*, but fled to Europe when Hollywood-style moviemaking and the requirements of the role angered and frustrated her. That same year Italian director Mario Bava cast her in a dual role in his horror masterpiece, the aforementioned *Black Sunday*.

From that point it was off to the races as Steele worked steadily for the next nine years, appearing in Federico Fellini's *Otto e Mezzo* (*8 1/2*, 1963); *Le Monocle rit Jaune* (*The Monocle*, 1964, a spy comedy); Volker Schlondorff's *Young Törless* (1966, one of her best roles, as an oversexed beauty who initiates a young male student in the ways of the world); *Honeymoon with a Stranger* (1969, an American TV-movie)—and a plethora of horror thrillers: Roger Corman's *The Pit and the Pendulum* (1961, for many years, Steele's sole American feature); Riccardo Freda's *L'orribile Segreto del Dr. Hichcock* (*The Horrible Dr. Hichcock*, 1962) and its sequel, Freda's *Lo Spettro* (*The Ghost*, 1962);

Antonio Margheriti's *La Danza Macabre* (*Castle of Blood*, 1963); Margheriti's *Il Lunghi Capelli Della Morte* (*The Long Hair of Death*, 1964); Camillo Mastrocinque's *Un Angelo per Satana* (*An Angel for Satan*, 1965); Massimo Pupillo's *Cinque Tombe per un Medium* (*Terror Creatures from the Grave*, 1965); Michael Reeves' *Il Lago si Satana* (*The She Beast*, 1966) and Vernon Sewell's disappointing *Curse of the Crimson Altar* (1967, American-release title *The Crimson Cult*).

Steele also worked in episodic television in the early and mid-1960s, "guest-starring" on *Alfred Hitchcock Presents*, *Adventures in Paradise*, *Secret Agent* and *I Spy*. Most notable of her later TV appearances is a fine performance in a 1972 episode of *Night Gallery*, "The Sins of the Fathers."

Steele married Oscar-winning screenwriter James Poe in 1969, gave birth to a son in 1970 and went into semi-retirement. She was divorced from Poe in 1974 and returned to features, but now as a full-fledged cult actress recruited for showy roles in an odd mix of films that included Jonathan Demme's *Caged Heat* (1974, as the crippled warden of a women's prison); David Cronenberg's *They Came from Within/Shivers* (1975, as a lesbian whose kiss infects her female neighbor with a strange, slug-like parasite); Joe Dante's *Piranha* (1978), and a foolish slasher thriller called *Silent Scream* (1980). In addition, Steele took supporting roles in *I Never Promised You a Rose Garden* (1977) and Louis Malle's *Pretty Baby* (1978).

Following a stint as a script reader for MGM, Steele joined Dan Curtis Productions as associate producer of the mammoth 1983 TV miniseries, *The Winds of War*. She put her film experience and multilingual skills to good use, scouting locations and interviewing actors. Steele moved up to VP/producer status for the follow-up miniseries, *War and Remembrance* (1988). In 1991 she co-starred in a brief TV revival of Curtis' *Dark Shadows*. Today, the actress, slender and strikingly attractive in her 70s, divides her time between Los Angeles and Europe.

"Extreme" is an apt summation of the horror-film portion of Barbara Steele's career. Her ambivalence about this body of work is understandable; she has stated more than once, for instance, her desire to do comedy or to play "a housewife in a scruffy cardigan." Steele has found it difficult—and probably tedious, as well—to grapple with iconographic status, an intellectual conceit that has been foisted on her by others and that has no relationship to her real life. But like Robert Wadlow, the tallest man who ever lived; like the astonishing young Bardot; like the heart-stopping beauties of mythology, Steele has been cursed by nature. Her remarkable face and intensity of demeanor liberated her from anonymity, allowed her travel and a career and associations with fascinating people, but these same features also imprisoned her within severely limited emotional and stylistic boundaries.

The screen struggles to contain her power. No casting director would have dreamed of hiring her to play a mousy clerk or Gidget; Steele's reaction to being cast as a cowgirl opposite Elvis Presley was nothing if not sharply self-aware. Her 35-year search for a canvas large enough to accommodate her suggests that the horror film—with its requisite melodrama, violent sexuality and wild emotion—was a natural and perhaps inevitable stopping place. Regardless, Steele's career readily encourages "what if?" speculation. She would have been an impressive Mary Todd Lincoln, for instance, a deliciously unexpected *farceur* à la Kay Kendall, an intensely watchable heroine of a film by Michael Powell or Rainer Werner Fassbinder.

In the end, of course, reality is what it is. *Nightmare Castle* is a good film of its kind and a compelling showcase for one of cinema's most potent and fascinating personalities. If we can take instruction from the nature of Steele's horror film roles, if we can interpret her performances in the larger contexts of our own lives, relationships and the cultures that produced them, then Barbara Steele's career has not been imprisoning at all, but a thing of vigor, honesty and liberation.—David J. Hogan

The Brides of Dracula (1960)

There is no question about it: *The Brides of Dracula* would find itself in the top three or four best-ever Hammer films compiled by horror fans and it is also one of the most stylish vampire chillers ever made, carefully, even caressingly, directed by Terence Fisher, who lets his camera linger over those authentic period sets bathed in rich Technicolor, every so often treating us to a series of his customary jolts and shocks: vampire David Peel appearing before Peter Cushing in gray cape, fangs flashing and bloodshot eyes; a ghostly white female vampire, coaxed by demented sorceress Freda Jackson, clawing her unsteady way out of her earth-covered coffin; locked padlocks dropping from another coffin as vampire Andree Melly clambers out and approaches a startled Yvonne Monlaur; and Peel vampirizing a comatose Cushing in the old mill. Fisher shows us in masterly fashion how a movie on the undead *should* be conceived, instead of all those frenetic, blood-soaked farragoes that

The evil Baroness Meinster (Martita Hunt) finds her son a new victim in Marianne (Yvonne Monlaur) in *Brides of Dracula*.

appeared from the mid-80s onwards. Christopher Lee refused the part of Dracula in the production for fear of typecasting, so good-looking Peel, a stage actor at the time, was brought in to play a disciple of the Count, Baron Meinster, chained up in his sinister castle by his mother (a chillingly gaunt Martita Hunt) and inadvertently let loose by the unsuspecting Monlaur, who falls for his boyish charms. Cushing reprised his role as Van Helsing, journeying through Transylvania on a mission to eradicate vampirism, bringing his usual stamp of authority to the colorful proceedings. First seen coming to the aid of Monlaur after she has fled the Baron's castle. Cushing's early tussle with Peel in the castle mirrors the climactic battle in *Dracula* (but is not as memorable) as the two fight across a table; he then has the odious task of dispatching the unfortunate Hunt, who has been turned into a vampire by her own son, hinting at a hidden incestuous relationship between the pair. Naturally, Peel turns his attentions to the local girls' school, his coffin ensconced in a nearby mill as he romances the still unsuspecting Monlaur, who discovers what Peel is the hard way—combing her hair in the mirror, the vampire in full bestial glory stands behind her, hissing and snarling, but he casts no reflection *in* her mirror. The movie boasts two climaxes: the first when, following a fight in the mill, Cushing gets bitten by the bloodsucker and has to cauterize the wound with a red-hot branding iron, splashing holy water over the cut to prevent him from becoming one of the undead, and the second being the final confrontation with Peel, who receives a dose of holy water in his face, writhing in agony before Cushing leaps onto the sails of the windmill, forming the shadow of a cross over the vampire who perishes. Fair enough, *Brides* doesn't contain the significant set-pieces that made *Dracula* such an out-and-out influential archetype and Peel, although fine in the role of the Baron, lacked Lee's depth and screen authority which, had the six-foot-plus actor decided to star in the film, would have made it just that *little* bit classier. But these are minor quibbles that mustn't detract from the fact that *Brides* is superior Gothic Hammer fare in all departments, assisted enormously by Malcolm Williamson's threatening, organ-based score that heightens the creepy tension, particularly in the castle sequences. A massive hit for the company when first released and going the rounds for a non-stop 10 years in the U.K., it now seems strange that having received complimentary reviews from the critics, David Peel decided not to pursue a career in the cinema and quietly returned to stage work, disappearing into obscurity as quickly as he had made his mark.—Barry Atkinson

Brides boasts several great scenes including the wonderful sequence with Martita Hunt where she reveals her incestuous relationship with her own son the Baron. And we have the superb windmill sequence with the two vampires protected by their nurse Greta (Freda Jackson in a wondrous over-the-top performance) before the Baron appears. These are *Brides of Dracula*'s money sequences (along with perhaps the eerie resurrection sequence of Marie Devereux coaxed by the vampiric mid-wife Greta).—Gary J. Svehla

Calling Dr. Death (1943)/*Dressed to Kill* (1946)

She always had the exotic look of a sexy, angry, Shakespearean actress.

Patricia Morison had 39-inch-long auburn hair—the longest of any actress in Hollywood, and usually worn in a bun. She had fiery, blue/gray eyes, and the most sensual mouth of any lady in the movies. And there was a tinge of passion in her dramatics, which—spiked with this "vamp" look—made her a fascinating actress.

Perhaps inevitably, in 1940s Hollywood, she only truly had the chance to spark in B melodramas.

There was *Hitler's Madman* (MGM, 1943), a haunting, passionate movie, as much horror film as propaganda piece, with Patricia as the self-sacrificing village heroine who helps assassinate John Carradine's satanic Nazi.

There was *Calling Dr. Death* (1943), the first of Universal's notorious *Inner Sanctum*s, in which she was the madly jealous nurse who kills Lon Chaney's wife with a fire poker, and disfigures her face with acid.

And, perhaps most famously, there was *Dressed to Kill* (1946), Universal's final Sherlock Holmes film, with Patricia as foxy villainess Hilda Courtney—sparring with Basil Rathbone's Holmes, flirting with Nigel Bruce's Watson and slinking about London in furs and a chapeau that looks like a giant black toe.

Hilter's Madman had a fascinating production history. Seymour Nebenzal (who had produced 1931's *M*, with Peter Lorre) produced the film independently in the fall of 1942, under the title *The Hangman*, with PRC resources. Originally, Frances Farmer signed to star as Jarmila, a singing teacher in Lidice, who assists her lover (Alan Curtis) and father (Ralph Morgan) in assassinating Heydrich. However, the erratic Miss Farmer suffered one of her highly publicized breakdowns, and Nebenzal canceled her contract. Patricia signed on, and director Douglas Sirk began shooting the film several days before Halloween, 1942.

Of course, top-billed Patricia is a bit too glamorous for a Bohemian village singing teacher; yet she plays the role with a wonderfully effective sadness and sense of grim purpose. The assassination episode is truly exciting: Patricia riding her bicycle across the forest road, attracting Heydrich's lecherous eye; as he leers at her from his open car, Curtis blasts his machine gun, Morgan tosses his grenades and the car crashes over a hill.

Very moving is Patricia's own death scene; she and Curtis escape into the forest and mountains, tracked by Nazis—who fatally wound the heroine. Curtis takes the dying woman into a forest hut, where she dies in his arms ("You're crying!" she exclaims; "No I'm not," insists Curtis). She dies weeping; her lover buries her in the mountains. In Lidice, the horrible Nazi revenge begins. And as the film ends, the martyrs rise from the fiery destruction (Patricia curiously not among them) and beg the audience to avenge their deaths.

Calling Dr. Death (1943) was the first of Universal's *Inner Sanctum* horror films—a bizarre parade of B

Lon Chaney and Patricia Morison in *Calling Dr. Death*

potboilers, all hell-bent on presenting Lon Chaney as handsome, brilliant and desired by some of the loveliest ladies in Hollywood. Patricia Morison was the first actress to portray mad passion for Chaney; such beauties as Evelyn Ankers, Anne Gwynne, Lois Collier, Jean Parker, Brenda Joyce and Tala Birell all would follow in her high-heeled footsteps.

Patricia Morison truly snares the honors as Stella Madden, Chaney's lovesick nurse (a role originally fashioned for Gale Sondergaard, who was supposed to co-star with Chaney in all the *Inner Sanctum* films, but ultimately played in none of them). Patricia's Stella reveals in a climactic hypnotic spell that she murdered Chaney's wicked wife (Ramsay Ames) with a fire poker—then destroyed her face with acid. Certainly it's one of the most grim and shocking crimes in the Universal horror canon.

Patricia was at her most slinky in *Dressed to Kill*, the 1946 swan song of the Universal Sherlock Holmes series. She was master villainess Hilda Courtney—mistress of disguises, smoker of Egyptian cigarettes, and diabolic vamp who supplies Universal's own final challenge for Basil Rathbone's Holmes and Nigel Bruce's Watson.

Julian Emery (Edmond Breon), aka "Stinky," is a wealthy collector of music boxes and an old schoolmate of Watson. He has just removed his toupee for the night when he receives a telephone call from Patricia's Hilda Courtney—who seductively invites herself up for a drink. Breon has his toupee back on by the time Patricia makes her entrance—drop-dead gorgeous in a full-length dress and a remarkable white stole. Of course, Mrs. Courtney's interest is not in this old codger, but in his music boxes—one of which contains stolen Bank of England plates. Patricia turns up her vamp act, Breon moves in for a kiss and we see one of the most memorable death scenes in the Universal Holmes series: Hilda's accomplice (Harry Cording) tosses a knife into Breon's back, and he falls—dragging the villainess' white stole with him as it runs over her shoulders and down her arms like a giant, plunging snake. As Michael Brunas wrote about *Dressed to Kill* in the book, *Universal Horrors*: "Most critics seemed more interested in griping about the inappropriateness of the title. One wonders where these critics were looking when the sleek, elegantly coiffured Patricia Morison dispassionately retracted her ermine from under the body of poor old Emery... and then cold-bloodedly walked over him."

Patricia Morison is at her cold-hearted best in *Dressed to Kill.*

Thereafter, Patricia's Hilda Courtney is a deadly black widow of a villainess: performing a marvelous disguise bit as an old charwoman; making her way around London in the aforementioned sexy black dress, furs and big-toe hat (with partners-in-crime Frederic Worlock and Harry Cording); and sparring with Rathbone's Holmes:

Hilda: So fearfully awkward having a dead body lying about, don't you agree, Mr. Holmes?
Holmes: Another dead body shouldn't weigh too heavily on your conscience, Mrs. Courtney!

In the course of *Dressed to Kill*, Patricia's Hilda almost kills Holmes as her henchmen handcuff him to a pipe on a garage ceiling, filling the area with exhaust smoke; she also tricks Watson, flirting with him and planting a smoke bomb in 221-B Baker Street. However, Holmes and Watson foil her in the end, and she marches off, her head arrogantly held high—and still dressed to kill.—Gregory Mank

Countess Dracula (1971)/Ingrid Pitt
For a short time during the 1970s, Ingrid Pitt became the female horror movie icon for Hammer films and other production companies; however, her presence and performances were not properly assessed at the time.

Ingrid Pitt, portraying the evil Countess who bathes in the blood of virgins, acting under heavy layers of age makeup, only to emerge as her sensual self after taking bloodbaths, creates a nuanced and rich performance. As the Countess, mostly mute and hidden partially beneath a veil that covers her head, Ingrid Pitt slightly hunches over and moves stiffly to demonstrate her frail condition. But after emerging in the guise of her "daughter," after the actual daughter is imprisoned, Ingrid Pitt glows with a radiant sensuality that loves the camera. Never has Pitt looked more alluring or beautiful.

Ingrid Pitt as *Countess Dracula* with Sandor Eles

Countess Dracula, with its stark sequence of the nude Ingrid Pitt emerging from her tub, dripping blood as she attempts to hide her nudity, is a sequence for the ages. Unfortunately, this talky costume drama likes to shock us with the discovery of sexy nude virgin bodies in the closet, and though the set-up for murder is nicely atmospheric, the movie plays out at a much too slow a pace and the costume drama becomes too classy for its own good. Nigel Green, shortly before his suicide, submits another aristocratic performance that commands attention, but poor unfortunate hero (although he is tainted by enjoying the pleasures of the village prostitute after seemingly committing to the Countess' "daughter") Sandor Eles dies unfairly in the final minute of the movie before the irate villagers punish Countess Dracula once and for all. Ingrid Pitt's performance is mesmerizing and quite solid, with a remarkable contrast between her non-sexual Countess and blatantly erotic transformation into nude romper.

However, *The Vampire Lovers* is Pitt's classic horror portrayal and a film that grows richer with age. Touting direction by Roy Ward Baker and featuring a generally uninspired supporting performance by Peter Cushing (compare his role here as the General to his Baron Frankenstein performances or Van Helsing in the Dracula movies), *The Vampire Lovers* is not Terence Fisher's style of vampire fandango. Featuring lush period detail and costuming, *The Vampire Lovers* brings erotica to Hammer's vampire mythology, and does it quite tastefully. Ingrid Pitt, through the course of the movie, plays the same vampiric character operating under two different identities, both involving her so-called aunt leaving her at the home of an unsuspecting aristocrat, where she subsequently befriends a virginal daughter who becomes her next victim. (Even though Ingrid Pitt claims in printed interviews that vampires are not sexually motivated, all her primary victims are female and are slowly seduced, more so than attacked, and the look in Pitt's eyes before she bites Madeline Smith is sexual, pure and simple.) The nude romps, which seemed more flashy and sensational back in 1970, today seem more carefully crafted to demonstrate the seductive influence of evil, and how sexual seduction is similar to the seduction of evil. Ingrid Pitt, looking beautiful yet somehow infinitely sad and pale, almost haggard, captures the loneliness of the undead and demonstrates vampirism as both a sexual urge and also as a disease. Her performance resonates and grows richer over time. Here is not the typical Hammer Glamour model who frolics in the nude, for Pitt, though quite beautiful with a well proportioned body, was exotic and mature in a way that separates her from most of the other female fashion queens. For Pitt truly submits a multi-layered performance here. While *The Vampire Lovers* offers one beheading too many, its vampiric violence and well-filmed cinematographic atmosphere create a movie several cuts above the other typical Hammer productions of that time.—Gary J. Svehla

The Devil Commands (1941)

Gary J. Svehla in *Midnight Marquee 71/72* says, "In a gut-wrenching sequence, Karloff's wife dies tragically in a car accident, Karloff's spirit dying with her. Now his research turns to contacting the dead, and he hooks up with a fake spiritualist, a very domineering woman, Mrs. Walters, Anne Revere in one of the strongest female horror film performances of the 1940s." His opinion is seconded by David H. Smith in *Boris Karloff: Midnight Marquee Actors Series*, "As Mrs. Walters in *The Devil Commands*, Revere is the epitome of the clichéd turbaned 'ice princess,' supercilious, dominating the befuddled Blair with ease, her dark eyes glinting with greed. With a script that developed her character further, Revere could easily have outshone Karloff, and Mrs. Walters' ignominious death before the finale is a major failing of the film."—Gary J. Svehla

Devil Girl from Mars (1954)

Adapted from the stage play by John Mather and James Eastwood and looking very much *like* a stage play, this early British science fiction thriller has now gained something of a cult reputation among buffs and it's probably all down to one person—Patricia Laffan as Nyah, the Martian female sent to Earth to kidnap males for breeding purposes. The statuesque Laffan, previously known for her role as a mad empress wed to Peter Ustinov's equally mad emperor in MGM's *Quo Vadis*, looks an absolute treat in her black PVC cloak, incredibly short skirt, tights and boots, an S&M fan's dream come true! Reports of a meteor seen over Scotland are unfounded: it's Laffan's flying saucer that is showing up on radar screens. The alien has landed on the Inverness moors in Scotland to take back men to a Mars that has been decimated by atomic war, leaving only female survivors in a "matriarchy society." Placing a force field around a remote inn to prevent anyone from escaping, she terrorises and threatens the people staying there both verbally and physically, her laser gun reducing humans to ashes and Chani the robot firing off thunderbolts from his head to demonstrate his awesome power. A good cast was assembled to play the mix of British sterotypes: a socialite with a troubled past (a very young Hazel Court), the sexy barmaid (Adrienne Corri), a newspaper reporter (Hugh McDermott), a scientist (Joseph Tomelty) and a convict on the loose (Peter Reynolds). Likewise, Nyah's flying saucer is an impressive-looking craft when you consider the film's tight budget, almost, and I repeat, almost, up there with Harryhausen's models in *Earth vs. the Flying Saucers*. Even the engaging Chani, resembling a seven-foot-high refrigerator on clumpy legs, is on a par with similar robots in American sci-fi actioners. You know this production has "Made in Britain" stamped all over it when the landlady announces, amid all the mayhem and intrigue taking place, "Nothing like a good cup of tea in a crisis." Did she forget that Earth was under threat at that precise moment in time? But this all adds to the movie's quirkiness and endearing quality and Laffan is mesmerizing as the alien, spouting off streams of pseudo-scientific jargon with a perfectly straight and meticulously made-up face, only her eyebrows arching as she views the humans with utter disdain. After the group have unsuccessfully tried to shoot and electrocute Laffan, she boards her vessel with one male, the convict who, on instructions from the professor, sacrifices himself by tampering with the saucer's power source, thus causing it to explode, just as Nyah is heading toward London and more males to kidnap. Edwin Astley contributed a boisterous score (used in all the right places) to a well-made but largely forgotten British picture (it has never been screened on U.K. television) that has far more merit than many American B movies of the same period. —Barry Atkinson

Die! Die! My Darling!

When I watch Hammer's *Die! Die! My Darling!* (1965), I take it seriously despite the light-hearted opening credits and Wilfred Josephs' whimsical main-title theme. Then again, in the late 1960s, I took *Dark Shadows* and even *Batman* completely seriously. The amusing title sequence of *Die! Die! My Darling!* and the occasional harpsichord riffs within the film belie the fact that this thriller can provide shocks and suspense in addition to Grand Guignol camp. *Die! Die! My Darling!* owes as much to *Psycho* and *Homicidal* as it does to *What Ever Happened to Baby Jane?* and *Hush... Hush, Sweet Charlotte*.

Based on Anne Blaisdell's novel *Nightmare* and titled *Fanatic* in the U.K., *Die! Die! My Darling!* (U.S. title) is Richard Matheson's first produced script for Hammer Films. (His earlier *I Am Legend* screenplay *The Night Creatures* was discarded as being unable to pass the British censors.) *Die! Die! My Darling!* stars Tallulah Bankhead (another aging actress turning to horror in the 1960s) and Stefanie Powers (one and one-half years before *The Girl from U.N.C.L.E.*) with Donald Sutherland in a supporting role. Powers and Sutherland's careers were just beginning, but *Die! Die! My Darling!*, her *Batman* two-parter and a cartoon voice-over were Bankhead's final roles before her death in 1968. Bankhead's character of Mrs. Trefoile represents the dying mores of early 20-century life, while Powers' character of Patricia Carroll symbolizes the more relaxed standards of the burgeoning sexual revolution of the 1960s. Caught between the two was Mrs. Trefoile's son and Patricia's ex-fiancé Stephen, who killed himself as his only escape from his mother's fanatical repression—and also possibly from the subtly threatening, free-thinking "new woman" Pat, who had decided not to marry him. The character of Stephen never appears in *Die! Die! My Darling!*, although his portrait figures in the violent, melodramatic conclusion.

Now engaged to Alan Glentower (Maurice Kaufmann), a London television executive, Pat nevertheless feels obligated to pay a courtesy call to Mrs. Trefoile at her isolated, stifling manor house. When Pat arrives, she enters the oppressive, suffocating world of the ascetic Mrs. Trefoile and her odd assortment of servants—meek parlor maid Gloria (Gwendolyn Watts), frustrated married domestics Anna (Yootha Joyce) and Harry (Peter Vaughn), and slow-witted handyman Joseph (Sutherland). Mrs. Trefoile instantly disapproves of Pat, who wears short red dresses and lipstick, does not go to church regularly and may not be a virgin. Pat soon realizes that Mrs. Trefoile does not intend to let her leave the house and go back to her sinful life in London. Instead, Mrs. Trefoile will keep Pat locked away and intimidate, starve and beat her into submission so that Pat will be a suitable bride for Stephen in the afterlife. Pat may never see Alan or even freedom again!

Die! Die! My Darling! shows the influence of *Psycho*, as do so many psychological-horror films of the 1960s. There are violent outbursts, an overbearing mother and even a dead body in the fruit cellar. The film is an effective blend of the psycho-thriller and woman-in-jeopardy subgenres and another one of Richard Matheson's remarkable blends of suspense and dark humor. Tallulah Bankhead, as Mrs. Trefoile, gets my vote as a dangerous dame because of her maniacal obsessions, her hazardous gunplay and her over-the-top performance. *Die! Die! My Darling!* can be appreciated as both horror and camp.
—Jeff Thompson

Dracula's Daughter (1936)

"She was beautiful when she died—a hundred years ago." So spoke Professor Von Helsing (Edward Van Sloan) at the close of *Dracula's Daughter* (1936), a film that arguably features the most fascinating female villain from horror's "Golden Age."

This titular vampire is a monster of a very different stripe. Not only is she a rare feminine bloodsucker in a (at the time) male-dominated arena, but she's a *sympathetic* one as well. Gloria Holden's Countess Marya Zaleska is much more than a bloodsucking demon; she is a tortured soul, a pitiable victim (of her own despised heritage), as much as vicious victimizer. This sympathetic characterization adds a fascinating "monster-as-victim" subtext (a theme which makes the Frankenstein films so intriguing) to what could otherwise have become just another straightforward vampire yarn.

Though her very nature has made her cold and aloof, Zaleska's haughtiness carries a decidedly hollow ring. While her face may remain passive, her voice can readily quicken with excitement to betray the hope and longing

Gloiria Holden as *Dracula's Daughter*

gaze almost unfocused at times, as if her inner self were concentrating elsewhere, attempting to escape from her own nightmarish existence. At other moments her staring eyes dart about, almost desperately, as if searching for the escape she craves. When she talks of living "a normal life" in which she'll "think normal things," the faraway look in her eyes and half-smile on her lips speak of the hopeful expectations stretched out before her. After her moral defeat during the piano scene (in which she once again succumbs to the bloodlust), her servant Sandor holds up Zaleska's black cloak and ring (the symbols of her nocturnal cravings) so she can venture out to claim another victim. Holden hesitates, gazing at the despised garment in ambivalent fascination. Unable to resist the lure, she finally turns and allows Sandor to drape the damning cloak on her shoulders. Holden's face remains outwardly impassive, but her eyes and downward turn of expression betray a poignant sadness at her defeat.

Such appealing torment, coupled with the irresistible lure of vampirism (symbolizing power over both sex and death), makes this diabolical daughter one of the most intriguing female villains of the silver screen.—Bryan Senn

Ginger Snaps

Welcome to the new era of werewolf film! *Ginger Snaps* (2001), the low-budget but slick Canadian film that just happens to be the best werewolf movie produced since Joe Dante's *The Howling* a generation ago. And its sequel *Ginger Snaps 2: Unleashed* (2003), along with *Dog Soldiers* (2002), is a modern werewolf movie worthy of making audiences howl.

Ginger Snaps, written by Karen Walton and directed by John Fawcett, equates a young girl experiencing her first menstrual cycle with lycanthropy (a subtle metaphor for all the unnerving changes in her body, giving special meaning to the phrase "the curse").

It is the subtle and layered performances that bring to life 16-year-old Ginger (Katharine Isabelle, actually 18) and 15-year-old Brigitte/B (Emily Perkins, actually 22) and makes *Ginger Snaps* a modern horror classic. Perkins and Isabelle make *Ginger Snaps* an anomaly: a character-driven horror movie that relegates the werewolf to only two sequences. The girls and their antics carry the entire movie, aided in large part by pithy, intelligent dialogue that keeps these teens and their uncertainty and pain rooted in reality.

lurking beneath the cold countenance. Tortured soul she may be, but this reluctant vampire hasn't completely lost her sense of humor, for she displays a sharp wit that emphasizes her humanity. When psychiatrist/hero Jeffrey Garth makes a skeptical comment at a party, for instance, Zaleska cleverly disarms him with, "Possibly there are more things in heaven and Earth than are dreamed of in your—psychiatry, Mr. Garth."

Gloria Holden brings this tormented spirit to life with her restrained-yet-earnest performance, revealing the living being beneath the undead exterior. Holden truly uses her eyes to mirror her character's soul. She keeps her

For their school project the girls enact a series of photos/slides of the sisters dying horrible deaths. As Ginger gleefully declares, "Our deaths will *rock*," B answers, "You don't think our death should be *more* than *cheap* entertainment?" By movie's end the viewer will come to realize these individual quotes define the personality of each girl. Right from the start we learn that Ginger is a poseur, a drama queen, who romanticizes the concept of death, while odd-duck B cherishes life. These eccentric sisters are obsessed with their death pact to always be together. Ginger reminds B, "Suicide is the ultimate fuck you. Come on, it's so *us*. It's the pact!" B, referred to as "the dweeb" by a group of high school boys, tells Ginger, "the redhead with the rack," "It's so easy for you… you don't care." To which Ginger smiles and declares: "Dead by 16… out of the scene… together forever." The two girls lock their flat palms together, revealing slash marks on both their hands.

Their school slide project is revealed one day in class. One sister, face up, is impaled on a white picket fence, her eyes wide open; another shot shows a sister curled up underwater in the bathtub; another shows a sister crushed under the wheels of a car, blood oozing from her mouth; another shows a girl lying dead on the grass, a lawnmower on top of her, a cigarette still burning in her mouth; etc. In this manner the sisters gleefully celebrate their flipping-finger attitude and outcast status.

The required werewolf attack, shot in a park playground at night, comes as the sisters are planning to kill classmate Trina's dog and make it seem as though the beast that has slaughtered pets in the community has struck again. Blood begins to drip down Ginger's thigh as the girls find the devoured remains of a dog in the park. "B, I just got the curse," Ginger reveals in disgust. "You kill yourself to be different, but your body screws you. If I start hanging around tampon dispensers or start talking about PMS, just shoot me." Eerily, the hobbyhorse nearby slightly sways and all grows quiet as Ginger is suddenly attacked and dragged screaming through the nearby woods. B, her breathing heavy and labored, frantically searches, calling out her sister's name, but all she hears are screams in the distance. We can hardly see the beast that is attacking, only quick flashes of snout and teeth and fur. Finally B, armed with a branch, beats the beast off Ginger, and both girls run toward the road and safety, where the werewolf is splattered by a van driven by greenhouse keeper and likable drug dealer Sam (Kris Lemche). No Hollywood mythology (silver bullets) is at work here. In a marvelous follow-up sequence, B gets Ginger home, screaming in pain and covered in blood, huge claw marks running down her shoulder and chest. But within a minute Ginger declares she's not bleeding anymore and her wounds are already healing.

While Ginger's transformation to werewolf is slow, her transformation from outcast to sex queen is sudden, as she soon finds herself playfully attacking boys on the athletic field and smoking pot in the back of vans. However, Ginger is unnerved when she invites B into the school bathroom stall to show her tufts of hair growing out of her slash wounds. "I can't have a hairy chest, B, that's fucked!" Soon Ginger will also sprout a phallic tail.

But Ginger and B start to move further apart. Ginger becomes paranoid, thinking B is jealous of her expanding social/sexual cycle, but in reality B is simply worried about her sister's unnatural physical and personality changes. Ginger accuses B of being the monster with little green eyes, to which B answers in her totally honest way: "Yes, I always wanted to hemorrhage and be hairy and suck off Jason McCarthy!" Later that night, Ginger is in a car with Jason where she makes all the aggressive sexual moves. Jason, obviously not comfortable being used as a sex toy, cries, "Take it easy, we got all night." Ginger tells him to lay back and relax, as she tears his shirt off. Jason's last frantic words are, "Who's the boy here!!!" as Ginger's rough sex commences.

Yet Ginger is not as strong or as independent as she pretends, as she runs home to her sister and vomits blood in the toilet. Fearfully, Ginger admits, "Something is very wrong. I had this urge… I thought it was for sex, but it was to tear every fucking thing to pieces!!!" Admitting to herself that Jason's "the hero" and that I'm just "the freak, mutant lay," Ginger admits she killed the neighbor's dog to satisfy her urge, that she couldn't help herself, and that she feels "wicked," flashing her new wolfish teeth. B is forced to enlist Sam, the guy with the green thumb and interest in chemistry and, surprisingly, B. B

is the shrinking violet, her long, straight hair covering her face, her eyes darting downward when speaking, always reluctant to make eye contact. Sam comes up

with a potential cure: Aconitum (monkshood), a naturally growing poison (with blue flowers) that Sam describes as a natural detox that promotes the growth of red blood cells, similar to wolfbane.

But as Ginger transforms into a sexually active teen, she also grows jealous of B's attraction to Sam. When teen bitch Trina confronts B outside their yard and demands the return of her dog, the bestial Ginger grabs Trina from behind, playfully taunting and slapping her on her forehead. Ginger utters: "You play with your new friends, I'll play with mine… You asked for this, you picked Sam over me. Whatever happens now, it's your fault!" The fight escalates into the Fitzgerald kitchen and milk is spilled on the floor, and when Trina grabs a knife, she slips and cracks her head open on the counter, her blood blending with the puddles of milk as she crumples in death. Hiding the body in the freezer, the girls quickly stage one of their death photo shoots, pretending that the real blood is only for show as their parents rush into the kitchen. Mother Pamela utters: "I told you, *no* more deaths in the house!"

After digging the corpse out of the family freezer with an ice pick, Ginger longingly looks at the blood-matted corpse of Miss Popularity and asks B seriously, "Do you think she is pretty?" B just as seriously asks, "If I wasn't here, would you *eat* her?" Ginger, in disgust, mutters, "No! God! That would be like *fucking* her." Once again Ginger's confused violent/sexual urges baffle her. But these lines of dialogue demonstrate Ginger's inability to cope with all the changes her body is undergoing.

Later, Ginger, very feline, hovers menacingly over B. Ginger almost purrs, "You would love it, a little scratch, swap some juice… it would be our own pact, just like before, it's so *us* B!" But B tells her, "I'd rather be dead than be what you are!" Ginger reminds her, "We have a pact! Dead by 16!" When B refuses, Ginger tells her sister to stay out of her way.

That evening Ginger makes her grand entrance at the party at the greenhouse. Ginger's looks have changed as her hair is now blonde, her eyes appear animal-like, the structure of her face less human, her exposed stomach leathery. She is now a smoldering creature of sensuality and immediately makes a play to seduce the *unwilling* Sam, to win her sister back by proving Sam to be only a sex-obsessed creep (such is not the case). But since the medicine is back at their home, B has to get Ginger there, and the only way is for her to finish the new blood pact, cutting her hand, cutting Ginger's, and joining palms together (thus infecting B with the virus) to again win her sister's trust. "You got everything from me that isn't about you… now I *am* you," B bellows. To which frightened Ginger responds, "But what am I?"

By the movie's climax Ginger is no longer human. In the back of Sam's van, her body contorts and she spits up blood as her human shell becomes twisted and shed. Ginger finally loses the last vestiges of her humanity as she becomes the werewolf. The pulse-pounding finale features a slow trek through the darkened family home, Sam and B armed only with a flashlight and syringe of monkshood. Sam volunteers to administer the drug. But once out of the kitchen, Sam is brutally attacked, banged against furniture and dragged down to the cellar. B, gasping for breath, slowly leaves the kitchen and finds the still-intact syringe, which she clutches as she heads downward to find her sister. Downstairs B follows the puddles of blood until she hears Sam, who lies broken, beaten and near death on the floor. The werewolf hovers right over him as he sits bleeding, gasping, unconscious. B attempts to suck the blood from her fingers, but she vomits it all up crying, "I can't, I won't." The wolf grows more violent while Sam's body slumps over, apparently dead. B manages to fetch a knife from the drawer as the werewolf approaches her. "Come on, it's me…Ginger, please, it's me!" Then the determined B declares, "I'm not dying in this room with you… I'm not dying!" Philosophically B is declaring the fundamental difference that always existed between Ginger and her. As the werewolf approaches, its snout inches away from B's face, the animal suddenly slumps over, the knife now buried deep in the beast's torso. Tears well up in B's eyes as she scans her shared bedroom and sees the photos of her sister. B's face is bloodied and pained, the needle still held unused in her hand. The werewolf breathes slowly and B hugs the fiend that was her sister, even after its labored breathing ceases. The camera pans back to show the two sisters' beds in the background.—Gary J. Svehla

Sam (Kris Lemche) is attacked by the now completely transformed Ginger.

Ju-On

The ghost of *Ju-On* played by Takako Fuji is creepily haunting. She is shown crawling upward under bed covers toward her victim; she is shown bent and hovering over her victim who lies in bed; she comes upward between a victim whose hands cover her eyes; and most hauntingly, she crawls on her belly, snakelike, squirming, as though her backbone were broken, across the floor and down a staircase. And her easily identified calling card is her clicking, gurgling sound that announces her proximity to unaware victims.—Gary J. Svehla

House on Haunted Hill (1959)

Generally, the screen's most dangerous dames belong to the world of film noir (Barbara Stanwyck, Lana Turner, Lizabeth Scott, Jane Greer); however, the horror cinema also has had its fair share of despicable ladies (vampires and mad scientists alike, even daughters of Frankenstein and Dracula!). For me, the movie that instantly springs to my mind when I think of a dangerous dame is the noir/horror hybrid written by sharp-tongued Robb White, William Castle's *House on Haunted Hill*, released by Allied Artists in 1959.

Even though the movie was sold as a straight haunted house horror thriller, its roots are pure noir with a conniving millionaire, Frederick Loren (Vincent Price), hosting a house party where survivors who remain overnight receive $10,000. Curiously, all the invited guests express desperate needs for quick cash. However, the dramatic conflict does not only originate from the obvious "who will survive and who will not" question, but also from the unhappily married hosting couple, Mr. and Mrs. Loren (Carol Ohmart). She almost admits to poisoning her husband years ago, and he admits to hating her with a passion. As their under-control but venomous barbs go flying up in their bedroom as the nervous guests gather down below, Frederick wishes for his wife to get dressed to greet their guests, but she refuses, forcing Frederick to venture on alone. She does make a belated appearance later. But as is apparent, she openly defies her husband's wishes and does as she pleases, when she wishes.

Interestingly enough, it is slowly revealed that Annabelle Loren's secret lover, Dr. David Trent (Alan Marshal), is one of the invited party guests, and that

Carol Ohmart as the delightfully vicious Mrs. Loren gets her just deserts in *House on Haunted Hill.*

Mrs. Loren has concocted a bold scheme whereby all the spooky goings-on will unbalance the mind of pretty but naive Nora Manning (Carolyn Craig) so that Manning will accidentally shoot and kill Frederick in a well-staged course of events intended to drive the young heroine off the deep end (a chandelier falls near her, she gets trapped in a dark room, she is spooked by an elderly blind woman in the same room, she witnesses the suicide of Mrs. Loren [by hanging] yet watches her ghostly form return, floating in space with a rope slowing wrapping itself around her feet, etc.).

However, the even more sinister and corrupt Frederick Loren is able to anticipate all these moves, and while the innocent yet manipulated Nora does in fact shoot the startled Mr. Loren, her gun is filled with blanks. When Dr. Trent enters to dispose of the body by throwing it in the convenient acid bath in the cellar, Loren surprises and overpowers him, tossing him into the vat instead. Then using devious means to horrify (and kill) his own wife, Loren has manipulated a skeleton marionette which he uses to force his own wife to slowly back into the very same acid bath to meet her death. Disposing of the skeleton prop, the appropriately sad-faced host awaits the arrival of his party guests (who have temporarily been locked in a room upstairs), concocts a slightly altered story, and states he will gladly let the courts decide his fate.

True, this dangerous dame does get her comeuppance, but think of all the hell she caused for her party guests: staging her own death, cruelly putting innocent people into danger, forcing a young woman to seemingly commit murder, and callously plotting the murder of her husband so she can be free to run off with her lover. All of this while making vile threats to her husband about both past and future attempts on his life. The hatred that exists between husband and wife is stated in both thinly veiled and verbally clever ways, yet the absolute hatred is clearly evident in the cleverly executed dialogue given the actors.

A woman who is evil and plots to murder the man she believes unfairly oppresses her is one thing; involving the lives of innocent bystanders and manipulating them to do her dirty work is quite another. Horror cinema has seldom created a female character as thoroughly evil as Annabelle Loren from *House on Haunted Hill*, and it is a credit to the keen imagination of Robb White that he was able to populate the creaking haunted house/ghost genre with a *femme fatale* straight out of the world of film noir.—Gary J. Svehla

Homicidal (1961)

Homicidal is about greed and violence, and on that level unfolds like a standard thriller. But its special resonance arises from its preoccupation with a disturbing sort of sexuality that we instinctively know is "wrong"— not in a moral sense (other than the fact that Warren/ Emily is a killer, the script invites no particular negative judgment of him/her); rather, we recoil because of the ambiguity of Warren's sexuality. Part of our distaste is grounded in pity, for Warren—although born a girl— had been forcibly *transformed* into a boy by his father, and thus is the victim of a terrible crime.

At the same time, though, we're made aware that Warren has become complicit in his own transformation. In the film's final sequence, when the psychiatrist suggests that something peculiar happened during Warren's stay in Denmark, the script is hinting broadly at a sex-change operation—and not the male-to-female variety made famous in the early 1950s by George/

Christine Jorgensen, but the considerably more rare female-to-male transformation. Warren has undergone this change of his own free will and because of past abuse that he is powerless to resist. In a strange paradox, the killer is both powerful and powerless. In the final judgment, though, because Warren has consciously chosen to perpetuate his own victimization, he becomes an accomplice to his own corruption.

The final, and most potent, jab to the audience that arises from Emily/Warren's sexuality is the way the film equates ambiguous sexuality with physical violence. The character is male *and* female, both and neither, and thus (the film reasons) homicidally violent. It's this point of view that makes the central character's sexuality not merely puzzling but distasteful and threatening. Unorthodox sexual orientation, *Homicidal* tells us, is dangerous.

Castle originally planned to cast an actor in the dual role. He interviewed dozens of young men, most of them, according to his autobiography, gay and, one may assume, insufficiently masculine to carry off the deception. Dissatisfied with these candidates, Castle searched Hollywood talent agencies and casting offices, looking for an actress. Finally, an agent named Jerry Lauren phoned with news that he had just the woman Castle had been looking for.

William Castle changed Joan Marshall's name to Jean Arless in the gender-bending *Homicidal*.

The actress was a leggy blonde named Joan Marshall, who had co-starred with Dane Clark in a syndicated 1959 TV series called *Bold Adventure*. Castle described her as "strikingly beautiful" and possessed of "a strange, different quality." She had large eyes that bored into whomever she looked at, a full, sensuous mouth, a strong profile and marvelous bone structure highlighted by a square jaw and high, prominent cheekbones.

Castle was further intrigued by the relatively low pitch of Marshall's voice. After he described the role to her, he phoned Columbia makeup chief Ben Lane and asked him to turn the beautiful Marshall into a man. Castle sent the actress off to makeup. Two hours later, a slender young man entered Castle's office and asked to see the director. The young man was, of course, Joan Marshall; Castle was suitably impressed. He took her to a men's hairstylist in Beverly Hills where her long blonde hair was cut and dyed black. (This part of Castle's recollection seems doubtful, for to cut Marshall's hair before she had been formally cast—and, more importantly, before the shooting of her "Emily" scenes—is madness. A good guess is that the actress shot her female scenes first, and then was given the haircut so that she could do her "Warren" scenes.)

Castle goes on to claim that he had a mask maker he identifies only as "Ernie" devise an appliance for Marshall's nose, and another, more dramatic one, for her mouth, both of which gave her face an angular, masculine look. After taking casts of Marshall's hands, Ernie created hand appliances, as well. If the mysterious Ernie did all this, he did it anonymously, for only Ben Lane receives screen credit for makeup. (Of course, even in these waning days of the studio system, department heads nearly always received credit for work done by others.)

If casts of Marshall's hands were made, they were not featured in the film; in her Warren guise, Marshall spends most of her time with her hands hidden in her trouser pockets, a self-consciously "masculine" pose that is an unfortunate peculiarity of her performance.

At Castle's request, Marshall wore brown contact lenses over her blue eyes during Warren's scenes, and wore dark makeup suggestive of a suntan.

An uncredited actor did post-production dubbing of Marshall's voice in her scenes as Warren, a point Castle neglected to mention in his autobiography. Also unmentioned is the film's clever use of a male double

Violet Kemble Cooper (left) provides little warmth and comfort to her suffering son (Boris Karloff, fifth from left) in *The Invisible Ray* with Bela Lugosi.

whenever Warren walks away with his back to the camera and when the character is seen in long shot. The double was slender yet clearly male, and his presence reinforces our willingness to accept Warren as a man.

Finally, to add psychological weight to the illusion, Castle changed Joan Marshall's name to the androgynous "Jean Arless."—David J. Hogan

The Invisible Ray (1936)

The best sequences in the movie involve the teaming of Karloff and Violet Kemble Cooper as Mother Rukh, the stern white-haired woman who tells her son he is not good dealing with people and should work alone in his laboratory. She is absolutely correct, but her lack of motherly sympathy and her hard-nosed life lessons make her a truly fascinating character. At the movie's end when Janos confronts her pleading for comfort and advice, she flings her cane and smashes the bottle of antidote, spelling her son's destruction when he turns momentarily into a human fireball and burns away. Even among veterans, Cooper contributes a performance equal to Karloff and Lugosi (albeit of much shorter duration).—Gary J. Svehla

Suspiria (1977)

It is difficult to think of very many truly evil women in the horror genre. The great vampires such as Barbara Steele in *Black Sunday* and Gloria Holden in *Dracula's Daughter* are victims as well as predators. The same can be said of female monsters such as Sandra Harrison in *Blood of Dracula* and Marla English in *She-Creature*. Some very dangerous women in the genre were certifiably insane such as Catherine Deneuve in *Repulsion* and Adrienne Barett in *Daughter of Horror*. But is an insane person truly evil? I guess it all depends on how you look at it.

From my perspective, some good candidates for the genre's queen of evil would be Margaret Hamilton in *The Wizard of Oz*, Tallulah Bankhead in *Fanatic* (aka *Die! Die! My Darling!*), Gale Sondergaard in *The Spider Woman* and *The Spider Woman Strikes Back*, Hazel Court in *The Premature Burial*, Sharon Stone in *Basic Instinct* and maybe Bette Davis in *What Ever Happened to Baby Jane?* Of course, there are many others. When forced to choose, however, I must nominate the unbilled actress who portrays Elena Marcos in Dario Argento's classic *Suspiria*. Marcos is a witch who supposedly died about 70 years before the film begins, but who now serves as the queen of a coven of witches under cover of the ballet school, Tanz Akademie. Director Argento doesn't show us Marcos until the end of the picture. Throughout most of the film, she remains a hidden but no less permeating and palpable source of evil. Behind the artsy facade, Marcos engineers the brutal murders of innocent dancers and employees who learn too much. This heinous murdering of adolescents expecting protection from the school is a particularly loathsome betrayal.

In the film's finale, dancer Susan Banyon (Jessica Harper) discovers Marcos' lair in the depths of the Akademie and attempts to destroy the Black Queen. Several minutes of extreme horror begin in which Marcos raises a murder victim's corpse with pins in its eyes and sends it, knife in hand, after the terrified Banyon. Marcos' crackling voice is suitably menacing as she taunts and ridicules Banyon for wanting to kill the great and powerful Elena Marcos. When Banyon manages to plunge a knife into Marcos, the hitherto invisible witch appears in all her physical horror. As the jarring, throbbing, unnerving music of The Goblins dominates our senses much as Marcos' evil dominates the Akademie, the witch dies amidst a cataclysmic release of maleficent energy.

Using her talents to kill others in a quest for power and eternal life, Marcos is almost the personification of evil. *Suspiria* is scary stuff indeed. And for my money, you won't find a more dangerously evil woman anywhere in film than Elena Marcos.—Don G. Smith

The Tomb (1986)

Golda Meir once said, "Whether women are better than men I cannot say—but I can say they are certainly no worse." Too bad the Israeli prime minister passed away seven years before the release of *The Tomb* (1985), which tells the tale of Nefratis, an ancient Egyptian sorceress revived in modern-day Los Angeles, lusting for blood and immortal life. Her 84-minute saga might have changed the Russian-born political leader's opinion.

The brainchild of low-budget producer-director Fred Olen Ray, *The Tomb* started out as an attempt to finagle money out of New World Pictures, which at the time had optioned F. Paul Wilson's book for filming. By showing footage already shot, *auteur* Ray hoped New World would buy him off because of the title conflict, then use the footage later in some other, unrelated project.

But the best laid schemes of mice and B-movie impresarios often go awry, because Trans World Entertainment loved what they saw in the trailer (shot on faux Egyptian sets left over from a Wrangler jeans TV commercial) and bankrolled the rest. As it turned out, New World threatened to sue, but Ray had covered himself by copyrighting the title based on an H.P. Lovecraft story (which the movie wasn't). *The Tomb* is '80s sexploitation at its finest (just try to forget the incongruous nightclub striptease by the incredibly endowed Kitten Natividad), paying tribute to a number of horror movie predecessors and presenting the most merciless lady vampire ever on screen.

Roused from her eternal slumber by a couple of fortune hunters, Nefratis (Michelle Bauer) rips the heart from one (restoring her youth and beauty) and vows revenge on the other for stealing an ancient amulet she needs to stay alive. A sudden earthquake reburies the tomb and allows him to escape. She reappears in southern California, fetchingly dressed in a gauzy woven dress and open-toe sling-back pumps (which Ray likes to focus on as she stalks her human prey), fluent in English and modern ways.

Nefratis tracks down her tomb's surviving defiler (Richard Alan Hench) posthaste, inserting a live scarab into his chest to assert control over his will. He tells her he has sold the artifact to a collector, whom she seeks out and kills, drinking his blood.

The murdered man's son (David Pearson) and the nearsighted niece (Susan Stokey) of a rival Egyptian collector (Cameron Mitchell) join forces to solve the crime.

The pair call on an expert (John Carradine) in the field, who tells them of the horrors Nefratis perpetrated millennia ago. A priestess of Set, Princess Nefratis "sustained her magical energy by drinking the blood of the living." Her own fearful father has her buried alive and the location of her tomb made secret, for "her supernatural powers were matched only by her cruelty." In her ancient prime, Nefratis slaughtered newborn babies and drank their blood and (as the tomb scene vividly depicts) barehandedly tore the hearts out of full-grown men.

Eventually, the heroine finds herself about to be ceremoniously sacrificed to perpetuate Nefratis' life, even as the hero and the graverobber (freed from the evil princess' buggy enchantment) race to her rescue. "Her ancient fury sought its revenge," the ads for the movie warned us, so "their courage was our last hope!"

The Tomb has its tongue stuck so firmly in its cheek it's a wonder the tip doesn't poke through the soft tissue. The actors recite dialogue verbatim from *Plan 9 From Outer Space*, and almost all have names copped from characters in the Universal mummy series: The graverobber's guide is named Youssef from *The Mummy's Ghost*; the fortune hunter is named John Banning from *The Mummy's Tomb*; John Carradine played Professor Andoheb, from *The Mummy's Hand*; Susan Stokey played Helen from *The Mummy*. Cameron Mitchell, in a nod to the putative Lovecraftian origins of the story, played Howard Phillips.

In no small measure, it is Michelle Bauer as Nefratis that makes *The Tomb* so memorable. Born in 1958, the one-time *Penthouse* Pet of the Month (July 1981) used *The Tomb* as her escape from the soft-core bondage shorts that filled her resume till then and never looked back. Forget Linnea Quigley and Brinke Stevens. Unlike her highly polished and promoted rivals for '80s scream queen fame, Michelle Bauer had something else: an aura of accessibility. With dark curls, an outdoorsy glow and a smile that always seemed to be delighted with the goings-on, Michelle Bauer was a sex symbol unaware, the naughty-but-nice girl next door.

And even with last-minute deletion of gory violence and nudity (some of which turned up in *Beverly Hills Vamp* four years later), Michelle Bauer's performance still presents a vampire's malevolence incarnate. Nefratis is utterly ruthless. She is the complete (and welcome) opposite of the sympathetic vampire, like Milton's Satan fallen from God's grace, which the movies began to emphasize in the '70s and '80s.

Unlike her screen brethren, Nefratis has no pangs of guilt over her bloodthirstiness nor does she mourn for her lost humanity. Going against convention, she doesn't even fall for the hunky leading man in hopes he will lead her back to the straight and narrow.

At one point, confronted by a pair of customs agents (Peter Conway and Brad Arrington), Nefratis asks "Who the hell are you?" with such world weary contemptuousness it should become her signature line. Nefratis doesn't really care—they'll both be dead in a minute, no matter what they say. Though a little stilted in earlier dialogue, Michelle Bauer pulls this one line off so perfectly, all else is forgivable. She dominated *The Tomb* throughout.

The Tomb, made for $135,000, earned over three and a half million for Trans World, saving it from bankruptcy (the company had taken a financial bath with the abortive *Creature* the year before), and was definitely the breakthrough film for Fred Olen Ray, still a regular fixture in video stores. Though it may be dismissed nowadays for its camp humor and low budget, and hopefully forgiven its bigotry (the Egyptians are referred to as towel-heads and rag-heads), *The Tomb* survives as a two-fold vehicle: as a springboard to the B-movie mainstream for one actress, and for one of the most graphic depictions of female evil ever.—David H. Smith

Michelle Bauer as the evil Nefratis in *The Tomb*

The Wizard of Oz (1939)

Horror and science fiction films are arguably among the most sexist of film genres. So many memorable male monsters and villains have been featured over the years, from werewolves and mad scientists to mummies and visitors from outer space. But what of the ladies? Despite an intriguing wealth of possibilities, the golden age horrors that we all know and love were somewhat reticent when it came to offering great set-chewing, scene-stealing, villainous parts to the fairer sex. Only when I cast the cinematic net wider into the realm of fantasy and mysteries do I find distaff characters that can hold a candle to the Gothic monsters that forever haunt my movie screen. For who among us did not have their childhood dreams haunted by the specter of Ms. Hamilton's aptly named Wicked Witch, her face a mask of unrepentant evil, her voice gone mad with cackling laughter? Whether commanding forth her hellish army of flying monkeys or extending a bony finger to threaten helpless Dorothy, Hamilton's character tapped into the frightened recesses of my childhood imagination like few other film characters did. And like all memorable performances, this one conveyed a certain subtle truism—though life's challenges may seem insurmountable, with a little courage and enough perseverance they can be overcome. Like some nefarious, black-clad spider, Hamilton's performance left behind an impression as endearing and enduring as Lugosi's Dracula or Karloff's Frankenstein Monster.

Margaret Hamilton's appearance in *The Wizard of Oz* was another of those casting coups that MGM used to pull off with stunning regularity. The part seems so tailored for her it is difficult to imaging another performer in the role. (Gale Sondergaard, who was also reportedly up for the part, would have given an interesting though undoubtedly more restrained performance.) A veteran of over 70 films, Hamilton was one of Hollywood's busiest character actresses in the late 1930s and early 1940s, appearing in such diverse fare as *My Little Chickadee* and *The Ox-Bow Incident*. Comedy was arguably her forte, although film producers saw fit to cast her in all manner of roles. A typical Hamilton characterization would find her appearing as a peevish spinster, her sourpuss disposition suggesting

In real life Margaret Hamilton was as kind as she was wicked in *The Wizard of Oz*, where she is chasing Dorothy (Judy Garland) for the Ruby Slippers.

nothing less than a case of chronic constipation. The role of Miss Gulch from *The Wizard*'s opening reel is, in fact, typical of the performances in which she would specialize. That Hamilton could turn the fantasy level up a notch and create a character as memorable as her wonderfully Wicked Witch says much about the talents of this familiar but often overlooked character performer.

I have been told by Those Who Know that *The Wizard of Oz* was only moderately successful on its initial release and did not achieve classic status until it became a televised rite of spring. This might explain Hamilton's dearth of appearances in subsequent fantasy films; her filmography only indicates later roles in Universal's *Invisible Woman*, the William Castle kiddie matinee *13 Ghosts* and a voice-over (as Auntie Em!) in 1974's animated *Journey Back to Oz*. While old-time moviegoers may remember Margaret Hamilton primarily for her appearances as an irksome neighbor or a meddlesome maiden aunt, baby boomers are likely to forever think of her as the dark denizen of Dorothy's dream world. Speaking for myself, I know I could never watch one of her Maxwell House Coffee commercials without looking for a telltale broomstick hiding somewhere in the corner.

Perhaps someday, a talented and enterprising filmmaker will helm the quintessential cinematic version of J. Sheridan Le Fanu's *Carmilla* or bring to life one of Edgar Allan Poe's haunted and haunting heroines. Until then, Margaret Hamilton's Wicked Witch of the West stands unrivaled in my imagination as the ultimate expression of female evil.—Steve Thornton

Dominatrix Divas

MidMar Readers Pick Their Faves

Everyone loves those dangerous dames—what man can resist a woman in skintight leather with an evil gleam in her eye? And what woman can resist the thought of taking a whip to a man who asks her for the thousandth time where his shoes are? Whether you think of them as dominating dames, dominatrix divas, or witchy seductresses, *Movie Mystique* asked our readers to send us their favorite dominatrix divas—and we can't resist offering a tip of the cap to some of our favorite sexy sylphs.

Boris Karloff and Myrna Loy in *Mask of Fu Manchu*

•Jaded Exotics: Myrna Loy, yes, that sweet Nora Charles and also William Powell's screen wife many times over sizzles as the decadent Fah Lo See, who actually licks her lips when viewing the half-dressed hero sprawled helplessly before her in *The Mask of Fu Manchu* (1932*)*; Chat (Maggie Cheung), the tough-as-nails champion in *The Heroic Trio* (1993); Jen Yu (Ziyi Zhang) shines as an unwilling teenage bride-to-be who battles for her freedom in *Crouching Tiger, Hidden Dragon* (2000); Yasuhisa Yoshikawa (Jun Kunimura) is an even more unwilling fiancée in *Audition* (1999); Alex Munday (Lucy Liu) causes a stir when she poses as a dominatrix efficiency expert and struts into a geek-filled office in a hilarious scene in *Charlie's Angels* (2000).

•Scary Psychos: Mari Blanchard, as Kyra Zelas in *She Devil* (1957), is dying of tuberculosis and agrees to an experimental treatment which turns her into a deadly femme fatale; Irena (Nastassja Kinski) of the 1982 *Cat People* is a little less inhibited than her 1942 counterpart, as Nastassja Kinski puts the magnetism in animal; Sister Hyde (Martine Beswicke) brings out the kinky female side of Dr. Jekyll in *Dr. Jekyll and Sister Hyde* (1971); Gale Sondergaard as Zenobia Dollard snared drooling male audiences in her web in *The Spider Woman Strikes Back* (1946); Elizabeth Shelley (Patty Cullen) goes to pieces in *Frankenhooker* (1990); the movie's tagline is "from sluts to bolts"; shape-changing Mystique (Rebecca Romijn-Stamos) can be anything you want her to be in *X-Men* (2000); and let's not forgetTerminatrix Kristanna Loken in *T3*.

•Beware of Goddesses Bearing Gifts: No one could say no to the fabulous H. Rider Haggard–inspired babes-who-must–be-obeyed (aka She, Ayesha), which include Margurite Snow (1911); Betty Bythe (1921); Helen Gahagan (1935); Ursula Andress (1967); Sandahl Bergman (1987) (who also snaps a few whips in *Red Sonja* and *Conan the Barbarian*); plus Bella Darvi in *The Egyptian* (1954). Of course, we can't forget the exotic beauties who performed Cleopatra and happily ground men under their tiny golden sandals: Theda Bara (1917); Claudette Colbert (1934); Rhonda Fleming (*Serpent of the Nile*, 1953); Vivien Leigh (*Caesar and Cleopatra*, 1945); Sophia Loren (*Due notti con Cleopatra*, 1953) and Elizabeth Taylor (1963).

• In Space No One Can Hear You Scream: Private Vasquez (Jenette Goldstein) kicked some outer space butt in *Aliens* (1986); Leeloo (Milla Jovovich) took on porcine aliens in *The Fifth Element* (1997); Akima (Drew Barrymore) helped save the human race and tame Cale Tucker in *Titan A.E.* (2000); Carolyn Fry (Radha Mitchell) keeps panic-stricken crew and passengers in line in *Pitch Black* (2000); Dizzy Flores (Dina Meyer) holds her own against BEMs in *Starship Troopers* (1997); Serleena (Lara Flynn Boyle) is a ghastly outer space monster who disguises herself as a lingerie model in *Men in Black II* (2002); Ursa (Sarah Douglas) is indestructible in *Superman II* (1980); Space Girl (Mathilda May) in *Lifeforce* (1985); Lori (Sharon Stone) whips Arnold into submission in *Total Recall* (1990); Sil (Natasha Henstridge) is looking for a little mating action in *Species* (1995); Sarah Connor (Linda Hamilton) is mad as hell and isn't going to take it anymore in *Terminator 2* (1991); Nyah (Patricia Laffan) is looking for some breeding stock in *Devil Girl from Mars* (1954); *Cat-Women of the Moon* (1953) try seduction prior to grand theft spaceship; *The Astounding She-Monster* (Shirley Kilpatrick) was also looking for a little human companionship in 1958; Galaxina (Dorothy Stratten) has all her parts in the right place as an android in *Galaxina* (1980); android Pris (Daryl Hannah) puts her gymnastic skills to good use in *Blade Runner* (1982); Tank Girl (Lori Petty) hops to it with a kangaroo mutant in *Tank Girl* (1995); Edith Johnson (Melanie Griffith) proves real women are better than robots in *Cherry 2000* (1988); and Barb Wire (Pamela Anderson) is a bountiful bounty hunter in *Barb Wire* (1996).

• Itsy Bitsy Fur Bikinis: Kari (Martine Beswicke) keeps those pesky blonde slaves in control while seducing a new boy toy in *Prehistoric Women* (1967); Aunty Entity (Tina Turner) rules the roost in *Mad Max Beyond Thunderdome*

Pris (Daryl Hannah) is the deadly but doomed android in *Blade Runner*.

(1985); Martine Beswicke dons those furs again as Nupondi in *One Million Years B.C.* (1966); and Imogen Hassell isn't just stalking dinos in *When Dinosaurs Ruled the Earth* (1970).

• Who's That Vamp I Saw You With: Ingrid Pitt has her eye on Sandor Eles as *Countess Dracula* (1970); Magenta (Patricia Quinn) has an "interesting" relationship with Riff Raff in *The Rocky Horror Picture Show* (1975); Lillith (Angie Everhart) is a vampire madame in *Bordello of Blood* (1996); Marie (Anne Parillaud) is out to rid the world of human scum in *Innocent Blood* (1992); Miriam (Catherine Deneuve) depends on the kindness of lovers for her continued existence in *The Hunger* (1983); Lady Sylvia Marsh (Amanda Donohoe) puts the bite on a young Hugh Grant in *Lair of the White Worm* (1988); Diamondback (Jenette Goldstein) is "finger lickin' good" in *Near Dark* (1987); the Alien Queen (Florence Marly) delights in a spaceship full of yummy astronauts in *Queen of Blood* (1966).

• The Name Says it All: Bond Girls: Honey Ryder (Ursula Andress) *Dr. No* (1962); Pussy Galore (Honor Blackman) *Goldfinger* (1964); Fiona Volpe (Luciana Paluzzi) *Thunderball* (1965); Kissy Suzuki (Mie Hama) *You Only*

Live Twice (1967); Melina Havelock (Carole Bouquet) *For Your Eyes Only* (1981); *Octopussy* (1983) (Maud Adams); Jinx (Halle Berry) *Die Another Day* (2002)

While our lists could go on and on and on…we'll turn it over to our faithful readers:

I can't resist making lists, and, when it's a list of my top five fantastic-film dominatrixes (or FFDs), I'm practically *compelled* to (as in, "Yes, Mistress").

When she requested our input, Sue Svehla provided several superb examples of FFDs, such as Myrna Loy's Fah Lo See in *The Mask of Fu Manchu* (1932)—who salivates over the sight of men being whipped and of Terrence Granville (Charles Starrett), wearing little more than a diaper, bound before her—and Michelle Pfeiffer's Catwoman in *Batman Returns* (1992). Is there anything more erotic than cat-suited Pfeiffer straddling a supine Batman (Michael Keaton) and licking his face?

Rather than repeating Sue—and because my colleagues will probably write more eloquently than I about more well-known FFDs (none of whom I can think of)—I decided to try to come up with a few of the more obscure examples of the breed. I don't know if I succeeded (and may be beaten for my insolence), but here, in chronological order, are the five FFDs I'd most like to boss me around.

1. Patricia Laffan as Nyah, *Devil Girl from Mars* (1954). In the late 1950s, this British movie used to play on Detroit-area TV (over Windsor, Ontario's channel 9, I believe) all the time, so I got to see it more than once. I don't know which impressed me more—the boxy robot or the curvy devil girl, poured into black latex, replete with her severe hairdo and cape. She had a commanding presence—and was certainly commanding!

2. Shirley Kilpatrick as *The Astounding She-Monster* (1958). Another alien invades Earth in a tight-fitting costume (but this one photographed white). In a moment of adolescent wit, I dubbed this film "The *Ass*-tounding She-Monster," although that's unfair, since we rarely get to see the alien's behind. According to what could be apocryphal reports, the actress ripped her costume when filming began and, because the film's low budget didn't provide for costume replacement, she was forced to *back* out of rooms all the time, for, to turn around would have meant to reveal her—*ahem!*—assets. Is this story true or just one that's been repeated so often we *think* it's true?

3. Liana Orfie as the temptress Delilah in the Italian sword-and-sandal epic *Hercules, Samson, and Ulysses* (1964). What I most remember is the clingy black little number she wore, draped enticingly over her body and fastened by several gold (silver?) chains, which were all that covered her left (right?) side. (As you can tell, I wasn't paying close attention to the details.)

3A. Barbara Steele ought to fit *somewhere* in this category—but, although she sometimes played adulteresses and cruel wives (not to mention a cruel witch in *Black Sunday* [1960]), I don't know that she ever played an out-and-out FFD, even though her costume and makeup in *Curse of the Crimson Altar* (1968) might qualify her.

4. Elisabeth Brooks as Marsha Quist in Joe Dante's *The Howling* (1981). Brooks' Marsha certainly has the leather, the look and the proper attitude for an FFD. Since I like the movie so much, I had to include her here—although I wish the part had gone to porn queen Annette Haven, who would have been so much sexier in the role. (The oft-repeated story, at least over the Internet, is that Haven turned down the role because of the movie's "excessive violence." I don't know if that's true, but I just repeated it.)

5. Lena Olin as Mona Demarkov in Peter Medak's *Romeo is Bleeding* (1993). Hit-woman Mona is perhaps more of a femme fatale than an FFD, but please note that Leonard

Maltin's *Movie and Video Guide* says that the "film's stand-out virtue—and it's a doozy—is Olin's robust performance as a sadistic *dominatrix* [my italics] who ends up strangling her assailant between her thighs and tying him down to electrified bedsprings." So I guess she qualifies.

5A. But, just in case she doesn't: Sigourney Weaver as the Ripley-Alien clone in Jean-Pierre Jeunet's *Alien Resurrection* (1997) does. The resourceful, sensitive Ripley, newly reconstituted with Alien DNA in her makeup, becomes, in this film, a new being, swathed in leather and dedicated to the proposition of survival of the fittest—her survival. (Of course, before the movie's over, she does reveal a soft spot in her recreated heart for her *humalien* "grandson," who meets a horrible fate, and android Annalee Call [Winona Ryder], who doesn't.) It's a fine performance in a sadly underrated movie.
—Anthony Ambrogio

Sybil Danning in almost any of her films!
—Kevin Shinnick

Sigourney Weaver as the new and "improved" Ripley in *Alien Resurrection*.

We like Jamie Donahue from *Dead Hate the Living* and *Stop It, You're Killing Me*. She's the cat's pajama.
—KY

1. Michelle Pfeiffer as Catwoman in *Batman Returns*. Liked her outfit. I cried over her predicament, having been humiliated at jobs myself. Enjoyed her anger and seductive attitude toward Batman. I liked pretending I was she during the movie. (I don't really have a Catwoman outfit in my closet... hmm..?!)
2. Dyanne Thorne as *Ilsa She-Wolf of the S.S.!* Schlocky fun! My South Beach video store had the whole collection! Can't forget the fanboys rushing in droves to see Ilsa at Chiller!
3. Charlotte Rampling in (yikes) *The Night Porter*! I liked the outfit!! Also the German song she sang (?). In the midst of Women's Lib era, a *woman* director presents this gem that folks took too seriously and ran away from in disgust! If you want to be famous, always do something completely out of fashion!
4. Zoe Tamerlis (Mike Manik's [Chiller Theatre Expo photographer] fave actress) as *Ms. 45* in her dominatrix/nun outfit always catches my eye. I lived in a slum and I can relate to the crime and job anxiety of Anna, who unfortunately is handicapped and not a horror fan, therefore worse off than myself. It was fun watching her shoot bad guys. I wish that at the story's end she could've gotten away with it.
5. Maria Felix as *La General*. She slaps! She whips! She dominates armies, soldiers and even midgets. Renowned for her role as *Dona Barbara* (I'm really getting into this), she of the spurred boots, Mex hat, guns, riding horse with her midget servant. The army is realistically sweaty and dusty. She gets shot at the end to save her men.
6. I once saw a film that bears mention, based on the Sunday comic *The Phantom*. A handsome fellow riding a horse in the jungle wears an awful, purple outfit with black glasses. Fab action scenes! There's

a strikingly beautiful tan bad girl [Catherine Zeta-Jones], with long, glossy black hair. She's menacing the good girl and stealing her boots! It can't get any worse than that!
– Rose Solar

Barbara Crampton in Stuart Gordon's *From Beyond*— Why?? Because her "outfit" oozes menacing sexuality without resorting to full-on nudity. —Tim Hardin

There are so many great dark women in film history, it is tough, but before I vote, I must take my stand against the god-awful Halle Berry costume *Catwoman*. That thing is as laughable as the costume in the silent version of *The Bat*. At least that has the innocent distinction of being made in 1926.
1. Sarah Douglas in *Superman II*. Without a doubt the most beautiful, evil, dominating bitch this planet has ever seen. Sarah plays this role so cool, teasing men and effortlessly snapping their arms in arm wrestles, throwing them across rooms and kicking them out of sight in her dominatrix-style boots. What more can a man ask?
2. Pamela Anderson in *Barb Wire*. Talk about kick-ass. She rides a nasty Harley, carries around tons of weapons and beats the living crap out of anyone who challenges her. And it doesn't hurt to have Pam's body in that outfit :)
3. Joan Severance as *Black Scorpion*. This super-campy little 1995 film gives us the ultimate dominatrix super-heroine. Her outfit must be seen to be believed. And the bedroom scene is, perhaps, the only true scene in any such film listed in this article that reveals what men really see and think when they flock to watch their favorite dominating diva in a film.
4. Lynda Carter as *Wonder Woman*. It may be campy for today's audiences, but I guarantee young boys and men alike will still be totally turned on by one of the most beautiful woman of all. And with that golden lasso, she definitely enters the realm of Dominating Diva in style!
5. Michelle Pfeiffer as Catwoman in *Batman Returns*. This is the true catwoman—sexy, frisky and ready to cause havoc for all around her at a moment's notice. Most amazing is how she did half of those stunts herself in heels! This is a classic performance and an automatic for inclusion in such a category.
—Kenny Strong

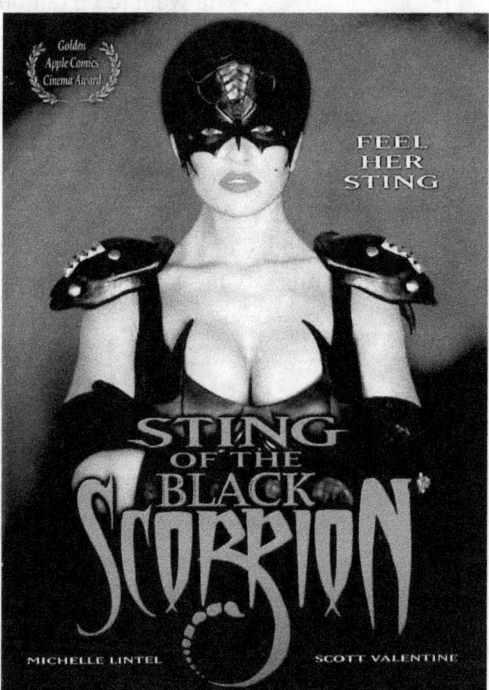

Well, in no particular order, here are my picks. Based on both fashion & bad-ass handling of men, I'd have to choose:
1. The Borg Queen (Alice Krige)— *Star Trek: First Contact*
2. The Evil Queen—Disney's *Snow White*
3. Vampirella [although she's never had a decent movie]
4. Xenia Onattop (Famke Janssen)— *Goldeneye*
5. Emma Peel (Diana Rigg)—*The Avengers*
6. Myrna Loy—*The Mask of Fu Manchu* [Let's face it, *no one* was more beautiful]. —Henry Guevara

Hmmm, this is a tough one since a Dominatrix Diva would actually require that she do some dominating—which leaves Carrie Anne Moss out in the cold as well as Elvira. The clothes do not make the DD. I also assume we are only referring to genre women. If not then Dietrich in *The Devil Is a Woman* wins hands down, followed by Hedy Lamarr in *The Strange Woman*…That said—
1. Myrna Loy in *The Mask of Fu Manchu*: Even though she needs male underlings to aid where a true DD needs only herself, never has the screen been so blatant about exactly where a dominant woman's head is at. Usually such a mind set is hinted at or implied. Not here. *Aayiii* indeed.
2. Honor Blackman from seasons 2 and 3 of *The Avengers*. Though very, *very* restrained, all dressed in head-to-toe leather with a confident no-nonsense attitude and

a tendency toward condescending smirking, certainly something is up here. While Blackman plays Cathy Gale so maturely, one also wonders if she would consider the act of domination somehow beneath her.
3. Diana Rigg from seasons 4 and 5 of *The Avengers*. A little less restrained, a little more blatant, though mitigated somewhat when she started wearing those odd pajama-like cat suits in season 5, still it does not take a psychiatrist to figure out that an evening with Mrs. Peel would probably be interesting.
4. Erin Gray from the film and season one of *Buck Rogers in the 25th Century*. All the confidence and maturity of Blackman but with the ability to switch to playful and mocking in an instant, thus setting up some nasty head game action.
5. Olivia Newton-John in *Xanadu*. Before she starts dancing with Gene Kelly and the cute cartoon animals, Newton-John spends the early part of the film playing the ice goddess to hapless male worm Michael Beck and somehow manages to twist him around her little finger while zipping about on roller skates. Very unsettling.

Equally unsettling would be Lorna Gray from the Republic serial *Captain America*. All done up in a severe 1940s business woman's attire and, while pleasant with the titular hero, when dealing with the villains, there is something else going on... especially when she pulls a snub-nosed revolver out of her handbag and starts blasting away. My my...—James J.J. Janis

1. Anita Pallenberg as the Great Tyrant/Evil Queen from *Barbarella* (1968). Loved her outfit.
2. Mathilda May as the Space Girl/Vampire in *Lifeforce* (1985). Loved her *not* wearing an outfit.
3. Alice Krige as the Borg Queen from *Star Trek: First Contact* (1996). No resistance here.
4. Natasha Henstridge as Sil from *Species* (1995). Obviously she would do *anything* for interstellar relations.
5. Allison Hayes as Nancy Fowler Archer from *Attack of the 50 Foot Woman* (1958). Whatever you want, dear.
Honorable Mention: Louise Jameson as Leela from the *Doctor Who* series.

She's a woman who can take care of both herself and you at the same time.
Second Honorable Mention: Jeri Ryan as Seven of Nine from *Star Trek Voyager*. A Trekker's dream comes true.—Joseph Higgins

1. Stacy Kane as portrayed by Meg Miles in *Satan in High Heels*. Not so much the fact that Ms. Kane goes through men like tissues makes her a dominatrix. Rather, it's how she skillfully manipulates those men; she really uses them. One of the finest exploitation films made.
2. Tura Satana's Varla in *Faster Pussycat! Kill! Kill!* My old girlfriend had been through the wringer with men in her past relationships, so the sight of Varla beating up and running over men excited her. Three go-go dancers inexplicably go on a kill-crazed rampage. Talk about female empowerment! Meow!
3. Essy Persson's character from *Mission Stardust*. Doesn't take any guff from hero Lang Jeffries' Commander Perry Rhodan. Also, she looks great in that form-fitting body suit.
4. Dyanne Thorne's title character from *Ilsa, She Wolf of the SS*. So classic, Ilsa became interchangeable in three unrelated (plot-wise) sequels. Ah, the perils of international intrigue. Glad I live in the suburbs.
5. Vulnavia, as played by Virginia North, in *The Abominable Dr. Phibes*. She doesn't even speak and men are willing to be tied up by her! Quiet but lethal, the perfect upstairs neighbor!—Douglas Brown

1. Shannon Tweed from *Electra*
2. Julie Strain in *Sorceress*
3. Honey Lauren in *Satan Was a Lady*
4. Monique Parent in *Bloodthirsty*
5. Linda Fiorentino in *Acting on Impulse* [*Eyes of a Stranger*]—Phil Holthaus

If I am reading this right, this refers to a particular kind of woman, those dangerous, demanding dames that festoon

Jessica Harper as Janet in the *Rocky Horror* sequel *Shock Treatment*, which couldn't capture the magic of *RH*.

film noir with femmes fatales. It calls to mind images of Irwin Klaw bondage films starring Bettie Page or the prima donna of the opera receiving her comeuppance at the hands of the mysterious Opera Ghost, aka the Phantom.

1. Selina Kyle (Michelle Pfeiffer), aka the Catwoman from *Batman Returns*, would be a good pick because she undergoes a radical change of personality after being pushed around as a mousy secretary. She definitely understands the sexy possibilities of vinyl, and also knows how to use sex as a weapon, with her own divided personality being a match for the equally divided personality of Bruce Wayne/The Batman.

2. "Let's face it, Mac, that basic Black is coming back!" I'll admit it, I'm a Jessica Harper fan, and while the film *Shock Treatment* is a mess, I do think Harper does a dynamite job as Janet Majors, the troubled wife of Brad Majors (Cliff De Young) in the problematic *Rocky Horror Picture Show* sequel. While Harper also got to show off her pipes and acting in the far better *Phantom of the Paradise*, I selected *Shock Treatment* because it also accentuates the dominatrix aspect as she is unscrupulously sexed up, ostensibly to aid her troubled hubby, but really as part of Brad's evil twin brother Farley Flavors' plan to make her a star on Denton TV.

3. Angelica Huston has provided a number of deliciously wicked performances to choose from: from her wicked stepmother in *Ever After* to the alien queen in *Captain EO* where she is a Giger-esque nightmare made flesh. The one for me, though, is her Miss Eva Ernst, the Grand High Witch in Nicolas Roeg's delightful adaptation of Roald Dahl's *The Witches*. (Given the excellence of this film, *Willy Wonka and the Chocolate Factory*, *Matilda*, and *James and the Giant Peach*, it is surprising that there aren't more adaptations of Dahl's wonderful work). Miss Ernst, like most witches, finds young children smell about as appealing as canine excrement and so has concocted a sinister plan to transform the babes of Blighty into vermin. Huston exudes a demanding, controlling, comic presence that truly renders her an adversary with which to be reckoned.

4. Reaching out to the extremes of diva-dom, it is hard to beat Heidi the Hippo from Peter Jackson's *Meet the Feebles*. Of course, it is a little problematic in that Heidi is a female character performed by two men—Mark Hadlow does her voice while Danny Mulhorn performs inside the body suit—but her showpiece climax as she machineguns everyone in sight while warbling "The Garden of Love" ensures her place as the ultimate in divas. Heidi may not be pretty, has a serious eating disorder and has been betrayed by Blech, but she is still the hugely talented star of the show that gets pushed too far. For the uninitiated, this is a riotously bad taste send-up of backstage musical dramas performed by muppet-like performers with genitals and real-life serious problems. Definitely, this film is not for all tastes.

5. Lastly we come to Nicole Horner (Simone Signoret) in *Les Diaboliques*, where the seemingly sympathetic Nicole is actually conspiring with her lover Michel Delasalle (Paul Meurisse) to drive his schoolteacher wife Christina (Vera Clouzot) insane. This effective French suspense thriller excels at its craft and inspired countless imitations. What could be more masterfullly manipulative than a fiendish plan to drive an unsuspecting cohort crazy, collect her inheritance and split the proceeds with her ex? The bathtub climax is truly chilling and has inspired scenes in *Fatal Attraction*, *Jacob's Ladder* and *What Lies Beneath*, but it has never been done better than in the original.
—Dennis Fischer

1. Myrna Loy, *The Mask of Fu Manchu*
2. Female alien Natasha Henstridge (Sil) from *Species*
3. Ingrid Pitt from *Vampire Lovers*, since I believe a vampire woman would fit the definition of a dominatrix
4. Susan Cabot from *The Wasp Woman*.
5. Halle Berry as Catwoman, following up on one of your good suggestions. A woman in black leather cracking a whip is my picture of a dominatrix.—Jeff Barker

1. Ever since she burned up the screen in *They're Playing with Fire*, Sybil Danning has been a mainstay in the role of (take your pick) barbarian queen, leather-clad dominatrix or space queen. She's very entertaining clutching with Christopher Lee in *Howling II*, although even her ample assets couldn't save Fred Olen Ray's *The Tomb*. But John Landis presented her perfectly in *Amazon Women on the Moon*.

2. Tura Satana's no-holds-barred performance as the leathered, lethal thrill-seeker in *Faster Pussycat! Kill! Kill!* leads the pack! She's also a lot of fun to watch as the dragon lady in Ted Mikels' *The Astro-Zombies*.

3. Brigitte Nielsen, introduced in Sylvester Stallone's *Rocky IV*, makes indelible marks in *Red Sonja*, where she holds her own in every way with Arnold Schwarzenegger, especially in screen appeal. Those leggy, tight-fitting skirt scenes in *Cobra* are also a highlight.

4. Alice Krige—Even with all of those well respected older stars in 1984's *Ghost Story*. Alice Krige gives the classiest performance of the film. Her performance in *Star Trek: First Contact* is genuinely creepy and has been recognized as such with her role being reprised in a number of *Star Trek* vehicles.

5. Eihi Shiina—A line from *Blade Runner*, "Talk about your Beauty and the Beast. She's both!" All right, Takashi Miike is no stranger to the audacious, but who could have been prepared for Eihi Shiina's truly psychoid character in Miike's *Audition*. Meek and menacing doesn't describe her. Being prepared isn't nearly enough. Run for the hills... if you can.

Special mention can be made of Kate Beckinsale and her form-fitting shiny black leather jumpsuit in *Underworld*. Even with all of the outstanding werewolves, she's the most eye-popping effect in the film.
—Ralph Kirchoff

Since this is a revised version of *BBV*, we thought we'd update our Dominatrix Diva list. Now modern film fans may think that is easy. Almost every genre movie out today features a tough female lead who can kick the ass of anyone or anything that lumbers into the scene. But will these characters be remembered and discussed like Ripley from *Alien*? I think not. I suppose we should be pleased that Hollywood is portraying women as strong characters, but they have sacrificed story for special effects and action. And as long as people keep buying tickets, they'll keep making crap. However, while genre movies haven't come close to the Golden, Silver or even Copper age of moviedom, we do have some memorable femmes fatales...

1. *Planet Terror*, the 2007 Robert Rodriguez film in which a group of survivors band together to fight zombies. This was part of the Grindhouse experiment by Rodriguez and Quentin Tarentino. The film contains the typical Rodriguez humor that will leave audiences laughing rather than quaking in terror, but with today's horror films, that's pretty much par for the course. Rose McGowan stars as Cherry, a kick-ass heroine whose amputated leg becomes a weapon as various items are used for the artificial limb, including a table leg and a machine gun.

2. *V for Vendetta* (2006) turned out to be one of my favorite genre films in a long, long time. Natalie Portman is outstanding as Evey, a girl who is rescued by a mysterious freedom fighter called V. Evey and V manage to take down a totalitarian dictatorship in a futuristic Great Britain.

3. *Avatar* (2009), the James Cameron mega-hit offered nothing new for readers of classic sci-fi, but everyone else was raving. Zoe Saldana made herself a star with her performance as Neytiri, one of the inhabitants of a planet that is coveted by evil white guys who are out to destroy the natives. For classic sci-fi fans it was "been there, done that," but the film won over both critics and audiences with amazing color, 3-D and art direction.

4. *True Blood* (2008), based on the Charlaine Harris books, started out great with heroine Sookie (Anna Paquin) falling in love with a vampire and kicking the ass of assorted supernatural villains that constantly try to attack her. Unfortunately, the stories pulled away from the novels and have substituted their humor for sex and gore.

Natalie Portman and Hugo Weaving in a classic horror film pose for *V for Vendetta*.

**If you enjoyed this book,
e-mail or write for a free catalog**

**Midnight Marquee Press, Inc.
9721 Britinay Lane
Baltimore, MD 21234
www.midmar.com**

mmarquee@aol.com

www.ingramcontent.com/pod-product-compliance
Lightning Source LLC
Chambersburg PA
CBHW081720100526
44591CB00016B/2441